Labour Law in Russia: Recent Developments and New Challenges

ADAPT LABOUR STUDIES BOOK-SERIES

International School of Higher Education in Labour and Industrial Relations

Series Editors
Tayo Fashoyin, University of Lagos (*Nigeria*)
Michele Tiraboschi, University of Modena and Reggio Emilia (*Italy*)

Guest Editors
Elena Radevich, National Research Tomsk State University (*Russia*)
Vladimir Lebedev, National Research Tomsk State University (*Russia*)

English Language Editor
Pietro Manzella, ADAPT Senior Research Fellow

ADAPT (www.adapt.it) is a non-profit organisation founded in 2000 by Professor Marco Biagi with the aim of promoting studies and research in the field of labour law and industrial relations from an international and comparative perspective. Our purpose is to encourage and implement a new approach to academic research, by establishing ongoing relationships with other universities and advanced studies institutes, and promoting academic and scientific exchange programs with enterprises, institutions, foundations and associations. In collaboration with the Centre for International and Comparative Studies on Law, Economics, Environment and Work (DEAL) at the Marco Biagi Department of Economics of the University of Modena and Reggio Emilia, ADAPT set up the International School of Higher Education in Labour and Industrial Relations, a centre of excellence which is accredited at an international level for research, study and the postgraduate programs in the area of industrial and labour relations.

Labour Law in Russia: Recent Developments and New Challenges

Edited by

Vladimir Lebedev and Elena Radevich

CAMBRIDGE SCHOLARS
PUBLISHING

Labour Law in Russia: Recent Developments and New Challenges,
Edited by Vladimir Lebedev and Elena Radevich

This book first published 2014

Cambridge Scholars Publishing

12 Back Chapman Street, Newcastle upon Tyne, NE6 2XX, UK

British Library Cataloguing in Publication Data
A catalogue record for this book is available from the British Library

ISBN (10): 1-4438-6746-2, ISBN (13): 978-1-4438-6746-7

TABLE OF CONTENTS

LIST OF ILLUSTRATIONS

LIST OF TABLES

FOREWORD

ELENA RADEVICH AND VLADIMIR LEBEDEV

Russia's transition towards a market economy in the early 1990s called for new approaches to the regulation of employment relations in the post-Soviet period in order to strike a balance between employers' interests and employees' rights in changed conditions. The adoption of the Labour Code of the Russian Federation (hereafter: LC RF) in 2001 contributed to solving the issue only partly, as in reality it was passed as a compromise between different political forces and consists of both provisions which can be implemented in the new context of the market economy and restrictions inherited from the planned economy.

The recent and ever-changing socio-economic conditions and the increasing complexity of the employer-employee relationship originating from globalization and technological progress called for the need to further develop Russian employment legislation, which resulted in substantial amendments made to the original LC RF in 2006, with the majority of its provisions being profoundly revised.

However, a thorough analysis of the changes under way shows that many aspects concerning the employment relations are still far from being addressed. This, in turn, indicates a research interest towards foreign, and in particular, European experience, which can be seen as a source for further improvement of Russian employment legislation.

The papers collected in the present volume of the ADAPT Labour Studies Book-Series consider the recent developments of the legal regulation of employment relations – as well as some closely related aspects – from a historical and comparative perspective, in order to provide some insights into these issues and examine the current challenges.

THE DEVELOPMENT OF RUSSIAN EMPLOYMENT LEGISLATION IN THE POST-SOVIET PERIOD

VLADIMIR LEBEDEV

1. Employment legislation in post-Soviet Russia experienced a progressive reduction in the number of rights which were earlier granted to employees as a group (*trudovoy kollektiv*) and trade unions that was later on reflected in the Labour Code of the Russian Federation passed in 2001.

The key objectives of employment legislation established by Art. 1 of the LC RF mainly have declarative contents. Thus, the main goals of Russian employment legislation are proclaimed in the following: "the coordination of the interests of the parties to the employment relationship with those of the state" and, in particular, in the legal regulation of "social partnership, carrying out collective bargaining and concluding collective 'contracts' and agreements; the participation of employees and trade unions in the definition of working conditions and the improvement of employment legislation in the cases envisaged by the law". The declarative character of these main objectives is reflected in the lack of adequate tools ensuring their implementation. Moreover, a dramatic reduction in terms of safeguards has been reported in comparison with those laid down in the Code of Labour Laws of the Russian Soviet Federative Socialist Republic of 1971 (hereafter: CLL RSFSR).

In accordance with Art. 7 of the CLL RSFSR, a collective contract had to be signed by trade union representatives within an organization on behalf of the employees as a group. This was preceded by employees' meetings (conferences) where they have discussed and approved the draft of a collective contract, and authorized trade unions to conclude a collective contract with management. At that time, the legislator treated employees as a plenipotentiary participant concluding a collective contract.

Yet the expression "employees as a group" (*trudovoy kollektiv*) is not even mentioned in Art. 40 of the LC RF. In the legislator's opinion, a collective contract is concluded between the representatives of the employer and those of employees who produce a first draft of the contract that is not usually discussed in the employees' meetings (conferences).

Accordingly, employees are intrinsically excluded from the drafting and the adoption of key acts within an organization which is normally concerned with such aspects as: regulatory practices, systems and rates of remuneration; benefits and compensation; the adjustments to remuneration taking into account price growth, inflation levels and the achievement of the targets set by the collective contract; employment, re-training and dismissal procedures; working hours and time off, including issues concerning leave and its duration; the improvement of working conditions and job safety, especially those of women and youth; the observance of the employees' interests in the privatization of state and municipal-owned organizations; environmental safety and the protection of employees' health at work; the benefits for those employees who combine work and studies; the improvement of health as well as the recreation of employees and their family members; the partial or full payment for employees' meals; the monitoring of the implementation of the collective contract, the procedure for its amendment, the liability of the parties to an employment contract, the provision of adequate conditions for employee representatives, the procedure for informing employees on the implementation of the collective contract; the obligation to refrain from industrial action if the relevant terms and conditions of the collective contract are observed; other issues defined by the parties (Art. 41 of the LC RF).

In 1988, the CLL RSFSR was amended by the special chapter (XV-A) which regulated the participation of blue and white collars in the organization of work processes, established bodies of employees as a group, their rights and safeguards which were to ensure genuine employee participation in the business activity. Employees as a group decided "issues of production and social development". In accordance with relevant employment legislation, they took measures to improve work organization, quota-setting, remuneration and job safety.

The CLL RSFSR defined the powers of employees' meetings (conferences) in production. These meetings (conferences) established the council of employees as a group, approved economic and social development plans as well as the collective contract, confirmed internal working regulations *(pravila vnutrennego trudovogo rasporyadka)* and dealt with other important labour issues in the organization (Art. 235^1).

2. The CLL RSFSR granted extensive powers to the trade union representatives operating in the organization. Thus, in accordance with Art. 35 of the CLL RSFSR it was prohibited to terminate an employment contract without the consent of trade union representatives. As a general

rule, it was possible to dismiss an employee no later than one month after receiving the consent on the part of trade unions. Moreover, employment legislation did not provide for the possibility to appeal the refusal of trade union representatives to grant their consent to the termination of an employment contract. The violation of that rule always involved the employee's reinstatement, although such a one-sided approach was widely criticized in theory and practice. However, when the courts reinstated an employee, the requirement of Art. 35 of the CLL RSFSR was not fulfilled unless other circumstances were included.

The LC RF inherently deprived trade union representatives of their right to verify the lawfulness of an employee's dismissal and give consent to the termination of an employment contract. The legislator only gives the right to provide an opinion on the matter. In accordance with Art. 373 of the LC RF, at the time of making a decision regarding the possible termination of an employment contract of an employee who is a trade union member under items 2, 3 or 5 of part 1 of Art. 81 of the LC RF,[1] the employer shall send the elected body of the main trade union a draft of the order as well as copies of the documents motivating the decision. The opinion of the trade union has practically no influence on the employer's decision. The employer can dismiss an employee even if the trade union considers the dismissal to be groundless and (or) against current employment legislation.

Some minimum levels of protection are also given to the heads of the elective collegial bodies of an organization and its departments who are also full-time employees (Art. 374 of the LC RF). In some cases, while maintaining the dismissal order, it is necessary to obtain the consent of the relevant trade union representative body.

3. Current Russian employment legislation widens the employer's room for manoeuvre, while reducing the safeguards for employees to be restored among their legal rights if infringed. This should come as no surprise, considering the legislator's concern for entrepreneurship which appears to be reasonable taking into account that between the last and the current century, entrepreneurship reported a decrease, especially in the engineering industry, producing a limited number of scientific achievements and lower investments.

At this stage the protective function of the courts in Russia is dwindling and employees rarely resort to labour dispute review bodies to

[1] This includes: redundancies or job cuts in an organization; the employee's failure to meet the job requirements due to a lack of qualifications, as certified by an evaluation procedure; the employee's repeated and unjustified failure to fulfill his/her duties, if preceded by a disciplinary penalty inflicted by the employer.

protect their rights. It is more and more common to think that it is almost impossible for employees to protect their rights violated by the employer by bringing the case before the court.[2]

4. Employers usually start neglecting employment legislation immediately after the conclusion of the employment contract. The LC RF defines an employment contract as an agreement between an *employer* and an *employee* (Art. 56). Yet in legal terms, this definition does not make any sense taking into account that in the terminology established by the LC RF "employee means a natural person who has entered into employment relations with an employer" (Par. 2, Art. 20 of the LC RF), while "employer means a natural person or a legal entity (organization) that has entered into employment relations with an employee" (Par. 4, Art. 20 of the LC RF).

Pursuant to Art. 57 of the LC RF, the following terms must be included in the employment contract: the place of work (i.e. the name of the employer); the job function; the date of commencement of work and, if a fixed-term contract is concluded, its term and the reasons for concluding a fixed-term employment contract under the LC RF or another federal law; remuneration (basic wage, extra payment, and incentives); working hours and rest periods (if different from those established for other employees); bonuses for operating in harmful and/or hazardous working conditions if the employee is hired to perform work in such conditions, including a description of working conditions; the terms and conditions defining the nature of work (mobile, travelling, en route, or any other kind of work); the reference to mandatory social insurance for the employee under the LC RF and other federal laws; other terms and conditions in the cases envisaged by employment legislation and other labour-related provisions.

Employers violate Art. 57 of the LC RF as they avoid specifying the employee's job functions, basic wage or remuneration rates, and other terms of payment. In other cases, employees are partly paid under the table so employers can save on social contributions and taxes.

---

[2] The Russian Federation ranks among the top places in the number of applications submitted to the European Court of Human Rights; those filed from Russian citizens account for a quarter of the total figure. In Russia, the European Court of Human Rights is viewed by employees as the last opportunity to exert their rights. As of 2010, the European Court of Human Rights handed down more than 500 rulings on the applications submitted by Russian citizens against Russian authorities (see Gerasimova, 2010, I. "Svoboda obedinenija v profsojuzy. Praktika Evropejskogo Suda po pravam cheloveka [Freedom of association in trade unions. The practice of the European Court of Human Rights]," in Gvozdickikh, A. (Moscow: CSTP), pp. 4-5).

5. Par. 3, Art. 37 of the Constitution of the Russian Federation establishes that anyone shall have the right to work in conditions which meet safety and hygiene requirements, to receive remuneration which is equal to at least the minimum wage without any discrimination whatsoever and to be protected against unemployment.

These constitutional provisions are detailed in the Labour Code of the Russian Federation. Thus, Art. 3 of the LC RF prohibits employment discrimination: employment rights and freedom should be ensured to anyone, regardless of sex, race, colour of skin, nationality, language, origin, property, family, social status and occupation, age, place of residence, attitude to religion, political views, affiliation or failure to affiliate with public associations, and other factors not relevant to the professional qualities of the employee. On reflection, this statement is the only attempt made by the legislator to tackle discrimination in the context of employment law.

Some safeguards for certain categories of employees are provided at the national level, yet they are not always ensured by employers. In some cases, employees themselves do not know about such guarantees. The awareness-raising activity in relation to employment legislation carried out by some public organizations (for example, "*Znanie*") was narrowed down in the post-Soviet period and has not been restored since then, both for a lack of interest on the part of employers and because of limited financial resources at the national level. An attempt was made by trade unions (inspectorates and trade union committees) which proved unsuccessful, since their activity mainly aims at the restoration of the employees' rights which have been infringed by the employer rather than the prevention of breaches of employment legislation.

The issue of discrimination, which is increasingly urgent in contemporary Russia, is still not considered important by the legislator, although there are reasons to believe that it will become a decisive factor in the years to come.[3] Discrimination in the Russian Federation depends

[3] See ILO. 2003. *Time for Equality at Work. Global Report Under the Follow-Up to the ILO Declaration on Fundamental Principles and Rights At Work. Report of The Director-General*. Geneva: ILO. http://www.ilo.org/global/publications/ilo-bookstore/order-online/books/WCMS_PUBL_9221128717_EN/lang--en/index.htm; ILO. 2007. Equality at Work: Tackling the Challenges. Global Report Under the Follow-up to the ILO Declaration on Fundamental Principles and Rights at Work. Report of the Director-General. http://www.ilo.org/global/publications/ilo-bookstore/order-online/books/ WCMS_082607/lang--en/index.htm; *Diskriminacija v sfere truda: teorija i praktika: nauchno-prakticheskij sbornik [Discrimination in the Sphere of*

on a range of factors, including objective ones. Firstly, it relates to the increasingly dissatisfaction among Russians with their underestimation as the dominant nation in between other nations subject to the Russian Federation (Federal entities such as the Republic of Tatarstan, the Republic of Moldova, the Chechen Republic, the Republic of Dagestan, and so on).

Secondly, it can be explained by the migration flows from neighbouring countries, with many people who enter the country illegally. Migrants are usually given low pay and are employed in low-skilled or semi-skilled jobs. As a general rule, employers hiring migrant workers do not respect their rights, do not pay them their full wage and do not comply with safety requirements.

The relevant authorities, particularly in Moscow, are not interested in tackling and preventing discrimination based on one's immigration status, being more concerned with the provision of statistics on the number of migrant workers, their identification and deportation. Recently, the proposal to introduce a visa system within Central Asian and Transcaucasia has gained ground, along with that of assigning criminal liability to those employers who hire illegal immigrants.

Thirdly, in many cases the protective function of employment law is not as effective as it should so long as employees who are provided with some benefits at the national level are not aware of them and employers seek to avoid their granting. The Labour Code of the Russian Federation lays down some special provisions regulating the employment of certain categories of workers, among others women and young people under the age of eighteen (Chapters 41 and 42 of the LC RF). These provisions determine the range of statutory safeguards which are usually ignored by employers. Moreover, employers generally avoid hiring employees who are protected by additional safeguards, in particular, those which limit the range of potential jobs for such employees. Thus, Art. 253 of the LC RF sets some limitations on the use of female labour in heavy jobs, occupations featuring harmful and/or dangerous working conditions, and underground jobs, with the exception of intellectual work and work performed in the sanitary and consumer services sector. Further, and taking account of their physical constitution, women cannot be employed in jobs involving the lifting and the moving of heavy objects. Similar

---

Employment: Theory and Practice: Theoretical and Practical set of Art.s]. Moscow: CSTP. 272.

provisions are stipulated in relation to employees younger than eighteen[4] (chapter 42 of the LC RF).

Moreover, current legislation makes provisions for pregnant women and for women with children younger than 18 months to be assigned to other occupations (Art. 254 of the LC RF). Upon submission of a medical certificate, pregnant women can demand to reduce the amount of work performed or to be given another occupation which does not involve adverse working conditions of the employer who will retain the average wage of their previous position.

Part-time workers and those on fixed-term contracts might also be subject to discriminatory practices. Accordingly, they also need further legal protection.[5]

6. Recently, the implementation of "a decent work agenda" has been extensively debated in the Russian legal literature.[6] However, taking into account the foregoing issues, it is very likely that "a decent work agenda" will only constitute a slogan or a scientifically substantiated principle based on the cooperation between employers and employees. As is generally known, their interests are competing, in particular, if we talk about the correlation between the employer's profits and employees' wages, as well as the financial support of health care, etc. Striking a balance between them might take decades but it will be the starting point in the planning of an effective and decent work agenda.

---

[4] It is the government of the Russian Federation that establishes the range of prohibited jobs for these workers.

[5] See, for example Radevich, E. 2013. "Zaschita trudovykh prav chastichno zanyatykh rabotnikov [Protection of Part-time Workers' Employment Rights (Italian Experience)]," *Aktual'nye problemy trudovogo prava i prava social'nogo obespecheniya:* Proceedings of the fifth International Conference, Moscow: Prospekt, 253-258; Radevich, E. 2013. "Pravovaya zaschita rabotnikov po srochnym trudovym dogovoram [Legal Protection of Fixed-term Workers]," *Profsoyuzy i aktual'nye problemy trudovogo, korporativnogo i social'nogo prava:* Proceedings of the 2nd International Conference, Minsk: Mitso, 133-135.

[6] In 2013, the conference "Puti realizacii v Rossii programmy dostoinogo truda i dostoinogo social'nogo obespecheniya [The ways of implementation of the Decent Work Agenda in Russia]" was held by Lomonosov Moscow State University, the Ministry of labour and social protection of the Russian Federation, the Association of Russian lawyers and the Federation of independent trade unions. More than 200 participants from Russia, Sweden, Bulgaria, Azerbaijan, Kyrgyzstan, Latvia, Lithuania, Belarus, Kazakhstan, Ukraine, etc. have attended this conference. It was concluded that it was necessary to improve employment legislation considering the strategic directions formulated in the ILO Decent Work Agenda.

Moreover, a decent work agenda cannot be considered in a merely exploitative manner. In other words, its meaning should not be exclusively limited to such issues as payment rises, job safety maintenance and social partnership although they are undoubtedly important.

The ILO Declaration on Social Justice for a Fair Globalization of 10 June 2008[7] lays down the objectives through which the Decent Work Agenda is expressed, in particular:

a) promoting employment by creating a sustainable institutional and economic environment in which: individuals can develop and update the necessary capacities and skills they need to enable them to be productively occupied for their personal fulfilment and the common well-being;
b) developing and enhancing measures of social protection, social security and labour protection (healthy and safe working conditions; wages and earnings policies, hours and other conditions of work, designed to ensure a just share of the fruits of progress to all, and a minimum living wage to all the employed and those in need of such protection);
c) promoting social dialogue and tripartism as the most appropriate methods to increase the effectiveness of labour law and institutions, including the recognition of the employment relationship, the promotion of good industrial relations and the development of effective labour inspection systems;
d) respecting, promoting and realizing the fundamental principles and rights at work, which are of particular significance, as both rights and conditions are necessary for the full realization of all the strategic objectives.

At the 97th session of the International Labour Conference (Geneva, 10 June 2008) a declaration was made about the universality of the Decent Work Agenda: "all Members of the Organization must pursue policies based on the strategic objectives—employment, social protection, social dialogue, and rights at work". Therefore, the Decent Work Agenda and the methods of its implementation should be established at the national, regional[8] and local level.

---

[7] The ILO Declaration on Social Justice for a Fair Globalization on 10 June 2008. http://www.ilo.org/global/about-the-ilo/mission-and-objectives/WCMS_099766/lang--en/index.htm.

[8] Some measures were taken in this connection. On 25 January 2013 the following regional program was adopted: "Programma Federacii profsoyuzov Respubliki Bashkortostan, Objedineniy rabotodateley Respubliki Bashkortostan, Pravitel'stva

An analysis of the issue of the Decent Work Agenda at the organisational level which overlooks the labour process and the relationship between the parties is doomed to be ineffective. Any labour process requires the cooperation of employees and is based on their volitional action or inaction. This system is reflected in the production process of an organization, where efficiency is ensured by the activity of the employer and the employees (or their representatives). Decent work in such conditions can be ensured not only through objective factors (for example, the technical advances used in the labour processes), but also through the personal characteristics of the parties involved: their training levels, and their (professional and legal) expertise. Decent work will emerge where the interests of flexible employees and those of thoughtful employers will coincide.

To ensure decent work, an employer should:

a) promote the coordination between an organization and other entities (state and civil society);
b) cooperate with employees in the labour process;
c) meet legal and moral requirements.

The analysis of the relation between employers (or their representatives) and civil society and the state shows that decent work should also have an ideological character.[9] Establishing the conditions for decent work requires an ideological base, which should involve not only the employer, but also the state as a social partner, employers'

Respubliki Bashkortostan 'Dostoiniy trud v Respublike Bashkortostan' (na period do 2025 goda) [The program of Federation of trade unions of Bashkortostan, Employers association of Bashkortostan, and the Government of Bashkortostan 'The decent work in Bashkortostan' to 2025)]".
http://fprb.ru/download/economika_oplata_truda/programma_dostoyn_trud.pdf.
On 26 September 2012 the Krasnodar regional trilateral commission on the regulation of social and labour relations approved "Standarty dostoinogo truda [Standards of decent work]," providing some labour standards which should give employees and their family members decent work and life and adequate social security. http://docs.cntd.ru/document/462502910.

[9] Art. 13 of the Constitution of the Russian Federation concerning the media statements prohibits "ideologizing" social, economic and legal issues". In reality, Art. 13 of the Constitution of the Russian Federation prohibits establishing any ideology involving collectivity. At the same time ideologies as a system of ideas, notions, and conceptions which are shared by individuals or associations, including those of employers and employees have always existed and will exist in the future. The ideology of the decent work can be seen as a form of social consciousness, as well as the most important aim of labour cooperation.

associations, trade unions, political parties, etc. Decent work can be elevated to the state policy level, and disseminated in the relevant structures of civil society[10] as an essential part of the daily lexicon of their representatives. It is necessary to develop a system awarding the honorary title of "organization where the decent work agenda is implemented" and ensure its realization by providing material incentives (grants, honourable distinctions, tax rebates, and so on.). Today, such "militant" ideology is necessary for Russia. It would favour economic expansion and respect for one's work.

Employers' duties should also be connected with the implementation of the decent work agenda. Generally, they are determined by the peculiarities of the production process which also affect the selection process of employers' representatives as well as the recruitment process. Thus, on their part, employers should:

a) develop a respectful attitude of employees towards work, teams and colleagues. Management and its representatives should evoke a feeling of self-appraisal, making employees proud of working for a certain organization;

b) assign tasks in line with the employee's occupational skills;

c) pay staff on time and at a rate which ensures a decent standard of living, also considering the company's profitability;

d) establish working conditions which make it possible for an employee to increase or fulfil his/her professional level.

These duties can be fulfilled if employers and employees as a group manage to adopt them through legal acts at the local level, not only bringing the issue to the attention of relevant representatives, but prompting employees to set these duties as their own aims. The theory of flexible employees (*akribologiya*)[11] makes it possible to solve this issue.

7. The analysis of current employment legislation and practices points out the entropy of Russian labour law representing the whole Russian legal

---

[10] The implementation of the Decent Work Agenda at national level will depend on national needs and priorities and it will up to member states, in consultation with representative organizations of workers and employers, to determine liability. To this end, they may consider, among other things: the adoption of a national or regional strategy for decent work, or the establishment of a set of priorities for the integrated pursuit of the strategic objectives (see the ILO Declaration on Social Justice for a Fair Globalization on 10 June 2008).

[11] See Lebedev, V. M. 2000. "Akribologiya (obschaya chast') [Akribologiya (essentials)]. (Tomsk: Tomsk University Publishing House), 116 p.; Lebedev, V. M. 2008. "Trudovoe pravo i akribologiya (osobennaya chast') [Employment law and akribologiya (special part)]. (Moscow: Statut), 133 p.

system. In the post-Soviet era, especially at the beginning of the current century, Russian law has been changed substantially. The feverish lawmaking process affects almost every branch of law and even their basic provisions (e.g. codes).

The legal entropy in contemporary Russia challenges the fundamentals of civil societies such as the supremacy of law and equality before the court, ensuring the full and real implementation of people's rights, etc. All of these deviations from the basic elements of civil societies, including those in the sphere of employment and social security law, are objective and based on a range of factors. Firstly, they are based on the violation of the principle of separation of powers. The legislative initiatives put forward by the executive bodies, as well as initiatives (e.g. opinions) of the President of the Russian Federation are always converted into laws and regulatory acts.[12] The rest of the employment legal regulations are established through regulatory acts, the efficiency of which is not analyzed by the legislative body. Further, legal entropy is based on the non-compliance of the organization and activity of courts and law-enforcement entities with basic norms, especially when the principle of legality is separate from the principle of rationality. Finally, in contemporary Russia, questioning justice is typical when important aspects concerning how to disobey the law are raised.

The most important and obvious manifestations of such entropy concerning employment law is that the state, employers and trade unions avoid implementing decent working conditions at the local level. This has a number of consequences: cosmetic initiatives (conferences and events) replace real action; the seamy will of the ruling regime is introduced by means of employment legislation; the protective function of employment law is limited and is followed by the narrowing down of employees' rights and those rights which are granted to small businesses; employment discrimination increases, in particular, against migrant workers; the legal mechanisms of protection of certain groups of workers (women, employees younger than eighteen and those working in harmful and/or hazardous working conditions) are sequentially being destroyed.

---

[12] The Russian Opinion Research Center conducted research on social and political approval in the year following the presidential elections. From the fourth quarter of 2012 to the third quarter of 2013, the approval rate of the main legislative body—the State Duma—declined by 10%. More than two thirds of respondents disapproved of its activity. The rest of respondents considered that it was possible to perform legislative activity without the State Duma, relying on the lawmaking activity of the President of the Russian Federation and that of the Government of the Russian Federation.

References

Gerasimova, I. 2010. *Svoboda obedinenija v profsojuzy. Praktika Evropejskogo Suda po pravam cheloveka* [Freedom of association in trade unions. The practice of the European Court of Human Rights]. A. Gvozdickih (ed.). Moscow: CSTP.

ILO. 2003. Time for Equality at Work. Global Report under the Follow-up to the ILO Declaration on Fundamental Principles and Rights at Work. Report of the Director-General. Geneva: ILO. http://www.ilo.org/global/publications/ilo-bookstore/order-online/books/WCMS_PUBL_9221128717_EN/lang--en/index.htm.

—. 2007. Equality at Work: Tackling the Challenges. Global Report under the Follow-up to the ILO Declaration on Fundamental Principles and Rights at 22Work. Report of the Director-General. Geneva: ILO. http://www.ilo.org/global/publications/ilo-bookstore/order-online/books/WCMS_082607/lang--en/index.htm.

—. 2008. Declaration on Social Justice for a Fair Globalization on 10 June 2008. http://www.ilo.org/global/about-the-ilo/mission-and-objectives/WCMS_099766/lang--en/index.htm. Geneva: ILO

Lebedev, V. M. 2000. "Akribologiya (obschaya chast') [Akribologiya (essentials)]. (Tomsk: Tomsk University Publishing House), 116 p.

Lebedev, V. M. 2008. "Trudovoe pravo i akribologiya (osobennaya chast') [Employment law and akribologiya (special part)]. (Moscow: Statut), 133 p.

Radevich, E. 2013. "*Pravovaya zaschita rabotnikov po srochnym trudovym dogovoram* [Legal protection of fixed-term workers]," *Profsoyuzy i aktual'nye problemy* trudovogo, korporativnogo i social'nogo prava: Proceedings of the 2nd International Conference, Minsk: Mitso, 133-135.

—. 2013. "*Zaschita trudovykh prav chastichno zanyatykh rabotnikov* [Protection of part-time workers' employment rights (Italian experience)]," *Aktual'nye problemy trudovogo prava i prava social'nogo obespecheniya:* Proceedings of the 5th International Conference, Moscow: Prospekt, 253-258.

Regional Trilateral Commission on the Regulation of Social and Labour Relations "Standarty dostoinogo truda [Decent Work Standards]: the Agenda of Krasnodar Regional Trilateral Commission on the Regulation of Social and Labour Relations (26 September 2012). http://docs.cntd.ru/document/462502910.

Trade Union Federation of Bashkortostan, Employers Association of Bashkortostan, and the Government of Bashkortostan. "Dostoiniy trud v Respublike Bashkortostan (na period do 2025 goda)": Programma Federacii profsoyuzov Respubliki Bashkortostan, Objedineniy rabotodateley Respubliki Bashkortostan, Pravitel'stva Respubliki Bashkortostan [Decent Work in Bashkortostan (to 2025): Program of Trade Union Federation of Bashkortostan, Employers Association of Bashkortostan, and the Government of Bashkortostan] (25 January 2013). http://fprb.ru/download/economika_oplata_truda/programma_dostoyn_trud.pdf.

THE DEVELOPMENT OF RUSSIAN LABOUR LAW IN THE 21ST CENTURY: A COMPARATIVE SKETCH OF REGULARITIES AND TRENDS

ANDREY LUSHNIKOV

The development of civilization as a whole as well as of any of its components (and the law is an indissoluble component of any civilization) represents difficult, multilevel and multiple factor processes. In this regard, within academic research, we observe the consecutive implementation of three cogitative operations:

1. The detection of the regularity of developments of legal phenomena, both generally, and specifically.
2. The definition, on the basis of revealed regularities of trends, of further development of legal phenomena.
3. Full compliance of expert and legislative activity to revealed trends.

This article is an attempt at revealing the main regularities of development within the legal phenomena in the field of employment law. Further, the definition on the basis of the revealed regularities of trends of development of the labour law in the 21st century will be made.

Before discussing the problem at hand, we will briefly define our understanding of legal regularities and trends, what they are in general and what makes them distinct from one another.

There is a dearth of literature on legal regularities in Russia. However, a number of publications present the opportunity to formulate the determination of legal regularities. According to the most widespread notions, it is fair to speak of legal regularities as objective, systematic stable relations of factors and phenomena in certain environments.

Trends are closely connected with legal practices. It is obvious that any subject of theoretical knowledge consists not only of empirically perceived aspects, but also of inherent objective trends, discovered only at the level of scientific abstraction. It is possible to consider a tendency as the main direction of further development which can over time become standard practice.

We will further consider the precondition of the distinction of trends of the development of labour law, basing our discussion on trends already revealed. We observe that analyzed regularities and trends of global character (if it be exact, rather characteristic of economically developed countries of the West) in many respects coincide with that which is occurring in Russia. However, the latter have certain features that are determined by the set of social, economic and political development of Russia.

At the turn of the 21st century, the development of labour law in the West, as well as in Russia came to new qualitative level. Labour law of the workers in the 20th century, was suited to the industrial society or even the post-industrial society it was created in. The 21st century began as an information society emerged. This society is not based on production (industrial), or the public organization of work, but on a new public organization of which the boundary lines are yet to be outlined. Labour law formulated in the 20th century does not keep within the framework of a new public organization of work which has been dictated upon by conditions of the information society. Nowadays adherents of the concept of the post-industrial (information) society as well as sceptics agree on one thing: there have been revolutionary changes in employment that inevitably call for change in labour law and corresponding legislation.

This leads us to discussing the formation of the post-industrial (information) organization of work as the prevailing tendency that has become an expected regularity which has for the most part defined the further development of labour law. However, this organization of work has no universal character. In fact, a number of States remain in the industrial period, with some still progressing towards industrialization.

Thus, at the beginning of the new millennium the development of labour law was decisively influenced by two planetary processes, namely social regularities having these characteristics:

1) A technical revolution combined with an accelerated social evolution resulting in a post-industrial society.

2) The process of globalization inseparably linked with the above. Modern Russian researchers[1] play special attention to this.

In this context there was a release of a collection of essays, "Labour Law in the Post-Industrial Era"[2] by leading scientists from the West: Great

---

[1] See: Morozov, P. E. 2012. *Sovremennye tendencii razvitiya zarubezhnogo trudovogo prava v usloviyah globalizacii* [Current Trends of Development of the Foreign Labor Law in the Conditions of Globalization]. Moscow: Prospekt. 256 p.

Britain, Germany, France, and the Netherlands. These were all authors of this peculiar manifesto of the future changes. The books conclusions and future forecasts have stood the test of time. It is important to note that one of the co-authors, the German researcher, V. Doybler repeatedly reported in Russia on the trends related to the development of labour law in industrialized countries[3].

Similar to the aforesaid but even more representative with regards to the structure of participants, was the collective research study presented in the book: "The Idea of Labour Law".[4] Leading scientists—experts in a sphere of the labour law of the countries of the West from Great Britain, the USA, Canada and Germany presented their ideas. The majority of this research is devoted to detection of regularities and trends within the development of labour law. A similar key collection of essays in "Labour Regulation in the 21st Century: In Search of Flexibility and Security" (Vilnius, 2011, in English, Lithuanian and Russian languages) was written by a number of leading scientific researchers from the West with a group of Russian scientists (L.Yu. Bugrov, S. Yu. Golovina, K.N. Gusov, A.M. Kurennoy, M. V. Lushnikova, etc.). Also worthy of mention is the collection of articles in "Labour Law of Russia and European Union Countries" (M, 2012).

Furthermore, in April 2013, a conference hosted by the Kiev National University and the Institute of State and Law of NAN of Ukraine[5] was devoted to research of the development of labour law.

Domestically, in Russia, I. Ya. Kiselev (1932-2005) was the first to investigate trends of the development of labour law in the foregoing

---

2 Wedderburn of Charlton, K.K.W., Sinzheimer, H. ed. 1994. *Labour law in the post-industrial era: essays in honour of Hugo Sinzheimer.* Aldershot: Ashgate. 152 p.

3 See: Doybler, V. 1995. "*Tendencii razvitiya trudovogo prava v promyshlenno razvityh stranah* [Tendencies of Development of the Labor Law in Industrialized Countries]," Paper presented at the Moscow State Law Academy, Moscow, Russia, October, 1994, *Gosudarstvo i pravo* [State and Law], No 2: 103-109. In September 2012 he made the report "Current Trends of Development of the Labor Law of Germany and Euro—Crisis" at the Higher School of Economics (Moscow, Russia) (not published).

4 Davidov, G., Langille, B. ed. 2011. *The idea of Labour Law*. New York: Oxford University Press. 454 p.

5 See: Inshina, N.I., Khutoryan, N.M., Scherbina, V.I. ed. 2013. *Tendencii razvitiya nauki trudovogo prava i prava social'nogo obespecheniya* [Tendencies of Development of Science of the Labor Law and Law of Social Security], Papers presented at the 1st International Theoretical and Practical Conference. Kiev: Nika-Centr, 676 p.

manner. He noted that the transition to a post-industrial, information society created a crisis in the traditional labour law of the West. "Some lawyers, sociologists, and politicians note that as our social environment shifts towards a post-industrial society, there is a challenge for labour law to survive and it is doomed to extinction, or at least its independent existence is under threat"[6]. However, as the author fairly noted, in the 21st century labour law will overcome its challenges, and be revived on a new basis. A niche will be defined for it laying out the subject, its methods, basic principles and it will lead to significantly improved tools. It is likely that improvements in labour law due to the development of human civilization will become a leading branch of law[7].

I. Ya. Kiselev considered changes in the coverage of labour law (a tendency towards the expansion of labour law), the legal regulation of labour relations (that is an emphasis on flexibility, diversification, and a reduction of authoritative methods of regulation within labour relations at the expense of intensive development of local regulations, i.e. corporate labour law) and the increasing relevance of international labour standards in conjunction with the standardization of labour law at a global scale, which are key innovations in the sphere of labour law[8]. These trends have gained recognition amongst Russian labour law experts[9].

Furthermore, the main trends in the development of Russian labour law viewed in the context of regularities of global development in employment relations will be considered. In our opinion, the main trends of development of labour law are:

1. The recognition of the importance of labour rights and the widening of the scope of labour law.

---

[6] See: Lushnikov A.M., Lushnikova, M. V. 2009. *Kurs trudovogo prava* [Course of the Labor Law]. V.1. Moscow: Statut, 223-262; Lushnikova, M. V., Lushnikov, A.M. 2006. *Ocherki teorii trudovogo prava* [Sketches of the Theory of the Labor Law]. St. Petersburg: Yuridicheskiy centr Press, 103-146, etc.

[7] Kiselev, I.Ya. 2003. *Noviy oblik trudovogo prava stran zapada (proryv v postindustrial'noe obschestvo)* [New Shape of the Labor Law of the Countries of the West (Break in Post-Industrial Society)]. Moscow: Intel-Sintez, 12.

[8] See: Kiselev, I.Ya. Op. cit.

[9] See, e.g.: Golovina, S.Yu. 2007. "*Sovremennye tendencii v trudovom prave Rossii*" [Current Trends in the Labor Law of Russia], Paper presented at the at the Moscow State Law Academy, Moscow, Russia, January 2006, *Sovremennye tendencii v razvitii trudovogo prava i prava social'nogo obespecheniya: sbornik materialov konferencii* [Current Trends in Development of the Labor Law and the Law of Social Security: collected reports of the conference]. Moscow: Prospect, 9-27.

2. A shifting of valuable priorities within the content of labour rights to the sphere which ensure the full development of an individual.
3. The provision of labour mobility for workers by means of labour laws, a creation of a special type of "transnational" and "supranational" labour relations.
4. An increase in flexibility (including differentiation and individualization) in legal regulation of labour relations in combination with provision of labour rights.
5. The harmonization of individual and collective labour rights on the basis of an expansion of the sphere of social partnership.
6. Priority of international labour standards.

These trends cannot negate the continuity of century old processes of the formation and development of labour law. Moreover, they reflect an all-legal and specific regulation within the development of labour law. These trends, undoubtedly, have a major impact. The subject and methods of labour law are the key factors which make it possible to consider labour law as a separate branch of law. Accordingly, the first three trends and partly the fourth are connected with the formation of the subject of labour law in a post-industrial era. The next ones affect changing methods of legal regulation within labour relations in the 21st century.

1. Let us begin with the recognition that there needs to be an expansion of the coverage of labour law. To a certain degree this is a foundational trend based on the regularity that can be traced to the mid-20th century.

However, the universality of this regularity has not been accurately expressed yet. It is connected with the definition of a place for labour rights in the system of human rights in an information society. It is remarkable that the Universal Declaration of Human Rights of 1948 (Art. 23-25) recorded a rather extensive list of labour rights, including the right to work, the right to freely choose work based on fair and favourable working conditions, equal payment for equal work, to freely create labour unions, and to rest[10].

Within a system of social human rights determined by the International Convention on Economic, Social and Cultural Rights of 1966 (Art. 6-13) labour rights take precedence[11]. That is within the right to work, right to fair and favourable working conditions, and right to creation of labour unions. The 1961 European Social Charter (in a 1996 edition) assigns 18

[10] See: Universal Declaration of Human Rights (UDHR) of 1948.

[11] See: International Covenant on Economic, Social and Cultural Rights of 1966.

labour rights to a worker. Among the traditional labour rights, the right to vocational guidance, vocational training, information and consultation, the right to participate in the definition and improvement of working conditions and the production environment, and the protection afforded to migrant workers are now well-established. It is important to note that the European Social Charter was ratified on June 3, 2009 (with some exceptions) by the Russian Federation[12].

In the opinion of the experts of the International Labour Organization (ILO), it is necessary to take a global approach to a "threshold of rights", i.e. to provide a set of minimum human rights which are ensured to anyone regardless of one's employee status and which cannot be sold or bought[13]. Respectively, any state is obliged to provide the minimum set of labour rights as defined by norms of international law. We will return to this problem when considering the sixth trend.

Personal (civil) rights and freedoms, together with political rights (i.e. first-generation human rights) form the basis for second-generation human rights—economic and social rights, including labour ones. Between generations of the rights there is the following correlation. Personal rights include the following: the right to life which finds expression in labour law in the right to work and for labour protection; the right to dignity becomes the right for protection of honour and dignity at work; the right to freedom and security, within labour law becomes freedom to work, a ban on forced labour and the right to the protection of personal data.

Similar situations concern the political rights and freedoms which in labour law correlate with the right of workers to participate in the management of the organization, the right to association (freedom of the unions, associations), and the right to a strike. A distinctive feature of economic and social rights is their dependence on their realization from the economy and resources of the state. In the International Pact on economic, social and cultural rights of 1966 it is especially emphasized that these rights have to be provided for gradually and in "the maximum limits of available resources" (Art. 2).

Some academics only refer to the political and civil rights as inalienable rights of a person and consider them as a means for derogation and "restraint" of the political power of the State. At the same time, they emphasize that security of economic and social rights is weaker than political and civil ones. They relate this with the realities of the market

[12] *Russian Newspaper* (newspaper). 2009. June 5.

[13] "*Mezhdunarodnye trudovye normy kak global'nye obschestvennye blaga*" [International Labor Norms as Global Public Benefits], *Mezhdunarodniy obzor truda 141* [International Review of Work], No. 1-2:185-186.

economy and reduction of the possibility of the state to influence economic processes. Respectively, second-generation rights cannot be protected in a judicial manner as a court will not note a civil claim only because those rights are ensured by the Constitution by reason of the absence of the specific respondent. As a result, social rights are recognized by legal standards, rather than by legal norms.[14]

In this case it is possible to observe the following. First, a realization of the principle of freedom, a foundation of human rights, has one more basic component—the opportunity to use this freedom. It is obvious that freedom can be paralyzed by poverty, an elementary lack of means. Legal guarantees of formally recognized rights and freedoms, and the social function of the State are necessary tools. We agree with O.E. Leyst that working conditions represent a component of a way of life within society and in this sense their legal regulation has to be guided by prospect, taking into account the development of socio-political and economic realities.[15] It is possible to say the same about first-generation human rights. In a number of developing countries, the introduction of a general democratic election – the restriction of the state intervention in public life when ignoring traditional values – has had harmful consequences concerning the establishment of military dictatorships and political crises. But this does not mean "relativity" of the political and civil rights. It testifies to the need of compliance of the mechanism of their realization to a condition of society and the state.

Secondly, at times the inexhaustibility of human rights is a consequence of the inexhaustibility of human nature, and approaches to this problem should be based on the concrete understanding of history. Absolute inalienable rights do not exist, any right can be limited, not in the sense of possessing a right but rather in the context of its realization. Eventually, a ban on the abuse of rights is fixed in a number of the international acts, starting with the Universal Declaration of Human Rights of 1948 (Art. 30). This ban is expressed in the Constitution of the Russian Federation (Art. 17). Even first-generation rights can be limited in realization during military operations, in conditions of emergency. Moreover, weak states which are not breaking any human rights cannot guarantee their observance. History teaches us that in conditions of mass

---

14 See, e.g.: Alekseev, S. S. 1999. *Pravo: azbuka-teoriya-filosofiya* [Law: Alphabet-Theory-Philosophy]. Moscow: Statut, 621-622; Baglay, M. V. 1998. *Konstitucionnoe pravo Rossiyskoy Federacii* [Constitutional Law of the Russian Federation]. Moscow: Norma, 216, etc.

15 See: Leyst, O. E. 2002. *Suschnost' prava* [The Essence of the Law]. Moscow: Zertsalo-M, 31-32.

unemployment, social instability and impoverishment of the rest of people, the population itself is ready to promote refusal of the first-generation rights. In this case, political freedom can be associated within the public consciousness with the "freedom to starve" as it was in Germany on the eve of coming to power of Hitler[16]. Further, the Russian revolution of 1917, and the coming to power of fascists in Italy and national socialists in Germany serve as recent history to confirm this. The former German politician, Chancellor V. Brandt is quoted as saying, "It is difficult to present the right to life and integrity of human beings where hunger and poverty prosper".[17]

Thirdly, labour rights should be implemented, considering the specific country's economic situation. Thus, the minimum wage, the salary of a civil servant, the level of guarantees and compensation in undeveloped states will be low. However, taking into account the appropriate economic levels, those rights should be ensured to a worker. In this connection second-generation rights indeed need to be "translated" into concrete rules of law, consolidating social and labour rights. In particular, it concerns minimum labour rights which should be guaranteed by the state regardless of economic and political conditions. According to a number of experts, a global approach is necessary for "a threshold of the rights", i.e. a set of the minimum rights on which any person, irrespective of his/her status as an employee can rely on and which (if picturesquely said) cannot be sold or bought.[18]

Fourthly, judicial protection of labour rights is essential, in particular, to avoid any arbitrariness of officials. Thus, item 1 of Art. 15 of the Constitution of the Russian Federation defining its direct action with Art. 30, 37, 39 which fix basic social rights can mean only one thing: these rights can be directly and judicially ensured.

Finally, to connect inalienable rights of an individual only with restraint of absolute power of the state taking into account the democratic basis of Western countries is almost impossible. Free elections and some form of control of civil society over the state allow the latter to cease from being an all-consuming "leviathan". It is obvious that the individual has to be protected from absolute power of the state. It seems odd that the

---

16 See: Lushnikova, M. V. 1997. *Gosudarstvo, rabotodateli, rabotniki* [State, Employers, Workers]. Yaroslavl: Podati, 20-23.

17 *Izvestiya* (the newspaper). 1987. June 22.

18 "*Mezhdunarodnye trudovye normy kak global'nye obschestvennye blaga*" [International Labor Norms as Global Public Benefits], *Mezhdunarodniy obzor truda 141* [International Review of Work], No. 1-2:185-186.

restriction of state intervention into private life should be the main task of the state.

These rights extend to parties of an employer-employee relationship. Moreover, they are connected with the existence of recommendatory, estimated basic provisions, such as: fair and favourable working conditions, a decent standard of living, etc. As stated in the International Pact on economic, social and cultural rights, "an ideal of the free human person, is one free from fear and this needs to be enjoyed under conditions under which everyone can use the economic, social and cultural rights, as well as their civil and political rights".

Universality of the labour rights based on the unity of the natural, legal and positivistic beginnings allows us to extend this institute to other scopes of professional labour activity which are other than traditional wage labour (for example the work of professional athletes, work of the civil and municipal servants, etc.). It is a matter of expansion of coverage of standards of the labour law for the purpose of social protection of labour rights of these categories of workers. Neither civil nor administrative law establishes safeguards for labour rights as a main function. Analysing foreign legislation and practice of its application, I.Ya.Kiselev notes the emergence of "quasi-workers" to whom to some extent labour rights are guaranteed.[19]

This trend is already reflected in Russian labour legislation, in particular in Chapter 54.1 "Features of Regulation of Work of Athletes and Trainers" in the Labor Code of the Russian Federation (further Labor Code of the Russian Federation) 2001. According to current legislation, it is labour legislation (with some peculiarities) that regulates the work of municipal employees, or individuals in alternative civil service and employment contracts are signed with prosecutors.

2. Another trend that can be traced back to the last century is the shift of priorities from the content of labour rights to the development of one's personality. Such trend is standard practice in Western countries. This direction in further development of labour rights is connected with a shift from viewing the worker simply as an 'economic' person towards viewing them as one with personality. Invaluable priorities of human rights are increasingly shifting from the sphere of economic and physical safety towards the sphere of subjective health and "quality of work life".

Personal rights of a worker, such as the right to vocational training and professional development, the right to career advancement, the right to

[19] See: Kiselev, I.Ya. 2003. *Noviy oblik trudovogo prava stran zapada (proryv v postindustrial'noe obschestvo)* [New Shape of the Labor Law of the Countries of the West (Break in Post-Industrial Society)]. Moscow: Intel-Sintez, 17-21.

moral encouragement, an assessment of work achievements, the right to inviolability of private life and protection of personal data, the right to information on working conditions, the right to protection of advantage in the workplace and protection against mobbing (moral prosecution at work) have gained special importance. Following on from I.Ya.Kiselev, it is possible to repeat that standards of labour law are encouraged to add and deepen protection of the personal non-property rights and other non-material benefits, carried out by civil law, in relation to features of labour relations. They are encouraged to provide the rights and freedoms of the person during labour activity and thus to form the status of "the social citizen".[20]

The above listed labour rights of the worker have a personal dominant, pronounced character of the non-material benefits of the individual protected by the law. All these personal benefits unite the following criteria: 1) non-material personal character, 2) inalienability. Within a legal mechanism of realization and protection of the personal labour benefits these rights act as a legal instrument for safeguarding the personal sphere of a worker.

It is important to note that amongst Russian labour law academics, the issue of creativity and freedom of creativity for workers as a non-material benefit has become a subject of interest for representatives of the Perm School of the Labor Law.[21] They consider creativity as an element of a worker's duty to comply with labour legislation in the employer-employee relationship. Moreover, "creative attitude" is peculiar to any kind of labour activity. It is a matter of professional creativity, which legal guarantees—benefits and advantages—are provided by labour legislation as well as local regulations.[22]

It is especially important to focus our attention on the right of a worker to vocational training. It is remarkable that in Western countries it is becoming more widespread to include training in the employment contract.

---

[20] See: Kiselev, I.Ya. 2003. *Noviy oblik trudovogo prava stran zapada (proryv v postindustrial'noe obschestvo)* [New Shape of the Labor Law of the Countries of the West (Break in Post-Industrial Society)]. Moscow: Intel-Sintez, 44.

[21] See: Bugrov, L.Yu., Khudyakov, S.S., Varlamova, U.V., Goncov, N.I. 1995. *Tvorchestvo i trudovoe pravo* [Creativity and Labor Law]. Perm: Perm GU, 132 p.; Mikhaylova, N.S. 2003. *Trudovoe pravo i tvorchestvo prepodavateley vuzov* [Labor Law and Creativity of Teachers of Higher Education Institutions]. Perm: Perm GU, 112 p. etc.

[22] See: Bugrov, L.Yu. 1992. *Problemy svobody truda v trudovom prave Rossii* [Problems of Freedom of Labour in the Labor Law of Russia]. Perm: Perm GU, 147-176.

The ILO's recommendation No. 195 "Human Resources Development: Education, Training and Continuous Training" (2004) notes that education, training and continuous training have to be an integral part of any country's social policy. Moreover, member states have to recognize the right of each citizen to education and vocational training and, in cooperation with social partners, provide availability of continuous training to all.

The 21st century is considered that of "information society". In this regard "information labour rights" of workers and employers demand their interpretation and a theoretical justification. Their analysis has allowed us to claim an emergence of a new institute within labour law with the similar name.

It is already remarkable that the Labor Code of the Russian Federation includes Chapter 14, the "Protection of Personal Data of a Worker" with more current changes made to the code by the Federal Law from July 2, 2013 No. 185-FL which should be considered as a major step forward.

At the international level, the questions that arise are not centred on the right to work, but on the right to decent work. Thus, the main report of the General Director of the ILO in 1999 was called "Decent Work" and one more report of 2001—"Reducing the Decent Work Deficit". Four measurements of decent work were respectively allocated: the fundamental principles and the rights in the workplace, employment, social protection, and social dialogue[23]. We will still return to this matter when considering the sixth trend.

According to the Russian researcher Z.S. Bogatyrenko, in connection with the adoption of the concept of decent work, the new trend in the development of rule-making at the ILO is focused on an integrated approach to development of the international legal rules on the basis of adoption of comprehensive (frame) conventions[24].

In this regard corresponding change of the legislation, starting with the Constitution of the Russian Federation is necessary. It is important to remember that there is still no right to work, but only the right to freedom

---

[23] International Labour Conference, 87th Session, 1999. *Report of the General Director: Decent Work.*

[24] See: Bogatyrenko, Z.S. ed. 2007. *Mezhdunarodnaya organizaciya truda: konvencii, dokumenty, materially* [International Labor Organization: Conventions, Documents, Materials], Delo I servis, 33. See also: Korneev V.O. ed. 2012. *Dostoiniy trud—osnova social'noy politiki* [Decent Work—a Basis of Social Policy]. Moscow: FNPR, 42 p.; Kolosova R.P., Lubiova M. Ed. 2009. *Dostoiniy trud—kluchevoy resurs innovacionnogo razvitiya* [Decent Work—a Key Resource of Innovative Development]. Moscow: MGU, 272 p., etc.

of work (par.1, Art. 37). The right to work is enshrined in the Labor Code of the Russian Federation (Art. 2) as a component of the principle of freedom of work, that from a theoretical point of view, is more than strange. Possibly, not only the right to work (it is already in the Universal Declaration of Human Rights and in the International Pact on the Economic, Social and Cultural Rights, the norms of which are obligatory for the Russian Federation) but also the right to decent work in the context of the above should be determined in these acts.

3. Provision within labour law of labour mobility for workers and a creation of a special type of "transnational" and "supranational" labour relations is another trend which corresponds with the increasing globalization of the law, its unification and standardization. However, for labour law it has a number of specific features.

Labour mobility, according to economists, is connected with professional, regional and international modulations (movement) of the workforce. In our opinion, from the perspectives of labour law, labour mobility means the opportunity for a worker to change the employer and to conclude a new employment contract with a new employer nationally or abroad.

"The external iron curtain" closeness of the Soviet economy dictated a narrow sphere of external migration of the workforce. Today the situation has essentially changed. The 21st century is a century of globalization when the term "world economy" has become conventional. The process of interaction between States increases through internationalization of capital and simplification of workforce migration.

The general approach to globalization, its reasons and consequences are rather ambiguous. The General Director of MBT on globalization at the end of the 20th century noted the following: "The adaptation of national economies and national institutes to global changes and also the adaptation of global changes to needs of people has become the main problem of the next decade […] globalization turned "adaptation" into the general phenomenon both for rich and poor countries. It changes the structure of development, changing the nature of long-term categories of economic growth and a form of a system of distribution of income. If these trends of our days are not controlled, they will put before us the greatest threat—instability caused by the growing inequality […] The global economy without a reliable social support will be fragile and politically unacceptable".[25]

[25] International Labour Conference, 87th Session, 1999. *Report of the General Director: Decent Work*, 6-7.

The General Assembly of the UN at the 24th special session which took place in Geneva, in June, 2000 accepted the special principles of policy directed on maintenance of social stability in the world. In February, 2002 under the aegis of the ILO the World Commission on Social Consequences of Globalization which finished its work in 2004 was created. The commission noted that discussions on globalization came to a standstill, the public opinion on this problem was split and the international obligations in this part, as a rule, are not fulfilled[26].

Interstate models were to a lesser extent connected with "flexible" regulation of the employment relations. This refers to the formation of a global labour market which has no frontiers, entailed emergence of a so-called "network of employment" (the network teleworker, the remote worker and so forth). An example of such a new network worker is the Russian or French programmer who works for the firms on the other end of the world, for example, in the USA or Australia. He directs there the final product—the program, and from there also receives a salary. All this does not keep in line with labour legislation of the last century. It is remarkable that the Federal Law of April 5, 2013 No. 60-FL included in the Labour Code of the Russian Federation, Chapter 49.1, the "Specific features of Regulation of Work of Remote Workers".

Globalization has led to the matters of external (international) workforce migration. At the turn of the millennia international migration became an aspect reflecting the development of globalization trends in various areas of activity of the world community. Such concepts as "external workforce migration", "guest workers", "border workers", etc. are gradually becoming legalized. It is really a global process that is realized at all levels.

For example, the World Trade Organization (WTO)—Russia became a member in 2012—suggested the addition of international labour agreements with a so-called social article that the export country has to carry out common standards in the sphere of employment[27]. It has to promote alignment of positions of the participating states of the WTO, promote not only free movement of goods and capital but also workers.

Thus, for the last the common standard for the purpose of prevention of "social dumping" (i.e. reduction of a salary and deterioration of working conditions in one country in comparison with another) has to be

---

[26] See: Report of the World Commission on the Social Dimension of Globalization. *A Fair Globalization: Creating Opportunities for all (2004)*. Geneva: ILO. C. IX, 25, 26, etc.

[27] See: *Russian Newspaper* (the newspaper). 2000. January 28.

observed. At the same time it would encourage the raising of requirements related to labour legislation of underdeveloped countries.

Thus, the creation of uniform standards of employment at a rather high level corresponds to interests not only of workers in economically developed countries but also to interests of employers. The aggravation of the world competition demands an establishment of the uniform "rules of the game" allowing to balance positions of employers of the different countries from the point of view of costs for labour. The standards of labour rights have to have not only global character but also the corresponding legal mechanism of their support, realization, first of all, by means of activity of the ILO. That these problems are addressed today at the WTO, EU and some other international organizations, is encouraging. However, it testifies to a certain weakness of the ILO.

Moreover, economically developed countries are not capable or do not wish to assume responsibility for observance of labour law of migrants. It is enough to say that the Convention of the UN on protection of the rights of workers—migrants and members of their families, accepted in 1990, was hardly ratified by 20 minimum necessary states. Respectively, it only came into force on July 1, 2003. In the European convention on a legal status of workers migrants (1977) in Art. 1 this category of workers is treated more narrowly than in acts of the UN and covers only citizens of contracting states without affecting illegal migrants.

So, in EU countries foreigners with the status of "recognized immigrants" are subdivided into two categories. One possesses the right of continuous accommodation to their territories and unconditional access to workplaces. For such migrants this access is provided on the same conditions as for citizens and natives of any European Union country. The other category of immigrants who do not possess the right of free movement can only rely on limited access to the labour market. To find work they need permission which is valid for a limited time, it can be limited to the territory where the person is allowed to work, an industry, or even an occupation.

In accordance with the formulation of Art. 1 of the Labor Code of the Russian Federation, the Russian legislator guarantees labour rights and freedoms only to citizens. It means that these guarantees do not extend on immigrant workers. The Russian Federation has not ratified the above-named Convention of the UN and the Convention of the ILO No. 143 on the rights of migrant workers (1975). It is important to note that the General agreement between the All-Russian Associations of Labour Unions, the All-Russian Associations of Employers and the Government of the Russian Federation for 2008-2010 provides ratification during the specified period of the Convention of the ILO No. 97 "Migration for Employment Convention" (1949) and called for the above Convention of the ILO No. 143 (1975) to be ratified. However, it still has not occurred. The solution of this problem has to be carried out taking into account the economic opportunities of the state and the priority of employment for the Russian citizens.

Thus, the development of an international labour market, and the development of a system legally regulating migrant workers at national and international level became one of the main reasons for migration. Labour migration in the 21st century is a global challenge that has to be approached through labour law, irrespective of one's nationality and place of residence.

4. An increase in flexibility (including differentiation and individualization) in legal regulation of labour relations in combination with provisions of labour law of the worker.

The need to strengthen flexibility of the state and legal regulation of the labour market in the West arose in the last few decades by objective requirements of the modern economy. Its survival as a necessary and important social tool considerably depends on the ability of modern labour law to gain flexibility. A similar position is now supported by a number of Russian experts.[28]

Prior to the start of the 1970s, industry was the main sphere of employment both for western and Soviet society. This type of production is characterized by the technocratic organization of work and management. At the turn of the century industry lost its position in attracting labour, and this loss can accurately be traced. This reference has shifted from the primary sector (production) to the secondary and tertiary (an exchange and

---

[28] See in details: Korkin, A.E. 2013. *Netipichnye trudovye otnosheniya: zaemniy trud, telerabota i rabota po vyzovu. Pravovaya priroda* [Atypical Labor Relations: Loan Work, TV Work and Work on a Call]. Moscow: Infotropik, 208 p.; Lushnikov, A.M. 2012. "Yuridicheskaya konstrukciya «gibkobil'nosti»: netipichnye trudovye pravootnosheniya" [Legal Design of "Flexicurity": Atypical Labor Legal Relationship], *Vestnik trudovogo prava i prava social'nogo obespecheniya* [Bulletin of Labor Law and Social Security Law], No. 6: 56-67; Radevich, E.R. 2013. *Rasshirenie sfery primeneniya nestandartnoy zanyatosti kak sredstvo obespecheniya gibkosti v ispol'zovanii naemnogo truda* [Expansion of Application of the Sphere of Non-Standard Employment as an Instrument for Ensuring of Flexibility in Use of Wage Labor], Paper presented at the 1st International Theoretical and Practical Conference *Tendencii razvitiya nauki trudovogo prava i prava social'nogo obespecheniya* [Tendencies of Development of Science of the Labor Law and Law of Social Security]. Kiev: Nika-Centr, 344-348, etc.

services) sectors. As a result, a new type of production has emerged (flexible innovative production) along with and new post-industrial organizational models.

The radical updating of technology in terms of a computerization, informatisation, automation, and the introduction of flexible production systems has entailed essential changes in the sphere of the organization of work: Taylorism and Fordism have been overcome through an introduction of the organization of flexible productions. It caused structural changes in the labour market in the form of the emergence of non-standard forms of employment: work away from of the main office including teleworkers; temporary agency work; part-time work; job sharing; flexible working time agreements; reduced working weeks, and temporary employment. In developed countries between 15 to 30% of workers are in such forms of employment. In economic literature the flexibility of legal regulation of labour relations corresponds with the need of legal support for non-standard forms of employment. Standard employment is considered as full-time employment for which an open-ended contract of employment is concluded. Work is carried out at the employer's premises and under the employer's direct control and supervision. Respectively, all forms of employment deviating from the described standard are considered as atypical, or non-standard.

Strengthening flexibility in the regulation of the labour relations, and the expansion of the sphere of legal differentiation and contractual regulation raises a question of flexibility's limits on the agenda. Such limits have to be established, first of all, by 1) the universally recognized norms and the principles of the international labour law 2) the principles of labour law as a separate branch of law (a discrimination ban in the labour relations, a ban on forced labour, etc.), 3) the minimum level of labour rights and safeguards established by the law (national standards for labour rights, the minimum wage, the maximum duration of overtime work, minimum holiday, etc.).

In this context it is far from clear why the Russian legislator tends to forbid temporary agency work in the Russian Federation. The last attempts at the very end of 2012 and during the summer of 2013 were unsuccessful; however, the matter has not left the agenda. It is necessary to legalize this form of non-standard employment, although with some reasonable restrictions which should protect employee rights and legitimate interests.

It is obvious that flexibility has to be combined with security (so called flexicurity) and to be favourable for an employee, as well as to be based on balance of interests of all parties of the labour relation. Moreover, in certain cases labour legislation has to be more rigid. It concerns, at least:

1) the protection of the personal non-property rights of workers discussed above, 2) the protection against discrimination, including gender,[29] 3) job safety.

5. Harmonization of individual and collective labour rights because of the expansion of the sphere of social partnership.

This trend is connected with the expansion of the sphere of social dialogue (social partnership), and the adaptation of collective labour relations to the economic realities of the 21st century.

The beginning of the 21st century was marked by essential changes, shifts in public organization of work, and strengthening of the individual and contractual (private) beginnings in legal regulation of labour relations. As a result, a decrease in the role of labour unions of workers, or their professional solidarity occurred. This trend is connected with social regularity of an individualization of public relations and their legal regulation. In general it preserves at the beginning of the 21st century. Thus, the individualization of labour relations is inevitably reflected in the destiny of collective labour relations.

Thus, the ILO considers that it is impossible to offer a uniform ideal model of social partnership which would promote social and economic growth better than other models. The ILO in conventions and recommendations defined the main forms and levels of cooperation of workers, employers and the state as well as legal principles of their social partnership. The international standards of collective labour rights make provisions for the formation and development of national models of social partnership.

The legal means of social partnership depending on national features range from consulting forms of cooperation of social partners prior to the adoption of joint decisions to collective agreements/contracts, and cover rank-and-file participants at the company and national level.

Globalization of the labour market will inevitably lead to an enrichment of the content of the international mechanism of social partnership. In the last century there was an interstate level of social partnership by means of activity of the ILO and other international organizations, associations (The Council of Europe, the European Union, the CIS, etc.). At the end of the 20th century the practice of concluding international collective agreements became widespread. This level of regulation of transnational labour relations will have further

---

[29] See in details: Lushnikov, A.M., Lushnikova, M.V., Tarusina, N.N. 2006. *Gendernoe ravenstvo v semie i trude: zametki yuristov* [Gender Equality in Family and Work: Notes of Lawyers]. Moscow: Prospekt, 288 p.

development.[30] The next trend is partly connected with these processes as well.

6. Priority of the international labour standards.

This trend is based on the international, universal concept of human rights and is closely associated with an increase of the role of the generally recognized principles and standards of international labour law in a globalizing world. Current literature points to an increase in the authority of international labour standards, many of which embody the generally recognized principles and norms of international law, act as national law and even have priority over national law. We observe that the mechanism of directly ensuring international legal protection of individual labour rights and signs of transformation of regional labour standards in national law, for example, in the countries of the European Union, is occurring.[31] In these conditions former ideas of the unlimited sovereignty of the national state in regulation of labour relations have lost significance.

It is important to emphasize that certain changes within Russian legislation are a direct consequence of ratification by Russia of international treaties, first of all, ILO conventions. Thus, ratification in 2010 by our country of the Convention No. 187 on "Occupational Safety and Health" (2006) led to the Federal Law of July 18, 2011 No. 238-FL[32] which amended Art. 209, introducing the notion of "occupational risks" and how to manage them.

The international labour standards received the fullest expression in conventions and recommendations of the ILO. As Z.S. Bogatyrenko rightly states, the present stage of improvement of rule-making activity of the ILO is inseparably linked with the adoption of the Declaration on the Fundamental Principles and the Rights in the Sphere of Work and the Mechanism of its Realization (1998)[33] and also the concept of decent work.[34]

---

[30] See: Shuraleva, S. V. 2012. *Pravovoe regulirovanie individual'nykh i kollektivnykh trudovykh otnosheniy v transnacional'nykh korporaciyakh v Rossii* [Legal Regulation of the Individual and Collective Labor Relations in Multinational Corporations in Russia]. Perm: Perm GU, 195 p.

[31] See: Gusov, K.N., Lyutov, N. L. 2013. *Mezhdunarodnoe trudovoe pravo* [International Labor Law]. Moscow: Prospekt, 115, etc.; Kiselev, I.Ya. 2005. *Sravnitel'noe trudovoe pravo* [Comparative Labor Law]. Moscow: Prospekt, 4, et al.

[32] *Russian Newspaper* (the newspaper). 2011. July 22.

[33] *Russian Newspaper* (the newspaper). 1998. December 16.

[34] Bogatyrenko, Z.S. 2003. "*Noveishie tendencii v normotvorcheskoy deyatel'nosti Mezhdunarodnoy organizacii truda*" [The Latest Tendencies in Rule-Making

As already stated above, at the beginning of the 21st century the ILO's main task is to implement the concept of decent work. The statistical basic indicators of the objective measurement of decent work were developed by the International Bureau of Work at the ILO and allow to value the correspondence of the state of labour relations in certain countries with declared objectives. The concept of decent work includes six aspects.

Firstly, it concerns the term *"employment opportunities for women and men"* that means that both women and men can seek work which is understood in a broad sense as all forms of economic activity, including self-employment, unpaid family work and work whether in the informal or formal sector.

Secondly, *it concerns the idea about work* in the conditions of freedom which stresses that work is to be freely performed and that some forms of employment are unacceptable in the 21st century, in particular, forced labour, slave labour and the worst forms of child labour. Freedom also refers to the right of workers to freely organize without any discrimination.

Thirdly, *productive work* is essential for workers so that they have a means of livelihood for themselves and their families. It also provides for sustainable development and competitiveness of enterprises and states.

Fourthly, *the concept of justice at work* refers to the necessity of fairness and equal opportunities at work. It includes freedom from discrimination at work and in recruiting, as well as the opportunity to balance work with family life.

Fifthly, *security at work* refers to the guarantee of health, pension, a means of livelihood, financial compensation and protection in case of illness or other unforeseen circumstances.

Finally, *dignity at work* requires that workers should be treated respectfully and that they can participate in decision-making with regards to their conditions of employment. Thus, they have the opportunity to represent themselves and their collective interests.

International labour law is an important component of the international law of human rights. It is considered as a branch of international law, and principles and norms regulate cooperation of the states in ensuring human rights. In the 21st century, international law addresses individuals and respect of their rights[35].

Activity of the International Labor Organization], *Trud za rubezhom* [Work abroad], No. 3:129-158.

[35] See, e.g.: Lukashuk, I.I. 2005. *Mezhdunarodnoe pravo. Chast' Osobennaya* [International Law. Special Part]. Moscow: Volters Kluver, 432 p.; Lukasheva, *E.A. ed. 2002. Prava cheloveka: Itogi veka, tendencii, perspektivy* [Human Rights:

The main priority of international relations for the 21st century is to create a base of world order. The recognition of rights and freedoms of individuals are to be held as of supreme value and should be considered a duty of the state and the world community.[36]

References

Alekseev, S.S. 1999. *Pravo: azbuka-teoriya-filosofiya* [Law: Alphabet-Theory-Philosophy]. Moscow: Statut, 712 p.

Baglay, M.V. 1998. *Konstitucionnoe pravo Rossiyskoy Federacii* [Constitutional Law of the Russian Federation]. Moscow: Norma, 752 p.

Bogatyrenko, Z.S. 2003. "*Noveishie tendencii v normotvorcheskoy deyatel'nosti Mezhdunarodnoy organizacii truda*" [The Latest Trends in Rule-Making Activity of the International Labor Organization], *Trud za rubezhom* [Work abroad], No. 3: 129-158.

Bogatyrenko, Z.S. ed. 2007. *Mezhdunarodnaya organizaciya truda: konvencii, dokumenty, materially* [International Labor Organization: Conventions, Documents, Materials], Moscow: Delo i servis, 752 p.

Bugrov, L.Yu. 1992. *Problemy svobody truda v trudovom prave Rossii* [Problems of Freedom of Labour in the Labor Law of Russia]. Perm: Perm GU, 236 p.

Bugrov, L.Yu., Khudyakov, S. S., Varlamova, U.V., Goncov, N.I. 1995. *Tvorchestvo i trudovoe pravo* [Creativity and Labor Law]. Perm: Perm GU, 132 p.

Davidov, G., Langille, B. ed. 2011. *The idea of Labour Law*. New York: Oxford University Press. 454 p.

Doybler, V. 1995. "*Tendencii razvitiya trudovogo prava v promyshlenno razvityh stranah* [Trends of Development of the Labor Law in Industrialized Countries]," Paper presented at the Moscow State Law Academy, Moscow, Russia, October 1994, *Gosudarstvo i pravo* [State and Law], No 2: 103-109.

Results of an Eyelid, Trends, and Prospects / Ed. by E.A. Lukasheva. Moscow: Norma, 573 p.

[36] See in details: Lushnikova, M. V., Lushnikov, and A.M. 2011. *Mezhdunarodnoe trudovoe pravo i pravo social'nogo obespecheniya* [International Labor Law and Law of Social Security]. Moscow; Lushnikova M. V. 2011. "Mezhdunarodnoe chastnoe trudovoe pravo: konceptual'nye podkhody" [International Private Labor Law: Conceptual Approaches], Russian Year-Book of the Labor Law, No. 7, 608-628, etc.

—. "Current Trends of Development of the Labor Law of Germany and Euro—Crisis," Paper presented at the Higher School of Economics (Moscow, Russia), September 2012 (not published).

Golovina, S. Yu. 2007. "*Sovremennye tendencii v trudovom prave Rossii*" [Current Trends in the Labor Law of Russia], Paper presented at the Moscow State Law Academy, Moscow, Russia, January 2006, *Sovremennye tendencii v razvitii trudovogo prava i prava social'nogo obespecheniya: sbornik materialov konferencii* [Current Trends in Development of the Labor Law and the Law of Social Security: collected reports of the conference]. Moscow: Prospect, 9-37.

Gusov, K.N., Lyutov, N. L. 2013. *Mezhdunarodnoe trudovoe pravo* [International Labor Law]. Moscow: Prospekt, 592 p.

Inshina, N.I., Khutoryan, N.M., Scherbina, V.I. ed. 2013. *Tendencii razvitiya nauki trudovogo prava i prava social'nogo obespecheniya* [Trends of Development of Science of the Labor Law and Law of Social Security], Papers presented at the 1st International Theoretical and Practical Conference. Kiev: Nika-Centr, 676 p.

International Covenant on Economic, Social and Cultural Rights of 1966.

International Labour Conference, 87th Session, 1999. *Report of the General Director: Decent Work*.

International Labour Conference, 87th Session, 1999. *Report of the General Director: Decent Work*, 6-7.

Izvestiya (the newspaper). 1987. June 22.

Kiselev, I.Ya. 2003. *Noviy oblik trudovogo prava stran zapada (proryv v postindustrial'noe obschestvo)* [New Shape of the Labor Law of the Countries of the West (Break in Post-Industrial Society)]. Moscow: Intel-Sintez, 160 p.

—. 2005. *Sravnitel'noe trudovoe pravo* [Comparative Labor Law]. Moscow: Prospekt, 360 p.

Kolosova R.P., Lubiova M. Ed. 2009.*Dostoiniy trud—kluchevoy resurs innovacionnogo razvitiya* [Decent Work—a Key Resource of Innovative Development]. Moscow: MGU, 272 p.

Korkin, A.E. 2013. *Netipichnye trudovye otnosheniya: zaemniy trud, telerabota i rabota po vyzovu. Pravovaya priroda* [Atypical Labor Relations: Loan Work, TV Work and Work on a Call]. Moscow: Infotropik, 208 p.

Korneev V.O. ed. 2012. 2012. *Dostoiniy trud—osnova social'noy politiki* [Decent Work—a Basis of Social Policy]. Moscow: FNPR, 42 p

Leyst, O. E. 2002. *Suschnost' prava* [The Essence of the Law]. Moscow: Zertsalo-M, 288 p.

Lukasheva, *E.A. ed. 2002. Prava cheloveka: Itogi veka, tendencii, perspektivy* [Human Rights: Results of an Eyelid, Trends, Prospects. Moscow: Norma, 573 p.

Lukashuk, I.I. 2005. *Mezhdunarodnoe pravo. Chast' Osobennaya* [International Law. Special Part]. Moscow: Volters Kluver, 432 p.

Lushnikov A.M., Lushnikova, M. V. 2009. *Kurs trudovogo prava* [Course of the Labor Law]. V.1. Moscow: Statut, 879 p.

Lushnikov, A.M. 2012. "Yuridicheskaya konstrukciya «gibkobil'nosti»: netipichnye trudovye pravootnosheniya" [Legal Design of "Flexicurity": Atypical Labor Legal Relationship], *Vestnik trudovogo prava i prava social'nogo obespecheniya* [Bulletin of Labor Law and Social Security Law], No. 6: 56-66.

Lushnikov, A.M., Lushnikova, M.V., Tarusina, N.N. 2006. *Gendernoe ravenstvo v semie i trude: zametki yuristov* [Gender Equality in a Family and Work: Notes of Lawyers]. Moscow: Prospekt, 288 p.

Lushnikova M.V. 2011. "Mezhdunarodnoe chastnoe trudovoe pravo: konceptual'nye podkhody" [International Private Labor Law: Conceptual Approaches], Russian Year-Book of the Labor Law, No. 7:608-628.

—. 1997. *Gosudarstvo, rabotodateli, rabotniki* [State, Employers, Workers]. Yaroslavl: Podati, 224 p.

Lushnikova, M.V., Lushnikov, A.M. 2006. *Ocherki teorii trudovogo prava* [Sketches of the Theory of the Labor Law]. St. Petersburg: Yuridicheskiy centr Press, 940 p.

Lushnikova, M.V., Lushnikov, A.M. 2011. *Mezhdunarodnoe trudovoe pravo i pravo social'nogo obespecheniya* [International Labor Law and Law of Social Security]. Moscow: Jurlitinform, 304 p.

"*Mezhdunarodnye trudovye normy kak global'nye obschestvennye blaga"* [International Labor Norms as Global Public Benefits], *Mezhdunarodniy obzor truda 141* [International Review of Work], No. 1-2:180-196.

Mikhaylova, N.S. 2003. *Trudovoe pravo i tvorchestvo prepodavateley vuzov* [Labor Law and Creativity of Teachers of Higher Education Institutions]. Perm: Perm GU, 112 p.

Morozov, P.E. 2012. *Sovremennye tendencii razvitiya zarubezhnogo trudovogo prava v usloviyah globalizacii* [Current Trends of Development of the Foreign Labor Law in the Conditions of Globalization]. Moscow: Prospekt. 256 p.

Radevich, E.R. 2013. *Rasshirenie sfery primeneniya nestandartnoy zanyatosti kak sredstvo obespecheniya gibkosti v ispol'zovanii naemnogo truda* [Expansion of Application of the Sphere of Non-Standard Employment as an Instrument for Ensuring of Flexibility in

Use of Wage Labor], Paper presented at the 1st International Theoretical and Practical Conference *Tendencii razvitiya nauki trudovogo prava i prava social'nogo obespecheniya* [Trends of Development of Science of the Labor Law and Law of Social Security]. Kiev: Nika-Centr, 344-348, etc.

Report of the World Commission on the Social Dimension of Globalization. *A Fair Globalization: Creating Opportunities for all (2004)*. Geneva: ILO. C. IX, 25, 26, etc.

Russian Newspaper (the newspaper). 1998. December 16.

—. 2000. January 28.

—. 2009. June 5.

—. 2011. July 22.

Shuraleva, S.V. 2012. *Pravovoe regulirovanie individual'nykh i kollektivnykh trudovykh otnosheniy v transnacional'nykh korporaciyakh v Rossii* [Legal Regulation of the Individual and Collective Labor Relations in Multinational Corporations in Russia].

Universal Declaration of Human Rights (UDHR) of 1948.

Wedderburn of Charlton, K.K.W., Sinzheimer, H. ed. 1994. *Labour law in the post-industrial era: essays in honour of Hugo Sinzheimer.* Aldershot. 152 p.

The Harmonization of Labour Legislation in Former Soviet Union States

Svetlana Golovina

Following the collapse of the USSR, the former Soviet republics began to unite once more, this time according to new principles which excluded dependency and inequality between states. On 8 December 1991, by signing the Agreement known as the Belavezha Accords, the Commonwealth of Independent States (CIS) was founded. The CIS is a regional international organization created in order to regulate the relations of cooperation between states which were formerly part of the Soviet Union. The CIS's founding document, signed by the presidents of Belarus, Russia and Ukraine, stated that the parties agreed to found the Commonwealth of Independent States based on the following principles: the historical community of their peoples, the connections between them, bilateral agreements, the pursuit of a democratic rule of law, the intention to develop their relations on the basis of mutual recognition and respect for state sovereignty. The founding members of the Commonwealth were Armenia, Azerbaijan, Belarus, Kazakhstan, Kyrgyzstan, Moldova, Russia, Tajikistan, Turkmenistan and Ukraine. Until 2009 Georgia also was a member of the CIS.

Part of the CIS's active cooperation has been to adopt a series of regulatory documents which have different degrees of obligation for different state parties of the Commonwealth. From amongst the legally binding acts it is worth noting the CIS Convention on Human Rights and Basic Freedoms of Man (26 May 1995) and the Agreement on the Regulation of Social and Labour Relations in Multinational Corporations Operating on the Territory of CIS State Parties (9 October 1997). The Charter of Social Rights and Guarantees of Independent State Citizens, approved on 29 October 1994 by the Resolution of the Inter-parliamentary Assembly of the CIS, also acquired a fundamental importance.

In Art. 1 of the aforementioned Charter it was proclaimed that the states shall form a single labour market. Citizens may move freely within the Commonwealth and have equal rights to paid employment and to pursue their personal and social needs on the territory of any state. States have an obligation to provide citizens with a series of social rights and guarantees including: the freedom of occupation and work throughout the economic community, free career guidance, education and vocational training as well as professional development, free assistance in finding suitable employment according to their vocation, abilities, training and education. States are also obliged to offer, in accordance with national legislation, additional employment guarantees for those who require social protection and have difficulty finding work including young people, single income families with several children or children with disabilities, people close to retirement, soldiers, disabled persons, the long-term unemployed, people who have served prison sentences or have had compulsory restrictions placed on them by courts, etc. The most important rights and guarantees in the world of work have been enshrined in the Charter: the prohibition of the unfair dismissal of workers, a limitation of 40 working hours per week, the right to paid annual leave, the prohibition of discrimination in the workplace, a limitation on deductions from wages as well as others.

Several model CIS laws (those regarding the protection of labour, collective agreements, employment agreements, personal data, etc.) and the Concept of Model Labour Code for the Commonwealth of Independent States (2000) were accepted by the states.[1] Although the model laws are only recommendations and do not constrain CIS state parties to bring their national legislation into conformity with their provisions, the fact that the states have adopted these laws voluntarily demonstrates their commitment to working together.

In 2000 five former Soviet Union states, Belarus, Kazakhstan, Kyrgyzstan, Russia and Tajikistan, established the Eurasian Economic Community (EurAsEC)[2] in order to effectively promote the creation of a single economic space, coordinating approaches while trying to integrate into the world economy and the international trade system. Creating a new union of states was a consequence of the objective process of the globalization of the world economy and of the further deepening of economic integration at an international level. The liberalization of external economic relations and the removal of administrative barriers

---

[1] For more acts of CIS linked to labour and related relationships, see Kiselev, I. Ya. 1999. *Sravnitel'noe i mezhdunarodnoe trudovoe pravo: uchebnik [Comparative and International Labour Law: Textbook]*. Moscow: Delo, 575-583.

[2] The agreement on the establishment of the Eurasian Economic Community was signed by the presidents on 10 October 2000 in Astana (Kazakhstan).

which previously prohibited labour migration caused an objective need for convergent approaches to the legal regulation of labour and a better integration of labour legislation in the united countries.

Following the creation of the Customs Union in December 2010 at the Eurasian Economic Community summit in Moscow, decisions about the creation of a Eurasian Union on the basis of the Common Economic Space of Belarus, Kazakhstan and Russia were reached. In October 2011 an agreement was signed to establish a free trade zone within the CIS. Some experts see this agreement as the starting point for the creation of new relations, as well as for increasing the total number of EurAsEC members.

One of the consequences of the establishment of the Customs Union was a reduction in the number of administrative barriers for labour migration between Russia, Belarus and Kazakhstan. On 19 November 2010, an agreement was signed in St Petersburg between the governments of the Republic of Belarus, the Republic of Kazakhstan and the Russian Federation regarding the Legal Status of Migrant Workers and Members of their Families ("the Agreement"). Art. 3 of the Agreement states that activities performed by migrant workers are to be organized by the employers in the state of employment without restrictions for the protection of the national labour market, and furthermore, migrant workers are not required to obtain permits in order to work in the territories of the states party to the agreement. The labour relations between a migrant worker and the employer are governed by the legislation of the state of employment in accordance with the Agreement and are defined in the employment contract.

The increase of migration has once again highlighted the need to coordinate the labour laws of states which are closely related to each other by common historical roots and modern economic relations. The current labour legislation of EurAsEC member states is, on the one hand, characterized by certain similarities, a uniformity of structure, the unity of the fundamental principles of the legal regulation of labour notwithstanding their separate legal institutions and separate legal structures. This can be explained by the fact that the labour codes in the various states have common legal roots going back to the Primary Legislation of the USSR and the Union Republics on Labour, adopted on 15 July 1970 and remaining in force until the collapse of the Soviet Union. On the other hand, an analysis of the legal framework of the Eurasian Economic Community in the field of labour regulation reveals the presence of a number of differences between the states such as, for example, those found in the terms of legal regulation, the quantity of labour guarantees for workers, the degree of normative elaboration of certain institutions and regulations, etc.

Labour legislation in the EurAsEC states is being continually reformed; codified laws have repeatedly adjusted by perfecting and clarifying existing rules and by the introduction of new articles and even whole chapters.[3] Over the past few years, the labour codes of EurAsEC countries have been supplemented with anti-corruption norms, the establishment of prohibitions, restrictions and additional duties for public officials,[4] as well as the definition of special grounds for the termination of their employment contracts.

In addition to the Labour Codes in EurAsEC countries there are a number of other important labour laws which concern professional unions, the employment of the population (in all EurAsEC countries), collective agreements and social partnerships (in Kyrgyzstan and Tajikistan), Employer Associations (in Russia and Kyrgyzstan) and Worker Health and Safety (in Kyrgyzstan, Russia and Tajikistan).

In a situation of increasing integration of EurAsEC member states and growing labour migration, it is vital to provide equal conditions of labour activity in the territories of all related countries. The solution to this problem may lie in finding a certain harmonization between national systems of labour legislation in order to balance the rights of citizens to decent work against cost.

The process of coordinating labour legislation in EurAsEC countries began with the adoption of the EurAsEC Inter-Parliamentary Assembly Regulations on 13 May 2009 (see No. 10-13), which approved the recommendations on the harmonization of labour legislation of EurAsEC member states. The recommendations were sent to the parliaments of the member states and to the Integration Committee of the Eurasian Economic Community to aid them in the coordination of national legislation and the improvement of a legal basis for the Community. The next step in the legal coordination of EurAsEC member states took place on 18 June 2004 in Astana where the Interstate Council of the Eurasian Economic Community signed the Treaty on the Status of the Basic Legislative Principles of the Eurasian Economic Community Legislation and on the Procedure for their Elaboration, Adoption and Implementation (the "Treaty").

---

[3] For example, in 2013 the The Labour Code of the Russian Federation was amended with Chapter 49.1 "Peculiarities of the regulation of distance workers' labour".

[4] The term "public official" is used in the United Nations Convention against Corruption signed on 31 October 2003.

According to Art. 2 of the Treaty, the principles for the development of the EurAsEC's legal base are: a) principles which are in conformity with the generally recognized principles and norms of international law, and b) principles which take into account the legal, socio-economic and other consequences of their implementation. The Basic Legislative Principles in the area of legal relations are to be developed by the EurAsEC Inter-parliamentary Assembly, proposed on the advice of the Interstate Council and accepted by an international agreement between EurAsEC member states (Art. 1 part 2 of the Treaty). Thus, thanks to their legal nature, the Basic Legislative Principles have become part of a multilateral international agreement created within the framework of the Eurasian Economic Community.

According to the very concept of the EurAsEC Basic Principles of Labour Legislation (approved with the Resolution of the EurAsEC Inter-parliamentary Assembly of 27 October 2010, No. 8) the Principles should be seen as a fundamental legal act of the Eurasian Economic Community which establishes the general principles of legal regulation in the field of labour.

The project of the EurAsEC Basic Principles of Labour Legislation is currently being developed in order to create a common labour market and to facilitate the free movement of labour in accordance with the plan of action created by the Common Economic Space of Belarus, Kazakhstan and the Russian Federation, and approved with the decision of the Interstate Council of the Eurasian Economic Community on 19 December 2009 (No. 35). The Basic Principles of Labour Legislation are essentially a regional legal instrument which defines legal policy in the labour sector for EurAsEC member states. As has been noted in literature, "regionalization is currently one of the trends of the development of modern relationships in the workplace".[5]

The coordination of labour legislation in the community states aims, first of all, to create interstate standards in the field of the regulation of labour relations and to improve national labour legislation. In this regard, while developing the EurAsEC Basic Principles of Labour Legislation it seems necessary to solve the following problems:

- how to modernize labour legislation in accordance with the demands of a market economy while maintaining fundamental guarantees in the world of work;

[5] Gusov, K. N, and N. L. Lyutov. 2013. *Mezhdunarodnoe trudovoe pravo [International Labour Law: A Textbook].* Moscow: Prospect, 129.

- how to create an effective mechanism for the protection of workers' labour rights, to ensure that violations of these rights occur as rarely as possible;
- how to aid the populations of EurAsEC members in finding employment, build equal opportunities and prevent discrimination in the field of employment and labour and eliminate all forms of forced or compulsory labour;
- how to best provide legal protection and support for women, minors, disabled people and vulnerable people.

In developing the EurAsEC Basic Principles of Labour Legislation the organization hopes to achieve two things. In order to create equal conditions for employment for all citizens of EurAsEC member states, it is necessary to eliminate any fundamental differences in the legal regulation of labour and labour relations between these countries. At the same time, one must bear in mind that employment law is part of the social sector and its provisions are aimed primarily at protecting the interests of employees; this is why, although conceptual differences in the regulation of labour and labour relations found in the Labour Codes of the EurAsEC member states do exist, it is important to aim for the conditions which are most favourable to the worker.

There is, however, an objective obstacle: the inequality of economic conditions and the peculiarities of national labour markets do not allow for the full unification of labour legislation as the question is not so much one of unification, but of harmonization. The most important aim of legislation is the search for a balanced approach to the development of common legal and labour norms. This raises another problem—how to maintain an adequate scope for the domestic regulation of labour relations in order to preserve national peculiarities and allow the legal traditions of EurAsEC member states to continue. In other words, the Principles must impose basic labour standards and guarantees for workers in order to create a foundation for the regulation of legal relations within the sphere of labour law. At the same time, EurAsEC states must retain the possibility to define specific provisions in national legislation, including by being able to increase guarantees for the rights of both workers and employers.

The main criteria for the development of the Principles must, of course, be their compliance with international labour standards, and it is advisable to take into account the regulations, conventions and recommendations of the International Labour Organization (ILO) on issues of labour relations and regulation. International labour standards can be regarded as a model for the EurAsEC Basic Principles of Labour Legislation. The constitutions of all EurAsEC member states include the necessity to take into account international standards (Art. 4 of the Constitution of the Republic of Kazakhstan, Art. 12 of the Constitution of the Kyrgyz Republic, Art. 15 of the Constitution of the Russian Federation, Art. 10 of the Constitution of the Republic of Tajikistan, Art. 8 of the Constitution of the Republic of Belarus).

However, it is of note that there is a difference between EurAsEC member states regarding the ratification of ILO Conventions. At the beginning of 2013 the Russian Federation had ratified 69 conventions (10 of which have been denounced), the Kyrgyz Republic, 53, Tajikistan, 49, Belarus, 49 (42 of which are in force) and the Republic of Kazakhstan, 21. However, all the states have ratified the eight core ILO conventions: No. 29 Forced Labour Convention (1930), No. 87 Freedom of Association and Protection of the Right to Organize (1948), No. 98 Right to Organize and Collective Bargaining Convention (1949), No. 100 Equal Remuneration Convention (1951), No. 105 Abolition of Forced Labour Convention (1957), No. 111 Discrimination (Employment and Occupation) Convention (1958) , No. 138 Minimum Age Convention (1973) and No. 182 Worst Forms of Child Labour Convention (1999). It should, however, be noted that the Republic of Kazakhstan has not ratified the very important No. 95 Protection of Wages Convention (1949).

The No. 143 Migrant Workers Convention has only been ratified by the Republic of Tajikistan. This does not, however, mean that it should not be taken into account while creating the general legislation act. These documents must be given careful consideration in the development of the EurAsEC Basic Principles of Labour Legislation, regardless of whether they have been ratified by all, some or none of the EurAsEC member states. It is correctly noted that "expanding the participation of EurAsEC countries in the ILO [is] the basis and condition for the development of a coherent legal policy on most aspects of labour regulation. The Principles, in their turn, by taking into account the positive and universal of international rules, are designed to revitalize state activity by bringing national rules into conformity with generally accepted standards of labour policy".[6]

In recent years ILO policy has been to promote the Concept of Decent Work, which is based on four key elements specified in ILO Conventions concerning fundamental rights at work: decent employment, decent wages,

---

[6] Abalduev, V. A. 2010. "Kodifikaciya trudovogo zakonodatel'stva EvrAzES — osnova soglasovaniya i sovershenstvovaniya nacional'noy pravovoy politiki v sfere truda [The Codification of EurAsEC Labour Legislation—the Basis of the Harmonization and Improvement of the National Legal Labour Policy]," *Trudovoe pravo v Rossii i za rubezhom [Labour Law in Russia and Abroad]*, No. 3: 14.

social protection and social dialogue. On 10 June 2008 the International Labour Organization adopted the Declaration on Social Justice for a Fair Globalization[7] and announced the universal character of the Decent Work Programme: all ILO member countries should pursue policies directed towards strategic goals and solutions in areas such as employment, social protection, social dialogue and workers' rights.

On a state level, decent work programmes are an agreement between the ILO and its national partners and include specific tasks identified for the joint action of partners over a three- or four-year period. The purpose of Decent Work is to contribute to the improvement of workers and their families' lives in practice. To date Decent Work Programmes have been signed by three EurAsEc member states (Kazakhstan, Kyrgyzstan and Tajikistan) and one observer state (Armenia).

In December 2012, an international high-level conference on decent work was held in Russia and, as a result, a programme of cooperation between the Russian Federation and the ILO for 2013-2016 was signed by the Russian Government, the Russian Union of Industrialists and Entrepreneurs, the Federation of Independent Trade Unions of Russia and the ILO. The main aim of this programme is to promote the further development of social and labour relations in the Russian Federation in order to achieve decent work by concentrating efforts in such areas as the expansion of employment and the creation of quality workplaces, social protection, payment and labour security, respect for international labour standards and fundamental principles and rights at work, and social dialogue.

As well as providing a basis for the development of the EurAsEC basic Principles, working with the ILO also facilitates consideration of the European Social Charter and practice of the European Union regarding the regulation of labour relations.

The EurAsEC Basic Principles of Labour Legislation act as a model of a codified act regulating labour and labour relations which can be used by member states in developing and adjusting their national labour codes and other regulations in the field of labour and employment. The Principles should not fundamentally contradict the pre-existing national legal regulation of labour relations, but should take into account the best and most advanced legislative accomplishments which have been made in

---

7 http://www.ilo.org/wcmsp5/groups/public/———dgreports/———cabinet/ documents/publication/wcms_100193.pdf (accessed 1 December 2013).

internationally and which have already proven to be socially and economically efficient.[8]

The relevance of developing the EurAsEC Basic Principles of Labour Legislation lies in the necessity to establish a common methodology for the legal regulation of employment relationships by taking advantage of the cumulative experience of EurAsEC member states in the field of labour legislation. To achieve its goals and objectives EurAsEC states must find a way to converge their legal approaches to the regulation of labour relations in order to improve the efficiency of legislation. According to the approved Concept of EurAsEC Basic Principles of Labour Legislation, not pursuing the aim of attaining a more careful regulation of labour relations and related areas could have serious consequences.

In accordance with established tradition, the labour codes of member states should maintain a familiar structure and make use of the EurAsEC Principles of Labour Legislation in both general and specific parts. The basic (initial) principles of the legal regulation of labour (goals, objectives, principles, ambits, sources, the characteristics of labour relations and their subjects), and the issues of social partnerships should be defined in the general part of legislation. The unique part which will be represented by all traditional institutions of labour law, is found in the Labour Code of each EurAsEC member state and concerns: employment contracts, working hours and rest periods, the payment and regulation of labour, guarantees and compensation in employment, vocational training, re-training and skills development, labour discipline, worker health and safety, the liability of parties of the employment contract, labour disputes, the supervision and monitoring of compliance with labour legislation, specific labour regulations for certain categories of workers (women, minors, persons with disabilities, and so on).

The aims of the EurAsEC Basic Principles of Labour Legislation are:

- the creation of favourable working conditions in order to improve the quality of human life;
- the establishment of state guarantees, labour rights and freedoms for the citizens of EurAsEC member states;
- the protection of workers' and employers' rights and interests;

[8] For more information about the content of EurAsEC Principles of labour legislation: Golovina S. Yu., 2008, "Perspektivi razvitiya trudovogo zakonodatel'stva v ramkah Evraziyskogo Ekonomicheskogo soobshchestva [Perspectives for the development of labour law in the framework of the Eurasian Economic Community]," *Rossiyskiy yezhegodnik trudovogo prava [Russian Yearbook of Labor Law]*, No. 4: 351-368.

- the implementation of international agreements and targeted programmes in the field labour and employment in EurAsEC member states.

To achieve these goals major problems must be solved by:

- the creation of the necessary legal conditions for achieving the optimal coordination of the interests of parties in labour relations and the interests of the EurAsEC member states;
- the legal regulation of labour and labour relations in order to increase the efficiency of production and the welfare of the people.

It is necessary to determine the place and role of the EurAsEC Basic Principles of Labour Legislation, as a fundamental international legal act, in the system of the sources of EurAsEC member states' national labour legislation.

The Principles should contain rules governing the conflict of laws which clarify which country's law will be applied in cases of labour disputes arising from a particular issue when this matter is not regulated in the Principles or referred to by the national legislative authority.

The possibility of defining the regulation of labour relations on a contractual basis (in collective agreements and stipulations, employment agreements), is also managed by the legislation of Commonwealth countries which guarantees that the inclusion of conditions in the contract which might weaken the position of workers in labour legislation is prohibited.

The tasks of defining the content of specific legal norms of EurAsEC labour legislation and finding a sort of "middle-way" which might satisfy all members of the Community are more complicated.

An analysis of the national labour codes leads us to draw a number of conclusions regarding the presence of discrepancies between the legal approaches of legislators to the regulation of labour relations in different member states. The fact that the labour codes of EurAsEC countries were written at different times has greatly affected their content and the quality of standards set. The "oldest" code (and therefore the one which can be considered least concordant with modern economic and socio-political realities) is The Labour Code of the Republic of Tajikistan which came into force on 15 May 1997. The Labour Code of the Republic of Belarus was adopted on 26 July 1999, that of the Russian Federation on 30 December 2001, that of the Kyrgyz Republic on 25 May 2004 and the Labour Code of the Republic of Kazakhstan was adopted on 15 May 2007. Exactly 10 years passed between the adoptions of the first Labour Code and the last. In modern legal terms, it is a long time. As one might expect these codes (that of Tajikistan and that of Kazakhstan) are the ones which present the most differences.

A comparative analysis of codified acts shows that the most similar in content are the Labour Code of the Russian Federation and that of the Kyrgyz Republic. The articles regarding legal regulation are almost identical (Art. 1 of the Labour Code of the Russian Federation and Art. 1 of the Labour Code of the Kyrgyz Republic). They do, however, use slightly different systems of labour law sources (there are no regional regulations in Kyrgyzstan, which, unlike Russia, is a unitary rather than federal state). The basic principles of the legal regulation of labour and labour relations only partially coincide. Art. 2 of the Labour Code of the Russian Federation, in contrast with Art. 2 of the Labour Code of the Kyrgyz Republic, does not contain the most important international principle laid down in the ILO Declaration on Fundamental Principles and Rights at Work (1998)—the effective abolition of child labour. However, in the Russian Labour Code the article regarding payment for labour as a fundamental principle is more in line with international standards than the corresponding article in the Labour Code of the Kyrgyz Republic. Let us compare: in Art. 2 of the Labour Code of the Kyrgyz Republic it is stipulated that "safeguards for the right to remuneration for labour in accordance with the employment contract, but not below the legal minimum wage". In Art. 2 of the Labour Code of the Russian Federation there is a different phrase — "safeguards for the right of every employee to timely and full payment of fair wages, providing a dignified existence for himself and his/her family, and not below the statutory minimum wage".

Russian law is closer to the international principle which is articulated as: the right to just and favourable remuneration ensuring a dignified existence for the worker and his/her family (par. 3 of Art. 23 of the Universal Declaration of Human Rights, 1948), remuneration ensuring as a minimum a fair wage and decent living conditions for the workers themselves and their families (Art. 7 of the International Covenant on Economic, Social and Cultural Rights, 1966), and the right to a fair remuneration which is sufficient for a decent standard of living of the working people and their families (Art. 4 of the European Social Charter, revised in 1996). The harmonization of the labour laws of EurAsEC countries is intended, above all, to develop principles of labour regulation common to all member states.

The EurAsEC member states have not yet fully implemented the principle of the prohibition of forced labour in their national legislation. For example, an employee's right to terminate a temporary employment contract before the expiry of its term is limited in Tajikistan (by Art. 45 of the Labour Code of the Republic of Tajikistan; the employee may only resign with good reason) and in Belarus (fixed-term employment contracts can be terminated early upon the request of the employee in the event of an illness or disability which prevents him/her from working, if the employer violates labour legislation, by a collective labour agreement and for other valid reasons—see art. 41 of the Labour Code of the Republic of Belarus). Art. 82 of the Labour Code of the Kyrgyz Republic limits the possibility of terminating fixed-term employment contracts before their end date. Should an employee terminate a temporary employment contract without valid reason, the employer may demand compensation from the employee equal to the amount stipulated in the employment contract, but not exceeding the employee's average monthly salary. Art. 52 of the Labour Code of the Republic of Tajikistan contains a condition regarding the payment of a penalty for the early termination of a temporary employment contract. Art. 348.12 of the Labour Code of the Russian Federation states that an employment contract may include the obligation to make cash payment to the employer in the case of an athlete's voluntarily redundancy without valid cause; the same also applies to the case of the dissolution of an employment contract by the employer for reasons related to disciplinary action in accordance with the sportsman's contract. The EurAsEC member states (except the Republic of Kazakhstan) have established direct restrictions, economic restrictions and even prohibitions on an employee's voluntarily redundancy, thus effectively violating the principle of an international ban on compulsory work.

In this regard, and as has been repeatedly noted in literature, national labour codes need to be appropriately adjusted. A number of Belarusian scholars believe that legislators "should reconsider some positions in order to harmonize national labour law with international law, for example, in the part of the termination procedure of fixed-term employment contracts by the employee",[9] and justify the need to increase the freedom of employees who wish to voluntarily resign their posts.[10] In order to follow the principle of the prohibition of compulsory work, EurAsEC member

---

[9] Urzhinsky, K. K. 2008. "Prinuditel'niy trud: mezhdunarodnoe pravo i nacional'noe zakonodatel'stvo [Forced Labor: International Law and National Law]" in *Labor codes of Russia and the Czech Republic (Comparative Legal Research)*, ed. Skachkova, G. S., (Moscow), 52.

[10] Tomashevskiy, K. L. 2009. *Ocherki trudovogo prava. Istoriya, filosofiya, problemy sistem i istochnikov [Essays on Labor Law. History, Philosophy, Problems of Systems and Sources]*, Minsk: BSU Izd. tsentr, 329.

states must remove legal restrictions on employees' rights regarding the dissolution of labour contracts.

There are, of course, other differences in the legal regulation of labour between the countries of the Eurasian Economic Community. Some are quantitative while others are qualitative (intrinsic). Art. 59 of the Labour Code of the Russian Federation, for example, lists over two dozen legitimate reasons for using fixed-term employment contracts, adding that other federal laws may establish further grounds for their use, whereas the Labour Code of the Republic of Kazakhstan does not contain such a list, stating only that an urgent employment contract can be signed for a period of no less than one year (with some exceptions). This is not to say that Kazakhstan *should* develop such a list. The Uniform Act, in the author's opinion, should not "chase" the legislator into certain frames. In order to harmonize labour laws it is more effective to set down clear limits regarding the legal regulation of a particular issue in the Principles. For example, instead of making a specific list of reasons to use a fixed-term employment contract, it would be more effective to set general criteria for determining the cases which an employer may make an employment contract for a given period of time.

An adequate coordination of legislation between EurAsEC member states can only be achieved through the harmonization of the states' Labour Codes which must be formulated in accordance with international standards.

In the case of the legal regulation of social partnerships, for example, the EurAsEC Basic Principles of Labour Legislation can only establish general principles: equality of the parties, respect and consideration for the interests of the parties, the parties' interest in participating in a contractual relationship, authorization of parties' representatives, the freedom of choice of issues to be discussed, the voluntary commitment by the parties, the liabilities for each of the parties, the obligation of carrying out said liabilities by the parties, control over the maintaining of commitments and responsibilities of the parties and their representatives for the non-fulfilment of obligations, transparency of decisions, state assistance in strengthening and developing social partnerships. The system and forms of social partnerships in a given state should be established independently, based on the characteristics of the territory, its political structure and established practice.

In accordance with existing practice in EurAsEC member states (comparative analysis of the Labour Codes of EurAsEC countries has shown that there are no fundamental differences in the procedures of making collective agreements and contracts), the Principles should contain rules governing collective agreements and contracts and should also fix the basic requirements for their content, including a rule on the inadmissibility of any norms which weaken workers' rights in comparison with international and national labour laws.

Rules on social partnerships must correspond to ILO Conventions No. 87 Freedom of Association and Protection of the Right to Organize (1948), No. 154 Collective Bargaining (1981) and also to the ILO Recommendation No. 91 Collective Agreements (1951).

The central part of the Principles includes the norms which apply to employment contracts. In all the Labour Codes of the EurAsEC member states the concept of an employment contract is formed using approximately the same format (characteristics of the employment contract, making an employment contract, changes in the employment contract, termination of the employment contract) which is used as a basis.

In order to harmonize the conceptual apparatus of employment contracts with the concepts contained in the Basic Principles of Labour Legislation, definitions of the most significant terms, e.g. "employee", "employer", "employment contract", "transfer", etc. must be formulated.

The definition of a "contract of employment" should include a description of its most important attributes: the parties of the agreement (employee and employer), the subject of the contract (carrying out work according to a defined labour function), the parties' main responsibilities (the employee agrees to submit to internal labour regulations, the employer agrees to give the employee work, ensure established working conditions and pay wages). As well as listing specific attributes, the definition should also include the distinctive features of the employment contract which allow it to be distinguished from other labour agreements, for example, from civil law labour contracts for fee-based services.

Specific requirements for the content of employment contracts must also be provided. The compulsory points are: the place of work, work function, start date and duration of validity (whether the contract is for a fixed term) and the terms of payment. This list of compulsory contents of employment contracts should be left open in order to permit the inclusion of other points through national legislation. Additional terms of employment contracts (for example, probation periods, the obligation to work after training carried out at the expense of the employer, the non-disclosure of secrets protected by law), must also be given in the national labour codes.

In the interests of employees, labour codes are expected to limit the possibility for employers to make fixed-term contracts by making the use of such contracts illegal unless the employer has reasonable motives for doing so.

The EurAsEC Basic Principles of Labour Legislation should constrain EurAsEC member states to impose an age restriction of 16 years for employment, permitting recruitment at an earlier age (15 and 14) only under certain conditions. In the latter case additional requirements regarding coordination with parents and other legal representatives of a minor should also be in place. It is necessary that further regulations governing employment contracts made with children under 14 years of age (which may occur in institutions such as cinema, circus, theatre, sports, etc.) be put in place in order not to cause damage to the health and moral development of the minor, and these are left to the discretion of the EurAsEC member states.

The creation of an article which ensures that employment contracts will contain nothing which may in any way compromise the equal rights and opportunities for the employee is also vitally important. This norm may take the form of a prohibition of unjustified refusals to make an employment contract, the denial of any direct or indirect restriction of rights or a ban on the establishment of direct or indirect benefits depending on circumstances which are unrelated to workers' qualifications.

The labour codes of EurAsEC member states list several reasons which justify the modification of an employment contract: translation, moving, changes to the conditions of an employment agreement (labour conditions) which are defined by the parties. These conditions should also be included in the Principles of EurAsEC labour law. A general definition of the term "transfer" must be provided, including the differences between "transfers" and "moving". Transfers are permitted with the written acceptance of the employee, except in cases which are provided for in the Principles.

A temporary transfer for work not provided for in the employment contract (the duration of which will be determined by the national laws of each country) made without the employee's written agreement is only permitted in emergency situations (natural disasters, industrial accidents, labour accidents, fire, flood, famine, epidemics, epizootics and other exceptional cases which threaten the life or normal living conditions of the population). This rule is consistent with international acts such as ILO Conventions No. 29 and No. 105 on Forced Labour.

On the other hand, moving an employee to another role in another organizational department or to work on a different machine (without changing the job function) is permitted without the employee's consent.

Changes to the conditions of an employment agreement which are determined by the parties be made as long as workers are given the following guarantees: 1) such alterations can only occur because of changes in organizational or technological labour conditions, and 2) the employer is obliged to notify the worker in written form in advance (the establishment of the period of notice is decided on by the state). Should an employee refuse to continue work under the new conditions the employment contract may be terminated.

The rules regarding the termination of an employment contract must provide a number of guarantees for workers. Firstly, a dismissal must be motivated (justified). In accordance with existing practice the legislations of EurAsEC member states include a list of reasonable grounds for terminating an employment contract. Secondly, it is necessary to define the procedure for dismissing a worker, including both general and specific guarantees for certain categories of workers. Events such as mutual agreement of the parties, the expiring of the contract, the employee's wish, the employer's wish and circumstances beyond the parties' control are considered reasonable grounds for terminating an employment contract in EurAsEC member states.

The Principles provide as a basic guarantee the prohibition of dismissing workers on the employer's initiative during a period of absence due to a temporary disability or annual leave. Other generally recognized rules and rights for an employee being dismissed on the employer's initiative are: prior notification of the dismissal, the obligation for the employer to take into account the opinion (either notification or consent) of the relevant trade union when dismissing trade union members, the offer of a transfer as an alternative to dismissal, severance payment and the right to a judicial review of an unlawful termination of the employment contract.

It would be appropriate to include in the Principles a guarantee which is already present in the Labour Codes of the Republic of Belarus and the Kyrgyz Republic, namely: during the period of notice for termination of the employment contract due to the liquidation of the organisation, the termination of an individual entrepreneur, downsizing or staff reduction, the employee is allowed one day off per week to seek new employment. The matter of wages for this day should be left to national legislation. This guarantee is provided in paragraph 16 of ILO Recommendation No. 166 on Termination of Employment (1982), according to which, during a period of notice of termination the employee should have the right to be exempt from work for a mutually convenient and reasonable length of time without the loss of wages in order to seek future employment.

The employee's right to terminate an employment contract (even at short notice) cannot be restricted by law or by the employer. If restrictions were permitted this would constitute a violation of the principle of freedom of labour. The Principles can only establish an employee's duty to promptly notify the employer of his or her resignation, leaving to the discretion of national codes the appropriate length of prior notice.

The concept of working time varies between the national legislation of the EURASEC countries. Let us start by noting the fact that there are different definitions of the term "working time", so in the Principles of Labour Legislation a definition of this legal category needs to be provided, indicating that it is not only the time during which an employee must perform his or her duties, but also some other periods . Art. 76 of the Labour Code of the Republic of Kazakhstan can be seen as an example as it lists what is considered working time.

The Principles classify normal working time (40 hours per week) and reduced working time (for some categories of workers), and regulate part-time work. The establishment of a forty-hour working week is fully consistent with the provisions of ILO Convention No. 47 on The Forty-hour Week (1935). However, this provision does not relieve employers from the obligation to develop and consistently implement policies aimed at the gradual reduction of working time. These provisions are contained in the ILO Recommendation No. 116 Reduction of Hours of Work (1962), which states that normal working hours should be gradually reduced without reducing wages in the appropriate cases.

Taking into account the position of the international community on this issue, it is interesting to examine the experiences of the Kyrgyz Republic and the Republic of Kazakhstan, the Labour Codes of which allow the establishment of fewer hours of work by collective agreement or by employment contract in accordance with relevant legislation.

The legal regulations of reduced working time in all EurAsEC member states share a common approach regarding guarantees for employees with reduced working capacity (persons with disabilities), workers under the age of 18 and workers who carry out work of a special nature. The difference in legislation between EurAsEC member states lies, above all, in the amount by which working time is reduced. The Principles define only the upper limit of reduced working hours, leaving the states the right to determine specific reductions. Another difference is the states' views of what is considered as "special kinds of work". In the author's opinion this subject does not require the coordination of legislation.

International legal acts relating to the reduction of working time (European Social Charter, the ILO Older Workers Recommendation No. 162 [1980], ILO Reduction of Hours of Work Recommendation No. 116 [1962], and others) establish the need for such guarantees for people engaged in hazardous work, minors, the elderly, disabled workers and workers employed in certain industries.

The legal regulation of part-time work involves distinguishing between different kinds of part-time work and different working conditions for part-time workers (in particular, the rules governing remuneration and the preservation of guarantees). The labour legislation of EurAsEC member states has a uniform approach to the definition of categories of workers to which the employer must provide the option of working part-time. The obligation for the employer to provide such a possibility for people with disabilities, pregnant women and those with family responsibilities, including people caring for sick family members, is in the requirements of international labour standards, and therefore this responsibility should also be imposed by the Principles.

An analysis of the labour legislation of EurAsEC member states has revealed a number of differences in the legal regulation of irregular working hours and overtime. Most states allow employers to determine a list of categories of employees for whom a longer working day may be established. A number of restrictions nonetheless need to be established in order to regulate the requirement of workers to work overtime, the duration of overtime work and the categories of workers involved. As an example, one can take the norms established in the Labour Codes of Russia, Belarus and Kazakhstan: the employer is permitted to require the employee to work overtime with the written consent of the employee. In exceptional cases, an employer may require an employee to work overtime without the latter's consent.

In order to limit the possibility of requiring certain categories of employees to work overtime, the rule might typically look like this: pregnant women, those under the age of 18, people with disabilities and women with children under three years of age may only be allowed to work overtime if they give their written consent and on the condition that such work is not prohibited to them for medical reasons.

International acts on labour concerning the procedure and conditions of requiring employees to work overtime address the need to increase the wages of employees working overtime, the need for certain restrictions, including a ban on requiring certain categories of employees to work overtime and the need to establish limits on the amount of overtime work any given employee can do.

The Principles of the legal regulation of workers' labour at night are currently governed by ILO Convention No. 171 on Night Work (1990) and ILO Recommendation No. 178 on Night Work (1990). According to these documents, the term "night work" means any work that is carried out for a period of no less than seven consecutive hours and including the interval between midnight and 5am. The definitions of night work by the EurAsEC members' Labour Codes as being between 10 pm to 6 am is therefore in line with international standards. The binding legal document for all member states of the EurAsEC is the Charter of Social Rights and Guarantees of Citizens of Independent States (1994), which provides a number of rules regarding night work. According to the provisions in this charter, people under 18 years of age, disabled workers and pregnant women are prohibited from working at night. In addition, the aforementioned charter states that working time must be reduced by one hour if the work is carried out as night work. These requirements should be taken into account when forming the rules on working time in the EurAsEc Basic Principles of Labour Legislation.

In the Principles of Labour Legislation various types of rest and their minimum duration are given. Common to all countries is the rule (guarantee) that workers shall have a weekly free "weekend", the exact details and provision of which shall be determined by each state in its national legislation. Similarly, in the national labour codes, non-working holidays are guaranteed. The Principles must prohibit the employer from forcing employees to work at weekends and on public holidays and, at the same time, specify the exceptions to this rule by defining the cases in which employees may be required to work at weekends and on public holidays without their consent.

Examples of these exceptional circumstances may include: the prevention of emergencies or accidents, dealing with injuries and property damage, working in emergency situations or other circumstances that could endanger the lives and health of the population. Work on holidays is also allowed, as work cannot be suspended in some circumstances such as in the case of emergency repairs and loading and unloading work, as well as work associated with the need for continued public service.

The Charter of Social Rights and Guarantees of Citizens of Independent States (1994) provides a number of restrictions on which categories of employers may require employees to work at weekends and on public holidays. These restrictions concern persons under the age of 18, disabled people, pregnant women, women with children under the age of 3, fathers raising children under the age of 3 years without a mother, and caregivers of children of the same age. It is recommended that measures be taken in order to fulfil the aims of the charter and that similar restrictions be established in the EurAsEC Basic Principles of Labour Legislation.

The Principles may also consider establishing a guarantee of the type found in the Labour Codes of the Russian Federation and the Republic of

Kyrgyzstan which states that if a public holiday should coincide with a weekend, the day "lost" to the public holiday is postponed to the next working day.

One of the most significant types of leisure time, and that with potentially the longest duration, is paid annual leave. The Principles must carefully regulate a number of elements relevant to paid annual leave such as minimum length, the minimum duration of employment which gives the employee the right to paid annual leave, the methods of calculating the length of service which gives the right to paid annual leave and how annual paid leave may be split.

The minimum duration of paid annual leave must be set according to the requirements of ILO No. 132 Holidays With Pay Convention (revised in 1970), which states that annual leave cannot amount to less than three working weeks per one year of work.

It is necessary to include in the Principles the traditional norm in EurAsEC countries that any public holidays which coincide with an employee's annual leave shall not be included in the number of days of said leave.

The Principles should also include a system of additional holidays, listing the types and specifying their minimum duration. The list of additional leave should be valid for the following types of workers: those working with harmful substances and/or working in hazardous working conditions, those carrying out work of special nature, those working in exceptional climatic conditions and those who have long working hours. Other additional leave may be granted to certain categories of employees, though the terms and conditions of this provision should be determined by national legislation.

It is necessary to coordinate rules regarding the minimum duration of employment which gives the employee the right to paid annual leave based on the ILO Convention No. 132 Holidays with Pay. This document establishes that the period in question cannot be more than six months. The rules regarding the calculation of work experience which gives the right to paid annual leave should be formulated taking into account item 5 of the aforementioned ILO Convention. Periods in which the employee is absent from work for reasons such as illness, accident or maternity leave should be taken into account when calculating the length of this period of work experience.

The Principles provide guarantees of financial security for the employee when he or she is on leave, particularly with the rule that annual leave should reflect the duration of the employee's employment and his or her average earnings. Article 7 of ILO Convention No. 132, according to which the amount payable to the employee on leave shall be paid to him or her *before* the period of leave begins, must be implemented.

The rule regarding how paid annual leave can be split must be accompanied by a guarantee specifying the minimum required length of one of the parts of the leave (14 calendar days). This corresponds to article 8 of ILO Convention No. 132.

The transfer or renewal of annual paid holiday (either by the employee or by the employer), and the withdrawal of an employee from leave should also be fixed in the Principles.

The right to remuneration for work is a fundamental right of the employee which has been raised to the rank of constitutional right (e.g. Art. 37 of the Constitution of the Russian Federation). In ensuring the right to a fair remuneration for work, a number of labour codes (the Labour Code of the Republic of Kazakhstan, the Labour Code of the Russian Federation, and the Labour Code of the Kyrgyz Republic) refer to several principles of international labour law. It is therefore appropriate that the EurAsEc Basic Principles of Labour Legislation prescribe all the basic guarantees of the right to remuneration for work, including those provided by international standards.

Firstly, the definition of the term "wages" must be clarified. Most states define "wages" as a reward for labour dependent upon the employee's qualifications, the complexity, quantity, quality and conditions of work, as well as the payment of compensation or incentives. This definition corresponds basically to the definition set out in ILO Convention No. 95 Protection of Wages (1949), but it ignores the fact that the international definition of wages contains another feature—wages are paid to the employee not only for work that has been performed but also for work which will be carried out. Taking into account both the ILO Convention No. 95 Protection of Wages and prevailing definitions in national legislation, the following may be considered an appropriate definition of the term "wages": "the remuneration paid by the employer to the employee for work that they have performed or will perform and dependent upon the qualifications of the worker, the quantity, quality, complexity and conditions of work, and the worker's performance, of an amount established by agreement of the parties in accordance with labour laws, collective contracts, agreements and local regulations". It would also be useful to clarify that wages include compensation (bonuses and allowances for working in conditions that deviate from the norm) and incentive payments (bonuses and allowances stimulating performance and other incentive payments).

In order to protect the rights of the employee regarding payment for labour and in order to prevent violations by the employer, the list of state guarantees on wages that every employer must provide to workers should be given in the Principles. The author believes it is necessary to generalize the experience of EurAsEC member states and to take into account the requirements of ILO Convention No. 95 in order to establish a system of state guarantees in the sphere of payment, which includes the following points:

- prohibition of pay discrimination and equal pay for work of equal value;
- wages should not be lower than the minimum wage, the latter being determined by national legislation;
- limitation of wages in kind;
- limitation on being able to make deductions from wages and on the amount which can be deducted;
- the frequency of payment of wages;
- measures to ensure the improvement of the real content of wages;
- state supervision and control for the full and timely payment of wages and the implementation of state guarantees of payment;
- the employer's liability for delays to the payment of wages and other sums due to employees;
- ensuring employees' wages in the case of the insolvency of the employer and his/her inability to pay;
- increasing of wages in conditions deviating from the norm (at a rate not lower than that stipulated in national law).

The most important guarantee is the one that bans paying workers less than the country's established minimum wage. The minimum wage is set by the state and cannot be standardized at an international level. The methodology of its determination should also be the prerogative of each EurAsEC member state. The ILO Convention No. 26 Minimum Wage-Fixing Machinery (1928) (ratified only by the Republic of Belarus), states that each member of the ILO which ratifies this convention shall have the right to determine the nature and form of the procedure for establishing the minimum wage, as well as its method of operation. The generalization of the legislation of EurAsEC member states can be formulated in the Principles common to all, with the rule that the basic criterion of a minimum wage is the minimum consumer budget (cost of living) of the workforce.

Furthermore, it is important to provide a rule concerning the increase in wages for work carried out in conditions deviating from the norm (e.g.

work done in exceptional climatic conditions, in areas contaminated as a result of industrial accidents, in unhealthy, dangerous and difficult conditions, overtime, work done at weekends and on public holidays, night work, etc.) All states must guarantee the employee the possibility of receiving higher wages if the carrying out of their work involves great physical cost, the possible deterioration of health, increased workload, or if it is carried out in periods usually dedicated to rest. The specific amount of the increase in wages should be determined by the legislation of each EurAsEC member state.

The venue and date of the payment of wages are also given in state guarantees. It is necessary to fix the rule which is established in all EurAsEC member states except Kazakhstan, that wages are to be paid every two weeks, and the specific terms of payment are set either in the by-laws or in the employment contract. Art. 12 of ILO Convention No. 95 establishes a general requirement for the periodic payment of wages—they must be paid regularly though the right to set the terms of payment is granted to national legislators or determined by collective agreements or arbitration procedures. However, Art. 22 of the Charter of Social Rights and Guarantees of Citizens of Independent States (1994) addresses this question differently by declaring that wages must be paid at least twice a month. The EurAsEC Basic Principles of Labour Legislation regarding how often wages should be paid must comply with international legal acts.

Wages shall be paid in the national currency of the host country and, as a general rule, to the employee in person. Wages are usually paid to the employee at the place of work (in the organisation), or, with the consent of the employee, the salary can be directly transferred to his or her bank account. According to ILO Convention No. 95, wages paid in cash should only be paid on weekdays and at the work place or nearby, unless national legislation, collective agreements or an arbitral body have stated otherwise or if these conditions cannot be met. It may often be more appropriate or convenient for the wages to be transferred directly to the employee's bank account (provided that the employee consents).

The Tajikistani Labour Code provides an important guarantee which can also be found in the Principles: if an employee is not at the place of work on the day he or she is due to be paid for work reasons (a business trip, a training course, seeing customers outside the work place, and so on), the employee may request that the employer, at his or her own expense, pay the wages via a bank transfer or to a nominated delegate of the employee. All of the above is in full conformity with the provisions of ILO Convention No. 95.

In order to comply with Art. 8 of ILO Convention No. 95, the Principles should contain an exhaustive list of the conditions under which and the extent to which deductions from wages may be permitted. Deductions may be allowed if the employer suffers some form of damage, for the return of unused advances (for example, when travelling on a business trip), with counting errors, etc. It is normal for the appropriate withholding to be 20% of wages, with a maximum limit of 50%, as provided for in Art. 23 of the Charter of Social Rights and Guarantees of Citizens of Independent States (1994).

The Basic Principles of Labour Legislation must resolve the issue of liability of employers for the delayed payment of wages and other sums to workers. The Russian experience may be of interest in this matter; Art. 142 of the Labour Code of the Russian Federation provides workers with the possibility to stop working if the payment of wages is delayed by more than 15 days.

The coordination of legislation in the field of guarantees and compensation is a rather complicated process, as is the establishment of employer responsibilities regarding financial costs incurred during the process of liberating an employee from work. These processes depend on the development of social partnerships in each country and on the economic resources of the employers and the states in general. Therefore, the issue of guarantees and indemnifications can only be partially resolved in the Principles.

The Principles must establish a list of cases of worker compensation and guarantees for: the performance of state or public duties, business trips, the donation of blood and blood components, when moving to a job in another district, the use of the employee's personal property in the interests of the employer and medical examinations. Special cases of guarantees and indemnifications shall be established by each EurAsEC member state (such as the provision in the Labour Code of the Republic of Kazakhstan of special protection for workers working in the field of environmental disasters and at risk from radiation).

The exact content of the specific guarantees and compensation should be determined by national legislation. It would be advisable for the Principles to recommend an average amount of money that employers should put by for medical examinations, training and blood donation as well as for collective negotiations and collective agreements.

The regulation of labour discipline issues cannot function without the creation of a common conceptual structure of this institute of labour law. Basic concepts common to all such as "labour discipline", "work schedule" and "serious misconduct" need to be defined and updated through coordination between EurAsEC member states.

The main document defining the work schedule is traditionally the Employment Policies and Procedures. The Principles should include the approximate contents of this local regulation, though the procedure for the adoption of rules shall be determined by national law on the basis of established practice.

It is important to consolidate the norms that an employer may not require an employee to perform work outside of his or her job duties, may not commit acts that are illegal or pose a threat to life and health and may not humiliate or demean the employee or others.

Since almost all the EurAsEC member states are in agreement on the list of disciplinary measures applicable to employees for a disciplinary offence, the Basic Principles of Labour Legislation specify three disciplinary penalties—a warning, a reprimand or dismissal on relative grounds.

The manner in which employees take part in disciplinary proceedings varies somewhat between EurAsEC member states, so it would be helpful it were described in the Principles: it is necessary to set a deadline for the application for disciplinary sanctions, to outline the duty of the employer to require an employee to provide an explanation of the offence committed and to clarify the procedure for the registration of closure. A limitation on the penalty which can be imposed on the employee (including in the form of dismissal) corresponds to the provisions of point 10 of ILO Recommendation No. 166 Termination of Employment (1982), according to which the employer should be deemed to have waived his/her right to terminate the employment of a worker for misconduct if he/she has failed to do so within a reasonable period of time after becoming aware of the misconduct.

The requirement of a written explanation from the employee complies fully with international law: Art. 7 of the ILO Convention No. 158 Termination of Employment (1982) (not ratified by any of the countries of the Eurasian Economic Community) states that the employment of a worker shall not be terminated for reasons related to the worker's conduct or performance before he is provided an opportunity to defend himself against the allegations made, unless the employer cannot reasonably be expected to provide this opportunity.

It is also worth clarifying that disciplinary punishments must be carried out within one year from the date of application, unless otherwise stated in national labour codes (for example, a time limit of six months is set in Kazakhstan). Penalties can be waived in advance at the employer's discretion, at the request of the employee, at the request of the representative body of workers or that of the employee's immediate supervisor. Any disciplinary action may be appealed in the manner prescribed for individual labour disputes.

In developing the regulations on safety at work, it is first of all necessary to take into account international standards in this area: ILO Convention No. 155 Occupational Safety and Health (1981) (ratified by the Russian Federation, the Republic of Belarus, Republic of Kazakhstan and the Republic of Tajikistan), ILO Recommendation No. 97 Protection of Workers' Health (1953), ILO Convention No. 161 Occupational Health Services (1985) (not ratified by the EurAsEC states), ILO Recommendation No. 81 Labour Inspection (1987), ILO Convention No. 187 Promotional Framework for Occupational Safety and Health (2006) (ratified only by the Russian Federation).

The Principles should provide common norms for EurAsEC member states in order to regulate labour relations and to ensure:

- the priority of the life and health of workers;
- state administration of worker health and safety;
- guarantees of employees' rights to health and safety;
- the establishment of responsibilities of all parties in the field of labour relations;
- international cooperation in the field of worker health and safety and the implementation of international agreements on the protection of labour.

In the Principles it is worth noting the basic requirements for health, safety, and in particular the safety of workers employed in the sectors of buildings, construction, the operation of machinery and technological processes, as well as those employed in the production of tools, materials and supplies. Relevant safety requirements for various types of work places and measures which can help to prevent accidents, maintain the health and lives of workers in dangerous situations, must be adopted. Where necessary, employees must not be allowed to carry out their work without previously undergoing mandatory medical or psychiatric examinations and they should be educated and trained in safe methods of working and how to perform first-aid in the workplace. Briefings on safety, on-the-job training and verifications of the employees' knowledge of safety and protection requirements should be carried out; employees who have not passed or attended such courses or briefings or who have not received adequate instruction should be suspended from work. Controls of the conditions in the workplace need to be organized, and individual and collective protection measures must be enacted correctly. Employees must be informed of the conditions of the workplace, of safety procedures as well as of the risks to their health, the compensation they can receive, compulsory social insurance against industrial accidents and occupational diseases, and of the procedure for the investigation of accidents in the workplace.

It is also necessary to provide the employee with the right to defend him or herself in the case of a breach of labour protection requirements by the employer, particularly by recognising the right to refuse to work in the case of danger to life or health as a result of violations of labour protection requirements.

The ILO Convention No. 155 makes it mandatory for the employee to notify the employer of any situation which threatens the life or health of the workers and this provision should be included in national legislation.

The legal regulation of the liability of the parties of employment contracts is very similar in all EurAsEC member states, so one can say that the harmonization of the concept has almost been achieved. However, the Basic Principles of Labour Legislation may continue to deepen the process.

Financial responsibility as a legal concept is based on the following principles:

- only the law may establish the terms and conditions of liability for the parties of employment contracts;
- the conditions of liability can be specified on a contractual level, but the employer shall always have greater liability than the employee and the employee cannot bear greater liability than that established by law;
- the termination of the employment contract does not relieve a party of the obligation to compensate for any damage caused to the other party during the period of employment.

The conditions set in employment contracts concerning liability should address the following issues: damage, illegal behaviour, the causal link between conduct and damage incurred guilt. Certain circumstances can exempt the employee from liability, such as a normal economic risk, force majeure, extreme necessity and self-defence, the employer's failure to provide adequate maintenance or storage conditions for property entrusted to the employee.

Cases of liability of the employer for damage caused to an employee and his/her property should be defined in national legislation, but it is worth noting the fact that the employer is responsible for damage resulting from illegally depriving the employee of the opportunity to work and for damage done to the employee's property. Furthermore, the employee must be given the chance to claim compensation for non-pecuniary damage caused by wrongful acts or omissions of the employer, including defamation of the employee.

As regards damage done to the life and health of the worker, compensation can come from a variety of sources (in some countries this responsibility lies with the employer, in others with specialized agencies—in Russia, for example, the Social Insurance Fund Against Accidents at Work and Occupational Diseases provides compensation). It is therefore appropriate not to include articles regarding this matter in the Principles of Labour Law but to allow national legislation to deal with this issue.

However, the employee is responsible for reimbursing the employer for direct actual damages, i.e., the real reduction or deterioration of the cash assets of the employer (including third party property for which the employer is responsible), and when it is necessary for the employer to cover the cost of acquisition or restoration of the property, or make unexpected payments. Compensation for the loss of profits is possible only in exceptional cases established by national legislation (for example, if the damage did not occur during the period of work).

In order to protect workers' rights it is necessary to establish the rule that an employee can only ever bear a limited liability, the degree of which shall be established in the national legislation. Only in exceptional cases, characterized by certain aggravating circumstances of the offence or entailing serious negative consequences, can the liability be fully attributed to the employee. Again, such cases will be established in national legislation.

The methods of providing compensation for damage caused to the employer must also be varied. Firstly, the employee may pay the damages voluntarily; secondly, the damages may in certain conditions specified in national legislation and on written instructions of the employer, be paid by withholding a certain amount of employee's wages, and thirdly, damages may be paid as a result of a judicial procedure for their recovery.

Provisions regarding the authorization of individual and collective labour disputes should also be given in the Principles.

The system of review of individual labour disputes (labour dispute committees created directly within the organization and by the court) does not differ between EurAsEC member states. The Basic Principles of Labour Legislation only discuss provisions for the resolution of labour disputes by commission in general terms and include the requirements for the composition of the commission (the principle of equal representation of the parties), the order of decision-making and the consequences of the decision committee (deadline for the implementation of decisions). The settlement of disputes in court should be governed by national law since the order of trial is established by the civil procedural legislation of each country. At the same time, the EurAsEC Basic Principles of Labour Legislation can provide a guarantee of the employee and the employer's rights. Section 3, Art. 8 of the ILO Convention No. 158 Termination of Employment (1982), states that a worker may be deemed to have waived his/her right to appeal against the termination of his/her employment if he/she has not exercised that right within a reasonable period of time after termination. It should be clarified that if the employee or the employer missed, for good reasons, the opportunity to apply to a body to examine the individual labour dispute, this period may be reduced.

The Principles should state that many types of disputes can only be addressed by the courts. These disputes should be the most important and difficult to deal with, such as those regarding reinstatement. However, the list must be open-ended, allowing for national legislation to specify the exclusive jurisdiction of the courts.

One can use the legislative experiences of the Kyrgyz Republic and the Republic of Belarus to establish a rule that if it is not possible to restore the employee to his previous job (because the title has been eliminated, the unit has been abolished or the organization closed, for example), the court will impose on the employer or his/her legal successor the obligation to provide the employee with financial compensation. The amount of such compensation should remain at the discretion of the EurAsEC member states (in Kyrgyzstan it is at least 12 times the average monthly wage, in Belarus it is 10 times the average monthly wage).

The Principles should describe the procedure for the settlement of collective labour disputes. According to ILO Recommendation No. 92 Voluntary Conciliation and Arbitration (1951), in order to promote the prevention and resolution of labour disputes between employers and employees, it is necessary to establish voluntary conciliation bodies appropriate to national conditions. In the Basic Principles of Labour Legislation it is advisable to fix a basic conciliation procedure which the parties can use to resolve a collective labour dispute. General procedures for the EurAsEC member states are carried out by the Conciliation Commissions and by labour arbitration.

The Principles must establish the main elements of conciliation;

- the bodies of reconciliation work on an equal basis;
- conciliation should be free and expeditious;
- during negotiations on reconciliation employees are not allowed to participate in strikes, and employers are prohibited from using a lockout;

- the creation of a labour arbitration body should be voluntary, but its decision on a collective labour dispute must be upheld by the parties.

The proceedings of reconciliation (including a rule on the timing) should be determined by national legislation.

In order to create effective labour arbitration bodies which will rule on disputes taking into account international laws and the laws of the EurAsEC member states, it is necessary to develop mechanisms which can enforce the binding nature of the decisions made by labour arbitration bodies. One can, for example, use the experience of the Republic of Belarus where such a rule exists; should a compulsory labour arbitration decision be violated by one of the parties involved in the dispute, the other party has the right to go to court in order to have the decision enforced (article 383 of the Labour Code of the Republic of Belarus).

The Principles should declare that workers can use their right to strike if the attempt to resolve the collective labour dispute by conciliation failed, as well as in cases where the employer ignores decisions made after conciliation or agreements made in the course of settling a collective labour dispute.

The right to strike must necessarily be limited for workers working in "essential" industries, but an alternative to this method of settling a collective labour dispute should be provided (the alternative may be the participation of the competent authorities in the resolution of the conflict). The procedure for a workers' strike shall be determined by national law, however, as general principles, we can specify the following:

- participation in a strike is voluntary;
- the employer has no right to discipline workers for participating in a strike unless it is found to be illegal and the workers did nothing to stop it;
- the wages of employees who refused to participate in the strike, but are unable to perform their job duties because of the strike, must be kept at the amount established by national legislation.

The decision on whether a strike is illegal can only be made by the court. This decision can depend on the violation of the procedure of the strike as well as on the threat to life and health.

It seems that the issues related to the supervision and control of compliance with labour legislation can only be regulated in the EurAsEC Basic Principles of Labour Legislation in very general terms as the structure of a system of state bodies exercising supervisory powers cannot intervene in domestic issues which are the exclusive prerogative of the state.

The concept of this body states that the Basic Principles of Labour Legislation which are the same for all EurAsEC member states, must provide a certain level of guarantees for those who require "special protection"—minors, women, persons with family responsibilities and the disabled. At the same time each state should be able to establish specific labour regulations for other categories of workers.

As has been demonstrated in practice, the problems associated with the use of hired labour are common to all the EurAsEC countries; these problems have been exacerbated by the growth of the informal sector of the economy hiring labour without issuing employment contracts, the active implementation by employers of contingent labour, the substitution of contracts of employment with contracts of a civil nature, the unwarranted use of fixed-term employment agreements used in the absence of centralized wage indexation mechanisms, the discrimination of migrant workers, and others. The task of the Eurasian Economic Community is not only to provide a legal framework for the free movement of citizens of the state parties within the Common Economic Space, but also to form a common legal regime for employment, working conditions, the payment of decent wages, and to create the conditions which are necessary for the implementation of international and national labour norms. All of these measures will help to contribute to a common labour market and the implementation of decent work in ex-Soviet states.

References

Abalduev, V. A. 2010. "Kodifikaciya trudovogo zakonodatel'stva EvrAzES—osnova soglasovaniya i sovershenstvovaniya nacional'noy pravovoy politiki v sfere truda [The Codification of EurAsEC Labour Legislation—the Basis of the Harmonization and Improvement of the National Legal Labour Policy]," *Trudovoe pravo v Rossii i za rubezhom [Labour Law in Russia and abroad]*, No. 3:13-15.

Golovina, S. Yu. 2008. "Perspektivi rasvitiya trudovogo zakonodatel'stva v ramkah Evraziyskogo Ekonomicheskogo soobshchestva [Perspectives for the Development of Labour Law in the Framework of the Eurasian Economic Community]," *Rossiyskiy yezhegodnik trudovogo prava* [Russian Yearbook of labour law], No. 4:351-368.

Kiselev, I. Ya. 1999. *Sravnitel'noe i mezhdunarodnoe trudovoe pravo: uchebnik [Comparative and International Labour Law: Textbook].* Moscow: Delo, 1999. 728 p.

Tomashevskiy, K. L. 2009. Ocherki trudovogo prava. Istoriya, filosofiya, problemy sistem i istochnikov [Essays on Labour Law. History,

Philosophy, Problems of Systems and Sources]. Minsk: BSU Izd. Tsentr. p. 335.

Urzhinsky, K. K. 2008. "Itel'niy trud: mezhdunarodnoe pravo i nacional'noe zakonodatel'stvo [Forced Labour: International Law and National Law]" in *Labour Codes of Russia and the Czech Republic (Comparative Legal Research)*, ed. Skachkova, G.S. (Moscow), 43-51.

THE COMPLIANCE OF RUSSIAN LABOUR LAW WITH INTERNATIONAL LABOUR STANDARDS

NIKITA LYUTOV

1. Introduction

Russia has ratified numerous international treaties related to the issue of labour rights: the 1966 UN Covenants on Human Rights[1] and other UN treaties concerning labour rights,[2] the Council of Europe acts,[3] a significant number of International Labour Organisation (ILO) Conventions,[4] several regional treaties within the Commonwealth of Independent States (CIS),[5] the Customs Union of Belarus, Kazakhstan, and Russia[6], to name but a few.

---

[1] International Covenant on Civil and Political Rights, 1966; International Covenant on Economic, Social and Cultural Rights, 1966.

[2] International Convention on the Elimination of All Forms of Racial Discrimination, 1965; The Convention on the Elimination of All Forms of Discrimination against Women (CEDAW), 1979; The UN Convention on the Rights of the Child, 1989; The UN Convention on the Rights of Persons with Disabilities, 2006; and others.

[3] The European Convention on Human Rights (ECHR), the European Social Charter (revised in 1996).

[4] See the ILO Normlex Database. http://www.ilo.org/dyn/normlex/en/f?p=1000:11200:0::NO:11200:P11200_COUNTRY_ID:102884 (accessed 15 February 2014).

[5] *Konvenziya Sodrujestva Nezavisimyh Gosudarstv o pravah i osnovnyh svobodah cheloveka [The Commonwealth of Independent States Convention on Human Rights and Basic Freedoms]*. 1995; and others.

[6] See among others *Soglasheniye mejdu Respublikoy Belarus, Kazakhstanom i Rossiyskoy Federatsiyey "O pravovom statuse trudyashihsya—migrantov i ih semey" ot 19 noyabrya, 2010 [The Treaty Between the Republic of Belarus, Kazakhstan and Russian Federation "On the Status of Migrant Workers and of Their Families", 19 November 2010].*

The text of these treaties is usually rather vague and flexible[7] and does not leave much scope for one to find discrepancies between national and international labour laws. Nonetheless, certain inconsistencies can be found in Russian labour laws and we will be examining these later on. There is also a widespread practice among international institutions to interpret international treaties, adopted under their auspices, in a particularly broad sense.[8] Discussions relating to the way in which these acts should be interpreted have been of great importance to modern international labour law, and have become even more relevant in view of the conflict between the employers' and employees' representatives at the International Labour Conference of 2012,[9] in which the employers' delegates made a statement to the effect that ILO controlling bodies, namely the Committee on Freedom of Association (CFA) and the Committee of Experts on Application of the Conventions and Recommendations (CEACR), have no mandate to claim that the right to strike is included in the freedom of association as long as there are no such direct provisions in the corresponding fundamental ILO Conventions (No. 87 and 98). This statement was made contrary to the customary practice that had been accepted by all ILO constituents for decades.[10]

---

[7] See more about the reasons and effects of flexibility in international labour standards in Javillier, J.-Cl. 2003. "Pour une Contribution des Universalitaires à la Dynamique des Normes Internationales du Travail" in *Changing Industrial Relations and Modernisation of Labour Law. Liber Amicorum in Honour of Professor Marco Biagi,* eds. Blanpain, R., and M. Weiss, (The Hague-London-New York: Kluwer Law International), 206-207; Servais, J.-M. 1986. "Flexibility and Rigidity in International Labour Standards," *International Labour Review* 125, No. 2:193-208.

[8] See more about the justifications of such an expansive interpretation from an international law perspective: Zuleeg, M. 1995. "International Organizations, Implied Powers," in *Encyclopedia of Public International Law, vol. 2*, ed. Bernhardt, R., (Amsterdam: Elsevier Science & Technology), 1312 and ff.

[9] See the materials of the 101th ILC at the ILO site: http://www.ilo.org/ilc/ILCSessions/101stSession/reports/lang--en/index.htm.

[10] See more on the issue: Ewing, K. D. 2013. "Myth and Reality of the Right to Strike as a "Fundamental Labour Right'," *The International Journal of Comparative Labour Law and Industrial Relations* 29, No. 2:145-166; Swepston, L., 2013. "Crisis in the ILO Supervisory System: Dispute over the Right to Strike," *The International Journal of Comparative Labour Law and Industrial Relations* 29, No. 2:199-218; La Hovary, C., 2013. "Showdown at the ILO? A Historical Perspective on the Employers' Group's 2012 Challenge to the Right to Strike," *Industrial Law Journal* 42, No. 4:338-368.

There is also a considerable number of soft-law acts containing provisions which are more effective and rigid than those found in international treaties, on the subject of labour. Although it is possible to find instances of non-conformity between Russian labour law and the various international labour standards, one must still bear in mind that the significance of these non-conformities varies considerably.

The differences between international labour standards and the Russian labour law system cover virtually all topics and issues of labour law. It would indeed take an entire book[11] to describe these differences in detail. This article will only deal with the major problems by illustrating the most serious and relevant examples of non-compliance, putting more technical or minor issues to one side.

2. Freedom of Association and Collective Bargaining

Collective bargaining and trade union freedoms are probably the most discussed and problematic issues of Russian labour law in the context of international labour standards. The most problematic gaps in Russian labour law in this respect are rooted in the country's Soviet past and in the current corporatist structure of industrial relations.[12] Workers in socialist countries were not permitted to strike or bargain individually over the terms of their labour contracts. Socialist trade unions were quasi-governmental structures and were therefore prohibited from acting in conformity with the market-economy principles of freedom of association most staunchly defended by the ILO. Trade unions were not acting as real collective bargaining agents as in capitalist systems and were therefore particularly criticized by market economy countries or the ILO.[13] This, however, does not mean that socialist trade unions were useless. They

[11] Such a book is published in Russian by the author, but it does not claim to cover all issues of the topic. See: Lyutov, N., 2012. *Rossiyskoye trudovoe zakonodatelstvo i mejdunarodniye trudoviye standarty: sootvetstvie i perspectivy sovershenstovaniya [Russian Labour Legislation and International Labour Standards: The Issues of Compliance and Perspectives for Modification]*. Moscow: Tsentr sotsial'no-trudovyh prav [Centre for Social-Labour Rights]. Available at "Center for social and labour rights" website: http://trudprava.ru/files/pub/rostrudzak.pdf (accessed 15 February 2014).

[12] See the special issue of *Comparative Labour Law and Policy Journal* dedicated to the transformation of the freedom of association in countries with corporatist traditions: *CLLPJ* 32, No.4, 2011.

[13] See Hepple, B., 2005. *Labour Laws and Global Trade.* Oxford and Portland, Oregon: Hart Publishing, 33.

were playing a *different role*. Instead of acting as a representative of workers, as is traditional the case in Western trade unions, socialist trade unions were rather an amalgam of an intermediary between the state and employees and a kind of "social ministry". According to the official Soviet labour law doctrine, workers in socialist countries, unlike their capitalist colleagues, did not need the right to strike. This was explained by the fact that socialist states officially belonged to the proletariat, i.e. the workers. All entities (employers) were state-owned and were declared to belong to the workers themselves which made any conflict of interests nonsensical.[14]

In addition to acting as a "transmission gear" of the communist party to the "masses" (i.e. workers) in Lenin's terms,[15] trade unions were also important social structures. Their major function was to control the social security, healthcare, leisure and tourism institutions—social security funds, assets, hospitals, sanatoriums, stadiums and so on. This huge patrimony was assigned to trade unions by the socialist state. Another function of trade unions was to negotiate the terms of collective agreements at plant-level with employers. The word "bargaining" would not be appropriate here—"consultation" would better describe the situation. The subject of bargaining was not generally wages (as these were established by the state), but additional benefits which could be obtained from the state's limited budget. As long as there was no right to strike, there was no need for any laws governing collective labour disputes or disputes of interest.

After the collapse of the Soviet Union, the USSR Confederation of Trade Unions (Russian abbreviation—VCSPS) was transformed into the Federation of Independent Trade Unions of Russia (Russian abbreviation—FNPR). According to its statement, the FNPR unites more than 95% of total union members in Russia, approximately 22 million employees.[16] Although this percentage may be an exaggeration, the FNPR is still by far the largest trade union organization in Russia. It "inherited" not only the VCSPS's members, but also, even more importantly, its property, including real estate worth billions of US dollars. The FNPR is frequently criticized for being more interested in maintaining close relations with state authorities than in defending the interests of employees. After the

---

[14] For more details of this doctrine see Aleksandrov, N. G., 1948. *Trudovoe pravootnoshenie* [Labour Legal Relations]. Moscow: Yuridicheskoe izdatel'stvo ministerstva yusticii SSSR, 129-163.

[15] Lenin, V. I., 1967. *Polnoe sobranie sochineniy* [Complete Works], 5th ed., Vol. 44. Moscow: Izdatelstvo politicheskoy literatury [Political Literature Editors], 349.

[16] FNPR official site: http://fnpr.ru/n/252/4890.html (accessed 15 February 2014).

change in regime, a number of new trade union federations were formed,[17] but they are incomparably smaller and much weaker at a political level than the FNPR.

The current system of trade union rights and collective bargaining is mainly regulated by two federal laws, the Labour Code[18] and the Act on Trade Unions,[19] and is very much influenced by the domination of the FNPR. This situation has led to several gaps between the regulations governing the freedom of association and collective bargaining in Russia and the international labour standards. These gaps mainly concern the following issues:

- a lack of regulations preventing the creation of employer-controlled "yellow" unions;
- virtually no statutory rules governing internal trade union democracy;
- the pro-majority union type of collective bargaining which leaves minority unions without any real possibility of independently taking part in collective bargaining.[20] This is especially problematic when one takes into account that minority unions are often the only truly independent representatives of workers;
- weak consultation and information rights. There are provisions in the Labour Code stating that employers must take into account the plant-level union opinion before implementing company-level acts and, in some cases, before dismissal.[21] There is, however, no real obligation to take part in any genuine negotiations: the obligation is limited to the exchange of information and hearing the opinion

---

[17] The main "alternative" trade union federation is the Russian Labour Confederation [Konfederatsiya Truda Rossii, KTR]. See its official site: http://www.ktr.su/ (accessed 15 February 2014).

[18] *Trudovoy Kodeks Rossiyskoy Federatsii* [Labour Code of the Russian Federation] of 30 December 2001, No.197-FZ.

[19] *Federalniy Zakon o professionalnih soyuzah, ih pravah i garantiyah deyatelnosti* [Federal Law on Trade Unions, their Rights and the Guarantees of their Activity], 12 January 1996.

[20] The main features of this system are based on the compulsory creation of a "joint bargaining unit' for all plant-level trade unions where the majority union decides on the demands to be presented in negotiations with the employer (Art. 37 of the Labour Code), and an *erga omnes* scheme of collective agreements (Art. 43, para. 3 of the Labour Code) discouraging workers from joining the minority union. There are a number of other norms in the Labour Code and Act on Trade Unions, which are aimed in fact at disfavouring unions not affiliated with the FNPR.

[21] The procedures are established in Art. 372 and 373 of the Labour Code.

of workers' representatives. Employers are then absolutely free to take any proposed action they wish.[22]

- serious restrictions on the right to strike.[23]

In the majority of situations, the cases of non-conformity of domestic labour law do not concern the direct provisions of the international treaties[24], but rather their interpretation by the ILO and CE controlling bodies. Nevertheless, the large number of such gaps, though each of them may not be a major problem when taken individually, creates a broad system of collective bargaining which is generally unfavourable to independent unions and the possibility of collective action. The number of strikes registered annually by the official statistics institution is therefore close to zero,[25] while independent sociologists talk about dozens of work stoppages (strikes, work stoppages provoked by the non-payment of

[22] The only exception to this rule is established in Art. 374 of the Labour Code and has been discussed further elsewhere. For more details see: Lyutov, N., and E. Gerasimova. 2014. "Non-trade Union Employees' Representation in Russia," in *Bulletin of comparative Labour Relations 85 "Workers' Representation in Central and Eastern Europe Challenges and Opportunities for the Works Councils' System"*, eds. Blanpain, R., Lyutov, N., (Aspen: Wolters Kluwer), 183-201.

[23] For more details see: Gerasimova, E. S. 2012. "*Poryadok razresheniya kollektivnyh trudovyh sporov i organizatsii zabastovok izmenen. Dostignuta li tsel'?*" [*"The Procedure for Collective Labour Disputes Resolution and Strikes' Performance has been changed. Has the Goal been Achieved?"*], *Trudovoe pravo* [*Labour Law*] 1:51-59.

[24] Except for the first, concerning the lack of regulations prohibiting the creation of employer-controlled unions which contradict the ILO Right to Organize, and the Collective Bargaining Convention, 1949 (No. 98), containing the provision that "...acts which are designed to promote the establishment of workers' organizations under the domination of employers or employers' organizations ... shall be deemed to constitute acts of interference" in the right of association (para. 2, art. 2 of the Convention). Nevertheless, according to the Russian Constitution (para. 4, art. 15), any international treaty ratified by Russia is considered to be a part of domestic legislation. This provision may therefore be applied directly by the court, although this is not widely practised in case-law.

[25] For example, in 2011 there were only two officially registered strikes and in 2010 none at all. See: *Federalnaya Slujba Gosudarstvennoy Statistiki* (Rosstat Rossii) [Federal Service on State Statics (Rosstat of Russia)]. Rossiysky Statisticheskiy Ejegodnik, 2012. Moscow, 2012. [Russian statistical annual, 2012] http://www.gks.ru/bgd/regl/b12_13/IssWWW.exe/Stg/d1/05-29.htm (accessed 15 February 2014).

wages, hunger-strikes, take-overs of the employer's facilities, etc.) taking place every month.[26]

It is not the aim of this article to describe the technical details concerning these non-conformities, but the high number of unofficial strikes and the discussions within the ILO[27] and CE[28] concerning complaints demonstrate that the current regulations governing collective bargaining do not act as an effective "safety valve" for social unrest and are not able to adequately and appropriately promote workers' rights.

3. Prohibition of Discrimination

The issue of anti-discrimination regulation is also deeply-rooted in Russia's Soviet past. In a situation where all businesses were state-owned and there was no freedom to negotiate the conditions of employment contracts, there was no economic motivation for employers to discriminate. Instead of anti-discrimination regulations the ruling principle was that of "equality and differentiation in labour law", which meant that labour legislation was applied equally to everyone, although some specific categories of employees (young people, women, people with family responsibilities, disabled people, and so on) were examined individually by legislators and distinct rules were set for them. This system was effectively equivalent to having regulations on the prohibition of discrimination and it included elements of affirmative action. Following the introduction of the market economy and the arrival of privately-owned enterprises, however, this old approach to equality proved to be no longer sufficient.

---

[26] See: Bizyukov, P. V., 2011. *Kak zashishayut trudoviye prava v Rossii: kollektivniye trudovie protest i ih rol' v regulirovanii trudovyh otnosheniy [How Labour Rights are Defended in Russia: Collective Labour Protests and Their Role in the Industrial Relations Regulation].* Moscow: *Tsentr sotsial'no-trudovyh prav* [Centre for Social-Labour Rights], 30-33. Available at: http://trudprava.ru/download/bizukov_kak_zaschitit_1pdf (accessed 15 February 2014).

[27] See Committee on Freedom of Association cases No. 2244, 2251, 2758 and others in the Normlex Database: http://www.ilo.org/dyn/normlex/en/f?p=1000:20060:0:FIND:NO:20060:P20060_COUNTRY_ID,P20060_COMPLAINT_STATU_ID:102884,1495812 and http://www.ilo.org/dyn/normlex/en/f?p=1000:20060:0:FIND:NO:20060:P20060_COUNTRY_ID,P20060_COMPLAINT_STATU_ID:102884,1495811 (accessed 15 February 2014).

[28] The most important case in the CE was that heard by ECtHR, "Danilenkov and others vs. Russia" [30.07.2007].

Although Russia is party to both ILO fundamental Conventions on Discrimination[29] and other international treaties on the same issue, and despite having also introduced an article on the prohibition of discrimination in the Labour Code,[30] Russia's case-law in matters of discrimination is notably under-developed. Unlike the majority[31] of labour law proceedings which are won by employees, discrimination cases are very rarely won by the applicant. The main reason for this is that there is no kind of *alleviation of the burden of proof* in discrimination cases. Each party in civil court proceedings has to prove the circumstances that it refers to.[32] This provision is in contradiction with the approach of the European Committee of Social Rights (ECSR) which is authorized to interpret the provisions of the European Social Charter (ESC),[33] although the plain text of the ESC does not contain clear norms regarding the burden of proof. In some cases the ECSR states that the burden of proof in discrimination cases must be alleviated for the plaintiff,[34] while in others it goes even further to say that it must be totally lifted from the claimant.[35] It seems that a total shift of the burden of proof in discrimination cases may have controversial effects and could, in certain situations, be used as a tool by employees who are not actually being discriminated against in reality, to attempt to abuse their rights. Nevertheless, it is necessary that the burden of proof in discrimination cases be, to a certain extent, alleviated for applicants, and that certain other measures are taken. The ILO Committee of Experts on Application of the Conventions and Recommendations (CEACR) has already made recommendations to

[29] The ILO Conventions No. 100 and 111.

[30] Article 3 of the Labour Code.

[31] There are no reliable statistics on the issue, though this opinion is shared by many practising labour lawyers.

[32] Art. 56, Grajdansky Protsessualniy Kodeks Rossiyskoy Federatsii [Civil Procedure Code of the Russian Federation].

[33] Art. 4, par. 3; Art. 15; Art. 19, par. 5; Art. 20 and 27 of the European Social Charter.

[34] Council of Europe. *Conclusions of the European Committee of Social Rights, 2002*, 24; Syndicat Sud Travail et Affaires Sociales v. France, Complaint N 24/2004, Decision on the Merits of 16 November 2005, par. 33.

[35] Council of Europe. *Conclusions of the European Committee of Social Rights, 2004*. P. 495; Council of Europe. *Conclusions of the European Committee of Social Rights, XIII-5*. 272-276.

Russia concerning the alleviation of the burden of proof, but the Russian Government has not acted upon these recommendations.[36]

The issue of who bears the burden of proof in discrimination cases is aggravated by the traditional administrative approach of the courts towards employment relations, leading to the misunderstanding of the very notion of non-discrimination. We take as an example a case in which the court understood that an employee was selectively dismissed because of his trade union activities. However, as valid formal grounds for dismissal had been given,[37] it was found that the employer was entitled to discipline the worker and was free to decide whether to discipline others or not.

There are other non-conformities between Russian anti-discrimination legislation and case law and international labour standards which lead to a poor level of protection against discrimination for employees. The ECSR requires that "*remedies available to victims of discrimination must be adequate, proportionate and dissuasive*".[38] Russian legislation concerning unfair dismissals (irrespective of their discriminatory nature) provides for the reinstatement of unfairly dismissed employees, payment of the wages lost and compensation for moral damages. However, the amount of this compensation, determined by the courts on a case by case basis, is usually negligible and can in no way be regarded as "dissuasive".

A further serious gap in anti-discrimination legislation is the weakness of special provisions regarding the prohibition of *victimization*, i.e. the repression by an employer of a complaining employee. According to the ECSR statement, in order to make the prohibition of discrimination effective, domestic law must provide, among other things, protection against dismissal or other retaliatory action by the employer of an employee who has lodged a complaint or taken legal action.[39] Russian legislation permits dismissal only on the grounds specifically mentioned in law[40] and obviously does not consider "revenge" as valid grounds for dismissal. In practice, however, an employer can state that the reason for

---

[36] International Labour Conference, 100th Session, 2011. *Report of the Committee of Experts on the Application of Conventions and Recommendations (CEACR). Report III (Part 1A)*. 496.

[37] He was dismissed for the second time for arriving late at work. Although all the employees of this company regularly arrived at work in the first 30 minutes after official start of the working day, only the trade union activist was sanctioned.

[38] Council of Europe. *Conclusions of the European Committee of Social Rights, 2006*, 29.

[39] Council of Europe. *Conclusions of the European Committee of Social Rights, XVI-1*. 313.

[40] This will be explained in more detail further on.

dismissal is one of those given in the Labour Code, and it will be up to the employee to prove to the court that the *real* reason for dismissal was different from the officially stated *legal* reason given by the employer. This issue is therefore also very much connected to the problem of the burden of proof in discrimination cases. There is a norm regarding the partial immunity from dismissal for the elected chairmen and vice-chairmen of plant-level trade unions, which states that such union officials may be dismissed only with the consent of the trade union confederation to which this plant-level union is affiliated.[41] However, this limited immunity was restricted even further by the Constitutional Court in 2009.[42] The Constitutional Court motivated its decision with the argument that the principle of immunity from dismissal limits the constitutional freedom of the employer to conduct business. It seems that the balance of labour rights and economic freedoms in this situation was greatly tilted in favour of economic freedoms, leaving employees with little chance of protecting their rights.

Another serious gap in Russia's anti-discrimination legislation is the absence of regulations regarding *indirect discrimination*. The prohibition of direct or indirect preferences or a limitation of rights is only mentioned in the conclusion of employment contracts.[43] There is neither a legally grounded explanation of what indirect discrimination means, nor any case-law on the subject. The CEACR has raised this issue with Russia but without success.[44]

Among other flaws in anti-discrimination law and its practice, one may cite the weakness of measures of *reasonable accommodation* of persons with disabilities, and even the absence of disability as a reason for which people may suffer discrimination.

Perhaps too much discussion concerning the non-compliance of Russian legislation with international labour standards is centred on the *list of professions prohibited to women*. Control bodies of the ILO[45] and UN (including the Committee on Economic, Social and Cultural Rights which is responsible for monitoring the International Covenant on

---

[41] Art. 374, Labour Code.

[42] Constitutional Court Ruling of 3 November 2009 No.1368-o-p.

[43] Art. 64, Labour Code.

[44] International Labour Conference, 100th Session, 2011. *Report of the Committee of Experts on the Application of Conventions and Recommendations (CEACR). Report III (Part 1A)*. 496.

[45] International Labour Conference, 100th Session, 2011. *Report of the Committee of Experts on the Application of Conventions and Recommendations (CEACR). Report III (Part 1A)*. 464.

Economic, Social and Cultural Rights, 1966)[46] have criticized Russia for having a legally established list of professions that cannot be performed by women which is too extensive and in certain cases goes beyond the protection of women's health and becomes discrimination.[47] Although it is not wrong to say that this list of professions should be modified so that it is not discriminatory, the amount of discussion that this issue has caused seems to distract the attention of both the public and international organizations from much more important issues of discrimination in Russia such as those previously described.

All these flaws in anti-discrimination legislation and case-law, and others besides, have led to the serious under-development of the protection of the employee's right not to be discriminated against in Russia.

4. Labour Inspection

Russia is party to the so-called "governance" or "priority"[48] ILO Labour Inspection Convention, 1947 (No. 81). This Convention contains, among others, the provision that "*Labour inspectors provided with proper credentials shall be empowered to: (a) enter freely and without previous notice at any hour of the day or night any workplace liable to inspection; (b) enter by day any premises which they may have reasonable cause to believe to be liable to inspection; and (c) carry out any examination, test or enquiry which they may consider necessary in order to satisfy themselves that the legal provisions are being strictly observed* ". The new act[49] was adopted in Russia in 2008 with the aim of protecting businesses

[46] United Nations. *Committee on Economic, Social and Cultural Rights. Report on the 46th and 47th sessions (2-20 May 2011, 14 November-2 December 2011). Economic and Social Council Official Records, 2012. Supplement No. 2. UN Doc. No. E/2012/22, E/C.12/2011/3*. New York and Geneva: United Nations, 2012. 37.

[47] There were also debates of this kind in Russian court practice. See the Supreme Court Case of 2 March 2009, No.GPI09-36 concerning the legality of the ban on women working as subway-train drivers.

[48] For instance, one of the 12 ILO Conventions monitored on a priority basis. On the issue of the classification of the ILO instruments see ILO Governing Body. *Working Party on Policy Regarding the Revision of Standards. Follow-up to the Recommendations of the Working Party. ILO Document GB.283/LILS/WP/PRS/1/2*. Geneva, 2002.

[49] Federal Law "*O zashite prav juridicheskih lits i individualnyh predprinimateley pri osushestvlenii gosudarstvennogo kontrolya (nadzora) i munitspalnogo controlya [On the Protection of the Rights of Legal Entities and of Individual Entrepreneurs Under State Control (Supervision) and Municipal Control]*" of 26 December 2008, No. 294-FZ.

from excessive regulatory control by the state and from extortion by state officials authorized to control business activity. This act contains the provision that the "planned inspection" of legal entities and private entrepreneurs may be performed no more than once in three years and that the entities inspected must be informed of the planned inspection at least three days in advance.[50] "Non-planned inspections" may only be performed after the public procurator's office has issued a sanction.[51]

The contradiction of this legislation with the ILO Priority Convention is evident. It is obvious that serious breaches in the labour law may be concealed by the employer if he or she is warned about the planned inspection. The non-conformity of this legislation with international labour standards is aggravated by the fact that labour inspections in Russia are institutionally very weak and are being weakened even further: in 2013 the State Labour Inspection limited the number of labour inspectors in Russia to 2,800 (i.e. one inspector per 25,000 workers) despite the fact that the number of workers' complaints to the labour inspection board has doubled over the last few years. This issue was discussed during an ILO mission to Moscow at the end of 2011, but it did not lead to any results.[52]

Besides contradicting an important international treaty, this act has not achieved its official goal: protecting small and medium enterprises from excessive control. Employers have a lot of bureaucratic obligations towards the state and have to issue many officially regulated acts covering their relations with employees, irrespective of the size of the business (these are written orders that must be issued for any action taken by the employer, special forms of "local normative acts" for various issues). Most of these requirements were adopted by the state during the Soviet era with an aim to regulate the activity of large-sized state-owned corporations. Currently, however, even an employer of a domestic worker or a market-trader employing just one person must, at least theoretically, abide by almost all of these requirements. In practice, this hardly happens and these small employers are completely unprotected against inspections which are unrestricted by the law in any way.

---

[50] Art. 8, par. 12 of Law No. 294-FZ.

[51] Art. 10, par. 5 of Law No. 294-FZ.

[52] ILO. 316th Session, Geneva, 1-16 November 2012. ILO Doc. No. GB.316/INS/9/1. *365th Report of the Committee on Freedom of Association. Appendix. Mission report Moscow, Russian Federation (10-15 October 2011). Geneva: ILO, 2012*. Par. 20, 387-388.

5. Wages

The most serious inconsistency between Russian law and international labour standards regards the payment of wages and specifically concerns the regulation of the *minimum wage*. The Labour Code contains a clause,[53] added for purely political purposes, stating that the minimum monthly wage cannot be lower than the official subsistence level.[54] However, at the very end of the text there is a "modestly hidden" article stating that this norm is to be enacted by separate federal law, i.e. it is not in force. Official trade unions[55] are making their voices heard, publicly demanding[56] that the relationship between the minimum wage and subsistence levels must be made legally binding. Nevertheless, as yet there have been no signs that this is going to happen in the near future. At the time of writing, the minimum wage in Russia is just 5,554 roubles per month,[57] roughly equivalent to 123 euros. Although Russia has ratified the European Social Charter, it has refrained from ratifying Art. 4 par.1 which establishes what is considered a decent minimum wage. This cannot be seen as surprising when one takes into account that the ECSR insists[58] that a decent minimum wage cannot be lower than 60% of the country's average wage, or, in exceptional cases and with due note of the cost of living in certain countries, no less than 50% of the average wage. The average monthly wage at the end of third quarter of 2013 in Russia was 29,730 roubles.[59]

---

[53] Art. 133, par. 1 of the Labour Code.

[54] The subsistence level is officially established by the government on quarterly basis; for the third quarter of 2013 it was 7,429 roubles. Government Resolution No. 1173 of 17 December 2013.

[55] See an explanation of the difference between "official" and "independent" (or "new" and "old") trade unions: Bizyukov, P. V., V. A. Bizyukova, K. V. Burnyshev, and I. V. Donova. 2004. *Mesto profsoyuzov v sisteme reuglirovaniya trudovyh otnosheniy [The Place of Trade Unions in the Regulation of Labour Relations]* Moscow: ISITO.

[56] References to this relationship as a "goal" are repeated in General Collective Agreements that are regularly concluded at the national level.

[57] Federalniy Zakon "*O vnesenii izmeneniy v statyu 1 Federalnogo zakona o minimalnom razmere oplaty truda" [Federal Law on Amending Article 1 of Federal Law on Minimum Wage]* of 2 December 2013 No. 336-FZ.

[58] Council of Europe. Digest of The Case Law of The European Committee of Social Rights, 2008. 43.

[59] Federal Service on State Statistics (*Rosstat Rossii*) official site. *Srednemesyachnaya nominalnaya nachislennaya zarabotnaya plata v tselom po ekonomike Rossiyskoy Federatsii* v 2000—2013 g. [Monthly average nominal wages in the economy of the Russian Federation in general in 2000-2013]:

The official minimum wage is only about 18.7% of this sum. Compared to EU countries with a roughly equal or even lower GDP per capita,[60] the minimum wage in Russia is 3 to 5 times lower.[61]

It is easy to see that current regulation regarding the minimum wage not only enables employers to keep the minimum wage unreasonably low, but also, given that the official subsistence level is unilaterally calculated by the government itself, provides the government with grounds for claiming that the Russian budget cannot afford to pay higher salaries. It is much more difficult to cite budgetary issues as the problem when the minimum wage is objectively related to the country's average wage. It is therefore not surprising that the neo-liberal lobby in the government persistently avoids the implementation of such a relationship. This approach is damaging the poorest regions of Russia where the issue of minimum wages could significantly alter the demand-oriented economy without negative consequences for employment levels, as the majority of workplaces in these areas are created in the state sector. Changing this system could also limit the huge disparities in income between the different regions of Russia.

6. Working Time

According to the Russian Labour Code, "normal" working time must not exceed 40 hours per week.[62] This provision is in line with the relevant international labour standards.

There are, however, special norms which allow these limits to be extended. The Labour Code provides employers with the opportunity to establish the so-called "*un-normalized working day regime*",[63] which means that the employer has the power to draw up a list of certain positions within the entity which may require the employee to

---

http://www.gks.ru/free_doc/new_site/population/trud/sr—zarplata/t1.doc (accessed 15 February 2014).

[60] Such as Croatia, Estonia, Latvia, Lithuania and Poland. See: International Monetary Fund. World Economic Outlook Database. http://www.imf.org/external/pubs/ft/weo/2013/01/weodata/index.aspx (accessed 15 February 2014).

[61] See World Bank. 2014 The International Finance Corporation. *Doing Business Report, 2014.* Washington: The World Bank. http://www.doingbusiness.org/~/media/GIAWB/Doing%20Business/Documents/Annual-Reports/English/DB14-Full-Report.pdf (accessed 15 February 2014).

[62] Art. 91 of the Labour Code.

[63] Art. 101, Labour Code.

"episodically"[64] work "beyond the normal working time". There are no clear limitations concerning which categories of workers may be required to work under this kind of regime. Nor are there any restrictions on how many extra hours one may work, nor any guarantees that the employee will be paid extra. The only provision given in the Code is that the employee be given another three-day paid annual leave.[65]

There are also norms governing the "*combination of work*", which may be "internal" or "external",[66] i.e. for one or several employers respectively. In the course of an "internal combination of work", an employee may sign an additional employment contract with the same employer but for a different position (which in practice may actually be the same role with a slightly different name) for a maximum of four hours a day and for no more than half of the normal working time.[67] For the "external combination of work" there is no requirement that the job be different, and although the same limitation on the maximum duration of the combined work is applied, there is no limit on the number of "extra employers" that one employee may have. In reality this means that an employee working for a corporation which conducts its activities through a number of legal entities may appear to be employed by different companies which are in fact, to all intents and purposes, just one employer. This employee's real wage payment would be shared by these fictionally independent employers (legal entities affiliated to each other). Given that the minimum wage is very low (see above), it is not usually difficult for the employer to establish such a system.

Although both the foregoing schemes are legal according to the Labour Code of Russia, they are nonetheless in contradiction with the ILO Reduction of Hours of Work Recommendation, 1962 (No. 116),[68] which includes a clear provision that all hours worked in excess of the normal working hours should be classed as overtime, unless they are taken into

---

[64] No one knows what the notion of "episodic" character of work actually means. The Federal Agency on Labour and Employment (Rostrud) which controls the activity of labour inspections in Russia, has issued an official letter in answer to the request made by non-governmental organizations, concerning the interpretation of the requirements of Art. 101 of the Labour Code, and specifically how many number of hours per day and times per week would not be considered a breach of this "episodic" character. The answer was based on the notion that such extra work "must not be systematic", i.e. this "answer" did not provide any explanation at all. In practice, it would totally depend upon the discretion of the labour inspector.

[65] Art. 119, Labour Code.

[66] Art. 60.1, Labour Code.

[67] Art. 284, Labour Code.

[68] Par. 16, Reduction of Hours of Work Recommendation, 1962 (No. 116).

account in remuneration according to custom. Needless to say, these flaws in Russian labour legislation lead to the serious abuse of the limits of working time.

7. Notice of Termination of an Employment Contract

Article 4, paragraph 4 of the European Social Charter[69] affirms that ratifying states shall recognize the right of all workers to a reasonable period of notice for the termination of employment except in the case of immediate dismissal for any serious offence.[70] The ESCR interprets this provision as a requirement for the parties of the ESC to establish legal provisions for the notice of all non-disciplinary dismissals, with the period of notice depending on the length of each employee's job tenure.[71] Making judgments in specific cases, the ECSR has ruled that: a week's notice for up to six months of service,[72] two weeks' notice for more than six months of service,[73] no less than one month's notice for more than one year of service,[74] thirty days' notice for at least five years of service,[75] six weeks' notice after ten to fifteen years of service,[76] eight weeks' notice after more than fifteen years of service,[77] are not consistent with requirements of article 4, par. 4 of the European Social Charter.

The notice of dismissal in Russian legislation is only applied to some grounds for dismissal, such as collective redundancy (two months' notice[78]) or the end of temporary employment contracts (three days' notice[79]) and these terms do not depend on tenure. Such rules are in clear contradiction with the requirements of Art. 4, par. 4 of the European Social Charter as it is interpreted by the ECSR. It must, however, be taken

---

[69] This paragraph has been ratified by Russia.

[70] Appendix to the ESC.

[71] Council of Europe. *Conclusions of the European Committee of Social Rights, XIII-3, Portugal*, 267.

[72] *Ibid.*

[73] Council of Europe. *Conclusions of the European Committee of Social Rights, XVI-2, Poland*, 616.

[74] Council of Europe. *Conclusions of the European Committee of Social Rights, XIV-2, Spain*, 684.

[75] Council of Europe. *Conclusions of the European Committee of Social Rights, 2003, Bulgaria*, 41.

[76] Council of Europe. *Conclusions of the European Committee of Social Rights, XIV-2, Ireland*, 398.

[77] *Ibid.*

[78] Art. 180, par. 2 of the Labour Code.

[79] Art. 79, par. 2 of the Labour Code.

into account that the requirements of the ESC have been elaborated for a completely different system of dismissal protection which is used in other CE countries but not in Russia. According to the Russian Labour Code the dismissal of employees is only permitted on the grounds that are directly stated in legislation (i.e. the specific list of serious disciplinary offences such as absence from work for more than four consecutive hours without just cause,[80] being at work in a state of alcoholic, drug or toxic intoxication,[81] theft,[82] and others), after numerous disciplinary breaches,[83] if a lack of qualifications is discovered during a formal evaluation carried out by the employer[84] or for a number of other reasons. There are also grounds for the employer to dismiss employees on his or her own initiative which are not associated with employee conduct, such as during the liquidation of a company or in staff reduction (i.e. redundancy),[85] as well as others.

In most EU countries workers are well-protected from the "harmful effects" of dismissal by the system of dismissal notices, the periods of which usually depend on the duration of job tenure. Russian legislation, however, protects employees from dismissal itself. While it may seem that the list of grounds for dismissal is interpreted in a more limited way in Russia than in EU countries, the system of dismissal notices and severance payments actually turns out to be more "employer-friendly".

As long as this system of specifically named grounds for dismissal is understood by social partners in Russia as being an effective cornerstone of employment protection legislation, it seems highly unlikely that it will be substituted with a system of dismissal notices in the near future.

Conclusion

This overview presents only some of the major inconsistencies between Russian labour law and international labour standards. This cannot be explained solely by the poor quality of Russian legislation, collective bargaining and court practice, but is also due to the extreme complexity of modern international labour standards and national law. One may indeed say that a significant number of instances of non-compliance can be found, to a greater or lesser extent, in any country.

[80] Art. 81, par. 6 (a) of the Labour Code.
[81] Art. 81, par. 6 (b) of the Labour Code.
[82] Art. 81, par. 6 (d) of the Labour Code.
[83] Art. 81, par. 5 of the Labour Code.
[84] Art. 81, par. 3 of the Labour Code.
[85] Art. 81, par. 1 and 2 of the Labour Code.

There are numerous illustrations of a more technical character concerning distortions in the interpretation of international labour standards in the context of domestic labour law which could not be included in this publication precisely because there are so many of them.

Nevertheless, the examples presented here which cover the basic human rights of workers show that fundamental changes to the laws governing collective bargaining, anti-discrimination policies, labour inspections, wages, working times and other rights must be made in Russia in order to make Russian labour law more consistent with international regulations.

This comparison also shows that the idea that international labour standards provide only the basic level of rights and that it is *national* labour law which establishes the higher standards, is no more than an illusion, at least in the case of Russia.

References

Aleksandrov, N. G., 1948. *Trudovoe pravootnoshenie [Labour Legal Relations]*. Moscow: Yuridicheskoe izdatel'stvo ministerstva yusticii SSSR.

Bizyukov, P. V., 2011. *Kak zashishayut trudoviye prava v Rossii: kollektivniye trudovie protest i ih rol' v regulirovanii trudovyh otnosheniy [How Labour Rights are Defended in Russia: Collective Labour Protests and Their Role in the Regulation of Industrial Relations]*. Moscow: Tsentr sotsial'no-trudovyh prav [Centre for Social-Labour Rights], 30-33. Available at: http://trudprava.ru/download/bizukov_kak_zaschitit_1pdf (accessed 15 February 2014).

Bizyukov, P.V., V. A. Bizyukova, K. V. Burnyshev, and I.V., Donova. 2004. *Mesto profsoyuzov v sisteme reuglirovaniya trudovyh otnosheniy [The Place of Trade Unions in the Regulation of Labour Relations]* Moscow: ISITO.

Council of Europe. 2008. *Digest of the Case Law of the European Committee of Social Rights.*

Ewing, K. D., 2013. "Myth and Reality of the Right to Strike as a 'Fundamental Labour Right'," *The International Journal of Comparative Labour Law and Industrial Relations* 29, No. 2:145-166.

Federal Service on State Statistics (Rosstat Rossii) official site. *Srednemesyachnaya nominalnaya nachislennaya zarabotnaya plata v tselom po ekonomike Rossiyskoy Federatsii* v 2000—2013 g. *[Monthly*

Average Nominal Wages in the Economy of the Russian Federation in General in 2000-2013]: http://www.gks.ru/free_doc/new_site/population/trud/sr-zarplata/t1.doc (accessed 15 February 2014).

Gerasimova, E. S., 2012. "Poryadok razresheniya kollektivnyh trudovyh sporov i organizatsii zabastovok izmenen. Dostignuta li tsel'?" ["The Procedure for Collective Labour Disputes Resolution and Strikes' Performance has been Changed. Has the Goal been Achieved?"], Trudovoe pravo [*Labour Law*] 1, 51-59.

Hepple, B., 2005. *Labour Laws and Global Trade.* Oxford and Portland, Oregon: Hart Publishing.

ILO. 316th Session, Geneva, 1-16 November 2012. ILO Doc. No. GB.316/INS/9/1. *365th Report of the Committee on Freedom of Association. Appendix. Mission report Moscow, Russian Federation (10-15 October 2011). Geneva: ILO, 2012.*

—. 2002. *Working Party on Policy regarding the Revision of Standards. Follow-up to the recommendations of the Working Party. ILO Document GB.283/LILS/WP/PRS/1/2.* Geneva: ILO.

ILO Normlex Database. http://www.ilo.org/dyn/normlex/en/f?p=1000:11200:0::NO:11200:P11200_COUNTRY_ID:102884 (accessed 15 February 2014).

International Labour Conference, 100th Session. 2011. *Report of the Committee of Experts on the Application of Conventions and Recommendations (CEACR). Report III (Part 1A).*

International Monetary Fund. *World Economic Outlook Database.* http://www.imf.org/external/pubs/ft/weo/2013/01/weodata/index.aspx (accessed 15 February 2014).

Javillier, J.-Cl. 2003. "Pour une Contribution des Universalitaires à la Dynamique des Normes Internationales du Travail" in *Changing Industrial Relations and Modernisation of Labour Law. Liber Amicorum in Honour of Professor Marco Biagi,* eds. Blanpain, R., and M. Weiss, (The Hague-London-New York: Kluwer Law International), 206-207.

La Hovary, C. 2013. "Showdown at the ILO? A Historical Perspective on the Employers' Group's 2012 Challenge to the Right to Strike," *Industrial Law Journal* 42, No. 4:338-368.

Lenin, V. I. 1967. *Polnoe sobranie sochineniy* [Complete works], 5th ed., Vol. 44. Moscow: Izdatelstvo politicheskoy literatury [Political literature editors].

Lyutov, N., 2012. *Rossiyskoye trudovoe zakonodatelstvo i mejdunarodniye trudoviye standarty: sootvetstvie i perspectivy sovershenstovaniya*

[Russian Labour Legislation and International Labour Standards: The Issues of Compliance and Perspectives for Modification]. Moscow: Tsentr sotsial'no-trudovyh prav [Centre for Social-Labour Rights]. Available at "Center for social and labour rights" website: http://trudprava.ru/files/pub/rostrudzak.pdf (accessed 15 February 2014).

Lyutov, N. and E. Gerasimova. 2014. "Non-trade Union Employees' Representation in Russia," in *Bulletin of comparative Labour Relations 85 "Workers' Representation in Central and Eastern Europe Challenges and Opportunities for the Works Councils' System"*, eds. Blanpain, R., N. Lyutov, (Aspen: Wolters Kluwer), 183-201.

Servais, J.-M., 1986. "Flexibility and Rigidity in International Labour Standards", *International Labour Review* 125, No. 2:193-208.

Swepston, L., 2013. "Crisis in the ILO Supervisory System: Dispute over the Right to Strike," *The International Journal of Comparative Labour Law and Industrial Relations* 29, No. 2:199-218.

United Nations. *Committee on Economic, Social and Cultural Rights. Report on the 46th and 47th sessions (2-20 May 2011, 14 November-2 December 2011). Economic and Social Council Official Records, 2012. Supplement No. 2. UN Doc. No. E/2012/22, E/C.12/2011/3*. New York and Geneva: United Nations, 2012.

World Bank, The International Finance Corporation. Doing Business Report, 2014. Washington: The World Bank. http://www.doingbusiness.org/~/media/GIAWB/Doing%20Business/Documents/Annual—Reports/English/DB14—Full—Report.pdf (accessed 15 February 2014).

Zuleeg, M. 1995. "International Organizations, Implied Powers" in *Encyclopaedia of Public International Law. Vol. 2*, ed. Bernhardt, R., (Amsterdam: Elsevier Science & Technology), 1312 and ff.

THE RUSSIAN MODEL OF A LEGAL MECHANISM OF SOCIAL PARTNERSHIP: COMPARATIVE AND LEGAL ANALYSIS

MARINA LUSHNIKOVA

1. Legal Models of Social Partnership

In foreign practice there are two main models of social partnership in the work sphere. The first model is applied in countries in the European Union and elsewhere. It is characterized by active intervention of the state in the regulation of labor relations, especially in Northern Europe, and is based on the principles of tripartism, which includes three levels: national collective agreements, branch (standard) and local (regional, factory) collective agreements. According to the International Labor Organization, these countries are moving in the direction of decentralization, while national and branch collective negotiations are losing ground. However, the European model of labor relations as a whole keeps its commitment to national consultations and negotiations. Europeans are not inclined to agree with excessive inequality, they believe that the state has to correct the social consequences of the functioning of the market economy, as well as providing social protection and the minimum guaranteed income.

The second model of social partnership, according to the terminology of the International Labor Organization, the "forcible model", arose in England and is now applied in countries such as: Canada, the USA, New Zealand, Australia and in the majority of the developing countries of Asia, Latin America and English-speaking Africa.[1] It is, as a rule, reduced to a grassroots level, namely the level of collective agreements of enterprises.

More specific and unusual negotiations and agreements are carried out at the regional and branch levels. Organizations of businessmen and labor unions interfere with the social and labor relations indirectly by actively participating in legislative and political activity. Within this model of social partnership which in its purist form is presented by the USA, social

[1] See: 72nd Session of the International Labor Organization. ILO: Geneva.

partners form (regulate) labor relations whereas the function of legislation (state) consists in the organization of collective negotiations and establishment of rules for social dialogue. The unification of Europe and European legislation became the reason for modification to the considered model. It demanded from Great Britain the provision of obligatory consultations on collective dismissals and working hours, and also the formation of bodies of working representation—councils of the enterprises.

2. Social Partnership in Countries on Post-Socialist Space of Central and Eastern Europe and the Former Federal Republics of the USSR

The crash of the socialist economic system in these countries became a considerable event at the end of the 1990s. Transition to market relations was accompanied by the crisis phenomena in economy, a decrease in the income levels of the population, etc. Due to these conditions in the post-socialist countries there was a question on the choice of a model for social dialogue in the work sphere. The majority of the countries, including Russia, made the choice for tripartite cooperation of social partners and the state, tripartite consultations and three-bilateral collective agreements and contracts at national, intersectoral, branch, territorial and local levels.

The choice of this model was affected considerably by the position of the International Labour Organization (ILO). A three-party division for the organization was also under construction on the principle of tripartite interaction of representatives of the governments, of the unions of employers and of labor unions from the participating state. Besides, the last experience of centralized state regulation of the socialist labor relations in a certain measure dictated preservation of this function in "state hands" but its realization has to take place in new conditions on the basis of consultations with social partners. In this regard, in the countries of post-socialist space where tripartite councils were created, the powers differ from country to country, but generally these bodies have the consultative or consultative and recommendatory status. In some cases, in their framework, general agreements (Hungary, the Czech Republic, Kazakhstan, Belarus, Russia, etc.) can be concluded. These tripartite bodies are used by the governments for consultations before the adoption of important decisions in the social and labor sphere, which include: the Council for Reconciliation of Interests in Hungary, created in 1990; the Commission on Coordination of Interests in Bulgaria (1990); Fund of the Social World in Poland (1993), etc. So, in Hungary the national tripartite Council carries out a number of functions: determination of the minimum wage for the next year; permission of collective labor disputes; participation in policy and legislation formation concerning work and employment. The majority of tripartite councils operate on legislative acts; few under the tripartite agreement. In Russia such permanent bodies of social partnership became three or bilateral commissions on regulation of social and labor relations.

"Construction from above", i.e. formation of this model by the state became another characteristic of the legal model of social partnership in post-socialist countries. Many researchers emphasize the fact that unlike the Western countries where social partnership resulted from a long and persistent fight for the rights of workers and their labor unions, i.e. "from below"; in the considered countries social partnership was spread "from above", as a mechanism of regulation of a labor market. In Russia, the Decree No. 212 issued by the President of the Russian Federation on November 15, 1991, titled "About Social Partnership and Permission of Labor Disputes (Conflicts)", was the first step towards the creation of a legal mechanism of social partnership. This Decree permitted multilevel systems of social partnership in the field of the social and labor relations and allowed labor conflicts. It included the following levels: national, territorial, branch and enterprise levels. Further steps towards the creation of a legal mechanism of social partnership were taken with the Act of the Russian Federation "About Collective Treaties and Agreements" (1992), which concretizes levels of social partnership based on the types of collective agreements and contracts concluded, establishes the procedure of collective negotiations, and offers an order to the conclusion of agreements and responsibility of the parties.[2]

Going back to the history of the formation of the legal model of social partnership in the post-socialist countries, it is necessary to stop and take a particular look at one of its feature: the insufficient independence and self-identification of social partners, especially representatives of employers.

As for labor unions, in all countries it is a difficult process; on the one hand, we observed the reforming of the former traditional labor unions created in the period of socialist construction, on the other hand, we observed the origin of new independent labor unions. In a number of countries this process was accompanied by split and confrontation in the trade-union environment. In Russia, dominating positions were kept by the reformed labor unions, today known as the Federation of Independent Labor Unions (FILU). The situation with other social partners, such as the

[2] *Vedomosti sjezda narodnykh deputatov i Verkhovnogo Soveta RF* [Bulletin of Congress of People's Deputies and Supreme Council of the Russian Federation]. 1992 . No. 17. P. 890.

unions of employers, was much more difficult. In the West such associations were created as a call, a reaction to the existence of trade-union movements, with domination of the state form of ownership. These unions of employers by principle could not spread in the countries of socialist orientation. In the majority of the countries the legal base of social partnership appeared before the formation of the self-sufficient structured party of social partnership—representatives (unions) of employers.

After their accession to the EU, the European post-socialist countries experienced one more form of social partnership: councils of enterprises had developed. These bodies of working representation generally operate on a local level. In the majority of the countries they work with labor unions, and less often are they created only where the trade-union organizations are absent. EU legislation provides the obligatory creation at the enterprise level for every EU Member State of bodies of hired workers allocated with advisory and information functions that will be explained below. A "multichannel" system of representation of worker interests, not only labor unions, but also bodies of working representation become widely spread.

A tendency of the development of a legal mechanism of social partnership in the considered countries is that the orientation to the models of social partnership is unified at the level of international legal standards. So, CIS countries with this perspective of the Model Law on social partnership, adopted at the twenty-seventh plenary session of Inter-parliamentary Assembly of the States, the resolution acts No. 27-14 of November 16, 2006.[3] The law defines the organizational, legal and economic bases of the functions of the social-partnership as the most important mechanism of regulation of social, labor and related economic relations, the purposes, the principles, levels, forms of social partnership, and the basic rights of social partners: on information, collective negotiations, etc. For European countries, and also the Russian Federation, a special role is played by the European Social Charter (1996, reconsidered). The parties of the Charter recognize the purposes of policy creation, the conditions providing implementation of the basic labor rights and the principles, including: the right of workers and employers to association, the right to collective negotiations and collective actions regarding protection of the rights, the right to information and consultation. These rights are the center of a legal mechanism of social partnership.

---

[3] *Informacionniy bulleten' Mezhdunarodnoy Assamblei gosudarstv-uchastnikov SNG* [Information bulletin of the International Assembly of the participating states of the CIS]. 2007. No. 39.

Thus, legal means of social partnership depending on national features vary in consulting forms of cooperation of social partners until the adoption of joint decisions, collective agreements and contracts and cover participants from a grassroots level of the enterprises and firms on a national level. The ILO considers that it is impossible to offer a uniform ideal model of social partnership which would promote social and economic growth better than other models. The ILO in conventions and recommendations defined the main forms and levels of cooperation of workers, employers and the state, as well as legal principles of their social partnership. The international standards of the collective labor law is the basis for the formation and development of national models of social partnership.

2.1. The Russian Model of Social Partnership

In our opinion, social partnership in essence means nothing more than a legal mechanism of regulation of collective labor relations. The Russian model of social partnership is reduced to a model of this legal mechanism out of which social partnership turns into nothing but a supported set of good wishes. In one article it is not possible to give specific and singular characteristics of the Russian model of a legal mechanism of social partnership; separate research or a special section for this purpose is required.[4] However, its contours can be shown through considerations on the different levels, the principles and the bodies of social partnership. Further on, we will concentrate on this aspect.

We will begin with the short explanation of the characteristic of the concepts pertaining to social partnership. In our opinion, there are two main conceptual approaches of legal mediation that take place today in the Russian science. According to the first approach, social partnership is considered a new institute of the general part of labor law[5] or as a new general institute of "social partnership", having a complex structure,

---

[4] See: Lushnikova, M. V. 1997. *Gosudarstvo, rabotodateli, rabotniki* [State, Employers, Workers]. Yaroslavl: Podati, 224; Lushnikova, M. V., Lushnikov, A.M. 2008. *Social'noe partnerstvo v sfere truda* [Social Partnership in the Work Sphere]. Yaroslavl: Yaroslavl universitet, 432; Lushnikov, A.M., Lushnikova, M.V. 2009. *Kurs trudovogo prava* [Course of the Labor Law]. V.1. Moscow: Statut, 8-219.

[5] See, e.g.: Geykhman, V.L. and I.K. Dmitrieva, 2011. *Trudovoe pravo* [Labor Law]. Moscow: Yurait, 122-123; Golovina, S. Yu. and M.V. Molodtsov, 2008. *Trudovoe pravo Rossii* [Labor Law of Russia]. Moscow: Norma, 116.

including sub-institutes of collective treaties and collective agreements.[6] Such treatment is in many respects based on a position of the legislator who has isolated the structure of the Labor Code (further—LC) of the Russian Federation in the special Section II "Social Partnership in the Work Sphere". In this regard, I.Ya.Kiselev (1932-2005) noted that "… the existence in the Code of the special section "Social Partnership in the Work Sphere" makes unique lines to our labor legislation".[7] The validity of such "uniqueness" raises doubts within many scientists engaged in the labor law field.

The second approach to legal mediation of social partnership is based on a broader definition of social partnership and the views of scientists adherent to this approach vary to some extent. Social partnership is considered as a function, the purpose of labor law. In the Labor Code of the Russian Federation, one of the main objectives of labor legislation is the creation of necessary legal conditions for the achievement of optimum coordination of the interests of the parties, labor relations, and interests of the state (Art. 1). I.Ya. Kiselev wrote about social partnership as a sociological and ethical concept, while the part of the "guarantor", who establishes a legal framework of dialogue with the social partners, is assigned to the legislator. He especially noted that "in international legal practice, particularly in acts and publications of the ILO, the term social dialogue", instead of "social partnership", is accepted by our legislator" and applied most often.[8]

The General Director of the International Labor Bureau presented the Global Report "Association in the Organization for Social Justice" (which we will see below). It was drafted according to the mechanism of implementation of the Declaration of the ILO on the fundamental principles and the rights in the work sphere. For the ILO the term "social dialogue" covers all types of collective negotiations, consultations and/or exchange of information between representatives of the governments, employers and employees, on matters representing the general interest and concerning economic and social policy. Labor conflicts also have to be resolved within labor relations by conducting collective negotiations,

---

[6] See: Kurennoy, A.M. ed. 2008. *Trudovoe pravo Rossii* [Labor Law of Russia]. Moscow: Yurist, 140-143; Smirnov, O.V. ed. 2008. *Kommentariy k Trudovomu kodeksu RF* [Commentary on the Labor Code of the Russian Federation]. Moscow: Knorus, 80-81.

[7] Kiselev, I. Ya. 2005. *Sravnitel'noe trudovoe pravo* [Comparative Labor Law]. Moscow: Prospekt, 251.

[8] Ibid.

carrying out consultations and by means of properly functioning mechanisms of prevention and settlement of disputes.[9]

A number of scholars define social partnership as a way of regulating social and labor relations between employees (their representatives) and employers (their representatives), based on the mutual recognition of interests of each of the parties and respect of these interests.[10] Social and partnership regulations together with collective and contractual regulations are a necessary component in the modern mechanism of legal regulation of labor and relations along with individual, contractual, public state and legal regulations.[11] V. M. Lebedev reasonably puts an equal sign between collective labor law and social partnership in the work sphere, however, he prefers to apply only the first of these terms.[12]

Social partnership is considered by many scholars engaged in the labor law field, also as the principle in the field of legal regulation of the work sphere. The development of the principle of social partnership demands improvements of collective and contractual regulations of the labor relations, creation and provision of systems of participation for the personnel in enterprise affairs, and, therefore, improvements in the collective means of legal regulation of work.[13] In the Labor Code of the Russian Federation social partnership is proclaimed as one of the basic principles of legal regulation of labor relations and other directly related relations (Art. 2).

In our opinion, social partnership should be considered as a legal mechanism for the regulation of collective labor relations which includes regulatory mechanisms.[14] This position gained support and was further

---

[9] See: Organizing for Social Justice: Global Report under the Follow-up to the ILO Declaration on Fundamental Principles and Rights at Work (2004). Geneva: ILO.

[10] See: Mavrin, S.P. and E.B. Khokhlov, 2012. *Trudovoe pravo Rossii* [Labor Law of Russia]. Moscow: Norma, 156 and further (the author of the chapter, Safonov, V.A.).

[11] See: Ibid, 52.

[12] See: Lebedev, V. M. ed. 2011. *Trudovoe pravo* [Labor Law]. Moscow: Norma, 78 and further.

[13] See e.g.: Mavrin, S.P., A.S. Pashkov and E.B. Khokhlov, ed. 1996. *Kurs rossiyskogo trudovogo prava* [Course of the Russian Labor Law]. Vol. 1. St. Petersburg: SPBGU, 160-161.

[14] Lushnikova, M. V. 1997. *Gosudarstvo, rabotodateli i rabotniki: istoriya, teoriya i praktika pravovogo mekhanizma social'nogo partnerstva (sravnitel'no-pravovoe issledovanie)* [State, Employers and Workers: History, Theory and Practice of a Legal Mechanism of Social Partnership (Comparative and Legal Research)]. Yaroslavl: Yaroslavl universitet, 224; Lushnikova, M. V. 1997. *Pravovoy mekhanizm social'nogo partnerstva v regulirovanii trudovykh i social'no-*

developed in the works of a number of scholars and practitioners.[15] We consider that, collective (social and partner) legal relationships by nature are derivative from labor legal relationships. Their subjects are collective (labor unions, the unions of employers, groups of workers), representatives and other participants (bodies of social partnership, representatives of the state, bodies on permission of collective labor disputes). These collective (social and partner) relations develop over the task of carrying out collective negotiations and as the conclusion of collective treaties and agreements; with participation of workers and their representatives in management of the organization, trade union representation and protection of the rights of workers; over mutual consultations and negotiations on questions of regulation of labor relations. These are all covered by the regulatory part of a legal mechanism of social partnership.

Collective labor disputes, violations of collective labor law are the basis to the emergence of collective (social and partner) guarding legal relationship on permission of the collective conflict. Guarding thus becomes part of a legal mechanism of social partnership which includes conciliatory and intermediary procedures of permission of collective labor disputes, including the right to strike.

The Model Law "About Social Partnership of the CIS" (2006) defines social partnership as an interaction of public authorities, associations of employers and labor unions by definition and the carrying out in life of the coordinated social and economic policy; policy in the field of labor relations, and also the bilateral relations between employers and the labor unions and the coordination of their interests directed on ensuring in an order determined by legislation. In fact, it is a focus of a legal mechanism of social partnership: norms, social and partner legal relationship and acts of realization of the collective rights of social partners.

---

obespechitel'nyh otnosheniy (sravnitel'no-pravovoe issledovanie) [Legal Mechanism of Social Partnership in Regulation of the Labor and Social and Security Relations (Comparative and Legal Research)]: the thesis, etc.

[15] See: Chucha, S. Yu. 2001. *Stanovlenie i perspektivy razvitiya social'nogo partnerstva v Rossiyskoy Federacii* [Formation and Prospects of Development of Social Partnership in the Russian Federation]. Moscow: Verdikt-1M, 312; Chucha, S.Yu. 2005. *Social'noe partnerstvo v sfere truda: stanovlenie i perspektivy razvitiya pravovogo regulirovaniya v Rossiyskoy Federacii* [Social Partnership in the Work Sphere: Formation and Prospects of Development of Legal Regulation in the Russian Federation]. Omsk: Omsk GU, 412; Soloviev, A.V. 2007. *Social'noe partnerstvo. Kommentariy k Trudovomu kodeksu RF* [Comment to the Labor code of the Russian Federation]. Moscow: Alfa-Press, 12-13.

In the Labor Code of the Russian Federation, in our opinion, the idea of legalization of social partnership as legal mechanism of regulation of collective relations is also traced. The code defines social partnership as a multilevel system of relationships based on the principle of a tripartism (Art. 23); and classifies the principles (Art. 24), the parties and participants of social partnership, the levels of social partnership (Art. 26), and the bodies of social partnership (Art. 35).

The Labor Code of the Russian Federation identifies the main forms of social partnership: 1) collective negotiations; 2) mutual consultations; 3) participation of workers in the management of the organization; 4) participation of the representatives of workers and employers with the permission of labor disputes (Art. 27). In fact, it is a matter beyond that concerning a legal mechanism for the implementation of collective labor law and duties by workers (their representatives) and employers (their representatives); it is equal to the protection of these rights in a conciliatory and intermediary order.

2.1.1. Levels of Social Partnership

The system of social partnership is a hierarchical structure of levels, based on certain principles. According to the Labor Code of the Russian Federation the system of social partnership includes the following levels: federal, interregional, regional, branch, territorial, local (Art. 26).

The ratio, interdependence of levels of social partnership to labor legislation is defined by the principle of a ban on the deterioration of the worker's position in comparison with labor legislation (Art. 9of the Labor Code). The legislator extends this principle of ratio among the different levels of social partnership: when workers agree with the established procedures and actions of several collective agreements at the same time, the conditions of the agreement become optimum for them (Labor Code of the Russian Federation Art. 48).

Each level of social partnership is characterized, first, by the corresponding authorized representatives of the workers, the employers (the all-Russian, regional, branch associations of employers, labor unions, etc.), the states and, secondly, the appropriate authorized bodies of social partnership.

Coming back to the question of levels of social partnership, we will note that in the initial edition of the Labor Code of the Russian Federation there was no interregional level of social partnership and the local level was only limited to the organizational level. The system of social partnership did not cover employers—individual entrepreneurs and workers who have signed the employment contract with these employers.

There was a question over the existence of the rights of the specified workers on collective negotiations, the conclusion of the collective agreement, participation in management of work, etc. This problem was resolved by entering the corresponding changes into the Labor Code of the Russian Federation (in an edition of June 30, 2006 Federal Law No. 90-FL). Meanwhile, there was also a discussion over collective labor law, including the right to collective negotiations of the workers who have signed the employment contract with employers individually and not being individual entrepreneurs. According to a number of experts, such workers in spite of the fact that the Labor Code of the Russian Federation does not directly allocate them with the collective rights in the sphere of social partnership, have the right to use them. This conclusion is based on the Constitution of the Russian Federation (Art. 55) and the universally recognized norms of international labor law. The right to conduct collective negotiations, as it follows the contents of the Convention of the ILO No. 98 "About Application of the Principles of the Right to the Organization and on Conducting Collective Negotiations" is derivative of the right to association. In turn, the right to association is among the basic civil rights (The International Covenant on Civil and Political Rights of 1966).[16]

To the levels of social partnership established by the Labor Code of the Russian Federation called above, it is necessary to add the international level: the international collective agreements in the multinational companies[17] and the international social and partner acts of the ILO and the international regional organizations (EU, the CIS, etc.).

In this regard the ILO developed and adopted the Three-parties Declaration of the Principles concerning multinational corporations and social policy (Geneva, on November 16, 1977, new edition on November 17, 2000). The purpose of this Declaration was the encouragement of a positive contribution on behalf of the multinational companies to economic and social progress and to minimize and overcome difficulties

[16] See: Mavrin, S. P. and A. K. Sviridov, 2006. *Novacii Trudovogo kodeksa i social'noe partnerstvo v Rossiyskoy Federacii* [Innovations of the Labour Code and Social Partnership in the Russian Federation], *Russian Year-Book of the Labor Law*, No. 2:159-160.

[17] See: Shuraleva, S. V. 2012. *Pravovoe regulirovanie individual'nykh i kollektivnykh trudovykh otnosheniy v transnacional'nykh korporaciyakh* [Legal Regulation of the Individual and Collective Labor Relations in Multinational Corporations]/ Perm: Perm universitet, 195 p.

which can be caused by different types of their activity. Finally, this Declaration which is addressed to the governments, the organizations of employers and workers, to multinational corporations is directed to the establishment of a new international economic order on the basis of the international standards of the UN and the ILO.

The corporate agreements concluded at the international level, including corporate agreements of the largest companies of Russia (JSC "Gazprom", Lukoil Oil Company, etc.) became a subject of special complex interdisciplinary research.[18]

Formation in the state territory of the CIS of multinational corporations required the conclusion of an agreement on the regulation of the social and labor relations in the multinational corporations operating in the territory of the participating states of the Commonwealth of Independent States (Bishkek, on October 9, 1997). According to S. Yu. Chuchi, the original combination of elements of the international and local levels of social partnership in multinational corporations allows to speak about formation in Russia of a new level of partnership which can be called corporate.[19]

The Model Law on social partnership of the CIS (2006), unlike the Labor Code of the Russian Federation expands the list of levels of social partnership, supplementing it with a level of financial and industrial groups and multinational corporations. Social partnerships in financial and industrial groups and multinational corporations are provided on the basis of international treaties (agreements) and by national legislation.

2.1.2. Bodies of Social Partnership

Bodies of social partnership are created on an equal basis according to the decision of the social partners and are allocated with necessary powers by representatives of the parties. Current legislation, which is a constant body of social partnership at all levels (except local) created three or bilateral Commissions for the regulation of social and labor relations.

Subject of their activity are not only matters of regulation of the labor relations, but also the relations in the sphere of social security, including social, pension, medical insurance, and also measures for social protection

---

[18] See: Krylov, K.D. ed. 2005. *Korporativnye soglasheniya v sfere social'no-trudovykh otnosheniy* [Corporate Agreements in the Sphere of the Social and Labor Relations]. Moscow: Prospekt, 288.

[19] See: Chucha, S. Yu. 2005. *Social'noe partnerstvo v sfere truda: stanovlenie i perspektivy razvitiya pravovogo regulirovaniya v Rossiyskoy Federacii* [Social Partnership in the Work Sphere: Formation and Prospects of Development of Legal Regulation in the Russian Federation]. Omsk: Omsk GU, 248.

of needy citizens and the unemployed. Regarding the bodies of social partnership the expression "regulation of social and labor relations" is used, which unites both the labor relations and the relations on social security. The power of the Russian tripartite commission was later provided by the special Provision on this commission,[20] by the law.[21] Its powers can be classified in four main groups:

1) the right to conduct collective negotiations and draft the general agreement;

2) powers in the rule-making sphere (has the right to develop and bring in federal public authorities in the order of the offer coordinated with them about adoption of federal laws and other regulations of the Russian Federation in the field of the social and labor relations; to take part in the preparation of drafts of normative legal acts in the field of the labor relations);

3) advisory competences regarding matters of social policy (has the right to carry out with the federal public authorities consultations on questions connected with the development and realization of social and economic policy);

4) information powers (has the right to request from executive authorities, employers and/or labor unions information on the concluding and concluded agreements regulating labor relations and collective agreements; to receive from federal executive authorities in an order established by the Government of the Russian Federation information about socially—an economic situation in the Russian Federation and subjects of the Russian Federation, necessary for conducting collective negotiations and preparation of the draft of the general agreement, the organization of control over the implementation of the specified agreement, regulations of the Russian Federation, and also drafts of federal laws and other regulations of the Russian Federation in area of the socially and labor relations, etc.)

Let us note that the Labor Code of the Russian Federation (in an edition of the Federal Law of June 30, 2006 No. 90-FL) provided the right to the considered bodies of social partnership on participation to formation and realization of a state policy in the sphere of work with a corresponding obligation of government bodies (federal, subjects of Federation), local

---

[20] Regulations on Russian Trilateral Commission on the Regulation of Social-Labour Relations: Decree of the President of the Russian Federation of January 21, 1997, *Russian Newspaper*. 1997. January 28.

[21] Federal Law of May 1, 1999 No. 92-FZ "On Russian Trilateral Commission on the Regulation of Social-Labour Relations", *Sobranie zakonodatel'stva RF* [Collection of the Legislation of the Russian Federation]. 1999. No. 18. Art. 2218.

governments to consider decisions of the relevant commissions on regulation of the social and labor relations or opinions of their parties according to drafts of the regulations (Labor Code of the Russian Federation Art. 35.1).

According to the principle of formation the tripartite commission is the body of social partnership formed by the all-Russian associations of labor unions, associations of employers and the Government of the Russian Federation. In our opinion, it is a non-state corporate structure *per se*.

Meanwhile, not only all material services of the Commission are assigned to the Government, but also a number of officials from the Commission are appointed by the Government: the responsible secretary and other employees of the Secretariat are appointed by the head of Government office. The president appoints the Coordinator of the Commission who is not a member of it. The structure of the Commissions on regulation of the social and labor relations is formed on the basis of the observance of the principles of an equal share and equality of the parties and of the power of their representatives. Each of these all-Russian associations of labor unions and the all-Russian association of employers registered in accordance with the established procedure, have the right to send one representative to be part of the structure of the relevant party on the Commission. The law limits the total number of representatives of the parties (no more than 30 people from each party) but the decision is made when consent is given by each of the three parties.

Regular branch, regional and other commissions on regulation of socially labor relations whose powers are defined by normative legal acts of subjects of Federation and local governments or social and partner industry acts respectively operate on other levels of social partnership.

Types of Bodies of Social Partnership. According to current legislation two types of bodies of social partnership have been created: temporarily operating bodies and permanent bodies. These bodies can be multipurpose or for one purpose. So, at a local level of social partnership representatives of the parties form the commission on conducting collective negotiations, on preparing drafts of the collective agreement and the conclusion of the collective agreement. It is a temporary body of social partnership whose purpose is conducting collective negotiations. At the local level target permanent bodies of social partnership (committees) on labor protection (Labor Code of the Russian Federation Art. 218) were also formed. These are created by initiative of the employer and/or by initiative of the workers or their representatives. Their structure includes representatives of the employer and representatives of the workers. The committee (commission) on labor protection organizes joint actions by the employer and workers on providing requirements of labor protection, injury prevention and occupational diseases, and also organizes checks of the conditions and labor protection in the workplaces.

The permanent commissions on regulation of social and labor relations which are formed at all levels of social partnership (except local) (Labor Code of the Russian Federation Art. 35) oversee the second group of bodies of social partnership. They are urged not only to conduct collective negotiations, prepare drafts of collective agreements and control their execution, but also to participate in the formation and realization of state policy in the work sphere, in the development and discussion of drafts of legislative and other types of regulations (Labor Code of the Russian Federation Art. 35.1). Regular bodies of social partnership are created with specific purposes, for example, for the coordination of positions of social partners in the sphere of employment or obligatory social insurance.

According to the Federal law of April 19, 1991 "About Population Employment in the Russian Federation" new committees were created to pursue decision making process regarding employment policies at a federal and territorial level with assistance from representative bodies and other government bodies (Art. 20).[22] On the basis of the Provision on Social Insurance Fund of the Russian Federation the structure of the board of fund joins representatives of the all-Russian associations of trade unions and associations of employers.[23]

In the considered classification of such bodies of social partnership it is possible to allocate these bodies especially based on the consideration of the labor disputes formed according to the principles of social partnership: the commissions on permission of individual labor disputes as a permanent body (Labor Code of the Russian Federation Art. 382), and the conciliatory commissions and labor arbitration as a temporary bodies created for allowing collective disputes (Art. 402 and Labor Code of the Russian Federation Art. 404).

2.1.3. Principles of Social Partnership

In the Labor Code of the Russian Federation of 2001, the legislator establishes a list of principles of social partnership (Art. 24). Many of them (equality of the parties, voluntariness of acceptance by the parties of obligations, the power of the representatives of the parties, freedom of

---

[22] *Sobranie zakonodatel'stva RF* [Collection of the Legislation of the Russian Federation]. 1996. No. 17. Art. 1915.

[23] *Sobranie zakonodatel'stva RF* [Collection of the Legislation of the Russian Federation]. 1994. No. 8. Art. 599.

choice in discussions on questions regarding the sphere of work, assistance from the state in strengthening and developing social partnership on a democratic basis, an control over the implementation of collective agreements) have something in common with the international legal principles of social partnership. Let us note that the Law Model of social partnership of the CIS contains a long list of principles of social partnership (Art. 3). Unlike the Labor Code of the Russian Federation, these principles require trust and integrity in the relations of the parties of the social partnership, assuming sincerity and constructability, which is an exception of any unjustified delay in the solution of urgent questions and they urge reach anyone's consent. Thus, the principle of a ban on the abuse of rights also penetrates well collective labor relations.

The international legal principles of social partnership are enshrined in UN acts (The Universal Declaration of Human Rights of 1948, the Covenant on Civil and Political Rights of 1966; The Pact About the Economic, Social and Cultural Rights of 1966) the Council of Europe (The European Social Charter) and also in basic normative documents of the ILO, which include: The Declaration on the Fundamental Principles and the Rights in the Sphere of Work of 1998; The Convention No. 87 "On Freedom of Association and Protection of the Right to the organization" (1948, it is ratified on August 10, 1956); The Convention No. 98 "On the Right to the Organization and on Conducting Collective Negotiations" (1949, it is ratified on August 10, 1956); The Convention No. 135 and the Recommendation No. 143 "On Representatives of Workers" (1971); The Convention No. 144 "On Tripartite Consultations for Assistance of Application of the International Labor Norms" (1976); The Convention No. 154 and the Recommendation No. 163 "On Assistance to Collective Negotiations" (1981); The Recommendation No. 91 "On Collective Agreements" (1951); The Recommendation No. 92 "On Voluntary Reconciliation and Arbitration" (1951); The Recommendation No. 94 "On Cooperation at the Level of the Enterprise" (1952); The Recommendation No. 113 "On Cooperation in the Branch and National Scale" (1960); The Recommendation No. 130 "On Consideration of Complaints" (1967); The Recommendation No. 129 "On Communications at the Enterprise" (1967), etc.[24]

---

[24] See: 1993. ILO: Conventions and Recommendations Accepted by the International Labor Conference. V. 1, V. 2. Geneva: ILO. The Russian Federation has ratified two conventions from the listed ones by now: Convention No 87 and Convention No 98.

Having analyzed the above-named international legal acts, we consider that the following international legal principles of social partnership reflect their contents:

The Principle of Freedom of Association and Protection of the Rights of Labor Unions and Other Representatives of the Workers. It includes the right of the workers and their businessmen to create an association or organization and the right to become members. The conditions necessary for the realization of this right are 1) free creation of the organization without preliminary permission and independent regulation of intra-organizational activities without the intervention of government bodies or other persons 2) prohibited discrimination on the basis of membership and prohibited refusal of introduction into the associations and refusal of asymmetric (primary) protection of the rights of labor unions and other representatives of workers.

The fulfillment of the right to association is directly connected with a lack of preliminary permission to create an organization. It does not mean absolute freedom. Necessary formalities and legal procedures are possible, but they should not interfere with the creation of the organization. The right of workers and businessmen to create organizations means a possibility of independent regulation of internal activities on the basis of certain Charters. According to Convention No. 87 (Art. 3), public authorities abstain from any intervention, from limiting this right or from preventing its lawful implementation. This convention also allows trade-union pluralism and does not exclude procedures recognizing the most representative labor union.

A ban on discrimination refers to a lack of any discrimination done by restrictions on the circle of people having the right to association (on the basis of a floor, a profession, nationality, skin color, race, religion or political views). The only exception is provided by Convention No. 87 (Art. 9) according to which each state independently defines in what measure the right to freedom of association is applicable to the armed forces and police. Meanwhile, the European Social Charter (1961, in an edition of 1996) further reflects the considered Convention of the ILO and does not allow any restrictions on the right of association on police officers. As for civil servants, as defined by this Convention, they can create organizations for the implementation and protection of their interests, though there was no say on the question of their right to strike.

At the same time, the Convention of the ILO No. 151 contains a number of provisions protecting the right to an organization of civil servants.

This principle also prohibits discrimination on the basis of belonging to an association at the workplace, promotion, compensation, etc. The rights of representatives of the workers at the enterprise are guaranteed by the ILO Convention No. 135 and Recommendation No. 143. Measures for the protection of the rights of the representatives can be taken in case of their dismissal.

The Convention No. 98 leaves a matter to the discretion of national authorities: the degree to which a guarantee to the right of association is applied concerning armed forces and police. The action of Convention No. 98 does not extend to "the civil servants occupied in government". In 1978, the ILO adopted Convention No. 151 "On the Labor Relations in Public Service". It extend the right to all persons employed by public entities if there are no perceived advantages from other international labor conventions.

Special attention is deserved for Convention No. 135, according to which, if at an enterprise level there are both representatives of labor unions and elective representatives of employees simultaneously operating, then there must be measures taken that are directed by cooperation. Thus, functions of the representatives of labor collectives should not include activities which are recognized as an exclusive prerogative to labor unions.

Principle of Bilateral and Tripartite Cooperation ("Bipartizm and Thripartizm"), Multilevel Cooperation. Originally this principle of the ILO considers work problems to be solved by representatives of a three-party structure: delegations from the governments of the states, trade unions and businessmen. The theory of tripartite consensus comes as a change to the theory of non-interference of the state in the relations between unions and employers, a characteristic of an early pre-monopolistic capitalism stage. This characteristic was reflected in the ILO Convention No. 144. In practice, in countries with a developed market economy the state assumes a role of social partner when signing national agreements concerning payment and working conditions, employment of the population, social protection, or the state regularly holds consultations with unions and employers regarding the same matters. For achieving the specified purposes, the tripartite commissions are given the status of state structures (for example, in Austria), or corporate status with consulting functions (for example, in Portugal).

The principle of tripartism according to the ILO Recommendation No. 113 means cooperation and effective consultations between the governments, the organizations of businessmen and workers on a branch and national scale. It is important that such ways of interaction of social partners are applied at all levels: at the enterprises, in branches, regions, and also at a national level.

If the cooperation among social partners is reduced to negotiations and consultations with organizations of workers and the organizations of employers without state participation, it is a matter of "bipartism". Thus, "bipartism and tripartism are not only ideological concepts, but also models of behavior for the participants of the collective and labor relations that are compliant with the international legal standards set by the provisions of the ILO Convention No. 150".[25]

The ILO committee on freedom of association notes that according to the Convention of the ILO No. 98, the definition of the level of negotiations is a matter left to the discretion of participants and has to be imposed by legislation.

The Principle of Powerful Representatives of the Parties—Social Partners means organizational and legal registration of powers on representation of interests by the participants or the parties of social partnership. According to the recommendation of the ILO No. 91 collective treaties (agreements) are signed by representatives of the parties, properly the elite, who are representatives according to the country legislation. Thus, as an important condition of efficiency of social dialogue among the partners these parties hold an organizational and legal form that gives them a powerful and imposing position.

The Principle of Voluntary and Equal Partnership and Ensuring the Right to Collective Negotiations. This in many respects predetermines the nature of a relationship amongst social partners. The ILO Convention No. 98 particularly underlines that where necessary, measures must be taken concerning the conditions of the country for encouragement and contribution to full development and the use of negotiating procedures on a voluntary basis between businessmen and the organizations of workers on the conclusion of collective agreements. Voluntariness of partnership is coordinated and is equal to that of the participants just like "different sides of the same coin". According to Convention No. 144, participants of social partnership have to be presented on an equal basis in any body through which mediation and consultations are carried out.

The Principle of Voluntariness and Equal Partnership Underlies Right Realization by the Parties on Collective Negotiations. The convention of The ILO No. 154 identifies negotiations as defining working conditions and employment by one businessman, a group of businessmen or several

[25] Kiselev, I. Ya. 1999. *Sravnitel'noe i mezhdunarodnoe trudovoe pravo* [Comparative and International Labor Law]. Moscow: Delo, 488.

organizations of businessmen on the one hand; and separate or several organizations of workers on the other. This shows that the subjects of collective negotiations are not only trade unions, but also other electoral bodies of workers.

The Convention of the ILO No. 154 and the Recommendation No. 163 state that it is necessary to provide assistance to collective negotiations that could take place at any level, in particular in enterprises, branch or all other industry levels or at regional and national levels; coordination between these levels has to be provided.

The Principle of Obligation and Appropriate Execution of the Collective Treaties (Agreements) Signed as a Result of Collective Negotiations. This principle gives stability to the legal mechanism of social partnership. All voluntary parties at collective negotiations have the obligations to reach a result, in other words the collective agreement. According to the Recommendation No. 91 such contracts are signed in writing by the representatives of the parties: between the businessman, group of businessmen or several organizations of businessmen, and one or several organizations of workers or representative of the workers in the absence of such organizations. The collective agreement extends to all workers of the enterprises covered by it if the contract does not further specify. Individual employment contracts which worsen the position of the worker in comparison to the collective agreement are to be considered invalid. In case it is needed to take into account the whole system of collective treaties existing in the country and in national legislation, there are measures for distribution of all or some provisions of the collective treaties on those enterprises which are not participating in the stipulation of the contracts, but have contracts in "production". The recommendation considers it necessary to impose control of the observance of conditions of collective treaties by the organizations of businessmen participating and the workers, bodies of inspectorate or the bodies that are especially created for this purpose.

The Principle of Conciliatory and Arbitration Trial of Labor Conflicts and Ensuring the Right of Workers and Employers to Collective Means of Protection. It assumes that, as a rule, peaceful methods of labor conflicts are permitted. Disputes are settled by an agreement between the arguing parties and with participation of intermediary and arbitration bodies.

According to the Recommendation of the ILO No. 163 (items 8) if necessary, there are measures corresponding to national conditions that can be taken during the process of settlement that help the parties with negotiations to resolve conflicts arising between them during collective negotiations on agreements and that concern specifically interpretation and application of the agreements. According to ILO Recommendation No. 92 the states are offered the voluntary option of creating bodies that focus on the reconciliation of the conflicting parties. Such bodies have to join representatives of employers and workers.

Conciliatory procedures have to be minimized on time of consideration and be carried out on a free basis. The parties have the right to resort to support from an independent arbitration body. In both cases during conciliatory and arbitration processes the parties are recommended to refrain from strikes and lock-outs.

The recommendation of the ILO No. 130 includes rules about consideration of individual complaints by workers. The process of consideration of a complaint represents an attempt of dispute settlement by the parties. If this does not yield result, disputes can be resolved by reconciliation, an appeal to judicial authorities or by means of other procedures provided in the collective agreement, and also by voluntary arbitration. At any stage of the trial the possibility of a dispute settlement by agreement of the parties must remain.

Collective means of protection include not only peace talks and arbitration trials, but also unilateral collective actions of participants. The right of workers to strike and the right of employers to lock-out concern this type of action. In the International Pact on the economic, social and cultural rights (1966) the right to a strike is guaranteed in the condition of its implementation according to laws of each country. The right of social partners to unilaterally protect themselves by collective means is more thoroughly formulated in the European Social Charter (Art. 6). This right also unites the right of workers to strike and the right of employers to lock-out. According to Art. 6 of this document "parties undertake the task of providing the right of workers and employers to collective actions in case of a conflict of interests, including the right to strike, on the condition that they observe the obligations from the previously signed collective agreements".

3. Problems and Prospects of a Legal Mechanism of Social Partnership in the Work Sphere in the XXI Century

The beginning of the XXI century was marked by essential changes, shifts in the public organization of work, strengthening of individual and contractual (private) conditions in the legal regulation of labor relations and, as the other side of the coin, a decrease in the role of labor unions and solidarity. Thus, the individualization of labor relations in modern conditions is inevitably reflected and is leading to collective labor relations. The general tendency of reduction in the membership of labor unions in many countries, the organizational difficulties which the unions of employers face and the deregulation of conditions of employment, according to a number of researchers, predetermine a decline of collective labor relations which are considered as a remnant of the past. Meanwhile, experts of the ILO, relying on generalizations about modern foreign practice of labor relations, see many signs that the associations of employers and labor unions can adapt to modern realities of the globalization of economy and the growing competition. They change structures and methods and improve the mechanisms of social dialogue.

Besides, practically in all components of a state there is a more active participation in the solution of social problems. All this testifies to the general tendency towards the development of a legal mechanism of social partnership and its adaptation in modern conditions.

Historical experience testifies to the hopeless attempts of removing contradictions between work and capital through mechanisms of state and totalitarian methods of legal regulation of social and labor relations. Any violent derogation from natural social development is fraught with social shocks. Lessons of the past have to be considered as difficult crisis situations that also accompany modern society. The orientation of a state policy towards methods of social partnership in regulation of social and labor relations proved to be efficient. It does not mean that a legal mechanism of social partnership is the panacea for all troubles. Its application has to be modified depending on the social and economic conditions of the society. Respectively, in conditions where there is an aggravation of a crisis situation, it is necessary to activate a role of the state and strengthen methods of state regulation of social and labor relations. A mechanism of social partnership itself does not exclude the state from the process of regulation of social and labor relations, but only complicates its role: from direct intervention to partnership with the unions of workers and employers. Considering the historical experience of Russia as well as many other countries, it is possible to claim that any, even reasonable state intervention in social and economic processes has to be limited or it could have a boomerang effect. State self-elimination from these relations though is not any less pernicious. In this regard the words of a known American historian A.M. Schlesinger can be quoted, "And still an inequality of the generation of the unregulated market, on the one hand, and horrors of totalitarian etatism on the other, do not leave to true democrats any other choice, except to search for diverse forms of coordination of efforts on behalf of the government, businesses and workers within free economy.[26]

The legal mechanism of social partnership will not lose importance in the XXI century since at its basis is consensus (coordination) of interests of workers, employers and the states, where the state acts as a social partner. The idea of social partnership, despite serious difficulties, remains a defining factor of stability in society. Moreover, according to a number of specialists of the International Bureau of Work of the ILO, during the modern period, the spreading of globalization of the markets forces each country to increase competitiveness of its producers. In this regard, participation of the state in the regulation of labor relations will keep extending. In globalization, an increased distribution will be gained by practice and participation of the state in collective negotiations and consultations in the form of a tripartism. Globalization of a labor market will inevitably lead to enrichment of the contents and the international mechanism of social partnership.

In summary, we will note that the Russian model of a legal mechanism of social partnership so far is not ideal and the changes made recently to the order of the conclusion of collective treaties, agreements and consideration of labor disputes (The Federal law of December 3, 2012 No. 234-FZ) have a solely cosmetic character. The efficiency of a legal mechanism of social partnership is influenced negatively by a number of social problems. Among them, first, is the unwillingness of employers to include in collective treaties social obligations when in the condition of economic and financial instability. Secondly, the absence of many small and medium-sized enterprises and the split in the trade-union environment in the form of contradictions between official trade unions and independent ones. Thirdly, and as a result, collective treaties on the regulation of labor relations at the level of the concrete organizations and the enterprises have a marginal role. The listed problems in a certain measure are dictated also by "defects" of existing Russian labor legislation. In inheritance from the last Soviet system of trade unions there was also the general membership of persons in one trade union when the trade union united and, therefore, represented interests of employees of administration (managers), of the head of the organization and of other hired workers. This is exactly the way that the Federation of Independent Labor Unions of Russia (FILUR), the right successor of the Soviet trade unions headed before the All-Union Central Council of Trade Unions (All-

---

[26] Schlesinger, A.M. 1992. *Cikly amerikanskoy istorii* [Cycles of the American History]. Moscow: Progress, 366.

Union Central Office of Trade Unions) functions today. Various independent and alternative trade unions that appeared later, practice other approaches without including in the ranks of heads of the enterprises or the organizations. This practice corresponds to the international principles where independence of labor unions of businessmen is provided including an association ban of one labor union of workers and administration. For example, in Denmark, under the law, the leading personnel of firms is forbidden to enter into the trade union uniting ordinary workers. In the USA trade unions that include positions relating to administration, even the most local link, have no right to act as representatives of workers in collective negotiations.[27] We believe that the reception of foreign experience in this part is necessary to show how the mentioned requirement for membership in labor unions and trade-unions representation, reflects the ILO Convention No. 87 ratified by our state, about freedom of association.

Besides, it is difficult to agree with the condition provided in the Labor Code of the Russian Federation for implementation of activity of labor unions on a possibility of compensation for the head of electoral trade-union body at the expense of the means and the size of the organization established by a collective agreement (Art. 377). We believe that it does not correspond to the international legal principles on the independence of trade unions. According to the ratified ILO Convention No. 98 "About the Application of the Principles of the Right to Organization and on Conducting Collective Negotiations" (1949) such actions are not allowed if their purpose is promoting the establishment of an organization of workers under the domination of businessmen or if their intent is to support organizations of workers by funding activities or by some other way that will put such organizations under the control of businessmen.

The act of the Russian Federation on labor unions provides that the relations of labor unions and their bodies with other representative bodies of workers are sustained on the basis of cooperation. Thus, the existence of other representative bodies of workers cannot be used to hinder the activities of trade unions (Art. 16). Trade unions have the right to propose candidates as representatives for election to other representative bodies of workers. Trade unions, with the authorization of the workers, have the right to have representatives in joint governing bodies of the organization.

But these rights only sound like a general wish, and it is not defined how far they have reached. In foreign models of cooperation among trade unions and representative bodies of workers, the participation of trade

---

[27] See: Kiselev, I.Ya. 1992. *Trudovoe pravo v usloviyah rynochnoy ekonomiki: opyt stran Zapada* [The Labor Law in the Conditions of Market Economy: Experience of the Countries of the West]. Moscow: Akademy truda, 59.

unions is guaranteed and provided through the established procedure for the formation of representative bodies.

Due to the arguments stated above, the confrontational option of interaction, for the bodies of trade unions and the representative bodies of the workers, provided in the Labor Code of the Russian Federation (Art. 31) according to which other representatives of workers can be chosen only in the absence within the organization of primary trade-union organizations, is also considered unacceptable. According to the Labor Code of the Russian Federation (Art. 29), the interests of workers at a local level are represented by primary trade-union organizations or by other representatives elected by those workers. The disjunctive conjunction "or" is what constitutes the beginning of a conflict, where there is recognition of one representative and denial of the other. In our opinion, it is not expedient to oppose trade unions or other representative bodies of workers, but rather to resolve the issue of obligatory participation of labor unions if those act within the organization to promote creation of representative bodies for the group of workers. According to the Convention of the ILO No. 135 and the Recommendation No. 143 if in one organization both, representatives of trade unions and elective representatives of labor collectives, exist at the same time, the state must take measures to encourage cooperation between them. The functions of the representatives of labor collectives should not include activities which are recognized as exclusive prerogatives of labor unions.

The Federal Law of November 27, 2002 No. 156-FL "About Associations of Employers"[28] provides the right of association of employers in the form of a non-profit organization, which is a legal entity from the moment of its state registration according to the federal law on the state registration of legal entities. Meanwhile, in our opinion, the problem with the creation of such law has to be solved on the basis of foreign experience, Conventions and Recommendations of the ILO, especially from the ILO Conventions No. 87 "About Freedom of Association and Protection of the Right to Organization", and Convention No. 98 "On the Right to Organization and Conducting Collective Negotiations". These conventions in an equal manner extend to the unions of workers, as well as the employers. In relation to the employers, the principle of freedom to create organizations without any distinction means that the legislation and the practitioners of each country ratifying the Convention, must establish equal conditions for all employers and a

---

[28] *Bulleten' Mintruda RF* [Bulletin of the Ministry of Labor of the Russian Federation]. 2002 . No. 12.

procedure for the creation of such organizations, without exceptions and without providing privileges. Differently, the organizations of employers, as well as the organizations of workers, are created without the preliminary permission from public authorities. Observance of some formalities (such as, registration) is admissible. However, they should not be difficult or time-consuming, but in practice must offer a chance for the authorities to refuse creation of the organizations at their discretion. For example, in the Law on Labor Relations of the Republic of South Africa (1995), equal demands are made to the unions of employers and the unions of workers (labor unions). They have to be independent and have the charter and the legal address in the territory of the Republic of South Africa (a national identity of the organization). Registration of these organizations is not obligatory, but allows the registered associations to participate in the collective labor relations regulated by this law.[29]

According to Art. 4 of Convention No. 87, the specified organizations are not subject to dissolution or temporary prohibition administratively. Experts of the ILO consider that the right to association means power over the choice of structure and organization structure, on development of its charter and regulations, on action program formation (Art. 3 of the Convention), and also on the creation of federations and confederations (Art. 5 of the Convention). Employers also possess the right to enter already operating organizations, only on the condition of submission to charters by the latter (Art. 2 of the Convention).

We believe that in the Law on Associations of Employers it would be expedient to enter the differentiated approach to state registration of such unions. Possibly there could be a limit on the notifications of registration of those associations of employers in which the charter has only a social function, i.e. where there is participation in the regulation of social and labor relations. There would be usual state registration concerning the rights of legal entities and to establish if the unions of employers have the authorized purpose specified, but also fulfill the purpose of protection of economic corporate interests. For the achievement of such associations, as a rule, special structures need to be formed providing members of association with services in training, of legal consultation and of protection of interests in arbitration courts, to granting market information, etc. Thus, the legal principle of non-interference of the state in internal relations of members of enterprise unions which independently within the

---

[29] See: Chernyaeva, D. V. 2006. "Sovremenniy etap razvitiya trudovogo prava YuAR" [Present Stage of Development of the Labor Law of the Republic of South Africa], *Trud za rubezhom* [Work abroad], No. 4: 124-125.

charter define the bases of membership in the organization, management structure, etc. remains in effect.

It is impossible to ignore one more problem: in existing Russian legislation there is a possibility of implementation of collective treaties through judicial and other government bodies. In the majority of the countries, collective treaties are legally binding acts for the parties. It means that the employer or workers have the right to address judicial authorities for compulsory execution of conditions regarding a collective agreement. In a number of countries such powers are reserved to special labor courts (Germany, Denmark, France, etc.), courts of law (for example, the USA) and only in Great Britain collective treaties are considered as “gentleman’s agreements” and have no validity. However, they remain invalid only until the parties declare that they wish the agreement to be legally provided. Thus, in the majority of countries, the appropriate execution of collective labor disputes is provided with a judicial claim form of protection. According to the Labor Code of France (Art. 135-6) the persons tied by the collective agreement, can make any claims about execution of contractual obligations or indemnification. A number of countries provide legal as well as administrative forms of protection. For example, in Italy labor inspectors of municipalities have the right to apply the administrative penalties whose severity increases in proportion to the term during which a violation by the employer on imperative conditions of collective agreements occurred and to the number of workers whose right was violated.

According to the Labor Code of the Russian Federation the contents of the collective agreement join mutual obligations of the parties: employers and workers. Meanwhile, an attentive reading of the law will reveal the unilateral character of these obligations. The unilateral contract generates, on the one side, the duties of the party, on the other side, the right. Legal duties, according to the collective agreement, in fact, are performed by only one party, namely the employer. Duties of the employer are provided with a sanction if the representative of the employer is guilty of violating its administrative and disciplinary responsibility or for the non-performance of the collective agreement. However, it is necessary to notice that the amount of an administrative penalty is transferred to the state budget, instead of the dissatisfied party, in this case a group of workers. Moreover, in itself, an administrative penalty is not yet a guarantee of ensuring the compulsory execution of conditions of the collective agreement and restoration of the violated collective rights. The court has no right to oblige the employer to carry out those actions which have to be executed under the contract.

Problems solving and the application of disciplinary measures is not part of the responsibility of the representatives of the employer. According to the Labor Code of the Russian Federation Art. 195, the employer is obliged to consider the statement from a representative body of workers claiming a violation by the head of the organization, the head of the structural unit, and their deputies on the conditions of the collective agreement, and to report about the results of this consideration. In case the facts concerning these violations are confirmed, the employer is obliged to apply disciplinary punishment which could end up in dismissal.

However, the employer has also the right to be limited, for example, by the announcement of remarks and the requirements of the considered article of the law that will be observed.

According to the collective agreement, the collective social and labor rights of workers are corresponded by duties of the employer and therefore are necessary not only for individual, but also collective means of protection of the rights of workers.

In existing labor legislation such collective means that force the employer to satisfy conditions of the collective treaty are represented by a strike. Workers have the right to go on strike as long as they observe the established conciliatory procedures and at any time during collective negotiations, near the conclusion of the collective treaty, and after its signing. The right to a strike, even if there is an obligation of refusal by the group of workers, is fixed in the collective treaty and its full implementation still remains in the hands of the employer. The Labor Code of the Russian Federation Art. 413, establishes when a strike is illegal, and when the criteria to understand such violation about refusal of strikes are not provided. Thus, the called obligation has a declarative character and is not provided with sanctions if violated. It confirms again our thesis about the unilateral character of the collective agreements.

References

1993. ILO: Conventions and Recommendations Accepted by the International Labor Conference. V. 1, V. 2. Geneva: ILO.

72nd Session of the International Labor Organization. ILO: Geneva.

Bulleten' Mintruda RF [Bulletin of the Ministry of Labor of the Russian Federation]. 2002 . No. 12.

Chernyaeva, D.V. 2006. "Sovremenniy etap razvitiya trudovogo prava YuAR" [Present Stage of Development of the Labor Law of the Republic of South Africa], *Trud za rubezhom* [Work abroad], No. 4: 123-128.

Chucha, S. Yu. 2001. *Stanovlenie i perspektivy razvitiya social'nogo partnerstva v Rossiyskoy Federacii* [Formation and Prospects of Development of Social Partnership in the Russian Federation]. Moscow: Verdikt-1M, 312 p.

—. 2005. *Social'noe partnerstvo v sfere truda: stanovlenie i perspektivy razvitiya pravovogo regulirovaniya v Rossiyskoy Federacii* [Social Partnership in the Work Sphere: Formation and Prospects of Development of Legal Regulation in the Russian Federation]. Omsk: Omsk GU, 412 p.

Federal Law of May 1, 1999 No. 92-FZ "On Russian Trilateral Commission on the Regulation of Social-Labour Relations", *Sobranie zakonodatel'stva RF* [Collection of the Legislation of the Russian Federation]. 1999 . No. 18. Art. 2218.

Geykhman, V. L., Dmitrieva, I. K. 2011. *Trudovoe pravo* [Labor Law]. Moscow: Yurait, 528 p.

Golovina, S. Yu., Molodtsov, M.V. 2008. *Trudovoe pravo* Rossii [Labor Law of Russia]. Moscow: Norma, 640 p.

Informacionniy bulleten' Mezhdunarodnoy Assamblei gosudarstv-uchastnikov SNG [Information bulletin of the International Assembly of the participating states of the CIS]. 2007 . No. 39.

Kiselev, I. Ya. 1992. *Trudovoe pravo v usloviyah rynochnoy ekonomiki: opyt stran Zapada* [The Labor Law in the Conditions of Market Economy: Experience of the Countries of the West]. Moscow: Akademy truda, 112 p.

—. 2005. *Sravnitel'noe trudovoe pravo* [Comparative Labor Law]. Moscow: Prospekt, 360 p.

—. 1999. *Sravnitel'noe i mezhdunarodnoe trudovoe pravo* [Comparative and International Labor Law]. Moscow: Delo, 728 p.

Krylov, K. D. ed. 2005. *Korporativnye soglasheniya v sfere social'no-trudovykh otnosheniy* [Corporate Agreements in the Sphere of the Social and Labor Relations]. Moscow: Prospect, 288 p.

Kurennoy, A.M. ed. 2008. *Trudovoe pravo Rossii* [Labor Law of Russia]. Moscow: Jurist, 467 p.

Lebedev, V.M. ed. 2011. *Trudovoe pravo* [Labor Law]. Moscow: Norma, 464 p.

Lushnikov A.M., Lushnikova, M.V. 2009. *Kurs trudovogo prava* [Course of the Labor Law]. V.1. Moscow: Statut, 879 p.

Lushnikova, M. V., Lushnikov, A.M. 2008. *Social'noe partnerstvo v sfere truda* [Social Partnership in the Work Sphere]. Yaroslavl: Yaroslavl universitet, 432 p.

Lushnikova, M.V. 1997. *Gosudarstvo, rabotodateli i rabotniki: istoriya, teoriya i praktika pravovogo mekhanizma social'nogo partnerstva (sravnitel'no-pravovoe issledovanie)* [State, Employers and Workers: History, Theory and Practice of a Legal Mechanism of Social Partnership (Comparative and Legal Research)]. Yaroslavl: Podati, 224 p.

—. 1997. *Pravovoy mekhanizm social'nogo partnerstva v regulirovanii trudovykh i social'no-obespechitel'nykh otnosheniy (sravnitel'no-pravovoe issledovanie)* [Legal Mechanism of Social Partnership in Regulation of the Labor and Social and Security Relations (Comparative and Legal Research)]: the thesis. 363 p.

Mavrin, S. P. and A.K. Sviridov, 2006. "Novacii Trudovogo kodeksa i social'noe partnerstvo v Rossiyskoy Federacii" [Innovations of the Labour Code and Social Partnership in the Russian Federation], *Russian Year-Book of the Labor Law*, No. 2:158-164.

Mavrin, S.P. and E.B. Khokhlov, 2012. *Trudovoe pravo Rossii* [Labor Law of Russia]. Moscow: Norma, 608 p.

Mavrin, S.P., Pashkov, A.S., Khokhlov, E.B. ed. 1996. *Kurs rossiyskogo trudovogo prava* [Course of the Russian Labor Law]. Vol. 1. St. Petersburg: SPBGU, 560 p.

Organizing for Social Justice: Global Report under the Follow-up to the ILO Declaration on Fundamental Principles and Rights at Work (2004). Geneva: ILO.

Regulations on Russian Trilateral Commission on the Regulation of Social-Labour Relations: Decree of the President of the Russian Federation of January 21, 1997, *Russian Newspaper*. 1997. January 28.

Schlesinger, A.M. 1992. *Cikly amerikanskoy istorii* [Cycles of the American History]. Moscow: Progress, 688 p.

Shuraleva, S.V. 2012. *Pravovoe regulirovanie individual'nykh i kollektivnykh trudovykh otnosheniy v transnacional'nykh korporaciyakh* [Legal Regulation of the Individual and Collective Labor Relations in Multinational Corporations]: the thesis. 156 p.

Smirnov, O.V. ed. 2008. *Kommentariy k Trudovomu kodeksu RF* [Commentary on the Labor Code of the Russian Federation]. Moscow: Knorus, 960 p.

Sobranie zakonodatel'stva RF [Collection of the Legislation of the Russian Federation]. 1994. No. 8. Art. 599.

—.1996. No. 17. Art. 1915.

Soloviev, A.V. 2007. *Social'noe partnerstvo. Kommentariy k Trudovomu kodeksu RF* [Comment to the Labor code of the Russian Federation]. Moscow: Alfa Press, 336 p.

Vedomosti sjezda narodnykh deputatov i Verkhovnogo Soveta RF [Bulletin of Congress of People's Deputies and Supreme Council of the Russian Federation]. 1992 . No. 17. P. 890.

Social Partnerships as a Means of Providing Labour Protection

Anastasiya Kashlakova

Labour protection relations are formed within the scope of contractual legal relations concerning "hired-labour employment", the subject of labour law. As a part of labour law, labour protection possesses certain features. On the one hand, legal regulations are aimed at protecting the life and health of employees in the course of their employment. This requires government intervention and entails setting imperative norms, mandatory for both employers and employees. On the other hand, labour protection relationships are formed between the parties and, as an element of contractual legal relations, labour protection should be clearly advantageous to both parties. This is achieved by ensuring freedom of contract. A proper combination of mandatory and non-mandatory rules increases the efficiency of legal regulation in this field. Labour law is directly aimed at the regulation of labour protection and must take into account the aforementioned aspects which, in turn, should govern the methods of regulating these relations. Thus, Art. 1 of the Labour Code of the Russian Federation (henceforth, the Labour Code) states that one of the goals of labour legislation is the creation of the necessary legal conditions to achieve an optimal coordination of the interests of the parties of employment relationship with the interests of the state. The coordination of the interests of the specified parties in the regulation of contractual relations takes place mainly through "permissive" methods, including social partnership.

Social partnership is one of the most important categories of labour regulation which can be explained by the nature of labour relations. According to Art. 23 of the Labour Code, a social partnership in this context refers to a system of relations between employees (or their representative organisations), employers (or their representative organisations), state bodies and local government bodies aimed at ensuring the coordination of the interests of employees and employers in labour and other relations in which they directly take part. Although social partnership norms are defined as an institute of labour law (bearing the same name), it can be argued that the creation of social partnerships is actually one of the main goals of labour law, with a view to ensuring the harmonization of the interests of the parties of the employment relationship, the interests of the state and the regulation of labour relations based on Article 1 of the Labour Code.

In the heterogeneous field of the legal regulation of labour relations, labour protection is of particular importance. Labour protection comes within the framework of those institutes of law where the interests of labour relations and the interests of the state clash most prominently.

Labour protection for employees is mainly provided by the norms which stipulate the protection of their life and health during employment, and, for employers, this may well entail some material expenses. The state also has an interest in the legal regulation of labour protection relations. Moreover, labour protection is one of the main reasons for the creation and existence of the state's social policy and consequently the development of labour legislation.

Such state interest in the regulation of labour protection relations has a historical grounding and was brought about by a series of factors. As we know, in the late 19th and early 20th centuries rapidly growing industry led to an increase in hired labour and its exploitation.[1] At the time, economic relations and the interests of company-owners in means of production which might increase the growth and development of the manufacturing industry, were contributing to creating a certain type of work environment. This in turn led to the growth of the working class which, as a result of unification and of a greater understanding of workers' inalienable rights, engaged in political activism to improve their social standing, lower the high mortality rate and gain the right to live a worthy life. Incessant clashes and conflicts threatened the stability of the state and eventually caused the state to act. The state's interest in the development of social policy was related to the need to ensure social stability which is impossible during a class struggle.

Another threat to social stability, in addition to the clashes between employers and employees fighting for their rights, was the fact that the failure to uphold workers' right to life in the late 19th and early 20th centuries increased the risk of epidemic diseases caused by insanitary

---

[1] See: Kiselev, I. Ya. 2001. *Trudovoe pravo Rossii. Istoriko-pravovoe issledovanie [Labour Law of Russia: Historical and Legal Research]*. Moscow: Norma, 3, 5, etc. [in Russian]; also *Kurs rossiyskogo trudovogo prava. Obshchaya chast', T. 1 [Course of Russian Labour law. General Part, V. 1]*, eds. Khokhlov, Ye. B. 1996. Saint-Petersburg: Izdatel'stvo Sankt-Peterburgskogo universiteta, 31. [in Russian].

working conditions at factories and plants. Better-off social groups were also running the risk of being affected by these diseases. Working in unhygienic conditions led to the health impairment of many workers, which consequently threatened the militarized state as its power was diminished. The risk of physical degradation particularly affected children working at factories and plants. This society built on family principles was further endangered by the perceived threat to morality constituted by men and women working night-shifts together and women being absent from their homes for 24 hours at a time.[2]

This situation was brought about by the state's liberal laissez-faire policy regarding economic relations, including labour relations, which caused the crisis of the principle of "freedom of contract" in the regulation of labour relations, making it necessary for the state to take an active part in the economy. It therefore followed that, in view of their significant value, labour relations needed to be regulated not only by means of labour contracts, but also by special legislation consisting largely of mandatory norms.[3]

The necessity for state participation in labour protection relations was also confirmed by the fact that individual rights ("first generation" rights), including, but not limited to, the right to life, had already been formulated during the period in question. However, given the prevailing situation, it became obvious that it would be impossible to provide the right to life—in other words, labour protection—without further definition and formulation of socio-economic rights. These considerations determined the main vectors of social reformation and the creation of "second generation" social, economic and cultural rights,[4] the enforcement of which was possible only with the involvement of the state.

It is of note that the legislation developed in the late 19th century which aimed to regulate the use of certain categories of worker, above all women and children, was known as "social legislation".[5]

---

2 See: Shershenevich, G. F. 2003. *Kurs torgovogo prava. T1: Vvedeniye. Torgovye deyateli [Labour Law Course. T.1: Introduction. Trade Figures]*. Moscow: Statut, 158. [in Russian].

3 Tal, L. S. 1913. *Trudovoy dogovor*: *Tsivilisticheskoye issledovaniye. Ch. 2 [Employment Contract: Civil Research. Ch.2]*. Yaroslavl: Tipografiya Gubernskogo Pravleniya, 235. [in Russian].

4 Lukasheva Ye. A. otv. red. 2003. *Prava cheloveka [Human Rights]: Uchebnik dlya vuzov*. Moscow: Norma, 200. [in Russian].

5 Khokhlov Ye. B. pod red. 1996. *Kurs rossiyskogo trudovogo prava. T. 1, obshchaya chast* [*Labour Law Course*. T. 1, General Part]. St. Petersburg: Izdatel'stvo Sankt-Peterburgskogo univesiteta, 31. [in Russian].

The state's interest in social harmony gave rise to the creation of labour protection norms all over the world. International labour legislation emerged as a consequence of the development and consolidation of human rights, especially the right to life, which is protected by labour protection norms. Thus, in the late 19th and early 20th centuries, progressive minds furthered the idea that it is essential to improve workers' working and living conditions. Gradually, this idea gained momentum and spread to different countries.[6] These tendencies were fixed in the International Labour Organization Constitution drafted in 1919 (with amendments and additions in 1922, 1945, 1946, 1953, 1962), aimed, among other things, at achieving social equality and the eradication of working conditions characterized by injustice, hardship and privation experienced by a large number of people, producing such a state of unrest that the peace and harmony of the world was imperilled. Working conditions should be improved through regulatory action in the field of labour relations. Historically, the protection of workers against sickness, disease and injury arising out of their employment has always been part of the ILO Constitution.[7]

The necessity for the state to participate in labour protection relations was clear and has been justified by history. Furthermore, it is important to take into account that the state is not just a mediator and protector of relations in the field of labour and employment, but is also directly concerned with the existence of such relations and the effectiveness of the relevant legal norms.

ILO data show that the negative consequences of neglecting labour protection norms can result in huge expenses incurred as a consequence of work-related illnesses. As a result, workers and their families lose their means of subsistence, there is a decline in their productivity and efficiency and medical-related expenses rise sharply. According to ILO estimates, 4% of the global gross domestic product (GDP), $2.8 billion, is lost annually due to industrial injuries and work-related diseases in the form of direct and indirect expenses covering injuries to workers, illness, sick leave, loss of working hours, lost earnings, disablement, welfare payments, medical expenses, property damage, loss of qualified workforce

---

[6] See Chernyayeva D. V. 2010. *Mezhdunarodnye standarty truda (mezhdunarodnoe publichnoe trudovoe pravo) [International Standards of Work (International Public Labour Law)]*: uchebnoye posobiye. Moscow: Knorus, 7-19. [in Russian].

[7] ILO. Guidelines on Occupational Safety and Health Management Systems (ILO-OSH 2001) SafeWork. Geneva: ILO. http://www.ilo.org/wcmsp5/groups/public/---ed_protect/---protrav/---safework/documents/publication/wcms_110496.pdf (accessed 10 November 2013).

and the cost of training new workers. In the European Union the expenses incurred due to work-related diseases amount to at least €145 billion every year.[8]

The negative consequences of neglecting labour protection norms, however, are not limited to adverse economic effects; they also impinge on the state's population policy and therefore on the health of the overwhelming majority of citizens. For example, the Declaration on Workers' Health approved in 2006 states that workers represent half of the global population and significantly contribute to the economic and social value of contemporary society. A substantial part of the general morbidity of the working population is related to work.[9]

Despite the fact that social policy and social legislation emerged from the necessity to coordinate the parties' interests in the area of hired labour, social policy currently incorporates not only the state's activity in this field, but also healthcare, education, welfare, and so on. In accordance with article 7 of Russia's Constitution, the Russian Federation is a social state, the policy of which is aimed at creating the necessary conditions for a worthy life and the unhindered development of man. Part 2 of article 7 of the Constitution of the Russian Federation declares that one of the goals of the social state is the protection of the labour and health of the population. Therefore, the conditions for a respectable life and the free development of man are created by the legal regulation of labour relations and in particular by labour protection regulations. The creation of a labour protection system is mentioned as one of the principles which can become the basis for the enhancement of social policy in the member states of the Commonwealth of Independent States (CIS).[10]

In summary, labour protection is not the only aim of state social policy but is certainly one of its main ones, and it entails corresponding state responsibilities in order to provide adequate labour protection. At the same time, the extent of state participation in contractual legal relations between

---

[8] The Prevention of Occupational Diseases. World Day for safety and health at work, 28 April 2013. ILO, 2013. Link: http://www.ilo.org/safework/areasofwork/workplace-health-promotion-and-well-being/WCMS_207663/lang--en/index.htm (accessed 10 November 2013).

[9] http://www.who.int/occupational_health/publications/declaration2006/en/index.html (accessed 15 November 2013).

[10] Rekomendatsiya Mezhparlamentskoy Assamblei gosudarstv-uchastnikov SNG, 16.05.2011 No. 36-11: Osnovniye napravleniya formirovaniya sotsialnoy politiki v gosudarstvakh-uchastnikakh SNG. Link: http://www.iacis.ru/upload/iblock/b51/11aa.pdf [in Russian] (accessed 5 September 2013).

employers and employees and the identification of the appropriate methods of labour protection are highly important. These matters are complex as a wide variety of factors such as state migration policy, the political activity of employees and their representatives, employer culture, mentality and the state of the economy, also play a role.

The major difficulty in achieving an optimal legal regulation, however, is that on the one hand, the subject of labour protection relations is the life and health of a person during employment, and on the other hand, labour protection relations fall within the terms of labour contracts, which cannot be fully governed by the state.

The economic weakness of employees requires greater state protection which grants them more rights and guarantees to find a balance between the interests of employers and employees.

At the same time, excessive state intervention in contractual relations contradicts the principle of contractual freedom, hinders business initiative and adversely affects the efficiency of norms in the area of labour protection. It is necessary to take into account entrepreneurs' economic rights when determining the degree of intervention in contractual relations which, if excessive, could result in a restriction of these rights. Employers' interests must be taken into consideration for several reasons.

The means of solving social problems lies in the society's living conditions, its economic basis. Consequently, social policy is inextricably linked to economic strategy and thus constitutes an integral part of general state policy. At the same time, various social factors affect the development of the economy as well as other spheres of life.[11]

The protection of the interests of employees' requires taking into consideration the interests of the other party in contractual relations—those of the employers. Moreover, the state dictates mandatory behaviour of employers towards their employees, i.e. employers are responsible to fulfil their obligations in the field of labour protection. In order to create a more complete social policy, the protection of workers' rights should be carried out with due consideration for the economic interests and constitutional rights of employers.

A social state guarantees the social and economic rights of the population, including not only labour rights, but also the right to be able to freely use one's abilities and property for entrepreneurial and economic activities not prohibited by law (Art. 34 of the Constitution of the Russian

[11] Pashkov A. S. 2006. *Izbranniye trudy po trydovomu pravu [The Chosen Works According to Labour Law]*. St. Petersburg: Izdatel'stvo Sankt-Peterburgskogo gosudarstvennogo universiteta, 417. [in Russian].

Federation), the right to private ownership (Art. 8 and 9 of the Constitution of the Russian Federation), and others.

Social responsibility should be to some extent also in the employers' economic interests. The transition from a focus on economic matters to accentuating social issues and the goal of complying with international social standards are noted as priorities for social policies in the Recommendations by the Inter-parliamentary Assembly of the CIS Member Nations, issued on 16 May 2011, No. 36-11.[12] It is stated that the CIS member nations should, when forming their social policy, take into account the functioning of major social development schemes, including by favouring an increase in funding for social programmes, a social orientation for economic development, an increase in the social efficiency of economic programmes, the strengthening of corporate social responsibility, social partnerships between different strata of the population, the promotion of equality and so on.

Therefore, when determining the degree of intervention in the area of labour protection, the state must work on the premise that labour protection is to be provided for employees, as it is their life and health one is aiming to protect, but should at the same time aim to preserve the employers' interests in these relations.

There is, however, no decisive answer to the question of labour protection methods, which is due, among other things, to the ambiguity of the very concept of labour protection. A substantial role in clarifying this concept is played by the International Labour Organization. Occupational safety and workers' health have been the ILO's major concerns since it was founded in 1919, and they continue to be fundamental concepts in the programmes the ILO adheres to in order to achieve the goals formulated in the Decent Work Agenda. For example, the Global Strategy on Occupational Safety and Health formulated by the ILO in 2003[13] states that decent work must be safe work. The Strategy emphasizes that the right to labour protection must be respected at all levels. The main, and historically the first, requirement of labour protection is protection from physical factors which means the absence of dangers in the workplace which could lead to occupational disease or cause potentially fatal injuries.

Following on from physical safety, labour protection focuses on mental health. According to Seiji Machida, director of the ILO Programme on

---

[12] http://www.iacis.ru/upload/iblock/b51/11aa.pdf [in Russian] (accessed 5 September 2013).

[13] Global strategy on occupational safety and health. Geneva. ILO, 2003 // www.ili.org/wcmsp5/groups/public/@ed_protect/@protrav/@safework/documents /publication/wcms_107535.pdf (accessed 10 November 2013).

Safety and Health at Work and the Environment (SafeWork), "creating safe and healthy working conditions is a challenge to which the ILO has been responding since it was founded in 1919. As our world develops, with new technologies and new patterns of work, the challenges change and new risks emerge. When safety and health measures are not followed or fail, accidents, injuries, diseases and even deaths may occur. This new list of occupational diseases reflects the state-of-the art development in the identification and recognition of occupational diseases in the world of today. The world's working population and their families will benefit from this new list".[14] The List of Occupational Diseases Recommendation 2002 (No. 194) contains a revised list which, for the first time ever, includes mental and behavioural disorders and post-traumatic stress disorder. This is an important step towards acknowledging a direct connection between work-related risk exposures and resulting mental and behavioural disorders.

The right to protection of physical, but also mental health, is repeated in many of the programme's declarations. The Declaration on Workers' Health approved in 2006[15] states that one objective is to achieve the maximum level of both physical and mental health for all workers. The 60th World Health Assembly in 2007 endorsed the Global Plan of Action on Workers' Health (2008-2017).[16] The Global Plan states that all workers should be able to enjoy the highest attainable standard of physical and mental health and favourable working conditions. The workplace should not be a place dangerous for health and well-being. A wider approach to labour protection, not limited to physical safety, is developed through a number of ILO conventions. The Occupational Safety and Health Convention of 1981 (No. 155,[17] which was ratified by the Russian Federation on 11 April 1998,[18] defines health in relation to work not as the mere absence of disease or infirmity, but all the physical and mental factors which affect the individual and which are directly related to safety and hygiene in the workplace. The Occupational Health Services

---

14 http://www.ilo.org/safework/whatsnew/WCMS_124671/lang--en/index.htm accessed (accessed 15 November 2013).

15 http://www.who.int/occupational_health/publications/declaration2006/en/index.html (accessed 15 November 2013).

16 http://apps.who.int/gb/ebwha/pdf_files/WHA60/A60_R26-en.pdf (accessed 15 November 2013).

17 http://www.ilo.org/dyn/normlex/en/f?p=NORMLEXPUB:12100:0::NO:12100:P12100_INSTRUMENT_ID:312300:NO (accessed 15 November 2013).

18 Russian Federation Federal Law No. 58-FZ of 11 April 1998.

Convention 1985 (No. 161),[19] contains several recommendations for the creation of a healthy working environment which facilitates the attainment of optimal physical and mental health in relation to work, and the adaptation of work to the capabilities of workers in light of their physical and mental state.

After physical and mental health have been ensured, it is possible to proceed to the third stage of labour protection: psychological comfort in the workplace. As well as physical dangers (biological, chemical, and so on), the ILO Global strategy on Occupational Safety and Health 2003,[20] and the ILO Global Programme on Safety, Health and the Environment 2003,[21] acknowledge the risk of psycho-social hazards in the workplace.

Occupational health and the quality of the individual's working life are clearly marked out among the Programme's main objectives. The International Programme for Better Working Conditions and Environment created by the International Labour Bureau mentions that concepts such as the connection between working conditions and the quality of a worker's life have been established.[22] The realization of the Programme's provisions will lead to a more careful treatment of workers' life and health, securing rest periods and leisure time and the possibility for each worker to develop their personal skills to their full potential.[23] One of the objectives formulated in the ILO Programme for Decent Work (1999)[24] is the employment of workers in occupations in which they will have the satisfaction of using their skills to the full and being able to make the greatest possible contribution to the common well-being.[25] In accordance with the ILO Guidelines on Occupational Safety and Health Management Systems (2001), decent work is safe work which should be done in conditions of freedom, equality, social security and human dignity.[26]

---

[19] http://www.ilo.org/dyn/normlex/en/f?p=NORMLEXPUB:12100:0::NO:12100:P12100_ILO_CODE:C161 (accessed 15 November 2013).

[20] ILO. 2003. *Global Strategy on Occupational Safety and Health.* Geneva: ILO. www.ili.org/wcmsp5/groups/public/@ed_protect/@protrav/@safework/documents/publication/wcms_107535.pdf (accessed 15 November 2013).

[21] http://www.wbcsd.org/web/projects/cement/tf3/ILO-SAFEWORK-GLOBAL-PROGRAM.pdf (accessed 15 November 2013).

[22] ILO. *Safety Measures, Occupational Health and production environment*, MBT Working Paper No. 68, Geneva: ILO.

[23] ILO Information Bulletin, 1976, No. 39:3.

[24] Somaviya, H. 1999. "Decent Work," ILO Working Paper No. 5. Geneva: ILO.

[25] Somaviya H. 2001. "Reducing the Decent Work Deficit—A Global Challenge," ILO Working Paper No. 7-8, Geneva: ILO.

[26] Guidelines on Occupational Safety and Health Management Systems (ILO-OSH 2001) SafeWork, ILO Geneva // http://www.ilo.org/wcmsp5/groups/public/---

In summary, nowadays both physical security and psycho-social security in the workplace are worldwide concerns. There is no doubt that the state needs to establish mandatory norms regulating physical security, although there is still some uncertainty regarding mental health and psychological comfort. An important question is what exactly the state strives to provide with respect to labour protection: whether it aims to ensure life and health *per se* (physical security), or whether it wishes to broaden its reach to the issues of mental health and psychological comfort in the workplace. During the early years of labour legislation, labour protection was understood as a system providing physical security to workers in the course of their employment. Due to the rudimentary state of labour legislation at the time, the state could only achieve its goals by imposing mandatory rules. It should be noted that physical security was and still is the first and foremost component of labour protection and without it the development of labour protection is meaningless. It is therefore natural to use mandatory norms in order to regulate this field.

However, the state, while establishing regulations for labour protection relations, must adapt legislation in order to meet current economic demands. Notwithstanding the fact that securing the life and health of contractual workers requires the establishment of compulsory standards, and even though security was provided by compulsory rules only during the early existence of social (labour) legislation, it is, in the current climate, impossible to rely solely on mandatory norms. The contractual nature of labour relations and the state of the current economy must be taken into account; if they are not, the very least we can expect is that these legal regulations will become more and more inefficient.

Furthermore, the area of labour regulation is notably critical and conflict-prone owing to the fact that the subjects of labour relations tend to have directly opposing interests. The degree of consideration which these interests are given determines the efficiency of the regulation of labour relations. One of the most efficient methods which is gaining more and more recognition internationally is that of social partnership. A state policy which addresses the interests of different social groups in order to maintain social harmony is inherent in the concept of a social state.

---

ed_protect/---protrav/---safework/documents/publication/wcms_110496.pdf (accessed 10 November 2013).

Securing labour rights and workers' interests via the social partnership system is one of the priorities for social policy enhancement in CIS member states.[27]

This is reflected in article 1 of the Labour Code of the Russian Federation, according to which one of the main tasks of labour legislation (as a direct tool of social policy), is the creation of the necessary legal conditions to achieve an optimal coordination of the interests of the parties of labour relations with the interests of the state. This social goal can be achieved by reaching agreements between the parties concerned, i.e. through a social partnership.

The state therefore establishes mandatory norms in order to guarantee the life and health of workers, including their physical security. All other labour protection issues should be resolved by means of a social partnership. Moreover, by establishing mandatory norms in the area of labour protection, the state has to take into account the contractual nature of labour relations. Consequently the state's interest in balancing the interests of the parties in labour relations manifests itself in the establishment of mandatory norms. This point is also expressed in international acts regulating labour protection.

Art. 3 of the ILO Promotional Framework for Occupational Safety and Health Convention No. 187 of 15 June 2006, for example, specifies that each member state shall promote a safe and healthy working environment by formulating national policy accordingly; shall promote and advance, at all relevant levels, the right of workers to a safe and healthy working environment. In formulating its national policy, each member state, in light of national conditions and practice and in consultation with the most representative organizations of employers and workers, shall promote basic principles of occupational safety. According to Art. 4, the national system for occupational safety and health includes, among others, arrangements to promote, at the level of the undertaking, cooperation between management, workers and their representatives as an essential element of workplace-related prevention measures.[28]

The priority of social partnership instruments in the regulation of labour protection relations is reflected in the papers of the Inter-

---

[27] Rekomendatsiya Mezhparlamentskoy Assamblei gosudarstv-uchastnikov SNG, 16.05.2011 No. 36-11: Osnovniye napravleniya formirovaniya sotsialnoy politiki v gosudarstvakh-uchastnikakh SNG. Link: http://www.iacis.ru/upload/iblock/b51/11aa.pdf [in Russian] (accessed 5 September 2013).

[28] http://www.ilo.org/dyn/normlex/en/f?p=NORMLEXPUB:12100:0::NO::P12100_ILO_CODE:C187 (accessed 15 November 2013).

parliamentary Assembly of the CIS Member Nations. The Recommendation by Inter-parliamentary Assembly of the CIS Member Nations: *Principal Directions for Social Policy Formation in the CIS Member Nations*[29] states that the realization of the principal goals of state policy in the area of working conditions and labour protection should be carried out by coordinated actions of government agencies, municipalities, employers and their associations as well as trade unions, their associations and other representatives elected by employees in the areas of safety and labour protection. Furthermore, one of the objectives of state policy formulated in the aforementioned document is the activation of employer associations and trade unions as the principal social partners, and the shift of the majority of decisions to this level.

Such consideration is necessary not only in guaranteeing freedom of contract and determining the rules of conduct in the area of labour protection concerning collective agreements and local normative acts, but also in the formulation of mandatory state norms, the efficiency of which is affected by providing for the employers' economic rights and interests.

One of the principal focuses of state policy in enhancing working conditions and labour protection, which is formulated in the Recommendation of the Inter-parliamentary Assembly of the CIS Member Nations: *Principal Directions for Social Policy Formation in the CIS Member Nations* of 16 May 2011, No. 36-11, is the effective realization of a tax policy which will be able to stimulate the creation of safe working environments and the development and application of safe working methods and technologies such as the production of individual and collective protective gear.

Alongside this, in accordance with Russian tax legislation, tax policy in the area of labour protection is aimed at encouraging employers to observe the mandatory norms of the applicable legislation, though there is a lack of norms stimulating the creation of improved legislation, relative to that currently applicable, governing the situation of workers. Part 1 of article 252 of the Tax Code of the Russian Federation, for instance, states that in order to pay the corporate income tax, the taxpayer shall receive a reduced income based on the amount of expenses incurred; these expenses include those associated with ensuring normal working conditions and safety measures as covered by the legislation of the Russian Federation (section 7 of article 264). Article 163 of the Labour Code classifies as normal working conditions, among others, labour conditions meeting the

---

[29] http://www.iacis.ru/upload/iblock/b51/11aa.pdf [in Russian] (accessed 5 September 2013).

requirements of labour protection and production safety. Thus, for the purpose of tax assessment, only expenses incurred to comply with the norms of applicable legislation, but not those additionally defined in the collective agreement, local normative acts can be accepted.

The Recommendation by Inter-parliamentary Assembly of the CIS Member Nations: *Principal Directions for Social Policy Formation in the CIS Member Nations* of 16 May 2011, No. 36-11, enumerates the following state policy objectives: the development of a labour protection management model compliant with market relations, the perception of labour protection as a significant reserve of production activity, the improvement of mechanisms ensuring employers' economic interests in arranging a safe working environment.[30]

Recent changes in Russian legislation appear to be more attentive in protecting the economic interests of employers. For instance, in part 2 of article 212 of the Labour Code of the Russian Federation, employers are charged with an obligation to perform a so-called "attestation procedure" of workplaces regarding working conditions. The attestation procedure is defined in the Procedure of Attestation of Workplaces on Conditions of Work, adopted by the Order of the Ministry of Healthcare and Social Development of the Russian Federation of 26 April 2011, No. 342n.[31]

Initially section 4 of the Order of 26 April 2011, No. 342n, ruled that all workplaces belonging to an employer must receive an "attestation". However, this was changed after an examination of the legislation by the Ministry of Economic Development and Trade of the Russian Federation.

The Ministry determined that some provisions of the Order unduly complicated entrepreneurship and investment activities. In particular, the Ministry considered it excessive to conduct "attestations" of workplaces which have no relevant statistics of loss or injury to workers. In addition, the Ministry suggested that an analysis of the opinions of the members of entrepreneurial society and subjects of business activities might lead to an improvement of certain provisions in the document.[32] Since 26 February 2013, employers have been obliged to conduct attestations only of workplaces which, due to the work involved, can be deemed as dangerous

---

[30] http://www.iacis.ru/upload/iblock/b51/11aa.pdf [in Russian] (accessed 5 September 2013).

[31] The Order of the Ministry of Healthcare and Social Development of the Russian Federation of 26 April 2011, No. 342n. *Rossiyskaya Gazeta*, 2011, No. 135, 24 June 2012 [in Russian].

[32] The Conclusion of 12 May 2012 on Inspection of The Order of the Ministry of Healthcare and Social Development of the Russian Federation of 26 April 2011, No. 342n [in Russian].

(sections 2, 4 of the Procedure of Attestation of Workplaces on Conditions of Work). The Procedure was accordingly revised by the Order of the Ministry of Labour and Social Security of the Russian Federation of 12 December 2012, No. 590n.

The encouragement of employers to respect such norms is one of the main directions for the improvement of labour protection regulation. Such encouragement, however, is important not only for employers but also for employees. The Global Plan of Action on Workers' Health (2008-2017) stipulates that the assessment and management of health risks in the workplace should be improved by defining essential interventions for prevention and control of mechanical, physical, chemical, biological and psycho-social risks in the working environment. The promotion of good health and prevention of non-communicable diseases should be further stimulated in the workplace, in particular by advocating a healthy diet and physical activity among workers, and promoting mental and family health at work.[33]

It thus follows that the legal regulation of labour protection requires state participation which manifests itself in the establishment of mandatory labour protection norms and the creation of conditions ensuring liberty of contract and respect for the interests of the parties of legal labour relations in the formulation of labour protection norms. It should be noted that contractual rules in the area of labour protection are important inasmuch as they can ensure labour protection not only in the sphere of physical security, but can also take into account other aspects of labour protection recognized worldwide.

It is, however, important to note that social partnership norms are not universal and do not involve all individuals (employers and employees) who have concluded an employment contract. In accordance with article 25 of the Labour Code the parties of social partnerships are employees and employers represented by authorized persons according to established procedure. From this rule it follows that the application of social partnership norms to a worker who has entered into an employment contract with an employer who is not a self-employed entrepreneur is impossible; the worker is not included in the collective body and the employer does not belong to an employers' association. Furthermore, home workers are also excluded from the collective body as they work outside of a "working environment". Additionally, according to article 310 of the Labour Code of the Russian Federation, a home worker may carry

---

[33] http://apps.who.int/gb/ebwha/pdf_files/WHA60/A60_R26-en.pdf (accessed 15 November 2013).

out work with the participation of members of his or her family. In other words, the extension of social partnership norms to this category of workers also contradicts the nature of a social partnership. Agency work has the particularity of a doubling of employers. Labour relations are established with one employer, but the work is done for another employer. Again, the extension of social partnership norms to such workers is prohibited.

In conclusion, social partnerships as a goal of social policy concerned with ensuring the coordination of the interests of employers, employees and the state is one of the primary methods of ensuring labour protection.

The state should create opportunities for the development of social partnerships, including the establishment of mandatory norms in the area of labour protection which should aim to regulate labour protection relations by taking into account the balance of interests of the parties to the employment contract. Categories of workers which are not included in the scope of social partnership norms should also be regulated by centralized and individual contractual norms.

References

Chernyayeva D. V. 2010. *Mezhdunarodnye standarty truda (mezhdunarodnoe publichnoe trudovoe pravo) [International Standards of Work (International Public Labour Law)]*: uchebnoye posobiye. Moscow: Knorus, 232. [in Russian].

Kiselev, I. Ya. 2001. *Trudovoe pravo Rossii. Istoriko-pravovoe issledovanie [Labour Law of Russia: Historical and Legal Research].* Moscow: Norma, 384. [in Russian].

Kurs rossiyskogo trudovogo prava. Obshchaya chast', T. 1 [Course of Russian labour law. General part, V. 1], eds. Khokhlov, Ye. B. 1996. Saint-Petersburg: Izdatel'stvo Sankt-Peterburgskogo universiteta, 573. [in Russian].

Pashkov A.S. 2006. *Izbranniye trudy po trydovomu pravu* [The chosen works according to the labour law]. St. Petersburg: Izdatel'stvo Sankt-Peterburgskogo gosudarstvennogo universiteta, 519. [in Russian].

Shershenevich, G.F. 2003. *Kurs torgovogo prava. T1: Vvedeniye. Torgovye deyateli* [Course of the labour law. T.1: Introduction. Trade figures]. Moscow: Statut, 480. [in Russian].

Tal L.S. 1913. Trudovoy dogovor: *Tsivilisticheskoye issledovaniye. Ch. 2* [Employment contract: Civil research. Ch.2]. Yaroslavl: Tipografiya Gubernskogo Pravleniya, 422. [in Russian].

Lukasheva Ye.A. otv. red. 2003. *Prava cheloveka* [Human rights]: Uchebnik dlya vuzov, Moscow: Norma, 448. [in Russian].

Global strategy on occupational safety and health. Geneva. ILO, 2003 www.ili.org/wcmsp5/groups/public/@ed_protect/@protrav/@safework /documents/publication/wcms_107535.pdf (accessed 10 November 2013).

Guidelines on Occupational Safety and Health Management Systems (ILO-OSH 2001) SafeWork, ILO Geneva http://www.ilo.org/wcmsp5/groups/public/---ed_protect/---protrav/---safework/documents/publication/wcms_110496.pdf (accessed 10 November 2013).

Rekomendatsiya Mezhparlamentskoy Assamblei gosudarstv-uchastnikov SNG, 16.05.2011 No. 36-11: Osnovniye napravleniya formirovaniya sotsialnoy politiki v gosudarstvakh-uchastnikakh SNG. Link: http://www.iacis.ru/upload/iblock/b51/11aa.pdf [in Russian] (accessed 10 November 2013).

Safety measures, occupational health and production environment, MBT Working Paper No. 68, Geneva: ILO.

Somaviya, H. 1999. "Decent Work," ILO Working Paper No. 5, Geneva: ILO.

—. 2001. "Reducing the Decent Work Deficit—A Global Challenge," ILO Working Paper No. 7-8. Geneva: ILO.

The Conclusion of 12 May 2012 on Inspection of The Order of the Ministry of Healthcare and Social Development of the Russian Federation of 26 April 2011, No. 342n [in Russian].

The Order of the Ministry of Healthcare and Social Development of the Russian Federation of 26 April 2011, No. 342n. *Rossiyskaya Gazeta*, 2011, No. 135, 24 June 2012 [in Russian].

ILO. 2013. *The Prevention of Occupational Diseases. World Day for Safety and Health at Work,* 28 April 2013. Geneva: ILO. Link: http://www.ilo.org/safework/areasofwork/workplace-health-promotion-and-well-being/WCMS_207663/lang--en/index.htm (accessed 10 November 2013).

http://www.who.int/occupational_health/publications/declaration2006/en/index.html (accessed 10 November 2013).

http://www.iacis.ru/upload/iblock/b51/11aa.pdf [in Russian] (accessed 10 November 2013).

http://www.ilo.org/safework/whatsnew/WCMS_124671/lang--en/index.htm accessed (accessed 15 November 2013).

http://apps.who.int/gb/ebwha/pdf_files/WHA60/A60_R26-en.pdf (accessed 15 November 2013).

http://www.ilo.org/dyn/normlex/en/f?p=NORMLEXPUB:12100:0::NO:12100:P12100_INSTRUMENT_ID:312300:NO (accessed 15 November 2013).

http://www.ilo.org/dyn/normlex/en/f?p=NORMLEXPUB:12100:0::NO:12100:P12100_ILO_CODE:C161 (accessed 15 November 2013).

http://www.wbcsd.org/web/projects/cement/tf3/ILO-SAFEWORK-GLOBAL-PROGRAM.pdf (accessed 15 November 2013).

http://www.ilo.org/dyn/normlex/en/f?p=NORMLEXPUB:12100:0::NO::P12100_ILO_CODE:C187 (accessed 15 November 2013).

http://apps.who.int/gb/ebwha/pdf_files/WHA60/A60_R26-en.pdf (accessed 11 September 2013).

THE HEAD OF THE COMPANY AND HIS LEGAL STATUS IN CONTEMPORARY RUSSIA

ELENA RADEVICH

The different aspects of entrepreneurship are widely investigated research topics in modern Russia, either from an economic or a legal point of view. This can be explained to a large extent by the effort to fill the gaps created in the planned economic system which, although with some differences, can be found in the Soviet Union from the early 1930s to the late 1980s.

During *perestroika* (1985-1991), some attempts were made to reform the planned economic system, by introducing elements which were peculiar to the market economy. At that time, public companies dominated the market, yet a number of private enterprises flourished in the form of cooperatives following the passing of the 1988 Cooperatives Act. A few years later in 1990, the Enterprises and Entrepreneurship Act was enforced, which regarded entrepreneurship as a relevant activity.

The innovative nature of these social relations called for a new legal framework. As a result, a range of legislative acts was enacted in the 1990s, which defined and regulated various forms of business, e.g. partnerships, joint-stock companies, limited liability companies, and cooperatives.[1] These provisions mainly concerned the foregoing legal entities and their corporate governance, chiefly the role of those in charge of running the business on a daily basis.

It is understandable that lawmakers paid attention to the role of those figures known as "managing director" or "chief executive officer" (CEO), who in Russia are generally termed "head of the organization"[2] (hereinafter referred to as "the head"). Evidently, the efficiency and the

---

[1] According to statistics, limited liability companies are the most widespread form of business in Russia. In October 2013, the share of limited liability companies out of the total number of commercial organizations exceeded 93% (*Statistics of Legal Entities.* Vestnik gosudarstvennoy registracii [Bulletin of State Registration]. http://www.vestnik-gosreg.ru/info_ul/ (accessed 8 March 2014)).

[2] More specific terms—e.g. "director", "general director", and "president"—are employed in everyday parlance.

existence of a business in the market economy mainly depend on the head's activity, which in turn, rests on its legal regulation. First, such regulation should promote the manifestation of the head's entrepreneurial talent, which should not be limited by overly stringent provisions.

Secondly, the interests of an organization must be properly safeguarded, since misconduct on the part of management may cause serious damages. Thirdly, notwithstanding his social status, the head's interests should also be protected by means of employment-related measures. Based on these considerations, the article affords an analysis of how current Russian legislation contributes to achieving these three objectives.

1. Russian Corporate Governance and its Peculiarities: A Hybrid System to Respond to National Needs

Before considering the legal regulation *per se*, it is necessary to clarify the position and the role of the head of an organization in the system of corporate governance. Depending on the structure of the board of directors, the international literature distinguishes between two basic models of corporate governance: the Anglo-American (or Anglo-Saxon) model and the Continental one.

The Anglo-American model, also known as the unitary model, is based on a single-tier board of directors. This structure is typical of the UK and the USA and does not presuppose a strict separation between supervisory and executive powers among its members. Conversely, the Continental model prevails in continental Europe and consists of a two-tier board of directors, i.e. an executive and a supervisory board. The former is responsible for running daily operations, while the latter mainly carries out monitoring functions.

The Russian system of corporate governance diverges from the models discussed above. At the early stage of the privatization process, lawmakers were in favour of the Anglo-American model. However, in the first years of the 1990s, it became obvious that this model could not be implemented in Russia, mainly because of the absence of efficient measures of external control. Such state of affairs emphasized the relevance of mechanisms of internal control in an organization.[3] As a result, lawmakers have created a peculiar hybrid system combining the features of the Anglo-American

---

[3] McGee, R. W., ed. 2008. *Corporate Governance in Transition Economies*. New York, NY: Springer, 259.

unitary model and the continental two-tier board models.[4] As it is in many Continental European countries, the Russian system of corporate governance provides for a two-tier structure of the board,[5] namely the supervisory board[6] and the executive board. Nevertheless, this system allows executive bodies to be members of the supervisory board; this would not be possible in the traditional continental two-tier board model, being that based on the clear separation between executive and supervisory functions.[7] The scope to be appointed as the head and the board member of the organization brings together the Russian system of corporate governance and its Anglo-American counterpart.[8]

However, at the international level, it has been rightly observed that comparing different systems of corporate governance only from a formal point of view might prove unsuccessful, since similar labels may refer to different structures.[9] Arguably, the Russian system of corporate governance

---

[4] Cepov, G. V. 2006. *Akcionernye obschestva: Teoriya i praktika [Joint-Stock Companies: Theory and Practice]*. Moscow: TK Velbi, 160-161.

[5] Strictly speaking, the establishment of the supervisory board is mandatory only in case of joint-stock companies where the number of shareholders with voting shares is higher than fifty. In other cases, establishing the supervisory board is entirely at the discretion of the founders of the organization (Par. 2, Art. 103 of the Civil Code of the Russian Federation of 1994; Par. 1, Art. 64 of Joint-Stock Companies Act of 1995; Par. 2, Art. 32 of Limited-Liability Companies Act of 1998).

[6] It is contradictory that in Russian legislation the terms "supervisory board" (*nabludatel'niy sovet*) and "board" (*sovet direktorov*) are used as synonyms (Par. 1, Art. 64 of Joint Stock Companies Act of 1995; Par. 2, Art. 32 of Limited-Liability Companies Act of 1998). Such identification, that the international literature defines as confusing, is further evidence of the hybrid nature of Russian corporate governance (Tricker, B. 2009. *Corporate Governance: Principles, Policies, and Practices*. New York, NY: Oxford University Press, 205).

[7] There are only two limitations. First, the number of the executive body members in the supervisory board should not be higher than 1/4 of its total number. Secondly, a person who acts as the sole executive body of an organization, i.e. its head, cannot be appointed as the chairman of the supervisory board (Par. 2, Art. 66 of Joint-Stock Companies Act of 1995; Par. 2, Art. 32 of Limited Liability Companies Act of 1998).

[8] Interestingly enough, the United Kingdom/Commonwealth model distinguishes between the board chairman and the chief executive officer, while in the United States these two positions are often held by the same person (Tricker, B. 2009. *Corporate Governance: Principles, Policies, and Practices*. New York, NY: Oxford University Press, 184).

[9] Chessell, M. 1996. "Sovet direktorov korporacii: kontrol' cherez predstavitel'stvo [The Board of a Corporation: Control through Representation]," in *Corporate governance: Owners, Directors and Employees of Joint-Stock Companies*

is more similar to the continental two-tier board model. This is because the majority of decisions in a business are made—or at least elaborated—by the executive board led by the head of the organization, while the supervisory board mainly exercises control over the executive one.[10]

2. The Different Approaches used to Define the Legal Status of the Head of the Organization

The different approaches used to determine the legal status of the head of the organization are either the result of his leading role in the system of corporate governance or the range of provisions regulating this function laid down in the Labour Code of the Russian Federation of 2001 [LC RF].

By and large, three main approaches can be identified. In this sense, many scholars are of the opinion that the head should be considered as an employee. This is because the LC RF dedicates a specific chapter (namely Chapter 43) to the legal regulation of his work.[11]

Chapter 43 introduces some innovative measures in Russian employment legislation. In fact, the need to regulate the activities of the head during Communism was not perceived as urgent. The reason for this was that the head was implicitly regarded as an employee of a state-owned enterprise with little power in terms of decision-making, profits and asset management.

However, Russia's transition towards a market economy caused significant changes in the tasks performed by the head. Now, it is believed that not only the profitability, but also the existence of a business depends to a large extent on his activity.[12] Further, the rules governing the head's

---

(Korporativnoe upravlenie. Vladel'tsy, direktora i naemnye rabotniki akcionernogo obschestva), ed. Chessell, M., (Moscow: John Wiley and Sons), 95-97.

[10] McGee, R. W., ed. 2008. *Corporate Governance in Transition Economies*. New York, NY: Springer, 281.

[11] See, for example: Bondarenko, E. N. 2004. *Osnovaniya vozniknoveniya trudovykh pravootnosheniy [The Grounds of Origin of Legal Employer-Employee Relationships]*. Moscow: Yuridicheskiy centr Press, 238; Goryachev, A.S. 2005. *Pravovoe polozhenie rukovoditelya kommercheskoy organizatsii* [The Legal Position of the Head of a Profit-Making Organization]: Phd thesis retrieved from the Digital Dissertation Library of the Russian State Library, 73 et al.; Zamorduev, D. G. 2005. *Rukovoditel' Organizatsii kak Spetsial'nyy Sub"ekt Trudovogo Prava [The Head of an Organization as a Special Subject of Employment Law]*, Phd thesis retrieved from the Digital Dissertation Library of the Russian State Library of the Russian State Library, 42 et al.

[12] Korshunova, T. Yu. 2004. "Osobennosti regulirovaniya truda otdel'nykh kategoriy rabotnikov [The Peculiarities of Regulation of Labour of Certain

functions must be carefully detailed, so as to protect the employer's interests.

This is because the violations committed by the head might lead to more serious consequences than those of ordinary employees. The rules governing the head's activities should also be flexible, so long as too stringent provisions may restrain his entrepreneurial talent. The introduction of Chapter 43 LC RF was intended to provide a legal response to these challenges.

The proponents of the "civil" approach have a different view, as they think that the head cannot be regarded as an employee who carries out a specific job, but as a component of the business.[13] However, the legal definition of the head runs counter to this assumption, being the head defined as a special employee[14] who runs a business and acts as its sole executive body on a day-to-day basis (Par. 1, Article 273 LC RF). Serving as the only executive body, the duties and responsibilities of which are regulated by civil law, is one of the main characteristics of the head when running an organization and does not affect his employee status.

Finally, a mixed approach exists which assumes that the legal status of the head is a halfway house between that of the employee and the self-employed as long as his contract contains provisions of both employment and of civil law.[15] This perspective is as fascinating as problematic, since Russian legislation does not regulate contracts which include provisions from different branches of the law.[16]

Categories of Employees]," *Trudovoe pravo*, No. 6:26.

[13] Boychenko, T. A., and E. R. Martirosyan. 2004. *Problemy trudovogo prava: prava i obyazannosti rabotodatelya* [The Issues of Employment Law: the Rights and Duties of an Employer]. Novosibirsk: Novosibirsk, 34, 47 et al.

[14] At present, in many countries legislation does not rule out the possibility for the head to be regarded as an employee, e.g. in the United Kingdom, the Netherlands, Spain, Brazil, Argentina, Australia (Berkowitz, P.M., Müller-Bonanni, T., & Reitz, A.E. 2008. *International Labor and Employment Law*. Chicago, CC: American Bar Association). This can be explained by the fact that despite their high social status, there are some circumstances (e.g. liquidation) under which heads need to be safeguarded by at least some employment protective measures.

[15] Glazyrin, V. V. 1992. "Predprinimatel'skiy kontrakt [An Entrepreneurial Contract]," *Khozyaystvo i pravo*, No. 7:107-113.

[16] Ogorodov, D. V. and M.Yu. Chelyshev provide a different view: a contract can lay down terms governed by different branches of law (Ogorodov, D. V., and M.Yu. Chelyshev. 2005. "Smeshannye dogovory v chastnom prave: otdel'nye voprosy teorii i praktiki [Mixed Contracts in Private Law: Some Issues of Theory and Practice]," *Zakonodatel'stvo i economika*, No. 10:53).

3. The Conclusion of an Employment Contract with the Head: Terms and Peculiarities

The provisions contained in Chapter 43 LC RF apply to the head of any organization, regardless of the business and ownership, with the exception of two cases, expressly referred to in paragraph 2, Art. 273 LC RF:

- The first exception concerns businesses run by sole proprietors. Given that Russian law does not allow a person to conclude an employment contract as an employer and an employee, it is not possible for a sole proprietor to enter into an employment contract due to the absence of a second party to the contractual relationship. The interpretation provided by a number of labour law scholars and practitioners is that sole proprietors who wish to perform the head's tasks fall outside the scope of chapter 43 LC RF, and are not covered by employment legislation, since they cannot be regarded as performing salaried employment.[17] In this case, in order to run a business, a sole proprietor will need to issue a written document stating that he will act as the sole executive entity.[18] However, some experts in company law believe that an employee-employer relationship originates between the sole proprietor and a running organization if the head performs work in accordance with a written resolution so long as such presumption does not contradict extant legislation.[19] Being that the case, the head can rely on some protective measures laid down in employment law concerning compulsory insurance schemes. Although widely criticized, one might

---

[17] Korshunova, T. Yu. 2007. "Osobennosti regulirovaniya truda rukovoditelya organizacii i chlenov kollegial'nogo ispolnitel'nogo organa organizacii [The Peculiarities of Regulation of Work of the Head of an Organization and Members of the Executive Board]" in *Kommentariy k Trudovomu kodeksu Rossiyskoy Federacii [Commentary on the Labour Code of the Russian Federation]*, ed. Orlovskiy, Yu. P., (Moscow: KONTRAKT, INFRA-M), 359.

[18] Letter No. 2262-6-1 of the Federal Agency on Labour and Employment of 2006; Letter No. 22-2-3199 of the Ministry of Health and Social Development of the Russian Federation of 2009.

[19] Shitkina, I. S. 2011. "Otdel'nye problemy pravovogo regulirovaniya obrazovaniya i deyatel'nosti edinolichnogo ispolnitel'nogo organa" [Some Issues on the Legal Regulation of Formation and Activity of the Sole Executive Body], *Khozyaistvo i pravo*, No. 4:3-17; Dzarasov, M., and D. Ogorodov. 2008. "Trudovoy dogovor s rukovoditelem khozyaystvennogo obschestva, gde on yavlyaetsya edinstvennym uchastnikom [The Employment Contract with the Head Who is the Sole Member of a Running Organization]," in *Korporativniy yurist*, No. 5:38-41.

note that the latter represents the most widespread approach in case law and is also welcome by many institutions at the state level.[20]

- The second exception concerns businesses that are run by another entity or a single entrepreneur upon conclusion of a civil contract. These relations are clearly regulated by civil law and fall outside the scope of employment law. In all other cases, a contract of employment needs to be concluded in writing with the person wishing to serve as a head.

The conclusion of the employment contract with the head features some distinctive traits. This is readily explained by the significance of the head's position and is mainly reflected in the specific criteria of the selection procedures, including certain statutory and qualifying requirements that candidates need to fulfill. In legal terms, the most significant one is that stipulated by the Administrative Code of the Russian Federation of 2001 which *de facto* prohibits those who have been disqualified for repeatedly violating employment legislation from being appointed as the head of an organization (Par. 2, Art. 5.27). Individuals who infringe labour laws and employers who hire a disqualified person commit an administrative offence and can be fined (Art. 14.23).

Unlike statutory requirements, the qualifying ones—e.g. education and work experience—are not prescribed by law but are laid down in the articles of association, local acts[21] or the employment contract. This makes it possible to take into account the specific features of the businesses at the time of establishing them.[22] The company's articles of association may also include provisions on some preliminary procedures which should be dealt with prior to the conclusion of the employment contract with the head, e.g. public competitions, elections or appointments (Par. 2, Article 275 LC RF).

Another feature is the scope to conclude a fixed-term employment contract with the head. As a general rule, open-ended employment

---

[20] For example, it is acknowledged that a female head who is also the sole proprietor is entitled to maternity allowances and parental benefits (Ruling of the Supreme Arbitration Court of the Russian Federation of 2006, No. VAS-6362/09; Letter of the Fund of Social Insurance of the Russian Federation of 2009, No. 02-09/07-2598P).

[21] According to Art. 8 of the LC RF, an organization-employer is allowed within its powers to issue local acts containing employment provisions.

[22] An exception to this general rule concerns the requirement of proper levels of education and work experience laid down in banking legislation in order to safeguard the customers' interests from the activity of inexperienced heads. If a candidate for the post of the head is not in line with the foregoing requirements, the application for the state registration of a bank and its licensing might be rejected (Par. 1, Art. 16 of Banks and Banking Act of 1990).

contracts are to be entered into in Russia. A fixed-term employment contract for a period not exceeding five years is usually concluded when it is not possible to establish employment relations of an indefinite duration due to the nature and conditions of work (Par. 2, Article 58 LC RF). Thus, a fixed-term employment contract is concluded in situations such as the substitution of an absent employee (e.g. for sickness), the performance of temporary work (up to two months), seasonal work, or tasks which go beyond the scope of the main business activity (e.g. reconstruction and installation works). Yet there are a number of cases which are listed in paragraph 2, Article 59 LC RF and include the head of a business where fixed-term employment contracts may be entered into without taking into account the foregoing factors, once the parties have given their consent.[23]

The terms of an employment contract concluded with the head are usually far more detailed than those of ordinary employees. By and large, two kinds of terms can be identified in Russian employment contracts: obligatory *(obyazatel'nye)* terms and additional (*dopolnitel'nye*) terms.

Obligatory terms, as the terminology suggests, must be specified in any employment contract. They are laid down in paragraph 2, Article 57 LC RF and include such elements as the place of work, the job title, the start date, remuneration, working hours, rest periods, and so forth. Besides obligatory terms, the parties can include additional terms to specify their binding nature, provided that these new contractual arrangements do not affect the employees' levels of protection ensured by current employment legislation.

The head's employment contract usually contains several additional terms, which can refer to either traditional[24] or specific issues. Taking into account that the head has unlimited access to confidential information—

---

[23] Voluntary consent is an important aspect. If the tribunal establishes that the head was forced to enter into a fixed-term employment contract, the latter will be converted into an open-ended one (Par. 13 of Decree of the Plenum of the Supreme Court of the Russian Federation of 2004 No. 2).

[24] Probation periods are illustrative of this aspect. The employee's probation period should not have a duration exceeding three months, whereas that of the head can last up to six months, being him regarded as a main figure in corporate governance (Par. 5, Article 70 LC RF). In accordance with Article 71 LC RF, probation periods cannot be included in an employment contract if selection procedures take place before its conclusion. As a result, the scope to include a clause concerning the head's probation period in a contract of employment is patently limited (see Tsindyaikina, E. P., Tsypkina, I. S. 2008. *Trudovoy dogovor: poryadok zaklucheniya, izmeneniya i rastorzheniya [An Employment Contract: Procedure for its Conclusion, Alteration and Termination]*. ed. Gusov, K. N., (Moscow: Prospekt), 72).

the disclosure of which may lead the company to experience substantial losses—his contract of employment usually includes a confidentiality clause prohibiting him from disseminating confidential information. The employment contract may also include a term allowing the head to take up paid jobs for other organizations so long as the head is *a priori* forbidden to combine work in different organizations without the permission of a relevant body (e.g. the board). This seems to be reasonable since holding multiple jobs may result in an increase of the head's working time as well as in a conflict of interests. In addition, the head cannot be appointed as a member of an auditing committee of a running organization (Article 276 LC RF).

4. The Specific Features of the Head's Liability

The special legal status of the head as an atypical employee becomes especially clear when considering liability to disciplinary action and the payment of compensation. As a general rule, employees' liability[25] for damage is limited and is calculated considering their average monthly wage, while heads bear full liability for direct and actual damage to a company[26] (Par. 1, Article 277 LC RF). This difference in assigning one's liability arises from the assumption that the head may cause greater damage to an organization in comparison with other employees. Accordingly, the head is legally obliged to pay damages to an organization even if not specified in his employment contract.[27]

The head and any other employee cannot be held liable when the damage is caused by unforeseeable circumstances, unexpected economic risks, extreme necessity or justifiable defence (Article 239 of the LC RF).

However, in considering the head's liability, the employer can fully or partially waive his right to claim compensation. This right does not depend on the type of business, although sometimes it can be limited by the owner of business assets (Article 240 of the LC RF).

There are also some specific features involving the head's liability to

---

[25] Pursuant to Russian employment law, this is a special form of liability and consists in the obligation on one party to the employment contract to compensate for damage caused to the other through wrongful acts (Art. 419 LC RF).

[26] Federal laws provide cases where compensation on the part of the head refers to both actual loss and loss of profit (Para. 2, Art. 25 of State and Municipal Unitary Enterprises Act of 2002; Para. 2, Art. 71 of Joint Stock Companies Act of 1995; Para. 2, Art. 44 of Limited-Liability Companies Act of 1998).

[27] Paragraph 9 of Decree of the Plenum of the Supreme Court of the Russian Federation of 2006 No. 52.

disciplinary action[28]. As a general rule, the employer has the right—rather than the obligation—to take disciplinary action against an employee if he committed a disciplinary offence. However, in relation to the head, Article 195 LC RF specifies that the employer must start disciplinary action against him in the event of a proven violation of employment laws and (or) provisions of collective agreements which are set out in writing by employee representatives.

5. Grounds to Terminate an Employment Contract with the Head

An employment contract with the head and any other employee can be terminated on different grounds, the general terms of which are laid down in Article 77 of the LC RF. Thus, like any other employee, the head can resign from his position (Point 3, Par. 1, Article 77 LC RF) providing a notice period which is longer than that required of ordinary employees.[29]

Such difference can be explained by the fact that finding a suitable candidate for top-management positions takes longer than filling a vacancy in non-managerial ones. According to Article 280 LC RF, the head has to give at least a 30 days' notice period as against the two weeks' period of notice that needs to be provided by other employees.

An employer might also be willing to terminate the head's employment contract. Yet unlike many foreign countries, an employer in Russia is allowed to dismiss an employee (including the head) on his own initiative only if valid grounds exist as those laid down in Article 81 LC RF, which are either of general or special nature. The latter includes two groups: 1) those concerning special categories of workers, thus including the head (Point 4, Par. 1, Article 81 LC RF; Point 9, Para. 1, Article 81 LC RF; Point 10, Par. 1, Article 81 LC RF) and 2) those applying to the head on an exclusive basis (Article 278 LC RF).

The employment contract with the head, his assistants and the chief accountant can be terminated within three months from the date of the change of ownership, that may take place: 1) by privatization of public and municipally-owned firms; 2) when the assets owned by the business

---

[28] Employees are held liable to disciplinary action in the event of the non-performance or poor performance of a task. There are three disciplinary penalties, established by par. 3, Art. 192 of the LC RF, namely 1) reprimand (*zamechanie*), 2) warning (*vygovor*) and 3) dismissal (*uvol'nenie*). All of these must be given in writing.

[29] The notice period should be provided in writing.

become state-owned; 3) when state-owned assets pass under the control of municipalities and vice versa; 4) when entities of the Russian Federation take over federal organizations and vice versa (Point 4, Par. 1, Article 81 LC RF). Under these circumstances, the head is entitled to compensation amounting to at least three average monthly wages (Article 181 LC RF).

Moreover, an employer can terminate the head's employment contract if the latter makes a groundless decision which results in the loss, the illicit use and damage to the organization and its assets (Point 9, Par. 1, Article 81 LC RF). The expression "groundless decision" is not defined in legislation; the employer assesses on a case-by-case basis if the head's decisions, as well as those made by his assistant and the chief accountant are groundless.

A contract of employment can also be ended in case of a one-off gross breach on the part of the head (Point 10, Par. 1, Article 81 LC RF). As with "groundless decision", the expression "gross breach" is not legally determined. If a legal dispute arises, the courts will decide case by case whether or not the violation is gross. The burden of proof that a breach took place lies with the employer. In general, the courts consider as gross those violations affecting employee health and safety or damaging the business and its assets.[30]

Particular grounds for terminating the head's employment contract are established by Article 278 LC RF. Consequently, an employment contract concluded with the head of an organization/insolvent institution may be terminated if he is removed from office in accordance with bankruptcy law (Point 1, Par. 1, Article 278 LC RF). The provisions of the 2002 Bankruptcy Act make it possible to remove the head from his office during two stages of insolvency proceedings, namely supervision (*nablyudenie*) and economic recovery (*finansovoe ozdorovlenie*).[31] During supervision, the interim administrator (*vneshniy upravlyayushchiy*) can submit a motion to an arbitration tribunal asking for the head's dismissal on the grounds of non-compliance with the provisions laid down in the 2002 Bankruptcy Act. If the motion is passed, the arbitration court rules that the head resigns from his position.

Point 2, Par. 1, Article 278 LC RF allows a body authorized by the business owner, the owner of the organization' assets, or the person/body empowered by the organization, to terminate the head's employer contract.

---

[30] Par. 49 of the Decree of 17 March 2004 No. 2.

[31] The Bankruptcy Act provides for five stages of insolvency proceedings: 1) supervision (*nablyudenie*); 2) economic recovery (*finansovoe ozdorovlenie*); 3) external monitoring (*vneshnee upravlenie*); 4) liquidation (*konkursnoe proizvodstvo*) and 5) comprehensive agreement (*mirovoe soglashenie*).

These entities are not obliged to motivate their decision, meaning that they do not need to provide facts justifying the dismissal. The practice to dismiss the head of the organization without providing any reasons is widespread worldwide, although in Russia its lawfulness is still under discussion. In 2005, the Constitutional Court of the Russian Federation issued a decree, the aim of which was to clarify this aspect.[32] On that occasion, the Constitutional Court concluded that lawmakers can establish special rules concerning the head's termination of employment, because his legal status is substantially different from that of other employees. In the opinion of the Court, the introduction of this dismissal procedure as laid down in point 2, paragraph 1, Article 278 LC RF is explained by the fact that, under certain circumstances, it is necessary to terminate the employment contract with the head to safeguard the owner's rights and legitimate his interests. For example, terminating a contract may be essential in the event of a change in the organization's development strategy or in order to increase management effectiveness. Yet the right to terminate an employment contract without a reason does not limit the head's right to take steps against possible arbitrary and discriminatory practices. If the head thinks his dismissal took place on discriminatory grounds, he can challenge it before the courts, which can rule in favour of his reinstatement.

Moreover, the scope for terminating an employment contract without just cause presupposes certain protective measures intended to strike a balance between the interests of the head as an employee and those of the company as an employer. One such measure is a ban on the termination of an employment contract during the head's temporary incapacity for work or when he is on leave, as laid down in paragraph 6, Article 81 LC RF.

Although such protective measure is not directly related to the termination of the employment relationship with the head of an organization, by virtue of point 2, paragraph 1, Article 278 of the LC RF, the Plenum of the Supreme Court of the Russian Federation concluded that it is also possible to apply the provisions of paragraph 6, Article 81 LC

[32] The Decree of the Constitutional Court of the Russian Federation of 15 March 2005 No. 3-P On Examination the Constitutionality of Point 2, Art. 278 and Art. 279 of the Labour Code of the Russian Federation and Indent 2, Point 4, Art. 69 of the Federal Law On Joint Stock Companies… (*Postanovlenie Konstitutsionnogo Suda Rossiyskoy Federatsii "Po Delu o Proverke Konstitutsionnosti Polozheniy Punkta 2 Stat'i 278 i Stat'i 279 Trudovogo Kodeksa Rossiyskoy Federatsii i Abzatsa Vtorogo Punkta 4 Stat'i 69 Federal'nogo Zakona "Ob Aktsionernykh Obshchestvakh"*…), published in the Collection of Laws of the Russian Federation, 2005, No. 13, Cl. 1209 ("Decree of 15 March 2005 No. 3-P").

RF[33] to this group of employees.[34]

Another initiative is the establishment of minimum compensation to be paid in case of termination of an employment contract pursuant to point 2, paragraph 1, Article 278 LC RF. According to Article 279 LC RF, in the absence of any *actus reus* (culpable action) on the part of the head, the amount of compensation—which should be at least equal to three average monthly wages—is determined by the terms of the employment contract.

Additional safeguards may be provided in the employment contract. For example, pursuant to point 2, paragraph 1, Article 278 LC RF, it is possible to include a clause relating to the notice period establishing compensation regardless of the reasons for terminating the employment contract.

In accordance with point 3, paragraph 1, Article 278 LC RF, termination can also take place on other grounds, which are specified in the employment contract concluded with the head. In practice, such obligations as to achieve certain financial and economic results, to set up production sites, or to realize different projects are frequently included in the contract of employment. Accordingly, failing to fulfil these obligations might cause the head to be dismissed. However, if the fulfilment of these obligations was unrealizable due to unforeseeable circumstances, the courts may rule that the dismissal is unfair.

Conclusion

To conclude, one can argue that the head of the organization in Russia is considered as an employee who, although his high social status, needs to and can rely on at least some of the protective measures provided by employment law. Yet the particular role of the head in corporate governance and the ability to influence decision-making in the organization cause this position to be regulated in a way which is different from that of other employees. His peculiar legal status as an atypical worker is evident, especially in those provisions concerning the conclusion and the termination of the employment contract, as well as the establishment of his liability to disciplinary action and compensation.

---

[33] The provisions provide a general ban on the termination of the employment contract at the employer's initiative when the employee experiences a temporary incapacity for work or when he is on leave (save for cases of liquidation of the organization or discontinuance of the economic activity on the part of a private entrepreneur).

[34] Para. 50 of the Decree of 17 March 2004 No. 2.

References

Berkowitz, P. M., T. Müller-Bonanni, and A. E. Reitz. 2008. *International Labor and Employment Law*. Chicago, CC: American Bar Association.

Bondarenko, E. N. 2004. *Osnovaniya vozniknoveniya trudovykh pravootnosheniy [The Grounds of Origin of Legal Employer-Employee Relationships]*. Moscow: Yuridicheskiy centr Press.

Boychenko, T. A., and E. R. Martirosyan. 2004. *Problemy trudovogo prava: prava i obyazannosti rabotodatelya [The Issues of Employment Law: the Rights and Duties of an Employer]*. Novosibirsk: Novosibirsk.

Chessell, M. 1996. "Sovet direktorov korporacii: kontrol' cherez predstavitel'stvo [The Board of a Corporation: Control through Representation]," in *Corporate governance: Owners, Directors and Employees of Joint-Stock Companies (Korporativnoe upravlenie. Vladel'tsy, direktora i naemnye rabotniki akcionernogo obschestva)*, ed. Chessell, M., (Moscow: John Wiley and Sons), 58-104.

Decree of the Constitutional Court of the Russian Federation of 15 March 2005 No. 3-P On Examination the Constitutionality of Point 2, Art. 278 and Art. 279 of the Labour Code of the Russian Federation and Indent 2, Point 4, Art. 69 of Joint Stock Companies Act… (Postanovlenie Konstitutsionnogo Suda Rossiyskoy Federatsii "Po Delu o Proverke Konstitutsionnosti Polozheniy Punkta 2 Stat'i 278 i Stat'i 279 Trudovogo Kodeksa Rossiyskoy Federatsii i Abzatsa Vtorogo Punkta 4 Stat'i 69 Federal'nogo Zakona "Ob Aktsionernykh Obshchestvakh"…), Collection of Laws of the Russian Federation, 2005, No. 13, Cl. 1209.

Decree of the Plenum of the Supreme Court of the Russian Federation of 17 March 2004 No. 2 "On the Application of the Labour Code of the Russian Federation by Courts of the Russian Federation" (Postanovlenie Plenuma Verkhovnogo Suda Rossiyskoy Federatsii "O primenenii sudami Rossiyskoy Federatsii Trudovogo Kodeksa Rossiyskoy Federatsii"), Bulletin of the Supreme Court of the Russian Federation, 2007, No. 3.

Decree of the Plenum of the Supreme Court of the Russian Federation of 16 November 2006 No. 52 On the Application by the Courts of Legislation Regulating Material Liability of Employees for Damage, Caused to an Employer (Postanovlenie Plenuma Verkhovnogo Suda Rossiyskoy Federatsii "O Primenenii Sudami Zakonodatel'stva, Reguliruyushchego Material'nuyu Otvetstvennost' Rabotnikov za Ushcherb, Prichinennyy Rabotodatelyu"), Bulletin of the Supreme

Court of the Russian Federation, 2007, No. 1.

Dzarasov, M., and D. Ogorodov. 2008. "Trudovoy dogovor s rukovoditelem khozyaystvennogo obschestva, gde on yavlyaetsya edinstvennym uchastnikom [The Employment Contract with the Head Who is the Sole Member of a Running Organization]," in *Korporativniy yurist*, No. 5:38-41.

Glazyrin, V. V. 1992. "Predprinimatel'skiy kontrakt [An Entrepreneurial Contract]," *Khozyaystvo i pravo*, No. 7:107-113.

Goryachev, A. S. 2005. *Pravovoe polozhenie rukovoditelya kommercheskoy organizatsii [The Legal Position of the Head of a Profit-Making Organization],* Phd thesis retrieved from the Digital Dissertation Library of the Russian State Library.

Korshunova, T. Yu. 2004. "Osobennosti regulirovaniya truda otdel'nykh kategoriy rabotnikov [The Peculiarities of Regulation of Labour of Certain Categories of Employees], *Trudovoe pravo*, No. 6:25-32.

—. 2007. *"Osobennosti regulirovaniya truda rukovoditelya organizacii i chlenov kollegial'nogo ispolnitel'nogo organa organizacii"* [The Peculiarities of Regulation of Work of the Head of an Organization and Members of its Executive Board] in *Kommentariy k Trudovomu kodeksu Rossiyskoy Federacii* [Commentary on the Labour Code of the Russian Federation], ed. Orlovskiy, Yu.P., (Moscow: KONTRAKT, INFRA-M).

Letter of the Federal Agency on Labour and Employment of 28 December 2006 No. 2262-6-1 (Pis'mo Federal'noi Sluzhby po Trudu i Zanyatosti), Normative Acts for an Accountant, 2007, No. 2.

Letter of the Fund of Social Insurance of the Russian Federation of 21 December 2009 No. 02-09/07-2598P (Pis'mo Fonda Sotsial'nogo Strakhovaniya Rossiyskoy Federatsii), Official Documents (weekly appendix to the newspaper "Accounting, Taxes and Law"), 2010, No. 15.

Letter of the Ministry of Health and Social Development of the Russian Federation of 18 August 2009 No. 22-2-3199 (Pis'mo Ministerstva Zdravoohraneniya i Sotsial'nogo Razvitiya Rossiyskoy Federatsii) (unpublished).

McGee, R. W. ed. 2008. *Corporate Governance in Transition Economies.* New York, NY: Springer.

Ogorodov, D. V., and M. Yu. Chelyshev. 2005. "Smeshannye dogovory v chastnom prave: otdel'nye voprosy teorii i praktiki [Mixed Contracts in Private Law: SomeI of Theory and Practice], *Zakonodatel'stvo i economika*, No. 10:50-53.

Ruling of the Supreme Arbitration Court of the Russian Federation of 5

June 2006 No. VAS-6362/09 (Opredelenie Vysshego Arbitrazhnogo Suda Rossiyskoy Federatsii) (unpublished).

Shitkina, I. S. 2011. "Otdel'nye problemy pravovogo regulirovaniya obrazovaniya i deyatel'nosti edinolichnogo ispolnitel'nogo organa [Some Issues of the Legal Regulation of Formation and Activity of the Sole Executive Body], *Khozyaistvo i pravo*, No. 4:3-17.

Tricker, B. 2009. *Corporate Governance: Principles, Policies, and Practices*. New York, NY: Oxford University Press.

Tsepov, G. V. 2006. *Akcionernye obschestva: Teoriya i praktika [Joint- Stock Companies: Theory and Practice]*. Moscow: TK Velbi.

Tsindyaikina, E. P., and I. S. Tsypkina. 2008. *Trudovoy dogovor: poryadok zakluchеniya, izmeneniya i rastorzheniya [An Employment Contract: Procedure for its Conclusion, Alteration and Termination]*, ed. Gusov,K. N., (Moscow: Prospekt).

Zamorduev, D. G. 2005. *Rukovoditel' Organizatsii kak Spetsial'nyy Sub"ekt Trudovogo Prava [The Head of an Organization as a Special Subject of Employment Law]*, Phd thesis retrieved from the Digital Dissertation Library of the Russian State Library of the Russian State Library.

Constitutional Court of the Russian Federation Act of 21 July 1994 No. 1-FKZ (Federal'nyy Konstitutsionnyy Zakon "O Konstitutsionnom Sude Rossiyskoy Federatsii"), Collection of Laws of the Russian Federation, 1994, No. 13, Cl. 1447.

Cooperatives Act of 26 May 1988 No. 8998-XI (Law of the Union of Soviet Socialist Republics "O Kooperacii v SSSR"), Bulletin of the Supreme Council of the Union of Soviet Socialist Republics, 1988, No. 22, Cl. 355.

Banks and Banking Act of 2 December 1990 No. 395-1 (O Bankakh i Bankovskoy Deyatel'nosti), Collection of Laws of the Russian Federation, 1996, No. 6, Cl. 492; 2013, No. 27, Cl. 3438.

Enterprises and Entrepreneurship Act of 27 December 1990 No. 445-1 (Law of the Russian Soviet Federated Socialist Republic "O Predpriyatiyakh i Predprinimatel'skoy Deyatel'nosti"), Bulletin of the Council of People's Deputies and the Supreme Council of the Russian Soviet Federative Socialist Republic, 1990, No. 30, Cl. 418.

Civil Code of the Russian Federation of 30 November 1994 (Grazhdanskiy kodeks Rossiyskoy Federatsii (chast' pervaya)), Collection of Laws of the Russian Federation, 1994, No. 32, Cl. 3301.

Joint-Stock Companies Act of 26 December 1995 No. 208-FZ (Federal'nyy Zakon "Ob Aktsionernych Obshchestvakh"), Collection of Laws of the Russian Federation, 1996, No. 1, Cl. 1.

Limited-Liability Companies Act of 8 February 1998 No. 14-FZ (Federal'nyy Zakon "Ob Obshchestvakh s Ogranichennoi Otvetstvennost'yu"), Collection of Laws of the Russian Federation, 1998, No. 7, Cl. 785.

Administrative Code of the Russian Federation of 30 December 2001 (Kodeks Rossiyskoy Federatsii ob Administrativnykh Pravonarusheniyakh), Collection of Laws of the Russian Federation, 2002, No. 1 (p. 1), Cl. 1.

Labour Code of the Russian Federation of 30 December 2001 (Trudovoi Kodeks Rossiyskoy Federatsii), Collection of Laws of the Russian Federation, 2002, No. 1 (p. 1), Cl. 3.

Insolvency (Bankruptcy) Act. of 26 October 2002 No. 127-FZ On (Federal'nyy Zakon "O Nesosotoyatel'nosti (Bankrotstve)" Collection of Laws of the Russian Federation, 2002, No. 43, Cl. 4190.

State and Municipal Unitary Enterprises Act of 14 November 2002 No. 161-FZ (Federal'nnyy Zakon "O Gosudarstvennykh i Munitsipal'nykh Unitarnykh Predpriyatiyakh"), Collection of Laws of the Russian Federation, 2002, No. 48, Cl. 4746.

TRANSNATIONAL EMPLOYMENT RELATIONS FROM A LEGAL SCHOLAR'S VIEWPOINT: TERMINOLOGICAL AND TAXONOMIC ISSUES

DARIA CHERNYAEVA

"[...] Juliet: What's in a name? That which we call a rose
By any other name would smell as sweet"
—Romeo and Juliet (II, ii, 1-2)

This paper offers an outline of the perception of "transnational employment relations"[1] in a legal context. It will analyse various doctrinal and legislative approaches to the definition of the phenomenon, as well as the usage of the terms employed in its naming, its key characteristics and classifications. The author will reveal and explore the reasons for the problems that arise in the interpretation and legal regulation of the phenomenon, and will suggest some possible solutions to them.

The paper will analyse several terminological aspects of the terms used in descriptions of and references to employment relations which could be seen as falling under more than one legal order (jurisdiction). The paper will also aim to prove the hypothesis that, from a legal point of view, a transnational employment relation can be described (and differentiated from a regular "national" employment relation) through the presence of elements in which "transnationality" manifests itself and the number of such elements in a particular relationship. From this viewpoint, we can divide all transnational employment relations into two groups according to whether the "transnationality" of its elements is connected with one (simple relationship) or more (complex relationship) countries (legal orders) except the observer's country (legal order).

[1] The term "transnational employment relations" in the title and the opening parts of the paper merely serves as a starting point for the study and a time/space saver to make references more compact. It should not be seen as an ideal or recommended naming of the phenomenon in question.

1. The Naming Problem Iceberg

The naming of the phenomenon of "transnational employment relations" is doubly controversial due to the fact that it combines two already ambiguous terms: "transnational" (which might sometimes be substituted for "international", "transborder"/cross-border, "inter-jurisdictional", etc.) and "employment relations" (which do have a precise meaning in the majority of national legal sources and even a recommended interpretation on an international level,[2] but may still be defined somewhat differently in different countries). While the lack of consistency in the definitions of the first part of the term (transnational) has enjoyed some scholarly attention, the problems which the second part of the term (employment relations) gives rise to are almost never discussed in such a context where two or more legal orders are involved. I therefore compare this terminology issue with an iceberg which has a clearly visible part (i.e. that which has been much discussed) while the bigger part of the problem remains hidden as it is rarely addressed either in doctrine or in research.

Due to publication constraints and in an attempt to control the level of both verbosity and abstraction, this paper will address only the first of the aforementioned aspects, i.e. those relating to the issue of "transnationality". I hope to continue this study and move on to the second part of the "iceberg" in other paper(s).

1.1. The Transnational Nature of Employment Relations: A Doctrinal Discussion

The term "transnational" dates back to Jeremy Bentham's understanding of "international law" (or, to be more precise, "international jurisprudence"), as dealing with the "conduct… [of] members of different states".[3] This understanding takes into account only the specifics of the parties ("subjects") of the relationship (i.e. its "subjective" aspect) but demonstrates no awareness of the possibility that its other aspects (i.e. object[s],[4] facts crucial to the definition of its nature or its procedural peculiarities), might have a similarly "international" character.

---

[2] See ILO Recommendation No. 198 concerning employment relationship (2006).

[3] Bentham, J. 1939. *An Introduction to the Principles of Morals and Legislation.* Hayes Barton Press, 276.

[4] It is widely known though that in his later works Bentham also addressed this issue. See Bentham, J. 1838-1843. "Principles of International Law," in *The Works of Jeremy Bentham*, ed. Bentham, J. (Edinburgh: William Tait. Vol. 2).

Nowadays legal scholars, being more experienced in dealing with various transnational legal issues, tend to include most of the other aspects of the relationship in its definition and description. W.W. Park, for example, states that "…characterization of a transaction as international or domestic might be made according to two principal criteria: the nature of a transaction or the parties' residence",[5] thus embracing both objective and subjective aspects of the phenomenon in question.

B. Hepple goes further by implicitly distinguishing "substantive" from "procedural" aspects and explaining "internationality" ("transnationality") in the context of labour disputes using a number of criteria. Amongst these criteria he names three which can be attributed to "substantive law" — a place of work that may be other than the place of the contracting parties' residence (objective criterion), the nationality, place of business or place of residence of the parties (subjective criteria), and two that can be attributed to "procedural law" — whether a domestic court applies foreign law (objective criterion) and whether it recognizes the jurisdiction of a foreign court (subjective criterion).[6] He also writes that "…the word "international" may be used to mark the distinction between the resolution of disputes that are truly national and those which, in some way, cross national boundaries, i.e., are transnational",[7] and warns readers against mixing up these issues of purely private international law (conflict of laws) nature with issues belonging to public international law.

However, these are rare examples of this terminology being addressed specifically in scholarly writings. Legal scholars (in Russia as well as abroad) demonstrate either unawareness of or indifference to the abundance of terms used in references to and/or in descriptions of the phenomenon of transnational employment relations.[8] There seems to be a widespread trend of referring to such relations with the most popular term

---

[5] Park, W. W. 2001. "Why Courts Review Arbitral Awards," *International Arbitration Reports* No. 16:27.

[6] Hepple, B. 2003. "Mapping International Labor Disputes: An Overview," in *Labor Law Beyond Borders: ADR and the Internationalization of Labor Disputes*, ed. The International Bureau of the Permanent Court of Arbitration (Kluwer Law International), 45.

[7] *Ibid.*

[8] Bisom-Rapp, S. "Exceeding Our Boundaries: Transnational Employment Law Practice and the Export of American Lawyering Styles to the Global Worksite," TJSL Public Law Research Paper No. 04-9 (note 3, at 2). Available at SSRN: http://papers.ssrn.com/sol3/papers.cfm?abstract_id=590942 (accessed 2 February 2014). Dowling Jr., D. C. 2001. "The Practice of International Labor & Employment Law: Escort Your Labor/Employment Clients into the Global Millennium," *The Labor Lawyer* 17:1-23; etc.

"international",[9] carrying the meaning Bentham defined almost two centuries ago (i.e. relations taking place between representatives of different nations, on an "inter-national" level). Contrary to their usual attentiveness to terminology issues, modern labour law scholars almost never go deep into the substantiation of this choice as if the term was comprehensible without any special explanations. This approach is justified to some extent because the naming "international employment relation" is one of the oldest among those applied to the phenomenon[10] and seems to be used as a generally recognized term. When the context is clear it rarely causes interpretational problems, especially among lawyers and scholars dealing with such relations on a regular basis.

However, when the context is not sufficiently clear and/or contains consonant terms that have another meaning, the naming "international

---

[9] Grušić, U. 2012. *The International Employment Contract: Ideal, Reality and Regulatory Function of European Private International Law of Employment*. A thesis submitted to the Department of Law of the London School of Economics for the Degree of Doctor of Philosophy, September 2012. London: London School of Economics. Available online: http://etheses.lse.ac.uk/583/1/Grusic_International_Employment_Contract_2012.pdf (accessed 2 February 2014); Colvin, A., and O. Darbishire, 2012. "International Employment Relations: The Impact of Varieties of Capitalism," in *Handbook of Research in International Human Resource Management*, eds. Stahl, G. K., Björkman, I., Morris, S. (Cheltenham: Edward Elgar Publishing); Bamber, G. J., and R. D. Lansbury, eds. 2010. *International and Comparative Employment Relations*. London: SAGE Publications; Morgenstern, F. 1984. *International Conflicts of Labour Law: A Survey of the Law Applicable to the International Employment Relation*. Geneva: International Labour Organization; see also in Russian: Shesteryakova, I. V. 2007. *Kollizionnye Normy i Mejdunarodnye Trudovye Otnosheniya [Conflict Rules and International Employment Relations]*. Saratov: SGAP; Kiselev, I. Ya. 2003. *Trud s Inostrannym Uchastiem: Pravovye Aspekty [Labour with Foreign Participation: Legal Aspects]*. Moscow: MCFER, 7-8; Dovgert, A. S. 1992. *Pravovoe Regulirovanie Mejdunatodnyh Trudvyh otnosheniy [Legal Regulation of International Employment Relations]*. Kiev: UMK VO.

[10] I managed to track it back to the 1960s (see Szászy, I. 1968. *International Labour Law: A Comparative Survey of the Conflict Rules Affecting Labour Legislation and Regulations*. Leyden: A. W. Sijthoff [translated from Hungarian]), though national scholarship written in languages other than English may contain older sources (see references to Gamillscheg, F. 1959. *Internationales Arbeitsrecht*. Berlin: Mohr Siebeck made in Birk, R. 1985. *Review: International Conflicts of Labour Law: A Survey of the Law Applicable to the International Employment Relation*. Morgenstern. F. *The American Journal of International Law* 79-4: 1120-1123 (at 1121).

employment relations" can lead to unwelcome confusion.[11] The main problem lies in the fact that the word "international" is polysemic and its meaning can vary according to the context in which it is used.

According to popular dictionaries, the word "international" generally has at least two principal meanings, and, to worsen the situation, the lists of meanings differ slightly between dictionaries of the same language[12] and between the languages themselves[13]. There are therefore reasons to believe that the problem with a uniform interpretation of this term exists in many languages.[14]

An analysis of the definitions given to the term "international" in some of the most popular explanatory dictionaries of various languages shows that, when used as an adjective, it may take on at least five meanings which can be classed into two, albeit disproportionate, groups:

1. a "between" group:
    1.1. general: occurring/existing/carried out between several nations;
    1.2. active:
        1.2.1. indirectly active: agreed on/sanctioned by several nations (for which there must necessarily be communication *between* them, they must be actively involved);
        1.2.2. directly active: used or available/intended for being used by several nations (people belonging to several nations);
    1.3. passive: affecting/related to several nations (as a result of which they may have something in common; they become passively involved);
2. a "beyond" group:

[11] See Dowling Jr., D. C. 2001. *Ibid.*, 3.

[12] See *Oxford Dictionary of English*. 2010. Oxford: Oxford University Press; *Merriam-Webster Online Dictionary & Thesaurus,* URL: http://www.merriam-webster.com/dictionary/international; *Collins Online Dictionary,* URL: http://www.collinsdictionary.com; etc.

[13] Compare with respective articles in Russian (Ushakov, D. N. 1937. *Orfographic Dictionary* Moscow: Uchpedgiz. Also available online, at http://ushakovdictionary.ru; Ojegov, S. I., and N. Yu Shvedova. 1999. *Explanatory Dictionary of the Russian Language*. Moscow: Azbukovnik; Kuznetzov, S. A., ed. 2000. *Comprehensive Explanatory Dictionary of Russian*. SPb: Norint), German (*DWDS Project—Digitalen Lexikalischen Systems der Berlin-Brandenburgischen Akademie der Wissenschaften*, URL: http://www.dwds.de), Spanish (*Diccionario de la lengua española* (*DRAE*) *es la obra de referencia de la Real Academia Española*, URL: http://www.rae.es/recursos/diccionarios/drae) and other dictionaries of other languages.

[14] Collier, J. G. 2001. *Conflict of Laws*. Cambridge: Cambridge University Press, 8.

2.1. effective beyond/reaching beyond/coming out of the national boundaries (borders of a particular country).

These lexical interpretations may also be classified in another way according to whether they focus on the subjective or the objective aspect of an issue in question:

1. the "subjective" interpretation is used to emphasize that the term "international" aims to be applicable/accessible to several nations so they must necessarily express their will and may even take part in its implementation; examples of this usage include "international organization" (the primary idea of which is to institutionalize and facilitate cooperation between several nations at either a governmental or non-governmental level), "international agreement" (which is wilfully concluded between several nations, often and traditionally (though not necessarily) represented by their official public authorities), "international public/private law" (which emphasizes that the particular branch of law focuses on the regulation of relationships between members of several nations representing their nations on either a public or private level), etc.; we can see that this interpretation is closer to the "between" meaning of the term;
2. the "objective" interpretation is used to emphasize that the term "international" aims to be applicable to several nations irrespective of their will and viewpoints; it is intended to be used in regard to several nations, but this aim may not necessarily be achieved; examples of such usage include "international passport" (which is supposed to be valid in several national territories but in calling it that we do not focus on whether any particular nation consider it valid on its territory), "international review" (which aims to cover several nations regardless of their consent and generally with no particular interest in their active and/or official participation), "international law" (when used as a general term and an antithesis to "national law" without going into details of its subjects, their will and nature), etc.; we can see that this interpretation is close to the "beyond" meaning of the term.

Further analysis may succeed in finding other (perhaps better) classifications. However, we can already see from the analysis shown above that the term is not only polysemicc, but that its polysemy may be interpreted or described in different ways. If we add to this the complexity of legal language itself, the picture becomes truly complete.

Now after the intricacy of the problem has been demonstrated, let us compare two notions which both contain the term "international":

- "international regulation of employment relations";

- "regulation of international employment relations".

In my experience even highly professional lawyers and legal scholars cannot always explain the difference between the two immediately after hearing them or seeing them written (for instance, in a conference agenda or in a master's program curriculum etc.). When one is given sufficient time to read/listen more carefully and attentively, (s)he understands that the first term reflects the first of the above-mentioned interpretations and involves only international legal norms (those established by international agreements, etc.) applied to any employment relation in general, while the second term demonstrates an example of the second interpretation and embraces all norms (both national and international, public and private) applied to the phenomenon. This example aims to show that confusion is almost inevitable when such terms are used side by side (a situation that occurs fairly often in the context of research and teaching in certain fields).

This difficulty in differentiation obviously does not favour a wider usage of "international employment relations" as a general term for the phenomenon of "transnational employment relations". However, we may recall the case of two similarly problematic consonant terms, "contract of service" and "contract for services" (acknowledged since the Romans)[15] which are still used side by side and still produce much confusion in everyday practice and sometimes even in courts.[16]

However, despite all the problems described, the above mentioned naming seems to be one of the most acceptable in terms of ease of interpretation in a particular context. All the other labels for the relations based on transnational labour are at least no less problematic.

If, for example, we took the term "transborder" (or "cross-border") to name the phenomenon (thus obtaining "transborder/cross-border employment relations"), we would have to further specify whether we mean internal borders between the federal subjects, regions or territories of a country or its external borders with other countries. This necessity would almost inevitably lead us to complementing the initial expression with the word "international" and finding ourselves back with all the problems listed above which this term brings about. However, if we refuse to do that, the term "transborder" ("cross-border") may cause misunderstanding in the case of a federative state (such as Russia, Germany or the USA) and

[15] Sohm, R. 1892. *Institutes of Roman Law*. Oxford: Clarendon Press, 311; McDonell, J. 1904. Classification of Forms and Contracts of Labour. *Journal of the Society of Comparative Legislation. New Series* 5-2: 253-261, at 255-256; etc.

[16] Freedland, M. 2003. *The Personal Employment Contract*. Oxford: Oxford University Press.

of a state with considerable political and/or legislative autonomy of its regions (like Spain or the UK). Therefore, in any case this term seems more suitable for another context in which the aim is to emphasize that we wish to differentiate and compare the two types of "transborderness" (intra-country and extra-country). At the same time, it remains inappropriate both as a single general term for the phenomenon we are discussing in this paper and as a name for any "international" (extra-country) relations. Further refinement of the term does not help a great deal as by resolving some problems it causes others. However, the term "cross-border employment relation(ship)" is found in labour law scholarship published in English.[17] Russian scholarship seems to be blessed with using it very seldom.[18]

As well as sharing the same problem of "borders" with the aforementioned tern, the term "inter-jurisdictional" (which also requires clarification of whether the word "jurisdiction" in this context represents a "territorial" or an "objective" jurisdiction and, should it be used in the territorial sense, whether the involved jurisdictions are of different regions within one country or of different countries), relates mostly to dispute resolution and procedural aspects, and thus cannot serve as a general term for the phenomenon. It is no surprise that this term is more widespread in private international law scholarship[19] where dispute solving and procedural issues play a significant role. Labour law scholars and students

---

[17] Evju, S., and T. Novitz. 2012. "The Evolving Regulation: Dynamics and Consequences," *Formula Working Paper No. 33*. Available online: http://www.jus.uio.no/ifp/english/research/projects/freemov/publications/papers/2012/WP33-Evju-Novitz.pdf (accessed 2 February 2014); Lazar, W. 2008. "Employment Agreements and Cross Border Employment: Confidentiality, Trade Secret, and Other Restrictive Covenants in a Global Economy," *Labor Lawyer,* 24-2: 195-211; Royle, T. 2006. "The Dominance Effect? Multinational Corporations in the Italian Quick-food Service Sector," *British Journal of Industrial Relations* 44-4: 757-779; etc.

[18] Dmitrieva, G. K., ed. 2010. *Mejdunarodnoe Chastnoe Pravo [Private International Law]*. Moscow: Prospekt.

[19] See MacDonald, K. 2009. *Cross-Border Litigation: Inter-jurisdictional Practice and Procedure* [e-book]. Canada Law Book; Available from: Bibliotheksverbund Bayern, Ipswich, MA (accessed 4 February 2014); Buxbaum, H. L. 2009. "Competition in the Private Enforcement of regulatory Law," in *Economic Law as an Economic Good: Its Rule Function and Its Tool Function in the Competition of Systems,* eds. Messen, K. M., M. Bungenberg and A. Puttler (Munich: Sellier European Law Publishers), 129-136; Chernichenko, O. S. 2003. *International Legal Aspects of the Jurisdiction of States*. PhD thesis. Moscow: Diplomatic Academy of the Foreign Ministry of the Russian Federation; etc.

may experience difficulties in the application of this term as there are almost no examples of its usage in either doctrine or practice in their field of specialization.

It is also mostly private international law scholars who argue that the phenomenon should be called "employment relations with a foreign element".[20] This term can be used either alone or with other labels.[21]

The specifics of the works using this wording backs the hypothesis that it has been borrowed from foreign (not Russian) private international law scholarship through works published in Russian (either in the original language or translated).[22] I assume that this wording may seem attractive because it allows one to avoid the confusing "international" sphere and to move towards the less problematic "foreign" one, which generally requires nothing more than a particular reference point. However, although this approach solves one problem it produces a further two.

Firstly, the term "foreign element" is problematic in itself. Inasmuch as the Russian labour law scholars see this term as somewhat alien and rarely make use of it in their papers, it was, again, private international law scholars, who formulated the main interpretation of this term in the Russian legal scholarship.[23] This interpretation follows a traditional

---

[20] Merrett, L. 2011. *Employment Contracts in Private International Law*. Oxford: Oxford University Press, 2; Morgenstern, F. 1984, *op. cit*; Belogubova, O. V. 2013. Koliziyni-pravove regulyuvannya trudovyh vidnosyn, uskladnenyh inozemnym elementom, v mijdunarodnomu sudnoplavstvi [Conflict Legal Regulation of Employment Relations Complicated by Foreign Element in International Shipping]", *Aktualni Problemy Polityky*, 50:120-130; Protasova, A. S. 2011. Коллизионное регулирование трудовых отношений, осложненных иностранным элементом: проблемы и перспективы [Conflict Regulation of Labour Relations Complicated by a Foreign Element: Problems and Perspectives]. *Vestnik Buryatskogo Universiteta*, 2: 224-227; Spektor, A. A. 2004. *Trudovye Otnosheniya, Oslojnennye Inostrannym Elementom, Kak Object Mejdunarodnogo Chastnogo Prava (Employment Relations Complicated by a Foreign Element as an Object of Private International Law)*. PhD thesis. Moscow: RGTEU; etc.

[21] Kiselev, I. Ya. 2003, *op. cit*.

[22] See Boguslavskiy, M. M. 1988. *Private International Law: A Soviet Approach*. Dordrecht: Martinus Nijhoff Publishers, 11-12; Luntz, L. A. 1973. *Kurs Mejdunarodnogo Chastnogo Prava [Course of Private International Law]*. Moscow: Yuridicheskaya Literatura, 140-170 (an analysis of foreign private international law doctrines, their interrelation and their influence on the pre-Soviet and the Soviet Russian private international law scholarship); Erpylyova, N. Yu. 2012 *Mejdunarodnoe Chastnoe Pravo [Private International Law]*. Moscow: Jurait, 26-30 (an analysis of existing studies of this notion in Russian scholarship).

[23] Erpylyova N. Yu. 2005. *Mejdunarodnoe Chastnoe Pravo [Private International Law]*. Moscow: Prospekt, 7-10, 25-29; Kolobov, R. Yu. 2006. *Osnovy Postroeniya*

private international law understanding according to which, in brief, the object of this branch of law is formed of relations, which include a "foreign element".[24] Labelling the discussed phenomenon as a subcategory of such relations, scholars apply this general interpretation to it and furnish it with the same distinctive, "foreign", element.

This approach has been criticized by A.A. Rubanov[25] who pointed out that the so-called "foreign element", while being apparent to many scholars, is not actually an element of a relationship at all, and should instead be considered more a characteristic of certain elements of a relationship, i.e. of its subjects (employer and employee) or its object (work/labour). Russian labour law scholars tend to support Rubanov's view, stating that the "foreign element" as it is described by its proponents cannot be found in a number of the relations in question.[26] They therefore abstain from using expressions that include "foreign element" at all or at least as a single name, and try to find other wordings to name the phenomenon, such as "employment relations with foreign participation".

Rubanov's approach does indeed solve many of the previously mentioned problems and, in my opinion, deserves serious consideration and wider application. This all the more so because, among other merits, it can be adapted to differentiate between the "foreign" and "international" nature of the described characteristic, and to attribute the latter to either a public field (e.g. international public service) or a private field (e.g. work for private transnational corporations) depending on the level at which the relations are established. The main disadvantage of calling the phenomenon an "employment relation having elements with foreign characteristics" is its complexity which almost destines it to remain known

---

i Funktzionirovaniya Mejdunatodnogo Chastnogo Prava [Foundations of Private International Law Building and Functioning]. PhD thesis. Irkutsk: IrkGU, 2006; Zvekov, V. P. 2004 *Mejdunarodnoe Chastnoe Pravo [Private International Law]*. Moscow: Jurist; Boguslavskiy M. M. 2002. *Mejdunarodnoe Chastnoe Pravo [Private International Law]*. Moscow: Jurist, 21; etc.

[24] Among the Russian private international law scholars the best description of this specifics is believed to be given by Luntz, along with the description of the aspects (or "structural elements") of such relations in which this element manifests itself. See Luntz, L. A. 1949. *Mejdunarodnoe Chastnoe Pravo [Private International Law]*. Moscow: Gosjurizdat, 9-14.

[25] Rubanov, A. A. 1984. *Teoreticheskie Osnovy Mejdunarodnogo Vzaimodejstviya Natzionalnyh Pravovyh System (Theoretical Foundations of International Interaction of National Legal Systems)*. Moscow: Nauka, 91-94.

[26] Kozlovsky, V. V. et al., eds.. 2000. *Trudovye Otnosheniya na Predpriyatiah s Inostrannym Uchastiem [Labour Relations at Enterprises with Foreign Participation]*. SPb: Sociologicheskoe obshchestvo im. M. M. Kovalevskogo.

to and used by a small group of scholars with a reasonable degree of understanding of the theoretical issues behind this naming.

Secondly, having a particular country as a reference point eliminates grounds for abstract consideration and generalization of the described phenomenon and its theorizing (making it nigh impossible without equally thorough consideration from all applicable reference points).

Unfortunately, those who use this wording almost never explain their choice nor critically assess other options. This leads us to conclude that wording which contains something "foreign" (no matter whether it is "element" or "participation") is acceptable only in national scholarship, which analyses the phenomenon from the position of a particular national legal system and legitimately sees anything outside its jurisdiction as "foreign". This approach is largely ineffective and irrelevant when describing the phenomenon from an entitative point of view and/or at a high level of theorization.

In the title of this paper I have used an alternative to the aforementioned wordings: a term which uses the word "transnational" instead of the problematic terms of "international" or "transborder" or something with "foreign element" or "foreign participation". This was done intentionally but was not meant to emphasize the flawlessness of the term. The word "transnational" sounds modern and allows a researcher or a practitioner to clearly distinguish this type of relation from anything existing on a truly international or supranational level. This term is also actively used in scholarly papers and books on transnational labour published in English[27]. At the same time, this term is almost non-existent in literature published in Russian, and when it is mentioned it is unaccompanied by any particular terminological explanations or

[27] Gunawardana S. J., and L. Mhando, 2014. "The Migration-Development Nexus, Women Workers and Transnational Employment Relations," in *The Oxford Handbook of Employment Relations*, eds. Wilkinson, A., Wood, J., Deeg, R. (Oxford: Oxford University Press); Fichter, M., and J. Sydow, 2009. "Organization and Regulation of Employment Relations in Transnational Production and Supply Networks. Ensuring Core Labor Standards through International Framework Agreements," Paper presented at the 15th World Congress of the International Industrial Relations Association (IIRA), Sidney, August 24-27, 2009. Track 4: Institutions, Processes and Outcomes. Available online: http://www.ilera-directory.org/15thworldcongress/files/papers/Track_4/Tue_W1_FICHTER.pdf [accessed 02.02.2014]; Rose, E. 2004. *Employment Relations*. FT Prentice Hall, Pearson Education Ltd, 223; Cherian, J. 1989. "Current Developments in Transnational Employment Rights." *Labor Law Journal 40*(5): 259-267; Forde, M. 1978. "Transnational Employment and Employment Protection," *Industrial Law Journal* 7-1: 228-238; etc.

comments.[28] Being quite a novelty for non-English languages, the naming seems to have struggled to enter non-English legal scholarship. It is also a bit of a tricky term due to the fact that it is closely associated with "transnational corporations" which are in no sense "representative employers" for transnational employment relations which have many other types of specific employers (e.g. a natural person with a *lex personalis* different from that of his/her employee(s), a national subsidiary of a foreign corporation, an international organization, etc.). Nonetheless, this term does seem to avoid the majority of problems mentioned above, being almost monosemic (at least in the context we are discussing here), understandable and simple. All this may explain its increasing usage, which has recently been observed in legal scholarship.

There are also other wordings, which have been suggested for or used as a name for the discussed phenomenon,[29] but their occurrence in published works is scarce. It is clear that there is still no one single term, which satisfies everyone. However, the name "transnational employment relations" seems to be the most generally acceptable, at least in English and until we find something more unambiguous.

1.2. The Transnational Nature of the Employment Relation: A Legislative "Patchwork"

The discussion briefly outlined above is only relevant to doctrinal literature. Current Russian legislation and other regulative instruments interpret the phenomenon as either containing a "foreign element" or being of a "transborder nature".

The term "foreign element" can be found only in the legislative provisions establishing the choice of law rules and defining legal status of various "entities": persons, places, organizations, etc. We can, for instance, find it in article 414 of the Code of Merchant Shipping of the Russian Federation which stipulates the choice of law rules for cases "[…]

---

[28] Kiselev I. Ya. 1999. *Sravnitelnoe i Mejdunarodnoe Trudovoe Pravo [Comparative and International Labor Law]*. Moscow: Delo, 7.

[29] See: Petrova, E. A. 2005. "Kollizionnye principy v trudovyh pravootnoshenijah s inostrannym sub'ektom [Conflict of laws principles in employment relations with a foreign subject]," *Juridicheskij Mir* 3: 76-77; Kiselev, I. Ya. 2003. *op. cit.* 8-11; Andrianova, M. A. 2002. *Pravovoe Regulirovanie Trudovykh Otnosheniy s Uchastiem Inostrantzev v Sistseme Mejdunarodnogo Chastnogo i Trudovogo Prava Rossii [Legal Regulation of Employment Relations with Participation of Foreigners in the System of Private International and Labour Law of Russia]*. PhD Thesis. Moscow: MGIMO; etc.

with the participation of foreign citizens or foreign judicial persons or complicated by a foreign element". It is also used in Part III of the Civil Code of the Russian Federation in article 1186 regarding the choice of law rules applicable to civil relations with the participation of "foreign persons" or complicated by a "foreign element", and in article 1204 regarding governmental participation in civil relationships complicated by a "foreign element". It is also found in par. 2.1, 2.2 and 3 of the Conception of Development of the Civil Legislation of the Russian Federation[30] devoted to amendments of the choice of law rules in the Civil Code of the Russian Federation, which, in some cases (such as the resolution of employment disputes or the definition of the person authorized to receive the unpaid wages of a deceased employee, and so on) are applicable to transnational employment relations as well.

It is logical for the same approach to be employed by the Russian judicial system, traditionally sluggish in the accommodation of all relatively new concepts. Although the Russian courts rarely resort to the term "foreign element" in their decisions, the Informative Letter of the Presidium of the Supreme Court of the Russian Federation No. 10 of 25.12.1996, mentions this term as a key feature of the relationship in question between a Belorussian company and a Russian company concerning the recovery of damages arising from the payment of disability pension fees for an injured employee of the plaintiff (the Belorussian company) to the Social Protection Fund of the city of Grodno (in Belarus).[31] There are also other examples in Russian case law in which courts have used this concept in their arguments on the applicability of the rules of the choice of law.[32]

Unfortunately, Russian legislation on transnational employment relations has not evolved to the same level of theorization and abstraction as general choice of law legislation has. It currently demonstrates no awareness of a "transnational employment relation" (or anything similar) as a general concept, but addresses only specific examples (or categories)

---

[30] Approved by the Presidential Council on the codification and further improvement of civil legislation on 07.10.2009.

[31] Par. 9 of the Informative Letter of the Presidium of the Supreme Court of the Russian Federation No. 10 of 25.12.1996

[32] See Decision of the Supreme Court of the Russian Federation No. AKPI12-1558 of 23.01.2013 concerning the civil servants' accommodation subsidy volume in the case of foreign residential property ownership; Decision of the Supreme Court of Arbitration of the Russian Federation No. VAS-7777/2010 of 07.11.2011 concerning the recovery of damages arising from a transnational freightage issue, etc.

of such relations: employment relations with foreign citizens employed in the Russian federation, secondment and assignments abroad (to some extent), taxation in particular cases of transnational employment relations.

At the same time the term "transborder", also found in Russian legislation and international treaties of the Russian Federation, relates mostly to "transactional" issues: transfers, transportation, air pollution, commercial transactions, etc. For example, this term is mentioned in article 12 of Federal law No. 152-FZ of 27.07.2006, "On Personal Data", and in Chapter III of the Convention for the Protection of Individuals with Regard to the Automatic Processing of Personal Data[33] concerning transborder data transmission. Both of these provisions are fully applicable to the personal data of employees that an employer may gather in regard to their employment. The same term is mentioned in the Rules on the Criteria of Labelling Markets as Transborder[34] setting the rules concerning breaches of the antimonopoly provisions of articles 12 and 15 of the Agreement on Unitary Principles and Rules of Competition[35] including those in the field of services and others. On an international level the most common approach is to adhere to the Civil Code choice of law provisions. The most relevant international instrument in this sense is the Decision of the Council of Heads of the CIS Governments, "On Interstates Program of Innovative Cooperation of the CIS Member States"[36], which touches upon issues of transnational intellectual property (and contains the concept of a "foreign element" in Direction 2.2 of the Decision).

2. Taxonomic Issues: Varieties of "Transnational Employment Relations"

Thus far, it seems that no single common classification or systematization of transnational employment relations has been suggested either in labour law or in private international law scholarship. Most classifications suggested in various studies are constructed ad-hoc on the basis of empirical data with little to no abstraction and little effort to develop a comprehensive, integral and consistent typology.

---

33 Council of Europe, 1981, signed by the Russian Federation in 2001 and ratified in 2013.

34 Approved by Decision No. 29 of the Supreme Eurasian Economic Council of 19.12.2012.

35 Signed by Russia, Belarus and Kazakhstan on 09.12.2010.

36 Adopted on 18.10.2011.

When dealing with transnational employment relations, private international law scholars do not actually bother to classify them. Instead, they describe the choice of law rules as applicable to a "typical" transnational employment relation and to several so-called "special situations" (which in some way differ from the "typical" one).[37]

Dealing with the phenomenon more closely, labour law scholars have at least presented some classifications. Thus, for example, in Japanese labour law scholarship[38] we find a "geographical" ("territorial") approach with a country-based reference point (Japan) which distinguishes three main categories, some of which are further divided into subcategories:

- "international employment relations within Japan" comprising (a) relations involving foreign workers and (b) relations involving foreign-affiliated companies;[39]
- "international employment relations outside Japan" comprising (a) relations in regard to the transfer of employees to foreign branches and subsidiaries and (b) relations in regard to employees on business trips abroad;[40]
- [relations regarding the] "transnational movement of the workforce" comprising no subcategories.[41]

Soviet scholarship seems to be not interested in the systemic study of transnational employment relations. The phenomenon was of rare occurrence then and so were the papers, which addressed specific issues in this field and did not present much effort in typology development.

Post-Soviet labour law scholarship inspired by the spurt in foreign relations of the new states, which had emerged on the former Soviet territory, produced at least two more or less consistent typologies. It is interesting to mention that both of them also have a "geographical" ("territorial") nature and a country-based reference point.

The first typology was suggested by A. S. Dovgert in a textbook, which was released almost immediately after the Soviet system had

---

[37] See Merrett, L. *op. cit.,* 259-310; Morgenstern, F. *op. cit*., 33-22.

[38] Yamakawa, R. 1996. "The Road Becoming More Traveled: The International Dimension of Japanese Labor Law. *Japan Labor Bulletin.* 35-09 [electronic resource]. URL: http://www.jil.go.jp/english/archives/bulletin/year/1996/vol35-09/05.htm (accessed 3 February 2014).

[39] We can see that this subdivision is based on the specifics of subjects (parties) of the relationship.

[40] We can see that this subdivision is based on the specifics of the object (place where the work is to be performed) of this relationship.

[41] Here the category in general again represents the specifics of the subjects (parties) of the relationship.

collapsed and several new states had emerged on the post-Soviet area. This typology reflects a transitional point in the development of the regional labour law scholarship, which was trying hard to find relevant terms and rules for the new economic reality. In that context professor Dovgert differentiated the following four types (categories) of "employment relations with a foreign element":

- work of local citizens for foreign employers on the territory of the former USSR and abroad;
- secondment of "our citizens" to work abroad;
- work for enterprises which are legal persons according to national law but are owned by "foreign capital" and included "into the orbit of transnational corporations";
- work of foreigners in the former USSR on various bases.[42]

We can see that Dovgert's typology bears obvious signs of the deficiency in empirical data, relevant terminology and experience in systematization of phenomena having transnational nature. This typology seems to be inspired by the spurt in foreign relations of the new post-Soviet states, but this time-specificity have made it short-lived and inapplicable in a context of a more developed economy. Now it has been almost forgotten and seldom cited in modern research.

Another—and a more well-known—typology has been suggested by Professor I.Ya. Kiselev about a decade ago. He divided transnational employment relations (or, to use his wording, "international labour") into five categories:

- work of Russian citizens abroad for Russian employers;
- work of Russian citizens for international organizations;
- labour migration of Russian citizens abroad (external labour migration);
- work of Russian citizens in their motherland for foreign firms or international organizations;
- work of the foreign citizens and stateless persons in Russia for employing organizations or natural persons.[43]

We can see that these all are empirical systematizations of the various types of transnational employment relations found in particular economic realities. However, the main value of these typologies is their degree of

[42] Dovgert, A. S. 1992. *op. cit.*, 5.
[43] Kiselev, I. Ya. 2003. *op. cit.*, 8.

similarity[44], which may allow for speculation as to whether an integral unified typology can be developed in this field.

Now that transnational employment relations are abundant and diverse and legal scholarship has, to some extent, familiarized itself with the phenomenon, we can attempt to apply a more systematic approach. Although a vivid exchange of viewpoints on this issue has not yet been initiated, I would suggest beginning the discussion with the typology of transnational employment relations which I have devised on the basis of the classic and well-developed concept of a "legal relation(ship)".

Private international law scholarship holds that a legal relationship consists of several "structural elements": (1) subjects (participating parties); (2) an object (a "matter of the relation") and juridical facts (facts which affect the relation in various ways, including engendering, changing or terminating them).[45] At the same time, when speaking of any transnational relations, the majority of scholars agree that the core feature of this type of relation is that their elements belong to two or more national legal orders (national legal regimes or jurisdictions), thus hypothetically implying a conflict of laws.[46]

Relying upon this general rule, I suggest, at least until a more consistent typology is introduced, dividing transnational employment relations according to the principle of whether the "transnationality" relates to one or more national legal orders ("degree of transnationality").

Thus, we get two distinct categories of transnational employment relations:

---

[44] Indeed, the subcategories of Yamakawa's first category correspond to, although do not exactly coincides with, the fourth and partly the first and the third Dovgert's categories respectively and Kiselev's last two categories, etc.

[45] First mentioned in Luntz, L. A. 1949. *op. cit.*; see also: Marchenko, M. N. 2007. *Problemy Obshhej Teorii Gosudarstva i Prava. Vol. 2. Pravo [Problems of General Theory of State and Law. T. 2. Law]* Moscow: Prospekt, 602; Golovistikova, A. N., and Ju. A. Dmitriev. 2005. *Problemy Teorii Gosudarstva i Prava [Problems of Theory of State and Law].* Moscow: Eksmo, 516.

[46] See: Stone, P. 2010. *EU Private International Law.* Cheltenham: Edward Elgar Publishing, 3; O'Brien, J. 1999. *Conflicts of Laws.* London, Sydney: Cavendish Publishing; Story, J. 1834. *Commentaries on the Conflict of Laws, Foreign and Domestic: in regard to Contracts, Rights and Remedies and Especially in regard to Marriages, Divorces, Wills, Successions, and Judgments.* Boston: Hilliard, Gray and Co.; see also in Russian: Pereterskiy, I. S. 1924. *Ocherki Mejdunarodnogo Chastnogo Prava RSFSR [Essays in Private International Law of the RSFSR].* Moscow: Gosudarstvennoe Izdatelstvo, 9-19; Luntz, L. A. 1949. *op. cit.*; Kiselev, I. Ya. 2003. *op. cit.*; Erpylyova, N. Yu. 2005. *op. cit.*

- "simple", in which no more than two national legal orders are involved;
- "complex", in which more than two national legal orders are involved.

An example of a simple transnational employment relation is that of an employment contract signed in Spain between a Chinese employee and a Spanish employer for work within the territory of Spain (or within the jurisdiction of Spain). Here the Chinese and Spanish legal orders may attempt to regulate the relationship depending on particular circumstances and approaches implemented in national legislation.

A complex transnational employment relation may be represented by a situation when the above mentioned Chinese citizen signs the same employment contract within the territory of Spain but with a US employer.

To make the relationship more complex we could add that the contract is signed in regard to a position in, for example, a Russian subsidiary of the US employer with regular business trips to Kazakhstan and India as an integral condition of this assignment. In general, it is initially impossible to say whether the relation produces a genuine conflict of laws and if it does, which of the national legal orders shall be applied to which element or aspect of the relationship. It is usually necessary to go deep into the international and national choice of law rules applicable to the particular case and its respective aspects, as well as into the relevant substantive law norms.

Apropos, it seems evident that the suggested typology does not have any specific "employment" or "labour" meaning and can be effectively applied to other kinds of transnational relations as well. It can, for instance, be used to classify transnational family relations, relations concerning transnational financial transactions, etc. The question of whether this and other relevant typologies have already been introduced in other branches of law and whether they can be borrowed from there and applied in the classification of transnational employment relations, may become a subject of further research.

3. The Place of Legal Norms Regulating the Phenomenon between (or within) other Branches of Law

In Russia the place of the legal norms which regulate transnational employment relations is perceived slightly differently in doctrinal literature and in legislation. Russian doctrinal writings present three approaches, according to which the phenomenon is perceived as (1) either a particular institution (an area or so-called "sub-branch") of private international law,[47] or (2) one of the basic institutions of the so-called "private international labour law" (or "private international employment law", which actually sounds the same in Russian),[48] or (3) an institution of both labour and private international branches of law.[49]

This assumption leads to the conclusion that the case of transnational employment relations creates a separate and complex sub-branch of both branches at once: a "private international employment law". This relatively new creation has borrowed its subjects from labour (employment) law, its specific choice of law rules from private international law and its object—labour implemented on the basis of an employment contract but embracing several national legal orders—from a combination of labour (employment) and private international law.

Despite this rather clear and obvious attribution, the law reflects it only to some extent and only in a few countries. Thus, the norms governing various aspects of transnational employment relations on an international level can be found in treaties concerning not only employment issues, but also those relating to education, tax and several other matters. However, when it comes to national legislation, there is a wide variation between countries. For instance, in the Russian regulative context the norms on transnational employment relations (or more precisely, on some of the aspects of some of their categories) can be found mostly in legislation on private international, employment and administrative law.

The level of corporate internal regulations demonstrates a more consistent approach as the relevant norms are for the most part divided between regulations on various aspects of regular (non-transnational) employment relations (i.e. concerning wages, benefits and compensations, leaves, business trips, and so on.)

---

[47] Erpylyova N. Yu. 2012. *op. cit.*, 435-436; Boguslavskiy M. M. 2002. *op. cit*, 34.

[48] Zvekov, V. P. 2004. *op. cit.*, 519-542.

[49] Andrianova, M. A. 2006. Aspekt trudovyh otnoshenij v mezhdunarodnom chastnom prave. O nekotoryh voprosah kollizionnogo metoda regulirovanija trudovyh otnoshenij s uchastiem inostrancev [Aspects of employment relations in private international law. On some questions of conflict of laws method of regulation of employment relations with the participation of foreigners), in *Aktualnye Pproblemy Mezhdunarodnogo Chastnogo i Grazhdanskogo Prava.* Moscow: Statut, 9-10; Bekyashev, D. K. 2008. *Mezhdunarodnoe Trudovoe Pravo [International Labor Law].* Moscow: Prospekt, 8-9; Zvekov V. P. *op. cit.* From 519 on.

If a national legislator approaches the task of the development of the regulations in the field, it may be advisable to choose a particular branch of law for the norms governing transnational employment relations.

Taking into account the active spread of the question around the globe and its continuing complication, the most advisable approach would be to enact a separate legislative act devoted specifically to the regulation of various types (categories) of transnational employment relations and containing blanket norms that lead to other relevant acts of legislation.

4. Conclusion

Transnational employment relations have developed to the point where particular generalization and systematization can be effectuated in order to make legislative amendments possible in the very near future. The author has shown that inconsistency in the terminology and taxonomy of this phenomenon may complicate the process of its systematization and further study, as well as attempts to regulate its legislation. This has been done from a comparative point of view on the basis of scholarship in both Russian and English.

The study has also revealed that scholars differ in their approaches to the classification of the types of the phenomenon and in the results they come to when supporting their systematizations with empirical data. The resulting typologies, made with little theorization, thus show inconsistency and lack integrity. This predetermines their inapplicability in the regulation of such a constantly developing phenomenon as transnational employment relations due to the lack of understanding of the particular elements which form the relation and can then be studied more closely and developed according to the growing variety of manifestations of the phenomenon.

There is also a problem regarding the relevant legal norms. Both scholars and legislators differ in their idea about which branches of law such norms should be attributed to and which principles shall be considered prevailing in the regulation of the phenomenon.

We can conclude that the time has come to pay closer and more serious attention to "transnational employment relations". This study has revealed that this widespread and constantly developing issue requires a consistent doctrinal and legislative approach.

References

Agreement on Unitary Principles and rules of competition. Signed by Russia, Belarus and Kazakhstan on 09.12.2010.

Andrianova, M. A. 2002. *Pravovoe Regulirovanie Trudovykh Otnosheniy s Uchastiem Inostrantzev v Sistseme Mejdunarodnogo Chastnogo I Trudovogo Prava Rossii [Legal Regulation of Employment Relations with Participation of Foreigners in the System of Private International and Labour Law of Russia]*. PhD Thesis. Moscow: MGIMO.

—. 2006. "Aspekt trudovyh otnoshenij v mezhdunarodnom chastnom prave. O nekotoryh voprosah kollizionnogo metoda regulirovanija trudovyh otnoshenij s uchastiem inostrancev [Aspects of Employment Relations in Private International Law. On Some Questions of Conflict of Laws Method of Regulation of Employment Relations with the Participation of Foreigners]," in *Aktualnye Pproblemy Mezhdunarodnogo Chastnogo i Grazhdanskogo Prava*. Moscow: Statut, 9-10.

Bamber, G. J., and R. D., Lansbury, eds. 2010. *International and Comparative Employment Relations*. London: SAGE Publications.

Bekyashev, D. K. 2008. *Mezhdunarodnoe Trudovoe Pravo [International Labor Law]*. Moscow: Prospekt.

Belogubova, O. V. 2013. Koliziyni-pravove regulyuvannya trudovyh vidnosyn, uskladnenyh inozemnym elementom, v mijdunarodnomu sudnoplavstvi [Conflict Legal Regulation of Employment Relations Complicated by Foreign Elements in International Shipping]. *Aktualni Problemy Polityky*, 50: 120-130.

Bentham, J. 1838-1843. *The Works of Jeremy Bentham*. Edinburgh: William Tait.

—. 1939. *An Introduction to the Principles of Morals and Legislation*. Hayes Barton Press.

Birk, R. 1985. "Review: International Conflicts of Labour Law: A Survey of the Law Applicable to the International Employment Relation," Morgenstern, F., *The American Journal of International Law* 79-4: 1120-1123.

Bisom-Rapp, S. Exceeding Our Boundaries: Transnational Employment Law Practice and the Export of American Lawyering Styles to the Global Worksite," TJSL Public Law Research Paper No. 04-9 (note 3, at 2). Available at SSRN: http://papers.ssrn.com/sol3/papers.cfm?abstract_id=590942 (accessed 2 February 2014).

Boguslavskiy M. M. 2002. *Mejdunarodnoe Chastnoe Pravo (Private International Law)*. Moscow: Jurist.

—. 1988. *Private International Law: a Soviet Approach*. Dordrecht: Martinus Nijhoff Publishers.

Buxbaum, H. L. 2009. "Competition in the Private Enforcement of regulatory Law," in *Economic Law as an Economic Good: Its Rule Function and Its Tool Function in the Competition of Systems,* eds. Messen, K. M., M. Bungenberg and A. Puttler (Munich: Sellier European Law Publishers), 129-136.

Chernichenko, O. S. 2003. *International Legal Aspects of the Jurisdiction of States*. PhD thesis. Moscow: Diplomatic Academy of the Foreign Ministry of the Russian Federation.

Collier, J. G. 2001. *Conflict of Laws*. Cambridge: Cambridge University Press.

Colvin, A., and O. Darbishire. 2012. "International Employment Relations: The Impact of Varieties of Capitalism," in *Handbook of Research in International Human Resource Management*, eds. Stahl, G. K., I. Björkman, and Sh. Morris, (Cheltenham: Edward Elgar Publishing).

Dmitrieva, G. K., ed. 2010. *Mejdunarodnoe Chastnoe Pravo [Private International Law]*. Moscow: Prospekt.

Dovgert, A. S. 1992. *Pravovoe Regulirovanie Mejdunatodnyh Trudvyh otnosheniy [Legal Regulation of International Employment Relations)]*. Kiev: UMK VO.

Dowling Jr., D. C. 2001. "The Practice of International Labor & Employment Law: Escort Your Labor/Employment Clients into the Global Millennium," *The Labor Lawyer* 17:1-23.

Erpylyova N. Yu. 2005. *Mejdunarodnoe Chastnoe Pravo [Private International Law]*. Moscow: Prospekt, 7-10, 25-29

—. 2012 *Mejdunarodnoe Chastnoe Pravo [Private International Law]*. Moscow: Jurait.

Evju, S., and T. Novitz. 2012. "The Evolving Regulation: Dynamics and Consequences," *Formula Working Paper No. 33*. Available online: http://www.jus.uio.no/ifp/english/research/projects/freemov/publications/papers/2012/WP33-Evju-Novitz.pdf (accessed 2 February 2014).

Lazar, W. 2008. "Employment Agreements and Cross Border Employment: Confidentiality, Trade Secret, and Other Restrictive Covenants in a Global Economy," *Labor Lawyer,* 24-2: 195-211.

Fichter, M., and J. Sydow, 2009. "Organization and Regulation of Employment Relations in Transnational Production and Supply Networks. Ensuring Core Labor Standards through International Framework Agreements," Paper presented at the 15th World Congress of the International Industrial Relations Association (IIRA), Sidney,

August 24-27, 2009. Track 4: Institutions, Processes and Outcomes. Available online: http://www.ilera-directory.org/15thworldcongress/files/papers/Track_4/Tue_W1_FICHTER.pdf [accessed 02.02.2014]

Freedland, M. 2003. *The Personal Employment Contract*. Oxford: Oxford University Press.

Gamillscheg, F. 1959. *Internationales Arbeitsrecht*. Berlin: Mohr Siebeck.

Golovistikova, A. N., and Ju. A. Dmitriev. 2005. *Problemy Teorii Gosudarstva i Prava [Problems of Theory of State and Law]*. Moscow: Eksmo, 516.

Grušić, U. 2012. *The International Employment Contract: Ideal, Reality and Regulatory Function of European Private International Law of Employment*. A thesis submitted to the Department of Law of the London School of Economics for the Degree of Doctor of Philosophy, September 2012. London: London School of Economics. Available online: http://etheses.lse.ac.uk/583/1/Grusic_International_Employment_Contract_2012.pdf

Hepple, B. 2003. "Mapping International Labor Disputes: An Overview," in *Labor Law Beyond Borders: ADR and the Internationalization of Labor Disputes*, ed. The International Bureau of the Permanent Court of Arbitration (Kluwer Law International).

Kiselev I. Ya. 1999. *Sravnitelnoe i Mejdunarodnoe Trudovoe Pravo [Comparative and International Labor Law]*. Moscow: Delo.

—. 2003. *Trud s Inostrannym Uchastiem: Pravovye Aspekty [Labour with Foreign Participation: Legal Aspects]*. Moscow: MCFER.

Kolobov, R. Yu. 2006. *Osnovy Postroeniya i Funktzionirovaniya Mejdunatodnogo Chastnogo Prava [Foundations of Private International Law Building and Functioning]*. PhD thesis. Irkutsk: IrkGU.

Kozlovsky, V. V. et al., eds. 2000. *Trudovye Otnosheniya na Predpriyatiah s Inostrannym Uchastiem [Labour Relations in Enterprises with Foreign Participation]*. SPb: Sociologicheskoe obshchestvo im. M.M. Kovalevskogo.

Kuznetzov, S. A., ed. 2000. *Comprehensive Explanatory Dictionary of Russian*. SPb: Norint.

Luntz, L. A. 1949. *Mejdunarodnoe Chastnoe Pravo [Private International Law]*. Moscow: Gosjurizdat.

—. 1973. *Kurs Mejdunarodnogo Chastnogo Prava [Course of Private International Law]*. Moscow: Yuridicheskaya Literatura.

MacDonald, K. 2009. *Cross-Border Litigation: Interjurisdictional Practice and Procedure* [e-book]. Canada Law Book; Available from: Bibliotheksverbund Bayern, Ipswich, MA.

Marchenko, M. N. 2007. *Problemy Obshhej Teorii Gosudarstva i Prava. Vol. 2. Pravo [Problems of General Theory of State and Law. T. 2. Law]*. Moscow: Prospekt.

Merrett, L. 2011. *Employment Contracts in Private International Law*. Oxford: Oxford University Press.

Morgenstern, F. 1984. *International Conflicts of Labour Law: A Survey of the Law Applicable to the International Employment Relation*. Geneva: International Labour Organization

O'Brien, J. 1999. *Conflicts of Laws*. London, Sydney: Cavendish Publishing.

Ojegov, S. I., and N. Yu. Shvedova. 1999. *Explanatory Dictionary of the Russian Language*. Moscow: Azbukovnik.

Park, W. W. 2001. Why Courts Review Arbitral Awards. *International Arbitration Reports,* No. 16:27.

Pereterskiy, I. S. 1924. *Ocherki Mejdunarodnogo Chastnogo Prava RSFSR [Essays in Private International Law of the RSFSR]*. Moscow: Gosudarstvennoe Izdatelstvo.

Perkins, S. J., S. M. Shortland. 2006. *Strategic International Human Management: Choices and Consequences in Multinational People Management*. Cogan Page Ltd.

Petrova, E. A. 2005. "Kollizionnye principy v trudovyh pravootnoshenijah s inostrannym sub'ektom [Conflict of Laws Principles in Employment Relations with a Foreign Subject]," *Juridicheskij Mir* 3: 76-77

Protasova, A. S. 2011. Коллизионное регулирование трудовых отношений, осложненных иностранным элементом: проблемы и перспективы [Conflict Regulation of Labour Relations Complicated by a Foreign Element: Problems and Perspectives]. *Vestnik Buryatskogo Universiteta*, 2: 224-227.

Rose, E. 2004. *Employment Relations*. FT Prentice Hall: Pearson Education Ltd.

Royle, T. 2006. "The Dominance Effect? Multinational Corporations in the Italian Quick-food Service Sector," *British Journal of Industrial Relations* 44-4: 757-779.

Rubanov, A. A. 1984. *Teoreticheskie Osnovy Mejdunarodnogo Vzaimodejstviya Natzionalnyh Pravovyh System [Theoretical Foundations of International Interaction of National Legal Systems]*. Moscow: Nauka.

Shesteryakova, I. V. 2007. *Kollizionnye Normy i Mejdunarodnye Trudovye Otnosheniya [Conflict Rules and International Employment Relations]*.

Saratov: SGAP.

Sohm, R. 1892. *Institutes of Roman Law*. Oxford: Clarendon Press, 311.

McDonell, J. 1904. “Classification of Forms and Contracts of Labour,” *Journal of the Society of Comparative Legislation. New Series* 5-2: 253-261, at 255-256.

Spektor, A. A. 2004. *Trudovye Otnosheniya, Oslojnennye Inostrannym Elementom, Kak Object Mejdunarodnogo Chastnogo Prava [Employment Relations Complicated by a Foreign Element as an Object of Private International Law]*. PhD thesis. Moscow: RGTEU.

Stone, P. 2010. *EU Private International Law*. Cheltenham: Edward Elgar Publishing.

Story, J. 1834. *Commentaries on the Conflict of Laws, Foreign and Domestic: in regard to Contracts, Rights and Remedies and Especially in regard to Marriages, Divorces, Wills, Successions, and Judgments*. Boston: Hilliard, Gray and Co.

Szászy, I. 1968. *International Labour Law: A Comparative Survey of the Conflict Rules Affecting Labour Legislation and Regulations*. Leyden: A.W. Sijthoff.

Ushakov, D. N. 1937. *Orthographic Dictionary* Moscow: Uchpedgiz. Also available online, URL: http://ushakovdictionary.ru.

Yamakawa, R. 1996. “The Road Becoming More Traveled: The International Dimension of Japanese Labor Law. *Japan Labor Bulletin.* 35-09 [electronic resource]. URL: http://www.jil.go.jp/english/archives/bulletin/year/1996/vol35-09/05.htm (accessed 3 February 2014).

Zvekov, V. P. 2004 *Mejdunarodnoe Chastnoe Pravo [Private International Law]*. Moscow: Jurist.

EMPLOYEE LIABILITY TO DISCIPLINARY ACTION IN SOCIAL AND EMPLOYMENT RELATIONS

ELENA BOLTANOVA

1. Determining one's responsibility is an important mechanism to safeguard individual, collective, and state interests, and to maintain law and order. In general, specific forms of liability are in place to help ensure the proper execution and application of the law. In the sphere of socio-employment relations it serves as an incentive for employees and employers to properly perform their duties. Statutory sanctions and their implementation make it possible to better organize the activities of society and workers.

Any kind of liability in the sphere of socio-employment relations is intended to protect individual rights, freedom, and the legitimate interests of the parties, to maintain law and order in the field of social labour, and to prevent future violations. In this area, the measures of disciplinary liability are the most widespread. Despite the different approaches to legal responsibility described in the relevant literature, one can assert that liability to disciplinary action is a different form of responsibility which falls within the scope of employment law. Some distinctive features of disciplinary responsibility are usually considered: the specific object and subjects; the specific ground for disciplinary action which is regarded as a disciplinary offence; the particular sanctions that can be applied to an offender (e.g. disciplinary penalties); the specific procedure for imposing and appealing disciplinary penalties. The specificity of the foregoing elements and of socio-employment relations is illustrative of the special nature of this form of liability.

There are different approaches to the legal nature of the relationship between the employer (a public entity) and such officials as judges, prosecutors and civil servants, as well as to the branch of law which should regulate this relationship. Some scholars argue that these relations can be considered as an employment relationship falling within the realm of employment legislation, therefore, special disciplinary action can be taken in case of offences. Conversely, other scholars think that such relations entail a different form of liability.[1] Still other scholars are of the opinion that judges' liability to disciplinary action amounts to constitutional legal responsibility.

2. Socio-employment relationships develop as a result of people's purposeful activity, either employees who perform their job or employers who wish to achieve some socially-significant results and take some steps relevant to the purpose, e.g. employing and ensuring proper working conditions.

Employment relationships are relations based on an agreement between an employee and an employer regarding the individual performance of a task on the part of the employee in exchange of remuneration. They require employee compliance with internal working regulations and proper working conditions which must be ensured by the employer, as stipulated in employment legislation and other labour law provisions, collective agreements and employment contracts (Art. 15 of the Labour Code of the Russian Federation, hereafter—LC RF).

Employee compliance with the internal working regulations is particularly important in the legal definition of the employment relationships. Art. 21 of the LC RF also specifies that the employee shall perform *bona fide* his/her duties enshrined in the employment contract, abide by internal working regulations and maintain discipline at work.

Internal working regulations are complex to define as consisting of a range of elements. They can be considered as a series of requirements regarding the employees' behaviour at work established by the employer within the limits of his authority which is defined by the state.[2] The most important requirements for employees, the provisions intended for the organization of technological process and for safeguarding safety at work are included in internal working regulations.

---

[1] In his thesis on the judges' liability to disciplinary action Aulov, V. K. considers it as a distinct form of legal responsibility and points out that "the breach of the ethical code on the part of public officers has some distinctive traits which are also regulated through special norms" (see: Aulov, V. K. 2012. *Disciplinarnaya otvetstvennost' sudey: genezis, ponyatie i procedura* [*Disciplinary responsibility of judges: its genesis, definition, and procedure*]. Moscow: Thesis, 14). On the contrary Eremina, S. N. argues that judges' liability to disciplinary action is regulated by employment legislation (see: Eremina, S. N. 2011. "Disciplinarnaya otvetstvennost' sudey cherez prizmu nauki trudovogo prava" *Rossiyskiy sudia [Russian judge]*, No. 2:32-36).

[2] See: Lebedev, V. M., T. M. Fakhrutdinova, and I. V. Chernyshova, 2008. *Vnutrenniy trudovoy rasporyadok*. Moscow: Statut, 26-29.

Internal working regulations (as an act) contain provisions laying down the norms of behaviour which are mandatory for all the employees in an organization, including those which define recruitment and dismissal procedures; the rights, duties and responsibilities of the parties to the employment contract; working time, rest periods, incentives; and the sanctions to be faced by the employees. Aside from internal working regulations, some categories of workers in certain sectors (e.g. transport workers) have to comply with more stringent disciplinary rules enforced by the Government of the Russian Federation in accordance with federal laws.

3. From an etymological point of view, the term "liability to disciplinary action" comes from the word "discipline". Labour discipline means conformity to a code of behaviour which is obligatory for all employees and which is defined in accordance with the LC RF, federal laws, collective agreements, internal rules and employment contracts (Art. 189 of the LC RF).

Internal working regulations are fixed by different acts as well as by an individual employment contract and, therefore, their content varies, although being similar to one another. This is because of the unifying effect of the normative legal acts and the business activities, e.g. the need for employees to be coordinated not only within the organization but also with other external subjects. An example of this is working time: whereas employees operating in different organizations nationwide start working at the same time, those who maintain relationships with international partners might begin to work later or earlier in consideration of different time-zones.

Employers need to elaborate effective rules regulating employee behaviour taking into account the peculiarities of the working process, with employees who have to follow these rules. Their failure to comply with them might result in a breach of labour discipline and disciplinary action as a result of such misconduct.

4. In the case of a disciplinary offence, that is in the event of the employee failing to perform his/her duties or to perform them properly, an employer may impose disciplinary sanctions upon such an employee (Art. 192 of the LC RF).

The Plenum of the Supreme Court of the Russian Federation in its Decision of 17 March, 2004 No. 2 "On the Application of the Labour Code of the Russian Federation in Court Practice"[3] explains the term

---

[3] *Bulleten' Verkhovnogo suda RF [Bulletin of the Supreme Court of the Russian Federation]*. 2004. No. 6.

"non-performance or poor performance of his/her duties by an employee" as breaches of legal requirements, obligations laid down in the employment contract, violations of internal working regulations, job descriptions, employers' instructions or technical instructions, etc. Examples of such misconduct include:

- any unjustified absence from work or from the workstation for a period longer than four consecutive hours in a working day or for the whole working day. If a dispute arises about the employees' place of work and this is not detailed in the employment contract or in any local provision, the place of work shall be considered that where the employee must be in order to perform his/her work which is under the employer's direct or indirect control.
- the unjustified refusal on the part of the employee to perform his/her duties subsequent to amendments to working standards so long as according to the employment contract an employee shall perform his/her duties and follow the internal working regulations laid down by the employer. It should be remembered that the refusal on the part of the employee to continue his/her work in connection with the amendments of the terms of an employment contract which an employer had to introduce due to some organizational or technological changes (Art. 74 of the LC RF) cannot be considered as a breach of labour discipline. However, such refusal makes it possible for the employer to terminate the employment contract under other circumstances;
- the unjustified refusal to undergo medical examination for certain categories of employees, as well as the refusal to undertake health and safety training during working time in order to obtain a work permit.

5. An offence is usually defined in legal theory as an unlawful act for which guilt and legal responsibility are attributed. In this sense,

- it is an act, notably a volitional action which can also result from one's inaction;
- an offender is found guilty if he/she has committed an act deliberately or carelessly;
- an act is an offence and, therefore, it is unlawful if violates the legal prescriptions.

On this last point, it should be noted that although the legal definition of "disciplinary offence" does not include the notion of "unlawfulness", any disciplinary offence is seen as unlawful. In employment law, the approach to the unlawful nature of an act is based on the specificity of the rights and duties of the parties to the employment relationship and is not limited by the general theoretical idea of unlawfulness of the action or the inaction violating legal norms.

Committing disciplinary offences implies a violation of labour discipline the requirements of which are laid down in the legal as well as in the local provisions established by an employer within an organization (for instance, internal working regulations) and in the terms of the employment contract. Therefore, according to Art. 9 of the LC RF "the regulation of employment relationships or closely connected relations may be implemented through the terms and the amendments made to collective agreements and employment contracts".

The requirements to labour discipline concern working hours, the protection of employee health, the preservation of employer property, and so on. The employee's failure to carry out his/her duties or to perform them properly independently when such duties are established (either by employment legislation, local rules, or employment contracts) amounts to unlawful behaviour from a party to the employment relationship.

In some cases the unlawful nature of an employee's act should be further acknowledged by someone who is not a party to the employment relationship. Accordingly, employees who have been accused of larceny (including minor theft), embezzlement, misappropriation, intentional damage or destruction of property can be dismissed only if these violations take place at their place of work and if employees are found guilty by a court ruling or a resolution from an official authority that is empowered to apply administrative sanctions.

6. In formal terms, the following are regarded as the factors that should be taken into account in any offence—including disciplinary ones: the perpetrator, the mental component, the target and its objective nature.

A perpetrator of disciplinary offences can be an employee, i.e. a person who has concluded an employment contract. The employment law literature draws a distinction between "general perpetrators" (i.e. any employee) and "special perpetrators". The latter include workers in some economic sectors (for example, rail transport workers, maritime transport workers, and those operating in atomic energy organizations) for whom liability to disciplinary action is established by federal laws, specific rules and regulations, which apply alongside the provisions of the LC RF. This is due to the special nature of these positions—which are highly-responsible roles—and to the fact that their disciplinary offences can have particularly significant consequences.[4]

All employees are required to comply with internal regulations. Such compliance points to their lawful behaviour and makes it possible to assess whether the duties are carried out properly.

The mental component of the disciplinary offence is the employee's feelings of guilt, namely the perpetrator's mental attitude towards the unlawful action and its consequences. Guilt may come in the form of intentional or negligent acts. Disciplinary offences are usually committed because of negligence.

Objectivity relates to the employee's unlawful behaviour, the socially harmful consequences (if any) and the direct causal relationship between them.

When evaluating the foregoing aspects, it is necessary to take into account the relationship among individuals in terms of mutual rights and duties. Not only have employees to adhere to labour regulations, but the employer as well, who has to set the best conditions allowing the former to perform their jobs.[5]

7. Legal opinion usually categorizes offences considering their seriousness, dividing them into crimes and other offences, including disciplinary ones. The latter can also be divided into different groups depending on their perpetrator, mental component, target, objectivity and so on.[6]

---

[4] See *Ustav o discipline rabotnikov rybopromyslovogo flota RF [Regulations on Discipline for Fishing Fleet Employees]* approved by the Decision of the Government of the Russian Federation from 21 September, 2000 No. 708. In accordance with its provisions, a disciplinary offence implies a violation committed by an employee on shipboard, in service premises or within a fishing company. The range of disciplinary penalties is broader in comparison with those established by the LC RF. The regulations also establish how to implement such measures.

[5] The Supreme Court of the Russian Federation upheld a lower court decision according to which the reprimand received by an employee (the plaintiff) from the employer (the defendant) was considered as unfair, so long as the employer did not provided the necessary conditions to maintain discipline at the workplace, violating Art. 189 of the LC RF (see *Apellyacionnoe opredelenie Verkhovnogo Suda RF [Appeal Decision of the Supreme Court of the Russian Federation]* of 9 November, 2012 No. 60-APG12-7).

[6] See, for example, Fedin, K. A. 2007. *Pravonarushenie v sfere truda kak osnovanie privlecheniya k disciplinarnoy otvetstvennosti po normam trudovogo prava [An offence in the sphere of employemntemployment as a ground for*

V. M. Lebedev reasonably classifies disciplinary offences into three types: 1) guilty violation of technology regulations; 2) insubordination and failure to comply with the requirements of the employer (e.g. non-compliance with the instructions given by the head of an organization); 3) the purposeful breach of rules on working time and time-off (namely violating work schedule, arriving late at work and so on).[7]

8. The Labour Code of the Russian Federation provides for different types of disciplinary actions: a reprimand (*zamechanie*), a reproof (*vygovor*) and, whereas applicable, dismissal (*uvol'nenie*). This range cannot be considered as exhaustive, but other sanctions laid down in federal laws, specific rules and regulations can be applied only to special categories of workers. Thus, according to the Regulations "On the Discipline of Railway Transport Workers", established by the Order of the Government of the Russian Federation No. 621 of 25 August 1992, the employer can impose upon the employee who committed a disciplinary offence the following disciplinary measures, which add to those established by the Labour Code of the Russian Federation:

1) the withdrawal of the license to train drivers and their assistants to operate the locomotive, with the assignment to another position upon their consent;

2) the dismissal from positions connected with the operation of railways, railway transport enterprises, etc. with the assignment to another positions upon the employee's consent.

In addition to the cases envisaged in the LC RF, the Regulations "On the Discipline of Railway Transport Workers" sets forth that a transport worker can be dismissed in the case of a serious disciplinary offence which endangers the management of railways and shunting operations, transportable goods, luggage and other belongings and people's life and health.

Case law concerning employee liability to disciplinary action mostly refers to their dismissal and reinstatement. This explains the workers' unwillingness to engage in conflict with their employer, being the latter the stronger party to the employment relationship. However, employees

---

disciplinary responsibility in accordance with provisions of employment legislation], thesis, Chelyabinsk, 46.

[7] Lebedev, V. M. 2011. "Disciplinarnye vzyskaniya [Disciplinary Penalties]" in *Trudovoe pravo [Labour Law]*, ed. Lebedev, V. M. (Moscow: Norma), Infra-M, 235-236.

might at times decide to bring the case before the court to ask for the revocation of other disciplinary charges against them.[8]

Dismissal is the most severe measure which can be inflicted to an employee who has violated a disciplinary rule. The grounds for dismissal can be established only by the Labour Code of the Russian Federation or by other federal laws. In accordance with the LC RF, employees can be dismissed in the following cases:

- Repeated and unjustified failure to perform their duties;
- A one-off gross violation of their duties, including:

a) unjustified absence from work during the whole working day or for more than four consecutive hours;

b) working under the influence of alcohol or drugs at the workplace (either at their workplace strictly speaking, in any area regarded as being part of the employer's organization, or in any facility where employees have to perform their job following the employer's instructions);

c) the disclosure of secrets protected by the law known to the employee in the performance of his duties, including the disclosure of other employees' personal information;

d) theft at the workplace, embezzlement, wilful damage to property determined by a court ruling or a body (an officer) empowered to hear cases regarding administrative offences;

e) the violation of health and safety requirements resulting in severe consequences (e.g. industrial accidents and disasters) or that is acknowledged to have caused a serious hazard;

- culpable actions by the employee handling money or valuables causing the employer to lose confidence in the employee;
- failure to avoid or to settle a conflict of interests involving the employee. This includes the provision on the part of employees, their spouse and/or underage children of false or incomplete information about income, expenses and property commitments; failure to mention the existence of an account/deposit opened with a bank outside the Russian Federation; failure to refer to foreign financial instruments which are either used by employees, their spouse or underage children in the cases provided by the law of the Russian Federation, whereas causing the employer to lose trust in the employee;
- an immoral deed committed by an employee engaged in educational activities that is incompatible with the work performed;

---

[8] The issuing of a severe reprimand towards an employee was overturned by Decision No. 45-66 of 10 November 2009 of the Saint Petersburg City Court. The reprimand was unlawful, since severe reprimand (*strogiy vigovor*) is not included in the list of sanctions laid down in Art. 192 of the LC RF.

- an unjustifiable decision made by the head of an organization (a branch or a representation office), by his deputies and the chief accountant which results in the loss, the illicit use and damage to the organization and its assets;

- a one-off gross breach on the part of the head of an organization (a branch, a representation office) or his deputies.

The Labour Code of the Russian Federation also identifies other grounds for terminating an employment contract:

1) a teacher's employment contract can be terminated in case of a repeated gross violation of the educational institution's charter in the academic year;

2) a sportsman's employment contract can be terminated as a result of a disqualification period of six months or more as well of the use of doping, even if happening once.

A disciplinary offence might result in only one form of disciplinary action (Art. 193 of the LC RF). This provision is in line with the underlying principles of legal liability and ensures that perpetrators are imposed only one penalty for the same offence. Accordingly, these sanctioning measures are not considered to violate human rights (see Decision No. 1314-O of the Constitutional Court of the Russian Federation of 17 July 2012).

9. Drawing on the assumption that a disciplinary offence is first and foremost detrimental to the employer's interests, special labour laws have been enforced at the national level that define the disciplinary penalties without a binding effect. This is because it is for the employer to establish the employee's liability to disciplinary action and the nature of the sanction.

Aspects such as the seriousness of the offence and the reasons causing the offence and the employee's behaviour, play a role in the employer's decision to attribute disciplinary liability. Art. 192 of the LC RF specifies that "while imposing a disciplinary penalty, one shall take into account the seriousness of the violation and the circumstances in which it took place."

A thorough assessment of an employee's act and his/her behaviour preceding and following the incident makes it possible for the employer not only to make a fair decision, but also to increase one's degree of responsibility, fostering a conscientious attitude on the part of employees towards their work. By factoring in all these aspects, the employer will be in the position to impose the most appropriate penalty in line with the law.

In this sense, a tribunal once ruled that "the right to choose the penalty among those established in employment legislation rests on the employer, who shall take into account the seriousness of the disciplinary offence, the circumstances in which it took place, and the employer's attitude before committing the offence".[9]

The Plenum of the Supreme Court of the Russian Federation affords a proper examination whereas a disciplinary penalty is challenged and the employee requires to be reinstated. At the time of bringing an employee before the court as allegedly liable to disciplinary action, the employer must ensure that principles such as fairness, equality, proportionality, lawfulness, guilt, and humanity are applied. To this end, the employer has to provide evidence not only of the disciplinary offence, but also of the fact that he has duly assessed the seriousness of the infraction, the circumstances under which it took place and the employee's attitude towards work.

If the court comes to the conclusion that a disciplinary offence has been committed and the employer has not dealt with all the foregoing aspects before dismissing the worker, the latter's claim to be reinstated is accepted. Yet the court cannot convert the dismissal into a different penalty, since according with Art. 192 of the LC RF, the imposition of a penalty is the preserve of the employer (Par. 53 of Decision No. 2 of the Supreme Court of the Russian Federation, 17 March 2004 "On the Application of the Labour Code of the Russian Federation in the Court Practice").

It is Art. 46 of the Constitution of the Russian Federation and other provisions implementing international regulations (e.g. Art. 8 of the Universal Declaration of Human Rights, Art. 6 of the European Human Rights Convention, Art. 14 of the International Covenant on Civil and Political Rights) that regulate this approach and ensure the judicial protection of individual rights and freedoms. National legislation has to safeguard the right to judicial protection, which should be fair, competent, comprehensive and effective.

When considering a case, the court should evaluate whether employers complied with the procedures of disciplinary penalties. Disciplinary proceedings consist of a set of logically-related steps. Every action must be documented and its implementation is limited. For example, prior to the imposition of a disciplinary penalty, the employer should request from the employee a written explanation regarding his/her violation. Should the explanation not be submitted to the employer within two working days,[10] then the employer can draw up a report explaining the facts.

---

[9] Decision of Moscow city court from 16 January, 2013 No. 4g-5/218/13.

[10] Prior to the amendments made to the Labour Code of the Russian Federation, the terms were not specified. They are certainly welcome, as long as time limits are established in advance.

Although Art. 193 of the LC RF does not establish the terms of implementation concerning stages of disciplinary proceedings, the employer has to comply with the general time requirements indicated in the Labour Code of the Russian Federation. More specifically, a disciplinary penalty shall be imposed no later than one month after the discovery of the offence and no later than six months after the day the offence was committed. If based on the results of an inspection and examination of financial and economic activity or an audit, the sanction should be imposed within two years of the offence. Such short-term limits ensure that employees can quickly and effectively exert their rights if they have been unlawfully imposed disciplinary penalty.

For the disciplinary measure to be enforced, the employer has to comply with certain duties (e.g. the request of a written statement on the part of the employee or of a medical report if the employee has operated under the influence of alcohol or drugs at the workplace), the infringement of which might prejudice the lawfulness of the final decision. The breach of these duties might lead the court to reject the employer's decision on employee liability.

Although in 2006 some amendments have been made to the Labour Code of the Russian Federation, the norms regulating the application of disciplinary penalties for an employee are still insufficient. For this reason, it is necessary to develop detailed procedures concerning the disciplinary penalties to be imposed in case of violations of the internal working regulations or other norms in force within an organization on the part of the employee (e.g. provisions governing special forms of liability). This would also safeguard the latter, ensuring equality of treatment in terms of human rights, freedom and when enforcing disciplinary measures.

References

Aulov, V. K. 2012. *Disciplinarnaya otvetstvennost' sudey: genezis, ponyatie i procedura [Disciplinary responsibility of judges: its genesis, definition, and procedure].]*. Moscow: Thesis.

Bulleten' Verhovnogo suda RF [Bulletin of the Supreme Court of the Russian Federation]. 2004. No 6.

Decision of Moscow city court from 16 January, 2013 No. 4g-5/218/13.

Decision of Saint Petersburg city court from 10 November, 2009 No. 145-66.

Eremina, S. N. 2011. "Disciplinarnaya otvetstvennost' sudey cherez prizmu nauki trudovogo prava" [Disciplinary Responsibility of Judges in the

Light of Employment Law Science]," *Rossiyskiy sudia [Russian Judge]*, No. 2:32-36).

Fedin, K. A. 2007. *Pravonarushenie v sfere truda kak osnovanie privlecheniya k disciplinarnoy otvetstvennosti po normam trudovogo prava [An Offence in the Sphere of Employment as a Ground for Disciplinary Responsibility in Accordance with Provisions of Employment Legislation]* Chelyabinsk: Thesis.

Lebedev, V. M. 2011. "*Disciplinarnye vzyskaniya*" [Disciplinary penalties] in *Trudovoe pravo* [Labour Law], ed. Lebedev, V. M. Moscow: Norma, Infra-M.

Lebedev, V. M., T. M. Fahrutdinova, and I. V. Chernyshova. 2008. *Vnutrenniy trudovoy rasporyadok [International Labour Order]*. Moscow: Statut.

Ustav o discipline rabotnikov rybopromyslovogo flota RF [Regulations on Discipline for Fishing Fleet Employees] approved by the Decision of the Government of the Russian Federation from 21 September, 2000 No 708. *Apellyacionnoe opredelenie Verhovnogo Suda RF [Appeal DecisionDecision of the Supreme Court of the Russian Federation]* from 9 November, 2012 No. 60-APG12-7).

THE TRANSFER OF UNDERTAKINGS IN THE RUSSIAN FEDERATION

OLGA CHESALINA AND ANDRÉ SCHARRER

The idea behind the regulations concerning the transfer of undertakings is that the mere change of ownership of a business should have no consequences for the employee.[1] Without adequate employment safeguards, the seller/transferor of an undertaking could dismiss all employees because he or she no longer needs them, and these employees would have no right to demand to be rehired by the buyer/transferee.[2] The European Union Directive 2001/23/EC[3] aims to provide protection for employees in the case of a transfer of an undertaking or a part of an undertaking. The Labour Code of the Russian Federation (henceforth "the Labour Code"), which came into force on 1 February 2002,[4] does not use the term "transfer of undertakings", but does provide certain regulations which are comparable to those of Directive 2001/23/EC.[5] The aim of this article is to examine the provisions of Russian labour legislation and to evaluate their effectiveness compared to that of the regulations in Directive 2001/23/EC.

---

[1] Thüsing, G. 2013. *European Labour Law.* Munich: C. H. Beck, 105.

[2] *Ibid.* p. 105.

[3] Council of the European Union. 2001. *Council Directive 2001/23/EC of 12 March 2001 on the Approximation of the Laws of the Member States Relating to the Safeguarding of Employees' Rights in the Event of Transfers of Undertakings, Businesses or Parts of Undertakings or Businesses (Official Journal L 82 of 22 March 2001, p. 16).* Brussels: European Union.

[4] Federal law No. 197 of 30 December 2001, published in: *Sobranie Zakonodatel'stva Rossijskoj Federacii* [Collection of Laws of the Russian Federation] (hereafter "SZ RF") 2002, No. 1 (Part 1), Art. 3; amended by Federal law No. 56 of 2 April 2014 (SZ RF 2014, No. 14, Art. 1548).

[5] Regulations regarding the legal consequences of transfers of undertakings are provided by the First part of the Civil Code of the Russian Federation (see footnote 6), and by the Federal Law on the Privatization of State Property and Municipal Property (Federal law No. 178 of 21 December 2001, SZ RF 2002, No. 4, Art. 251, amended by Federal law No. 291 of 2 November 2013, SZ RF 2013, No. 44, Art. 5630).

1. Differences in Terminology with Directive 2001/23/EC

1.1. Undertaking—Organisation

According to legal understanding in the European Union, and as expressed in Art. 1 sec. 1b of Directive 2001/23/EC, an undertaking is an "economic entity" in the sense of "an organized grouping of resources which has the objective of pursuing an economic activity, whether or not that activity is central or ancillary". In Russian law a corresponding concept of an "undertaking" can be found in Art. 132 of the Civil Code of the Russian Federation (henceforth "the Civil Code").[6] Art. 132 point 1 of the Civil Code defines an undertaking as "a complex of assets, used for the performance of business activities".[7] The term "assets" can be defined as a combination of things, rights and obligations (debts).[8] Art. 132 point 2 of the Civil Code states that the undertaking, or "a part of it", as a "complex of assets",[9] can be the "object of purchase and sale, of mortgage, lease and other deals". The undertaking may be part of a "juridical person" (legal entity), which the Russian law refers to as an "organisation".[10]

The term "organisation" is important because in contrast to Art. 1 sec. 1a of Directive 2001/23/EC, Russian law does not use the term "transfer of undertakings". The regulations of Russian labour law, applicable to cases of "transfer of undertakings" as understood in Directive 2001/23/EC, are

---

[6] Federal law No. 51 of 30 November 1994 (SZ RF 1994, No. 32, Art. 3301), amended by Federal law No. 129 of 5 May 2014 (SZ RF 2014, No. 19, Art. 2334).

[7] A business activity is, according to Art. 2 point 1 part 3 of the Civil Code, an "independent activity, performed at one's own risk, aimed at systematically deriving a profit from the use of the property, the sale of commodities, the performance of work or the rendering of services by the persons, registered in this capacity in conformity with the law-established procedure". The translations of the Civil Code in this text are taken from http://www.russian-civil-code.com/PartI/SectionI/Subsection1/Chapter1.html (accessed 26 January 2014).

[8] Krasheninnikov P. V., and B. M. Gongalo. 2013. Art. 132 in *Kommentariy k Grazhdanskomu kodexu Rossiyskoy Federatsii, chasti piervoy [Commentary to the Civil Code of the Russian Federation, Part 1]*, ed. Krasheninnikov P. V., (Moscow: Statut/Legal database Consultant-Plus).

[9] This "complex of asset", which forms the undertaking as a whole, is, according to Art. 132 point 1 sent. 2 of the Civil Code, treated as real estate.

[10] Barinov N. V. 2013. Art. 559 in *Kommentariy k Grazhdanskomu kodexu Rossiyskoy Federatsii, chasti piervoy* [Commentary to the Civil Code of the Russian Federation, Part 2], ed. Krasheninnikov P. V., (Moscow: Statut /Legal database Consultant-Plus).

contained in Art. 75, Art. 77, part 1, point 6 and Art. 81 part 1 point 4 of the Labour Code and they are applicable if one of the following events occurs:

- a change of proprietor of the assets of an organisation;
- a change of the department affiliation of an organisation;
- the restructuring[11] of an organisation.

The term "organisation" is not defined by the law. However, it may not be considered equivalent to the term "undertaking" in the sense of Directive 2001/23/EC. In the list of possible juridical persons given in Art. 48 of the Civil Code, the term "organisation" is used as synonym for a "juridical person". In this context it is also important to note that Russian law does not recognize any forms of associations or partnerships that are not considered to be a juridical person/organisation.

Therefore "undertakings", in the sense of Directive 2001/23/EC, are—in the terms used by Russian labour legislation as expressed in Art. 75, Art. 77 part 1, point 6 and Art. 81 part 1 point 4 of the Labour Code—either "assets of an organisation" or they may form an "organisation", which is the case for state-run and municipal undertakings, which, according to Art. 48 point 2 part 3 and Art. 113 point 1 of the Civil Code, are themselves organisations (juridical persons).

1.2. Part of an Undertaking—Structural Subdivision

As mentioned above, Art. 132 point 2 of the Civil Code states that "a part of" an undertaking can be the "object of purchase and sale, of mortgage, lease and other deals". The term "part of an undertaking" is, however, neither defined by Russian law nor referred to in Russian labour legislation. Just like "undertakings" in the sense of Directive 2001/23/EC, "parts of undertakings" are—in the terms used by the respective provisions of Russian labour law (Art. 75, Art. 77 point 6 and Art. 81 part 1 point 4 of the Labour Code) simply "assets of an organisation".

However, in the context of "parts of undertakings", one term used by Russian labour law is of particular note: "set-apart structural subdivision" ("*osoblennoje strukturnoje podraszdelenie*"). We shall now examine the contexts in the Labour Code in which this term is used.[12]

---

[11] Literally translated: "reorganisation".

[12] See Art. 40 parts 4 and 5, Art. 43 part 3, Art. 57 part 2 sec. 1, Art. 70 part 5, Art. 73 part 4 and Art. 81 part 4 of the Labour Code.

According to Art. 57 part 2 subpart 1 of the Labour Code, a labour contract must contain provisions regarding the place of work, including the "set-apart structural subdivision" in which the employee is to work.

Consequently, the transfer of the employee to another "set-apart structural subdivision" can only take place in accordance with the provisions of the Labour Code relating to the modification of the labour contract (in particular Art. 72 and Art. 72.1). "Set-apart structural subdivisions" include representations and subsidiaries (see Art. 55 of the Civil Code), but also any other division situated at "a place other than" the central administration of an organisation.[13]

In other provisions, the Labour Code uses the term "structural subdivision" ("*strukturnoje podraszdelenie*") without the prefix "set-apart" ("*osoblennoje*"). Accordingly, the term "structural subdivision" is not limited to subdivisions situated at "a place other than" the central administration. According to Art. 57 part 4 sec. 1 of the Labour Code, it is possible, but not obligatory, to include the name of the "structural subdivision" to which the employee is affiliated in the labour contract. Point 16 sec. 3 of Court Order No. 2 of the Plenum of the Supreme Court of the Russian Federation, "On the Application of the Labour Code of the Russian Federation by Courts of the Russian Federation" of 17 March 2004 (henceforth Court Order No. 2)[14], states that a "structural subdivision" can be a department, a production plant, etc. Furthermore, in juridical practice a certain amount of independence is required in order for a subdivision to be considered as such (its own management, separate financial equipment, and so on).

2. Statutory Requirements of Provisions of Russian Labour Law Applicable to the Transfer of Undertakings in the Sense of Directive 2001/23/EC

As we mentioned in section 1.1, the regulations of Russian labour law applicable to cases of "transfers of undertakings" as understood in Directive 2001/23/EC, do not use the term "undertaking", but instead "organisation"

[13] Khokhlov, E. B. 2008. *Trudovoe pravo Rossii [Labour Law of Russia]*. Moscow: Yurait, p. 275.

[14] Published in: Rossijskaja gazeta [Russian Gazette] (hereafter "RG") No. 296 of 31 December 2006. Amended by Court Order No. 63 of the Plenary Meeting of the Supreme Court of the Russian Federation of 28 December 2006 and by Court Order No. 22 of the Plenary Meeting of 28 September 2010 (RG No. 222 of 1 October 2010).

(juridical person). The first requirement for the application of Art. 75, Art. 77 part 1, point 6 and Art. 81 part 1 point 4 of the Labour Code is therefore the existence of an organisation (juridical person). The second requirement is, as previously mentioned, the occurrence of one of the following events (see Art. 75 of the Labour Code):

- a change of proprietor of the assets of an organisation,
- a change of the department affiliation of an organisation,
- the restructuring of an organisation.

2.1. A Change of Proprietor of the Assets of an Organisation

2.1.1. General Requirements

In order to understand the first case in which Art. 75 of the Labour Code can be applied, it is important to keep in mind that Russian civil law makes a distinction between the following forms of property: private property, state property, municipal property and other forms of property (Art. 212 point 1, Art. 48 of the Civil Code). According to Art. 213 point 3 of the Civil Code, commercial and non-profit organisations (juridical persons) are proprietors of the assets transferred to them by way of investments (contributions) made by their founders (participants, members), as well as of the property acquired by these juridical persons on other grounds. However, state or municipal unitary enterprises[15] and institutions financed by their owners for non-profit purposes (e.g. socio-cultural),[16] are not proprietors and only have the right to the economic management of the property (see Art. 113 et seq., Art. 120, Art. 294 et seq. of the Civil Code).

---

[15] State and municipal owned establishments are themselves organisations (juridical persons), see Art. 48 point 2 part 3 of the Civil Code. The assets of these "organisations", however, remain property of the Russian Federation, its subjects or of the respective municipality, see Art. 48 point 2 part 3 of the Civil Code and Art. 213 point 3 of the Civil Code.

[16] A special form of a non-economic organisation (juridical person) (see Art. 48 point 2 part 3 and Art. 120 of the Civil Code) which is founded by its owner for the realisation of cultural, social-cultural or other purposes of a non-economic character and is financed by him/her completely or partially. Art. 120 point 1 of the Civil Code specifies that assets transferred to these organisations shall not become their property and they only have the right of "operational management" in accordance with Art. 296 of the Civil Code.

A "change of proprietor of the assets of an organisation" can therefore only take place in the following cases:[17]

(a.) for organisations owned by private proprietors a "change of proprietor of the assets of an organisation" takes place when all of the assets of the organisation are assigned to a new acquirer. It does not matter whether the transfer of assets is the result of an agreement or of an execution imposed on the property of the former owner. What is important is that the legal owner of *all of the assets* has changed. This does not happen in the case of a share deal. Therefore, even if a stock company is sold by transferring 100% of the stock, no "change of the proprietor of the assets of an organisation" in the sense of Art. 75 of the Labour Code has occurred.

(b.) Another case in which the "change of proprietor of the assets of an organisation" of a privately owned company occurs is if an organisation is nationalised (see Art. 235 point 2 part 3 of the Civil Code).

(c.) The opposite case—the privatization of a state or municipal enterprise—also constitutes a "change of proprietor of the assets of an organisation" (see Art. 235 point 2 part 2 of the Civil Code). According to Art. 1 of the federal law, "On the privatisation of state and municipal property", privatisation is defined as the alienation of assets owned by the Russian Federation, its subjects or municipalities, to juridical or physical persons. According to Art. 17 point 3 of the aforementioned law, in the case of privatization the general rules of the Labour Code (Art. 75 et seq. and Art. 77, et seq.) apply with respect to the continuation of the labour relationship.

(d.) Finally, a "change of proprietor of the assets of an organisation" takes place when assets owned by the Russian Federation, its subjects or of municipalities are transferred to another state or municipal legal entity.

2.1.2. Problematic Constellations: The Transfer of Parts of the Assets of an Organisation (Parts of Undertakings in the Sense of Directive 2001/23/EC)

The wording of Art. 75 of the Labour Code ("change of proprietor of the assets of an organisation") implies that this regulation only applies if all the assets of an organisation (juridical person) are transferred to another owner.

The same wording is used in Art. 77 part 1, point 6 and Art. 81 part 1 point 4 of the Labour Code. According to this wording these provisions do

---

[17] See point 32 of Court Order No. 2.

not apply if only some of the assets of an organisation are transferred to a new owner.

The question therefore arises as to whether Art. 75, Art. 77 point 6 and Art. 81 part 1 point 4 of the Labour Code can be analogically applied to cases in which "parts of the assets of an organisation" forming a "part of the undertaking" are transferred to a new owner.

As a rule, Russian law allows the analogical application of its provisions (see Art. 1 point 4 and Art. 11 point 3 of the Code of Civil Procedure of the Russian Federation).[18] However, point 32 of Court Order No. 2 confirmed that Art. 81 part 1 point 4 of the Labour Code (the right of the employer to terminate the labour contracts of the chief executive, his or her assistants and of the chief accountant in the case of a "change of proprietor of the assets of an organisation", see 5.1 below), only applies if "all of the assets" of an organisation are transferred.[19] As a consequence, Art. 81 part 1 point 4 of the Labour Code cannot be analogically applied if only part of an undertaking is transferred to a new owner because the transferor keeps other parts of the undertaking as his or her property and has therefore not transferred "all of the assets" of the organisation to the new owner.

In reference to point 32 of Court Order No. 2, many courts have decided that Art. 75 of the Labour Code which regulates the transfer of employment relationships to the new owner of the "assets of an organisation", can only apply if indeed "all of the assets" of the organisation are transferred.

However, Court Order No. 2 refers only to Art. 81 part 1 point 4 of the Labour Code. An analogical application of this item of the Labour Code to the transfer of parts of undertakings would be detrimental to the chief executive, his or her assistants and to the chief accountant and would limit their right to use their labour capabilities (see Art. 37 point 1 of the Constitution of the Russian Federation). An analogical application of Art. 81 part 1 point 4 of the Labour Code to the transfer of parts of undertakings is therefore inadmissible, because, according to Art. 55 point 3 of the Constitution of the Russian Federation, the right of the employees to use their working capabilities may be limited only by the legislator[20] (and therefore not by courts by the analogical application of statutes).

[18] Federal law No. 138 of 14 November 2002 (SZ RF 2002, No. 46, Art. 4532), amended by Federal law No. 126 of 5 May 2014 (SZ RF 2014, No. 19, Art. 2331).
[19] See also Chikanova L. A. 2007. Art. 81 in *Kommentarij k Trudovomu kodeksu Rossijskoj Federacii [Commentary to the Labour Code of the Russian Federation]*, ed. Orlovskij, J. P., (Moscow: INFRA-M), p. 281.
[20] Mironov, V. I. 2009. *Trudovoe pravo [The Labour Law]*. Saint Petersburg: Piter Press, p. 676 et. seq.

The provisions of Art. 75 of the Labour Code are mostly favourable to employees, for example stating that the "change of proprietor of the assets of an organisation" cannot be considered reasonable grounds for terminating labour agreements with the organisation's employees (with the exception of the chief executive, his or her assistants and the chief accountant).

Moreover, it can be understood from Art. 75 of the Labour Code that labour relations are transferred from the transferor to the transferee as long as an employee does not refuse to continue performing his or her job functions for the new proprietor (Art. 75 part 6 of the Labour Code). An analogical application of Art. 75 of the Labour Code to the transfer of a part of an undertaking (a part of "the assets of an organisation") would therefore work in favour of the employees. As employees are in need of protection independently of whether "all the assets" of an organisation are transferred or not, we believe that under certain conditions an analogical application of Art. 75 of the Labour Code to the transfer of "parts of the assets" of an organisation is necessary. The Presidium of the Moscow district court explained these conditions in its decision of 25 October 2006[21] by applying Art. 75 of the Labour Code in a case in which a "structural subdivision" ("*strukturnoje podraszdelenie*"—see 1.2) of an organisation was transferred. An analogical application of Art. 75 of the Labour Code in cases of a transfer of a "structural subdivision" has also been recommended in literature.[22]

However, the decision of the Moscow district court of 25 October 2006 has not had any influence on other courts. Art. 75 of the Labour Code is still interpreted literally by the courts. In a number of court decisions regarding the transfer of assets from the state to municipalities, the courts have denied the application of Art. 75 of the Labour Code to cases in which a "structural

---

[21] Order of the Presidium of the Moscow district court No. 648 of 25 October 2006 in case No. 44g-384/06 which reversed the decision of the Moscow district court (court of second instance) of 16 March 2006, No. 33-1752, and confirmed the decision of the court of the Dolgoprudensk city court (court of first instance) of 8 November 2005.

[22] Mironov, V. I. 2006. Praktika novejshego trudovogo zakonodatel'stva. [The New Labour Legislation in Practice]. Moscow: Delo. p. 81; Novichkova, J. V. 2006. Osobennosti rastorzhenija trudovogo dogovora pri smene sobstvennika imushhestva, izmenenii podvedomstvennosti, reorganizacii [Specifics of termination of a labour contract in case of a change of the proprietor of the assets of an organisation, of the department affiliation of an organisation and of the restructuring of an organisation], Trudovye Spory [Labour disputes], No. 3: pp. 45-51 (47).

subdivision" of an organisation had been transferred.[23] It is argued that such a strictly limited interpretation of Art. 75 of the Labour Code is in line with Art. 132 and 559 of the Civil Code, according to which a "change of proprietor of the assets of an organisation" requires that all assets of an organisation be transferred to a new owner, including real estate, movables (equipment, inventory, raw materials, products), claims, debts and exclusive rights.

As a result of this strictly limited interpretation of Art. 75 of the Labour Code, this regulation will be inapplicable in the majority of cases because the transferor and transferee can simply agree not to transfer all of the assets of the organisation in question. In such a situation employees remain legally unprotected. Their employment contracts with the transferor, who does not need them anymore after the transfer of the undertaking, can be terminated in accordance with Art. 81, part 1, point 2 of the Labour Code (as a reduction of number of employees in the organisation).

This indicates a loophole in the Labour Code as far as the transfer of parts of undertakings is concerned.

2.2. Change of the Department Affiliation of an Organisation

The second alternative of Art. 75 of the Labour Code ("change of the department affiliation of an organisation") refers to cases in which a state or municipal enterprise which has been subordinated to a governmental body of the Russian Federation, its subjects or a municipality, is subordinated to another state or municipal body of the same entity. There is no change of ownership.[24]

2.3. The Restructuring of an Organisation

The third alternative in which Art. 75 of the Labour Code applies is the "restructuring of an organisation". The term "restructuring" is defined in Art. 57 of the Civil Code as the merger, affiliation, division, branching off or transformation of an organisation (juridical person). It is important to

---

[23] E.g. In its decision of 10 April 2007 in the case F03-A73/06-1/5571 the Federal arbitrage court for the Far Eastern district decided that a "change of the proprietor of the assets of an organisation" requires the transfer of "all assets" of the organisation in question.

[24] A case of a "change of the department affiliation of an organisation" which is very common in practice is that of research institutes or centres, clinics, teaching institutions, etc. which were subordinated to a certain state or municipal department and become subordinated to another department of the same entity.

note that, in this context, according to point 23 sec. 2 of Court Order No. 19 of the Plenum of the Supreme Court of Arbitration of the Russian Federation of 18 November 2003, "On some questions concerning the application of the federal law on joint stock companies" the transformation of an open joint-stock company into a closed joint-stock company is not considered to be a restructuring.[25]

According to its wording, the third alternative of Art. 75 of the Labour Code only applies to cases in which a restructuring has been carried out in accordance with the provisions of the Civil Code. This includes in particular the drawing up of a "divisional balance" in the cases of a division of an organisation and the branching off of part of an organisation (Art. 58 points 3 and 4 of the Civil Code). In the cases of a merger, affiliation or transformation of an organisation, a "transfer deed" must be drawn up (Art. 58 points 1, 2 and 5 of the Civil Code). Both the divisional balance and the transfer deed must contain provisions on the legal ceding of all obligations of the restructured organisation with respect to all its creditors and debtors, including any obligations disputed by the parties (Art. 58 sec. 1 of the Civil Code).[26]

According to Art. 57 point 4 of the Civil Code, an organisation shall be regarded as restructured (with the exception of cases of reorganisation in the form of affiliation) from the moment of the state registration of the newly created organisation. In the case of the restructuring of organisation in the form of another organisation's affiliation to it, the former shall be

---

[25] According to Art. 97 of the Civil Code and Art. 7 of the Federal law on joint stock companies (Federal law No. 208 of 26 December1995, amended by Federal law No. 410 of 28 December 2013 (SZ RF 2013 No. 52 [Part 1], Art. 6975) joint stock companies may be open companies (Russian abbreviation "OAO") or closed companies (Russian abbreviation "ZAO"). For closed joint stock companies a number of special provisions apply which create a stronger personal binding between the shareholders. Thus the transferability of the stocks to third parties is limited and open subscriptions to the stock are not possible, see Arzinger, R., and T. Galander. 2002. *Russisches Wirtschatfsrecht* [Russian economic law]. Berlin-Reinickendorf: GRUNDEIGENTUM-VERLAG GmbH. Chapter C. 9.1. The change of the limited liability company (Russian abbreviation "OOO") to a company with additional liability (Russian abbreviation "ODO") works differently. According to Art. 56 of the Federal law on limited liability companies (Federal law No. 14 of 8 February 1998, amended by federal law No. 282 of 29 December 2012 (SZ RF 2012 No.53 [Part 1], Art. 7607), this would be a case of a change of form and therefore a reorganisation in the sense of Art. 57 of the Civil Code.

[26] Translation in accordance with http://www.russian-civil-code.com (accessed 26 January 2014).

regarded as reorganized from the moment when an entry is made regarding the cessation of activity of the organisation which has become affiliated to it in the State Register of Legal Entities.[27]

Despite these formal requirements related to restructuring, the Kaliningrad district court did apply the third alternative of Art. 75 of the Labour Code in a case in which the assets of a "structural subdivision"[28] of an organisation (OAO[29] see "trade harbour Kaliningrad") were transferred to a limited liability company (OOO TPK), which had been founded by OAO for this purpose.[30] As the transfer of the assets from OAO to OOO TPK had been performed by way of several contracts of sale and several lease agreements there was no restructuring in the sense of Art. 57 of the Civil Code. The requirements for a restructuring, which would have been possible in the form of a "branching off", were not met, as no "divisional balance" had been drawn up and no such restructuring had been registered.

However, the Kaliningrad district court ignored the missing formal requirements of a restructuring (in particular of a "divisional balance") and held that a *de facto* restructuring had taken place as OOO TPK signed new labour contracts with the majority of the employees of the former "structural subdivision" and fulfilled the same functions for OAO as had previously been fulfilled by the "structural subdivision".[31]

---

[27] *Ibid.*

[28] See 1.2 above.

[29] See footnote 24.

[30] Decision of the Kaliningrad district court of 24 May 2002 in case No. 2-378/2002. This decision is reported by Lyutov, L. N. 2008. "Prava rabotnikov pri smene sobstvennika imushhestva organizacii: problemy rossijskogo zakonodatel'stva i normy Evropejskogo Sojuza [Workers' rights in the event of a change of the proprietor of the assets of an organisation: Problems of Russian legislation and regulations of the European Union]," in *Rossijskij ezhegodnik trudovogo prava [Russian Yearbook of Labour law]*, No. 4: pp. 467-494 (472).

[31] Lyutov, L. N. 2008. "Prava rabotnikov pri smene sobstvennika imushhestva organizacii: problemy rossijskogo zakonodatel'stva i normy Evropejskogo Sojuza [Workers' Rights in the Event of a Change of the Proprietor of the Assets of an Organisation: Problems of Russian Legislation and Regulations of the European Union]," *Rossijskij ezhegodnik trudovogo prava [Russian Yearbook of Labour law]*, No. 4: pp. 467-494 (472).

3. Consequences of the Transfer of an Undertaking for Individual Employment Relationships

3.1. General Consequences

The legal consequences of a "change of proprietor of the assets of an organisation", of the "change of the department affiliation of an organisation" and of the "restructuring of an organisation" for individual employment relationships are regulated in Art. 75 of the Labour Code.

Although it is not expressly stated that employment relationships in these cases are transferred, this can be concluded from the fact that Art. 75 of the Labour Code is part of Chapter 12 which is entitled "Modification of a Labour Agreement".[32] Art. 75 of the Labour Code therefore regulates cases of a change of one party of the contract or, in the case of a "change of the department affiliation of an organisation", the change of the name of one party of the contract.

Furthermore, according to Art. 75 parts 2 and 5 of the Labour Code, the "change of proprietor of the assets of an organisation", the "change of the department affiliation of an organisation" or the "restructuring of an organisation" cannot be considered grounds for the termination of labour contracts (with the exception of the labour contracts of the chief executive, his or her assistants and the chief accountant). This prohibition of the termination of labour contracts concerns the actions of the new owner of the undertaking, which also indicates that the law assumes that labour relationships will continue with the new owner.

Deviating from the previous version of Art. 75 part 4 (valid until October 2006)[33] the transfer of a labour contract of an employee no longer requires his or her approval (which could be declared implicitly by continuously fulfilling the duties in accordance with the labour contract).

If the employee does not want to work for the new owner of the undertaking, he/she can exercise his/her right to refuse to continue performing his/her job functions in accordance with Art. 75 parts 3 and 6 of the Labour Code (see 3.3 below).

When Art. 75 of the Labour Code applies, the labour relationship continues with the new owner of the undertaking. It does not matter

---

[32] In case of a "restructuring" this result can be derived directly from general civil law provisions. According to Art. 58 of the Civil Code the consequence of a restructuring is always a universal legal succession.

[33] On 5 October 2006 substantial changes of the Labour Code by Federal law No. 90 of 1 July 2006 came into force.

whether an employee was ill, on vacation or exempt from work during the previous duration of the labour contract. All that matters is the legal existence of an employment relationship at the time of the "change of proprietor of the assets of an organisation", the "change of the department affiliation of an organisation" or the "restructuring of an organisation".

However, Art. 75 of the Labour Code does not guarantee employees that, in the case of any of the three aforementioned events, labour contracts will not be altered either at all or for a certain lapse of time. The new employer can therefore modify the labour contracts in accordance with the general rules of the Labour Code.

Of course, according to these rules (Art. 72 of the Labour Code) the new employer cannot unilaterally decide to alter the conditions of the existing labour contract, including the transfer of the employee to a different job. A change is only possible with the written consent of the employee.

However, according to Art. 74 part 1 of the Labour Code, the terms of a labour contract may be modified on the initiative of the employer if the pre-existing terms cannot be upheld due to reasons relating to a change in organisational or technical working conditions (changes in production machinery and technologies, structural reorganisation of production facilities, etc.). Art. 74 part 2 of the Labour Code states that the employer must notify the employee in writing of any such change at least two months in advance. A change in organisational working conditions in the sense of Art. 74 part 1 of the Labour Code would be assumed, if, for example, the employer reorganises a manufacturing or other work process.

The second alternative of Art. 74 part 1 of the Labour Code ("change in the technological working conditions") would apply, if, for example, the employer were to introduce new or different technologies to the manufacturing process. The employer can also exercise these rights, provided by Art. 74 Labour Code, in the case of changes in organisational or technological working conditions resulting from a "change of proprietor of the assets of an organisation", the "change of the department affiliation of an organisation" or the "restructuring of an organisation".

3.2. Information of the Employees or their Representative Bodies

The Labour Code does not specifically oblige the employer to inform the employees or the undertaking's representative office of the trade union[34] of a forthcoming "change of proprietor of the assets of an organisation", "change of the department affiliation of an organisation" or "restructuring of an organisation". However, according to the general rule provided by Art. 21, part 1, sec 6 of the Labour Code, employees are entitled to receive complete and valid information on all of their labour conditions. In literature it is argued that on the basis of Art. 21 part 1, sec 6 of the Labour Code, employees are entitled to information about a forthcoming "change of proprietor of the assets of an organisation", "change of the department affiliation of an organisation" or "restructuring of an organisation" and about the consequences such events will have on them.[35]

3.3. Employees' Right to Object

According to Art. 75 parts 3 and 6 of the Labour Code, an employee has the right to refuse to continue performing his job functions in the case of any of the three aforementioned events. A notice of such a refusal has to be given to the employer in written form.[36] If an employee chooses to exercise this right, his or her labour contract will end in accordance with Art. 77 part 1 point 6 of the Labour Code. The former employer (the transferor of the undertaking) or, if this right is exercised *after* the occurrence of the events mentioned in Art. 75 of the Labour Code, the new employer (the transferee) does not even have to terminate the contract.

The Labour Code does not provide a deadline within which the employee has to exercise the right to refuse to continue performing his or her job functions. An analogical application of the time limit given in Art. 75 part 1 of the Labour Code has been recommended in literature.[37]

Art. 75 part 1 of the Labour Code states that the new proprietor of the assets of an organisation has the right to terminate the labour contracts of the chief executive officer, his or her assistants and the chief accountant within three months from the day of taking on the ownership of the

---

[34] See 4.2 below.

[35] Shajhutdinova, N. P. 2007. "Prekrashhenie trudovogo dogovora pri reorganizacii predprijatija putem prisoedinenija [Discontinuation of the labour contract in the case of reorganisation by merger]," *Trudovye Spory [Labour disputes]*, No. 2:61-63 (62).

[36] See also Chikanova L. A. 2007. Art.75 in *Kommentarij k Trudovomu kodeksu Rossijskoj Federacii [Commentary to the Labour Code of the Russian Federation]*, ed. Orlovskij, J. P., (Moscow: INFRA-M), 257.

[37] Mironov, V. I. 2009. *Trudovoe pravo [Labour Law]*. Saint Petersburg: Piter Press, p. 292.

organisation. This point is important in practice because if a deadline of three months were applied to an employee's right to refuse to perform his or her job, after this period of time the employee could only terminate his or her labour contract in accordance with the general (and indispensable) legal right of any employee to terminate his or her labour contract without providing a reason by giving two weeks' written notice to that effect (see Art. 80 of the Labour Code).

3.4. The Legal Position of the Transferor

3.4.1. Labour Relationship

As mentioned in 3.1 above, Art. 75 of the Labour Code treats the "change of proprietor of the assets of an organisation" and the "restructuring of an organisation" as cases of a change of one party of a contract: the former employer loses his position as a party of the labour contracts and the new employer becomes a party of the labour contracts.

Naturally, in the third case in which Art. 75 of the Labour Code applies ("change of the department affiliation of an organisation") the parties of the labour contract do not change. The labour contract is only changed in so far as the employer becomes a new representative (Art. 57 part 4 of the Labour Code), as another department of the employing organisation exercises rights and duties regarding the labour contracts.

3.4.2. Liability

As soon as a "change of proprietor of the assets of an organisation" in the sense of Art. 75 of the Labour Code has come into effect, the former employer is free of all duties of the labour contracts. Russian labour law does not provide joint or several liability for the old and new employers.

This also concerns any claims which may have already arisen prior to the date on which the "change of proprietor" or the "restructuring" became effective.

The same holds true also in the case of a "restructuring of an organisation", if, as a result of such restructuring, the former employer simply ceases to exist (e.g. in case of a merger or affiliation). However, in the case of a "restructuring of an organisation" in the form of a division or branching off, joint or several liability of the new legal entity or entities can arise for obligations of the restructured organisation in accordance with the general rules of the Civil Code.

4. Legal Consequences of the Transfer of an Undertaking for Collective Labour Law/Collective Bargaining Law

4.1. Legal Consequences for Collective Agreements and Collective Contracts

Russian labour law recognises both collective agreements and collective contracts.

According to Art. 45 part 1 of the Labour Code, a collective agreement is a legal act regulating socio-labour relations and related economic relations which is concluded between employees' and employers' representatives at federal, regional, industry (inter-industry) and territorial levels within the limits of their competence.[38]

According to Art. 40 part 1 of the Labour Code, a collective contract is a legal act regulating socio-labour relations within a single organisation. It is concluded between the employer and the employees' representatives.

Both collective agreements (agreements between associations of employers and trade unions) and collective contracts (agreements between the representatives of the employer and the representative of the employees in a single company) can be concluded for a maximum of three years (see Art. 48 part 1 and Art. 43 part 1 of the Labour Code). However, a minimum period for the validity of collective agreements and collective contracts is not required by Russian law. Usually, both collective agreements and collective contracts are concluded for a one-year period, but the parties are free to agree otherwise. Collective agreements and collective contracts become effective on the day they are signed or on the date agreed in the respective agreement or contract. At the end of their validity both collective agreements and collective contracts can be prolonged once for another maximum period of three years (see Art. 48 part 2 and Art. 43 part 2 of the Labour Code).

4.1.1. Collective Agreements (Agreements between Employers' Associations and Trade Unions)

A "change of proprietor of the assets of an organisation", the "change of the department affiliation of an organisation" or the "restructuring of an organisation" has no influence on the further validity of collective agreements. Russian labour law does not specifically regulate this matter.

---

[38] Translation in accordance with http://www.ilo.org/dyn/natlex/docs/WEB TEXT/60535/65252/ E01RUS01.htm#chap45 (accessed 26 January 2014).

This follows from the fact that neither party of the transfer of an undertaking can alter a collective agreement which has been concluded between the competent association of employers and the competent trade union for a certain region or branch of industry.

4.1.2. Collective Agreements (for a Single Company)

For collective agreements concluded between the representatives of the employer and the representative of the employees in a single company) Russian law does regulate some specific legal consequences:

(a.) If in the case of a "change of proprietor of the assets of an organisation", the "form of the property of the organisation" is also changed (in particular in cases where public property is changed into private property and vice versa,[39] e.g. nationalization or privatization) a collective contract will only remain effective for three months after the transfer of the rights of ownership (see Art. 43 part 5 of the Labour Code).

Both parties (the new owner of the company and the representatives of the employees) are entitled to propose a new collective agreement or the extension up to three years of the existing collective agreement (see Art. 43 part 5 and part 7 of the Labour Code). For cases in which the "form of the property of the organisation" remains unchanged as a result of a "change of proprietor of the assets of an organisation"—effectively for the more important cases of transfers of undertakings from one private owner to another private owner—the question of the further validity of collective contracts is not regulated by Russian labour law. In the authors' opinion, this gap in the statutes cannot be filled by an analogical application of Art. 43 part 5 of the Labour Code.[40] Russian labour law generally assumes that in the event of a "change of proprietor of the assets of an organisation" labour relationships continue with the new owner without any changes (see 3.1.). Therefore, for cases in which the "the form of the property of the organisation" is unchanged, the Labour Code contains no explicit regulations; both the terms and conditions of collective contracts and their duration remain unaffected by a "change of proprietor of the assets of an organisation".

[39] A "change of the form of the property" can only occur in the events (2) to (4) desribed in 2.1.1. above. The form of the property does not change when a privately owned company is transferred to another private owner or when a company run by a municipality is transferred to another municipality.

[40] For a different opinion Snigireva, I. O. 2008. "Art 43," in *Kommentarij k Trudovomu kodeksu Rossijskoj Federacii [Commentary to the Labour Code of the Russian Federation]*, ed. Gusov K. N., (Moscow: Prospekt), p. 130.

(b.) A "change of the department affiliation of an organisation" and a "restructuring of an organisation" in the form of a "transformation", i.e. in the form of a simple change of the juridical form of the organisation (e.g. change of a joint-stock company into a limited liability company) have no effect either on the terms and conditions of a collective contract or on its duration. In the event of the "restructuring of an organisation" in the form of a merger, affiliation, division or branching off, a collective contract will remain effective during the whole restructuring period (see Art. 43 part 6 of the Labour Code). According to Art. 43 part 7 of the Labour Code, either of the parties may propose to create a new collective contract or to prolong the existing one for a term of up to three years.

4.2. Functions of Employees' Representative Bodies in the Process of the Transfer of Undertakings and Afterwards

Effective from 19 May 2013,[41] a new section (sec. 8) was inserted in Art. 22, part 1 of the Labour Code. This section states that employers have the right to establish a "works council"—an advisory body which prepares proposals concerning questions of production, production processes, the implementation of new techniques and technologies, how to increase the effectiveness of production and the qualifications of employees. However, it is highly likely that such "work councils" will not be of any practical importance, because—apart from their mere advisory function—it is not obligatory for the employer to establish a "works council" for the undertaking and the employees do not have the right to demand the creation of such a body. Furthermore, even if a works council is established, according to Art. 22, part 1, sec. 8 of the Labour Code, it has no right to deal with questions which come under the authority of labour unions.

Therefore it is another body of employees' representation which is much more important: the elective body of the competent trade union. All employers must provide space in which sessions of the elective body of the competent trade union can be held (Art. 377 part 1 of the Labour Code). Any employers which have over 100 employees must offer the elective body of the primary trade union a permanent office including equipment, etc. The elective body of the competent trade union exercises many functions which are comparable to those of the works councils established in EU member states. However, the degree of participation of the elective body of the competent trade union in the case of the transfer of

[41] Federal law No. 95 of 7 May 2013 (SZ RF 2013 No. 19, Art. 2322).

the undertaking does not remotely equal the extent of employee participation laid down in the labour laws of EU member states in accordance with directive 2001/23/EC.

According to Art. 371 et seq. of the Labour Code, an employer shall make decisions with due consideration for the statement of the competent trade union, the elective body of the primary trade union or the relevant trade union in cases provided for in the Labour Code. However, a statement of the competent trade union or of its elective body within the company is not required in the event of the "change of proprietor of the assets of an organisation", the "change of the department affiliation of an organisation" or the "restructuring of an organisation". An obligation to take into account a statement of the competent trade union or of its elective body can be imposed on the employer by a collective agreement, a collective contract or a local normative act.[42]

Trade unions may have a certain degree of influence on an event such as the "change of proprietor of the assets of an organisation", the "change of the department affiliation of an organisation" or the "restructuring of an organisation", by using their right to control the conditions of the "labour and environment". According to Art. 20 points 2 and 3 of the Federal Law, "On trade unions, their rights and on the guarantees of their activity",[43] trade unions shall exercise control of the state of protection of labour and the environment through their bodies, their authorized persons (agents) for labour protection, and also their own labour-protection inspectorates. For these purposes they are granted the following rights:

- unimpeded access to an organisation, its structural subdivisions and workplaces manned by members of the given trade union,
- permission to take part in investigations of accidents at work,
- the opportunity to protect the rights and interests of trade union members on matters of working conditions, job safety in questions of the terms of employment, job safety, the compensation of harm caused to their health

[42] See also Korshunova, T. J. 2007. Art. 371 in *Kommentarij k Trudovomu kodeksu Rossijskoj Federacii [Commentary to the Labour Code of the Russian Federation]*, ed. Orlovskij, J. P., (Moscow: INFRA-M), p. 1115. "Local normative acts" are, according to Art. 8 part 1 of the Labour Code, local normative acts containing labour law norms adopted by employers, except for employers who are natural persons but not individual entrepreneurs, within the scope of their powers in accordance with the labour legislation and other normative acts containing labour law norms, collective contracts and collective agreements.

[43] See Federal law No. 10 of 12 January 1996 "On trade unions, their rights and on the guarantees for their activity" (SZ RF 1996 No. 3 Art. 148), amended by federal law No. 185 of 2 July 2013 (SZ RF 2013 No. 27 Art. 3477).

> by work accidents and also on other matters of protection of labour and the natural environment in conformity with federal legislation.[44]

In the event of the discovery of breaches of regulations which pose a threat to the life and health of employees, trade union bodies in an organisation and trade union labour-protection inspectors have the right to demand that the employer immediately eliminate these infringements, and simultaneously to request the Federal Labour Inspectorate to take urgent measures.[45]

5. Termination of Labour Contracts in Cases of Transfers of Undertakings

5.1. Prohibition of Dismissal

5.1.1. Dismissal on the Grounds of the Transfer of Undertaking

The dismissal of an employee on the grounds of the "change of proprietor of the assets of an organisation", the "change of the department affiliation of an organisation" or the "restructuring of an organisation" is expressively prohibited by Art. 75 parts 2 and 5 of the Labour Code.

In the event of a "change of proprietor of the assets of an organisation" the prohibition of dismissal does not apply to the chief executive of the organisation, his or her assistants and the chief accountant. According to Art. 75 part 1 of the Labour Code a new owner of the organisation's assets can terminate the labour contracts of these employees. Consequently, in the list of cases in which a labour contract can be terminated on the employer's initiative (Art. 81 of the Labour Code), the "change of proprietor of the assets of an organisation" is listed as a reason for termination of labour contracts with respect to the aforementioned employees (Art. 81 part 1 point 4 of the Labour Code).[46]

This right of the new employer to dismiss the chief executive of the organisation, his or her assistants and the chief accountant, is strictly

---

[44] Art. 20 point 2 of the law "On trade unions, their rights and on the guarantees of their activity, translation from http://www.ilo.org/dyn/natlex/docs/WEBTEXT/42900/64988/E96RUS01.htm (accessed 26 January 2014).

[45] Art. 20 point 3 of the Law on Trade unions, their Rights and on the Protection of their Activity (accessed 26 January 2014).

[46] See Decision of the Constitutional Court of the Russian Federation of 27 May 2010 No. 699-O-O.

limited to new owners who have taken on "all assets" of the organisation.[47] It is important to note that Art. 81 part 1 point 4 of the Labour Code cannot, even by analogy, be applied to the chief executive, his or her assistants and the chief accountant of a *structural subdivision* of the organisation (in particular representations and subsidiaries, see 1.2), a mistake which is widespread in practice.[48] Nor can these employees be dismissed when their role is carried out for a subsidiary and affiliated company of the organisation. Furthermore, this provision does not apply in the event of a "change of the department affiliation of an organisation" or of the "restructuring of an organisation".[49]

If the chief executive of an organisation has been hired on the basis of a service contract as permitted by the Civil Code, his or her contract can be terminated in accordance with the general civil law provisions.[50]

Another mistake which is very widespread in practice is that it is assumed that Art. 81 part 1 point 4 of the Labour Code can be applied in cases of a transfer of an undertaking by way of a share deal. However, in the case of a share deal no "change of proprietor of the assets of an organisation" actually takes place. According to Art. 66 point 1 and Art. 213 point 3 of the Civil Code, juridical persons (organisations) are the owners of the property which is transferred to them by way of the investments (contributions) made by their founders (participants, members), and also of the property acquired by these juridical persons in other ways. Even if 100 % of the shares of an organisation are transferred, the organisation itself remains the owner of its assets regardless of who the shares belong to. Therefore, in the case of a share deal the new owner of the shares cannot terminate the labour contracts of the chief executive of the organisation, his or her assistants or the chief accountant.

A new owner of all the assets of an organisation can terminate the labour contracts of the chief executive of the organisation, his or her assistants and the chief accountant within three months from the date of the acquisition of the property (see Art. 75 part 1 of the Labour Code). A

---

[47] See point 32 of Court Order No. 2.

[48] Orlovskij, J. P., A. F. Nurtdinova, and L. A. Chikanova. 2012. *Trudovoe zakonodatel'stvo: aktual'nye voprosy, kommentarii, raz'jasnenija [Labour Legislation: Current Issues, Comments, Clarifications: A Guide for Practice]*. Moscow: Yurait, p. 145.

[49] Chershinceva, E. A. 2013. *Voprosy i otvety [Questions and Answers]*. Legal database Consultant-Plus.

[50] Glazyrin, V. V. 2005. Art. 75 in *Kommentarij k Trudovomu kodeksu Rossijskoj Federacii [Commentary to the Labour Code of the Russian Federation]*, ed. Glazyrin, V. V., (Moscow: Examen).

notice of dismissal given after this three month period is invalid.[51] Should a valid notice of dismissal be given, the employer must pay the employee in question compensation amounting to three times his or her average monthly earnings (Art. 181 of the Labour Code), unless the parties agreed on greater compensation in the labour contract.

5.1.2. Dismissal on other Grounds

Art. 75 parts 2 and 5 of the Labour Code only prohibit the dismissal of employees on the grounds of the "change of proprietor of the assets of an organisation", the "change of the department affiliation of an organisation" or the "restructuring of an organisation" (with the above-mentioned exception for the chief executive, his or her assistants and the chief accountant in the first case).

However, the aforementioned events have no impact on the right of the employer to dismiss employees on other grounds stated in the Labour Code. In particular, an employer can dismiss employees if it is decided to reduce the staff of the organisation (Art. 81 part 1 point 2 of the Labour Code). Such a decision may be justified by economic, technical or organisational reasons.[52] In the case of a "change of proprietor of the assets of an organisation" such a reduction of staff will only be permitted after the state registration of the transfer of the property (Art. 75 part 4 of the Labour Code).

If an employer wishes to exercise his right to dismiss one or more employees, he or she must comply with Art. 81 part 6 of the Labour Code.

According to this provision it is prohibited to dismiss an employee (except for the cases of closing down an organisation or terminating the activity of an individual entrepreneur) during a period of temporary disability or leave of absence.

5.2. The Entitlement of Dismissed Employees to Re-employment

The provisions of Russian labour law concerning the "change of proprietor of the assets of an organisation", the "change of the department affiliation of an organisation" or the "restructuring of an organisation" deal

---

[51] Mironov, V. I. 2009. *Trudovoe pravo [Labour Law]*. Saint Petersburg: Piter Press, p. 315.

[52] If a representation or subsidiary which is situated at a place other than the central administration of an organisation or another "set-apart structural subdivision" (see 1.2 above) is closed, the labour contracts of the employees at this subdivison can be terminated in accordance with Art. 81 points 1 and 4 f the Labour Code.

with the question of whether the new employer is entitled to change or terminate employees' labour contracts. However, what if the former employer (i.e. the seller of the assets of an organisation) had already decided to reduce the staff of the organisation, perhaps because his or her original intention had been to liquidate the organisation before eventually finding a buyer?

In accordance with Russian labour law, such cases must be resolved in the following manner. After the decision to close down the organisation, the employer is entitled to reduce the organisation's staff in accordance with Art. 81 part 1 point 2 of the Labour Code. However, as soon as it becomes clear to the employer that the assets of the organisation can be sold and therefore the organisation does not need to be liquidated, the employer is obliged to correspondingly adjust measures concerning the staff. The employees in question will not need to demand re-employment because, due to the changed circumstances, their dismissal would be unlawful. The employees can demand further occupation from the buyer of the organisation's assets respecting the terms of their labour contracts which are transferred to the buyer in accordance with Art. 75 of the Labour Code (see 3.1.).

5.3. Judicial Proceedings in Cases of Disputes Concerning the Continuation/Unchanged Continuation of Labour Contracts

According to Art. 391 part 2 sec. 1 of the Labour Code, labour disputes concerning: the reinstatement of an employee in his/her position regardless of the grounds for the discontinuation of the labour contract, the transfer of the employee to another job or a change in wages during a period when the employee carried out lower-paid work, shall be heard directly by a court upon a petition by the employee. This provision applies regardless of the grounds for a claimed discontinuation of a labour contract, i.e. not only in the case of an employer giving a notice of dismissal, but also if the employer claims that the labour contract has ended because of an employee's refusal to work for the new owner of the undertaking (Art. 75 parts 3 and 6, Art. 77 part 1 point 6 of the Labour Code).

Art. 392 part 1 of the Labour Code gives the employee three months from the day the employee learned, or should have learned, of a violation of his or her rights in which to file for a court resolution to the dispute, or, in the case of disputes over terminations, one month from the day he or she was served with a copy of a termination order or the day his or her employment record book was released. No fees and costs are imposed on employees who file for court resolution.

If a dismissal or transfer to another job is deemed illegal by the court, it will order the employer to reinstate the employee in his/her previous job (Art. 394 part 1 of the Labour Code). In addition, the court may make a decision regarding the payment to the employee of his/her average earnings for the entire term of involuntary absence at work or the difference in earnings for the entire term of performance of a lower-paid task (Art. 394 part 1). Furthermore, in the events of a dismissal without legal grounds, a breach of the established dismissal procedure or an illegal transfer to another job, the court has the power to compel the employer to pay monetary compensation to the employee for the moral damage suffered (Art. 394 part 9). The amount of money to be paid as compensation is set by the court.

6. Burden of Proof

According to Art. 56 point 1 of the Code of Civil Procedure of the Russian Federation, each party involved in a dispute must provide proof of its reasons for claims and objections unless otherwise stipulated by federal law. Therefore, an employee who demands further employment from a new owner of the assets of the organisation he or she worked for would have to prove that "all assets"[53] of the organisation have been transferred.

If an employee was dismissed by the former employer or the new employer, the employer has to prove the existence of legal grounds for the dismissal. This procedure has been confirmed by point 23 of Court Order No. 2, according to which it is the employee whose labour contract has been terminated or changed by the employer and who wishes to be reinstated, who bears the burden of proof for demonstrating the illegal grounds for the termination/change of the labour contract as well as his or her compliance with the procedural requirements set forth by the Labour Code for such disputes.

7. An Evaluation of the Russian Regulations Applicable to the Transfer of Undertakings and Comparison with Directive 2001/23/EC

Russian labour legislation does not recognise the term "transfer of an undertaking". The regulations of Russian labour law, applicable to cases of "transfers of undertakings" as understood in Directive 2001/23/EC, are

[53] See 2.1.2 above.

contained in Art. 75, Art. 77 point 6 and Art. 81 part 1 point 4 of the Labour Code of the Russian Federation.

The regulations in Art. 75 of the Labour Code provide a certain degree of protection for employees in the case of a transfer of an undertaking or part of an undertaking. However, these regulations take a very formal approach to the subject matter and only apply if the transferor is a juridical person (an organisation) and only in the following events:

- a change of proprietor of "all" assets of an organisation,
- a change of the department affiliation of an organisation,
- the restructuring of an organisation (merger, affiliation, division, branching off or transformation).

The formality of this approach has three major differences compared to the regulations of Directive 2001/23/EC:[54]

- Firstly, the regulations of Directive 2001/23/EC on the transfer of undertakings do not only apply to juridical persons, but to any organised grouping of resources which has the objective of pursuing an economic activity (Art. 1 sec. 1 subsec. b Directive 2001/23).
- Secondly, the regulations of Directive 2001/23/EC also apply if part of an undertaking is transferred as long as this part is sufficiently structured and autonomous to be able to exercise an economic activity which pursues a specific objective and is not only limited to performing a specific employment contract.[55]
- Thirdly, and most importantly, the application of Directive 2001/23/EC is not strictly limited to cases in which all the assets of an entity are transferred. Even if no assets at all are transferred Directive 2001/23/EC can still apply if the transferred entity has retained its identity (Art. 1 sec. 1 subsec. b Directive 2001/23). Of course, in many cases a retaining of the identity of the entity will require the transfer of a substantial body of assets. However, the Court of Justice of the European Union has stated that an economic entity may, in certain sectors, function without any significant tangible or intangible assets and therefore the maintenance of the identity of such an entity following the transaction affecting it cannot, logically,

[54] For an overview of Directive 2001/23/EC and its implementation in the member states of the European Union see Thüsing, G. 2013. *European Labour Law.* Munich: C. H. Beck, p. 105 et seq.

[55] Decision of the Court of Justice of the European Union of 13th September 2007, Case C-458/05 (Mohamed Jouini and Others v Princess Personal Service GmbH), paragraph 31.

> depend on the transfer of such assets.[56] In such cases an entity may maintain its identity after it has been transferred as long as the new employer does not merely pursue the same activity as his predecessor but also takes over a major part of the employees, in terms of their numbers and skills, specifically assigned by his predecessor to a given task.[57]

Even if the requirements of Art. 75 of the Labour Code for a transfer of the labour relationship are met (e.g. because it can be proven that all assets have been transferred to a new owner), Russian labour law provides a lower degree of protection for those employees whose labour relationships are subject to the transfer than that which is provided by Directive 2001/23/EC.

Only the regulations concerning the prohibition of dismissal (Art. 75 sec. 2 and 5 of the Labour Code) are similar to the corresponding regulations of Directive 2001/23/EC. According to Art. 75 secs 2 and 5 of the Labour Code, a transfer cannot be considered grounds for the termination of labour contracts by the employer, which does, however, not impede dismissals made on technical or organisational grounds. A similar regulation is provided by Art. 4 sec. 1 Directive 2001/23/EC. In addition, the fact that certain leading employees (the chief executive officer, his or her assistants and the chief accountant) are excluded from this protection is similar to European law provisions. According to Art. 4 sec. 2 of Directive 2001/23/EC, member States may rule that the prohibition of dismissal shall not apply to certain specific categories of employees who are not covered by the laws or practices of the member states regarding protection against dismissal. However, in most cases, Art. 75 of the Labour Code will not apply due to the fact that transferor and transferee can easily prevent the application of this provision by excluding a part of the assets from the transfer.

[56] Decision of the Court of Justice of the European Union of 20 January 2011, Case C-463/09(CLECE SA v María Socorro Martín Valor and Ayuntamiento de Cobisa), paragraph 35.

[57] Decision of the Court of Justice of the European Union of 20 January 2011, Case C-463/09(CLECE SA v María Socorro Martín Valor and Ayuntamiento de Cobisa), paragraph 36.

References

Arzinger, R., and T. Galander. 2002. *Russisches Wirtschatfsrecht [Russian Economic Law]*. Berlin-Reinickendorf: Grundeigentum-Verlag GmbH.

Barinov, N. V. 2013. Art. 559 in *Kommentariy k Grazhdanskomu kodexu Rossiyskoy Federatsii, chasti piervoy [Commentary to the Civil Code of the Russian Federation, Part 2]*, ed. Krasheninnikov P. V., (Moscow: Statut /Legal database Consultant-Plus).

Chikanova, L. A. 2007. Art. 81 in *Kommentarij k Trudovomu kodeksu Rossijskoj Federacii [Commentary to the Labour Code of the Russian Federation]*, ed. Orlovskij, J. P., (Moscow: INFRA-M).

Glazyrin, V. V. 2005. Art. 75 in *Kommentarij k Trudovomu kodeksu Rossijskoj Federacii [Commentary to the Labour Code of the Russian Federation]*, ed. Glazyrin, V. V., (Moscow: Examen).

Khokhlov, E. B. 2008. *Trudovoe pravo Rossii [Labour law of Russia]*. Moscow: Yurait.

Korshunova, T. J. 2007. Art.371 in *Kommentarij k Trudovomu kodeksu Rossijskoj Federacii [Commentary to the Labour Code of the Russian Federation]*, ed. Orlovskij, J. P., (Moscow: INFRA-M).

Krasheninnikov, P. V., and B. M. Gongalo. 2013. Art. 132 in *Kommentariy k Grazhdanskomu kodexu Rossiyskoy Federatsii, chasti piervoy* [*Commentary to the Civil Code of the Russian Federation, Part 1]*, ed. Krasheninnikov, P. V., (Moscow: Statut/Legal database Consultant-Plus).

Lyutov, L. N. 2008. "Prava rabotnikov pri smene sobstvennika imushhestva organizacii: problemy rossijskogo zakonodatel'stva i normy Evropejskogo Sojuza [Workers' rights in the event of a change of the proprietor of the assets of an organisation: Problems of Russian legislation and regulations of the European Union]," *Rossijskij ezhegodnik trudovogo prava [Russian Yearbook of Labour law]*, No. 4: 467-494.

Mironov, V. I. 2006. *Praktika novejshego trudovogo zakonodatel'stva. [New Labour Legislation in Practice]*. Moscow: Delo.

—. 2009. *Trudovoe pravo [Labour law]*. Saint Petersburg: Piter Press.

Novichkova, J. V. 2006. "Osobennosti rastorzhenija trudovogo dogovora pri smene sobstvennika imushhestva, izmenenii podvedomstvennosti, reorganizacii [Specifics of termination of a labour contract in case of a change of the proprietor of the assets of an organisation, of the department affiliation of an organisation and of the restructuring of an organisation]," *Trudovye Spory [Labour Disputes]*, No. 3: 45-51.

Orlovskij, J. P., and A. F. Nurtdinova, and L. A. Chikanova. 2012. *Trudovoe zakonodatel'stvo: aktual'nye voprosy, kommentarii, raz'jasnenija [Labour Legislation: Current Issues, Comments, Clarifications: A Guide for Practice]*. Moscow: Yurait.

Shajhutdinova, N. P. 2007. "Prekrashhenie trudovogo dogovora pri reorganizacii predprijatija putem prisoedinenija [Discontinuation of a Labour Contract in the Case of Reorganisation by Merger]," *Trudovye Spory [Labour Disputes]*, No.2: 61-63.

Snigireva, I. O. 2008. Art.43 in *Kommentarij k Trudovomu kodeksu Rossijskoj Federacii [Commentary to the Labour Code of the Russian Federation]*, ed. Gusov K. N., (Moscow: Prospekt).

Thüsing, G. 2013. *European Labour Law*. Munich: C. H. Beck.

THE LABOUR OF PERSONS CONVICTED WITHOUT ISOLATION FROM SOCIETY: INTERNATIONAL STANDARDS AND THE ACTIVITY OF CRIMINAL-EXECUTIVE INSPECTORATES IN RUSSIA

NIKOLAY OLKHOVIK

1. Introduction

On the basis of international standards, the author of this article examines the legislative grounds and legislative limits, as well as organizational and legal conditions, for employing persons who have been given punishments without isolation from society, revealing the problems which exist in this sphere. The author will conclude that criminal-executive inspectorates, like European probation services, can favour the job placement of a convict by the execution of certain kinds of punishments without isolation from society, the control over the behaviour of conditionally convicted persons and those who have been given suspended sentences and the prevention of crimes and other offences being committed by persons who are registered with criminal executive inspectorates.

2. The Legal Grounds and Legislative Limits for Employing Persons who Have Been Convicted without Isolation from Society

This article is concerned with the obligation to work imposed upon those who have been convicted of a crime and whose punishments do not require them to be isolated from society (henceforth, "persons convicted without isolation from society"). In accordance with Art. 2 of the ILO Forced Labour Convention (1930, No. 29), the term "forced or compulsory labour" does *not* include "any work or service exacted from any person as a consequence of a conviction in a court of law, provided that the said work or service is carried out under the supervision and control of a public authority and that the said person is not hired to or placed at the disposal of private individuals, companies or associations”.[1]

A similar provision is included in the Labour Code of the Russian Federation of 2001 (henceforth “the LC RF”), according to which, as stated in Art. 4, the term forced labour (prohibited by the LC RF), does not include “work performed as a result of a court’s sentence which has become final under the supervision of the state bodies charged with observance of the legislation in execution of court sentences”. Therefore, work done by persons convicted without isolation from society is not considered to be forced labour if the obligation to work is stipulated in a sentence given by a court. According to current Russian legislation, such an obligation can only be imposed upon those persons who have been given penalties such as prison labour (*obyazatel’nye raboty*) or forced works (*prinuditel’nye raboty*) or upon those who have been given suspended sentences (*uslovno osuzhdennye*). The rest of those who have been convicted without isolation from society (who have been given a fine (*shtraf*), who have been deprived of the right to hold specific offices or to engage in specific activities (*lishenie prava zanimat’ opredelennye dolzhnosti ili zanimat’sya opredelennoy deyatel’nostiu*), who have had their liberty restricted (*ogranichenie svobody*) or whose punishment has been deferred (*otsrochka nakazaniya*) have the right to freedom of labour, including the right to work, which everyone can freely choose or freely agree to, the right to dispose of one’s capacity for work, to choose a profession and type of activity (point 1, Art. 37 of the Constitution of the Russian Federation, art. 2 of the LC RF).

At the same time, finding employment for those people who have been sentenced to prison labour or forced works and who must work in accordance with a court sentence is, in practice, problematic. First of all, the employment of such individuals is affected by the fact that people sentenced to prison labour are restricted in their right to the freedom of work by the imposition of an obligation to do prescribed work. Thus, among recidivists sentenced to prison labour, the number of those who have a certain speciality is three and a half times as much in comparison with the rest of those sentenced to this punishment. 38% of recidivists have specialized secondary education compared to 11.1% of the total number of offenders sentenced to prison labour. At the same time, the

---

[1] 1930. *Mezhdunarodnaya zaschita prav i svobod cheloveka [International protection of human rights and freedoms]*. Moscow: Yuridicheskaya literatura, 202.

work which they are made to do in accordance with their sentences does not correspond to their specialities. Moreover, if we take into account the fact that 55% of recidivists have breached the established procedure for serving their punishment and treat prescribed work negatively, it seems clear that when determining the type of prison labour a convicted person should be assigned to do and where he/she should be assigned to do it, criminal executive inspectorates would do well to take into account the convicted person's professional skills. However, this requirement should not be obligatory in all cases, otherwise there may be a risk of restricting the types and locations of free socially useful works, which are scanty enough as it is, and this could in turn eventually lead to the non-execution of a sentence. Nevertheless, it is necessary to oblige criminal executive inspectorates to consider the professional skills of a convicted person where possible in order to place him/her in a suitable kind of job.[2] Placing such an obligation on criminal executive inspectorates means that whenever they deliberate upon the punishment of a convicted person they must establish: a) the wish of a convicted person to work in a sector which is in keeping with his/her professional skills; b) the availability of appropriate workplaces and kinds of work amongst those approved by local self-government bodies. Only if both of these conditions are satisfied will it be possible to fulfil this obligation.

The need to establish these two conditions is confirmed by the practice of finding employment for juveniles who have been sentenced to prison labour. The results of our research revealed that 80% of juveniles who committed a new crime during the period of the execution of prison labour attended school at that time and 4% worked. If we add to the above information the fact that 32% of juveniles who committed a crime were not engaged in the execution of prison labour and 45% breached the established procedure for serving the punishment and treated the work experience negatively, there need be no doubt that legislative models and practice are far from perfect. The first problem lies in the very fact of sentencing juveniles to prison labour. Juveniles must carry out the labour during their free time, that is, when they are not studying. However, the question arises as to what should be considered "study-time": the time when they are studying at the educational institution, but should we also take into account the time which is used for private study? In practice, this

[2] Chubrakov, S. V. also pointed out that it is necessary to take into account the skills of a convicted person when determining the type of work they will do and where they will do it (see: Chubrakov, S. V. 2006. *Ugolovnoe nakazanie v vide obyazatel'nyh rabot [Compulsory Works as a Penal Punishment]*. Tomsk, 181–182, 185).

question is rarely asked. In our opinion, such a state of affairs can be explained solely by the wish to execute a sentence without taking into account the interests of the juvenile, that is, his/her right to education.

Therefore, approximately 87% of juveniles surveyed regularly skipped their lessons and lagged behind, while 80% actually committed a new crime during the period of the execution of prison labour. The second problem is linked to the fact that the list of workplaces approved by local self-government bodies for prison labour is not intended for juveniles.

This is because the workplaces in question are generally those of private companies and individual entrepreneurs, notwithstanding the fact that, according to Art. 2 of the ILO Forced Labour Convention, (1930, No. 29), any work or service exacted from any person as a consequence of a conviction in a court of law, if the said person is hired to or placed at the disposal of private individuals, companies or associations, should be considered as forced labour. A further problem lies in the lack of correspondence between the type of work prescribed to juveniles and legislative requirements.[3] Finally, there is also the issue of the refusal of many juveniles to carry out unskilled socially useful works at public places which are located in the district where they reside.

Therefore, the opinion of V. V. Lisauskaite and M. V. Sadovnikov, who believe it is necessary to elaborate a special programme for the execution of prison labour for juveniles which would allow for their different circumstances, ought to be accepted. The choice of the form of this punishment should be dependent upon the crime committed by the juvenile, his/her psychological characteristics and social environment.[4]

Moreover, it is necessary: a) via Art. 25 of the Criminal-Executive Code of the Russian Federation of 1996 (henceforth "the CC RF") to compel criminal executive inspectorates to take into account the requirements of Russian employment legislation, as well as the psychological and social peculiarities of juveniles when determining the type of compulsory works and the workplaces where they are to be carried out, without denying them of their right to education; b) to prescribe the

---

[3] See: Decision of the Government of the Russian Federation from 25 February, 2000 No. 163 "On approval of the range of jobs with harmful and/or dangerous work conditions where the employment of persons under the age of eighteen is prohibited".

[4] Lisauskaite, V. V., Sadovnikov, M. V. 2008. *Ohrana prav nesovershennoletnih i razvitie al'ternativnogo nakazaniya: sravnitel'no-pravovye aspekty [Protection of Minors' Rights and Development of an Alternative Punishment: Comparative Legal Aspects],* eds., Utkin, V. A., and F. Dunkel'. Tomsk: Izdatel'stvo "Pechatnaya manufaktura",121.

"failure to appear for registration at the criminal executive inspectorate without valid reasons" as a breach of the established procedure and the conditions for carrying out compulsory works.

The legal grounds and legislative restrictions regarding juveniles who have been sentenced to correctional works (*ispravitel'nye raboty*) are even more controversial. According to our data, none of the juveniles who committed a crime during the period of the execution of corrective works were working at the time of adjudication. More than half of them (57%) had not started work after the court passed the sentence either, i.e. they were not serving the punishment, while in the total number of juveniles who were sentenced to correctional works this rate does not exceed 7%.

The question arises as to the reasons for such varied figures. Might it be connected with the fact that according to the provisions of employment legislation and education legislation it should be impossible to engage this category of juveniles in correctional works? If this is so, what was the court's reasoning for giving them such a sentence? In accordance with Art. 63 of the LC RF an employment contract may be signed with persons who have reached sixteen years of age. In the case of those receiving general education or continuing their studies according to a basic general education curriculum in a form other than daytime study, or those who have left a secondary educational institution in compliance with federal legislation, an employment contract may be made with persons who have reached fifteen years of age for the purpose of carrying out light work that does not endanger their health.

With the consent of one of the parents or a guardianship body, an employment contract may be made with a young person who has reached fourteen years of age for easy work which does not endanger his/her health or interfere in the young person's studies. At the same time, in accordance with Par. 14, Art. 50 of the Law of the Russian Federation No. 3266-1 of 10 July 1992 "On Education", "the enlistment of students, pupils of civilian educational establishments without the agreement of their parents (persons acting in loco parentis) to works not envisaged by the education syllabus, is prohibited". This inherently means that assigning a penalty such as correctional works to persons who have reached fourteen or fifteen years of age is quite difficult. If this is indeed the case, might it not be better to specify in the Criminal Code of the Russian Federation (Art. 50 or Art. 88) that only juveniles who have already reached sixteen years of age may be sentenced to correctional works? In our opinion, a legislator's ruling to that effect would contribute to the uniformity of court practice[5], the differentiation of criminal responsibility and the punishment of juveniles of different age groups who have committed minor or relatively minor crimes.

When we come to the category of juveniles who were not engaged in the execution of corrective works but did commit a new crime, 25% of them had reached fifteen years of age and were studying, 33% had reached sixteen years of age of which 25% were studying and 42% had reached seventeen years of age of which 60% were studying. Therefore, taking into account Art. 63 of the LC RF and par. 14, Art. 50 of the Law of the Russian Federation "On Education", it is possible to conclude that there were no legislative limits to the work of two-thirds of persons having reached sixteen years of age and of 40% of persons having reached seventeen years of age who committed a new crime. In order to place juveniles between fifteen and seventeen years old in a job it was obligatory to obtain the consent of the juvenile and his/her parents (persons acting in loco parentis), however, neither the court nor the criminal executive inspectorate did this at the time of the juveniles' registration. Therefore, the existing practice of sentencing juveniles to corrective works and engaging them in the execution of such a punishment can hardly be considered satisfactory. At the same time, it is important to take into account the fact that in some cases criminal executive inspectorates cannot do what is necessary due to the absence of companies in the district where a juvenile resides and where he/she might work. This problem mainly concerns those who have been sentenced to compulsory or corrective works, especially if they are to be employed by a company which is run neither by the state nor the municipality. The point is that current legislation stipulates that contractual relationships must be made between state/municipal bodies and legal entities of other forms of property. Therefore, the approval of the range of companies where prison labour and corrective works can be undertaken presupposes the signing of an appropriate contract with the company. The practice of employing

---

[5] However, court practice on this matter is ambiguous. For example, a fifteen-year-old boarding school pupil who was given a fine for theft at the age of 14 and who committed another crime three months after the first sentence was passed, this time the theft of a mobile phone from a shop with heavy damages incurred by the victim, was convicted according to par. 2, Art. 158 of the CC RF to one year of corrective works with a charge of 15% of wages. At the same time, a pupil at an 'ordinary' school registered by the Juvenile Commission was convicted for the theft of another minor's mobile phone and was sentenced to conventional correctional works according to par. 1, Art. 161 of the CC RF.

people who have been sentenced to compulsory or corrective works indicates that, in reality, such contracts are very rarely concluded and this eventually leads to the decline of the number of workplaces where the aforementioned sentences can be served and therefore also to the reduction of the number of convicted persons for whom employment can be found.

Considering the competitive conditions of the labour market it is necessary to establish a quota system for those persons who are in particular need of social protection, including those who have been convicted of crimes. In the opposite case a certain segment of people will not have any means of subsistence and this, undoubtedly depending on the convict's personality, could lead to he or she reoffending.

3. Organizational and Legal Conditions for Employing Persons who have been Given Punishments without Isolation from Society

The established legal grounds for employing people who have been sentenced to compulsory or corrective works do not diminish the importance of the criminal executive inspectorates' activity regarding the importance of promptly finding a job placement for convicts serving a sentence or imposing other penal measures. However, as long as it is possible to take such actions only after the relevant court order and a copy of the sentence (a ruling, a resolution) have been given to the criminal executive inspectorate, it seems reasonable to dwell on the issue of timeliness of registration of a convict by the criminal executive inspectorate. This issue becomes even more significant when there is a substantial lapse of time between the day of the enforcement of the court's judgement, its acceptance and its execution. In the absence of adequate controls, convicts may not only attempt to evade the execution of the conferred sentence but may even commit a new crime. In our opinion, the chances of such a situation occurring depend on the legal gap in the criminal-procedural legislation which does not establish the exact term for the beginning of the execution of a sentence. In accordance with par. 4, Art. 390 of the Criminal-Procedural Code of the Russian Federation (henceforth, "the CPC RF"), "the sentence shall be presented for execution by the first instance court within three days from the day of its entry into legal force, or of the return of the criminal case from the court of the appeals or of the cassation instance". According to par. 1, Art. 391 of the CPC RF, "a ruling or a resolution of the court of the first or appeals instance shall enter into legal force and shall be presented for execution after an expiry of the term for filing an appeal against it by way of cassation, or on the day of passing the ruling by the court of the cassation instance". The court's ruling or resolution, not being subject to an appeal by way of cassation, shall enter into legal force and shall be presented for execution immediately (par. 2, Art. 391 of the CPC RF). The institution or body, upon which the execution of the punishment is imposed, shall immediately inform the court which passed the sentence of its execution (par. 5, Art. 393 of the CPC RF). This indicates that when prescribing the period of time between the presentation of a sentence (ruling, resolution) and its execution and imposing upon the criminal executive inspectorate the duty to promptly inform the court of the execution of the sentence, legislators do not take into account the possibility that allowing a significant amount of time to pass may not only lead to the previously described situation, but may, in some cases, make it formally impossible for the sentence to be executed. It therefore becomes necessary to stipulate in criminal-procedural legislation the period of time between the presentation of a sentence, its acceptance and its execution. Moreover, it is necessary to establish administrative responsibility in the Code of Administrative Offences of the Russian Federation of 2001 for any breaches of this term. Such provisions would effectively favour an increase in the effectiveness of the imposed punishment.

After a convict's registration, the criminal executive inspectorate explains to him/her "the order of execution of punishment and his/her rights and duties, specifies and verifies personal details and finds out data which are significant for the control of his/her behaviour". This information should then be confirmed with a signed statement by the convict. One should not underestimate the importance of this provision in order that the convict should understand that he/she is being monitored.

One of the indispensable conditions for engaging a convict in the execution of prison labour is his/her assignment to an organization where he/she shall carry out free socially useful works. The criminal executive inspectorate submits a copy of the court's sentence (the ruling, the resolution) and notifies the organization where the convict will serve his/her punishment. In practice, the administration of the organization where the convict will serve his/her punishment makes an employment contract with the convict. In our opinion, signing a fixed-term employment contract with a convict cannot be considered reasonable. Firstly, such an employment contract would not meet the requirements of employment legislation for the following reasons:

- federal laws, as well as Art. 59 of the LC RF which stipulates the range of persons with whom fixed-term contracts of employment can be made, do not allow for the possibility of signing a fixed-term employment contract with persons who have been sentenced to prison labour;

- a fixed-term employment contract is still a type of employment contract and should therefore contain the so-called essential (*suschestvennye*) terms of an employment contract which are stipulated in Art. 57 of the LC RF. These terms include the terms of payment. Therefore, contracts of employment in general, and fixed-term employment contracts in particular, imply payment. However, in terms of criminal and criminal-executive legislation, prison labour requires the performance of free socially-useful works;
- when a contract of employment is drawn up, certain aspects require the consent of the employee. A person who is sentenced to prison labour, however, cannot refuse to enter into the employment contract.

Secondly, the creation of an employment contract will not resolve the problem of indemnification should a convict sustain injury while carrying out prison labour. This indemnification will not be paid by the social insurance system as it presupposes not only an insured event, the signed employment contract, but also the payment of premiums to the social insurance fund from the relevant person's salary (wages). However, establishing the second condition is not possible since the payment of a salary (wages) to persons who have been sentenced to prison labour is not stipulated by law. Therefore, the most reasonable thing to do in this case is to apply the provisions of Art. 1064, 1084-1094 of the Civil Code of the Russian Federation. This approach to indemnification is universal. In other words it applies not only to persons who are parties to a contract, but also to other cases which are established by law. In this case, the responsibility to pay the indemnification lies with the person who sustained injury.

The aforementioned circumstances lead us to conclude that the official beginnings of a relationship between an organization and a convict for the execution of prison labour should not be made in the form of an employment contract.

In our opinion, this relationship should not be established with a contract, but by carrying out the following actions:

- a decision of the local self-government bodies, preconcerted with the criminal executive inspectorate, which includes the relevant organization in the range of the objects where prison labour can be served;
- a notice of the criminal executive inspectorate attaching a copy of the sentence and a time ticket.

The referral of a convicted person to an organization where prison labour may be served is an order (*predpisanie*) of the criminal executive inspectorate which is submitted to by the convict.

Following the arrival of the convicted person, the organization's administration determines the exact place where he/she will carry out the labour. In so doing the administration shall:

- acquaint the convict with the prescribed rules of work (*pravila vnutrennego trudovogo rasporyadka*), safety measures and occupational sanitation;
- assign an official who will control the execution of labour by the convict. This official shall keep a time ticket and notify the criminal executive inspectorate of the hours worked by the convict or of his/her evasion from the execution of the punishment;
- hand a convict a work order (orders) on the basis of the working standards.

Employing persons with suspended sentences is no less problematic. In accordance with par. 5, Art. 73 of the CC RF, when imposing a suspended sentence a court may place upon the person in question duties which are in some way linked to labour (the obligation to work, not to change his/her permanent place of residence without notifying the criminal executive inspectorate, etc.). However, during the last three years the imposition of such duties on those with suspended sentences is becoming less and less common in the practice of courts. Some judges believe that it is impossible to impose such duties on those with suspended sentences as this contradicts both the requirements of international legal standards regarding the prohibition of forced labour, as well as the Constitution and the Labour Code of the Russian Federation. This problem is not new. It was discussed and a reasonable decision was adopted ten years ago when convincing arguments were put forward in favour of the compliance of these duties with international legal standards which were contested then and should not be disputed now by the practice of courts.[6] Therefore, imposing the duty to work on conditionally convicted persons is not only valid, but also reasonable in terms of having an educational influence on the convicted persons through contact with their fellow workers.

The control of criminal executive inspectorates over the execution of the duties placed on convicted persons, including those duties which are

---

[6] Utkin, V. A. "Razvitie al'ternativ lisheniyu svobody v ramkah eksperimenta [Development of Alternatives of Imprisonment within an Experiment]," *Sodeistvie stanovleniyu mekhanizma realizacii al'ternativnykh mer nakazaniya v Rossiyskoy Federacii*: materials of the international seminar, Samara, 24–27 March 2002, 16.

linked to employment, is no less important than providing labour activity to convicts who have been sentenced to punishments which do not imply isolation from society. Nearly every convicted person sentenced to corrective works who went on to commit another crime had breached the established order of execution of this kind of punishment (failed to report for work or to appear before the criminal executive inspectorate without good reason, truanted or went to work in a state of alcoholic, narcotic or other intoxication), and/or had committed administrative offences.

Following the revelation of the aforementioned breaches, criminal executive inspectorates took certain measures regarding these convicts (a warning that the punishment of corrective works may be substituted by another punishment, the obligation to appear for registration, the presentation of a proposal for the substitution of this punishment submitted to a court). However, these measures have not proved sufficient.

In our opinion, this can be explained by the imperfection of current legislation and the activity of criminal executive inspectorates.

Thus, the current Criminal-Executive Code of the Russian Federation does not provide adequate measures intended to ensure that a convict respects the order and conditions of serving corrective works (for example, it does not allow criminal executive inspectorates to impose duties on the convicted persons at their registration, as previously occurred), and neither does it stipulate the threat of substitution of this type of punishment for those convicts who:

- regularly commit administrative offences against public order or offences which are similar to the crime he/she was convicted of;
- do not appear for registration or fail to appear before the criminal executive inspectorate or who flee from their permanent place of residence.

Taking into account that 72% of women-recidivists have not been working during the grace period, more than half are unmarried (60%), 43% have had secondary education or secondary special education, it is necessary to stipulate in Art. 82 of the CC RF the possibility for a court to impose on these women duties such as: working and not changing place of work without notifying the criminal executive inspectorate, undergoing a course of treatment for alcoholism or drug addiction where necessary (in the absence of contraindications for treatment) and others, as is stipulated in relation to those given suspended sentences and those who are paroled from institutions of confinement. It stands to reason that the range of such duties should not be exhaustive in order that for each individual case a court can decide whether it is necessary to impose on a woman specific duties, including those which are not specified by the law.

The fact that a third of conditionally convicted persons do not have a permanent paycheque is due not so much to the problem of unemployment as it is to their refusal to do a suggested job. Some proposals for a solution to this situation can be made. First of all, the criminal executive inspectorate has to make wider use of the possibility, provided by the law, to make a proposal before the court of imposing on convicts duties linked to labour. However, a radical solution to the problem of finding employment for convicts is possible only by law so long as current legislation does not provide provisions for the obligatory job placement of an unemployed convict. The aforementioned shortcomings need to be solved as early as possible by the introduction of relevant legislative amendments and the introduction of some elements of social work into the activity of the criminal executive inspectorates. The said circumstances indicate the need to create an effective mechanism for the job placement of convicts at a regional level and for fixing in criminal-executive legislation measures which will favour the execution of established requirements by a convict.

4. Job Placement of Convicted Persons and Social Work of Criminal Executive Inspectorates

The uncertain situation concerning the job placement of those convicted without isolation from society is also due to the fact that criminal executive inspectorates focus only on controlling whether the convicts are respecting the order and conditions of their punishments, and not on the resocialization of said convicts, their education and a change in their behaviour in general. According to the Order of the Government of the Russian Federation from 14 October, 2010 No. 1772-p "On Approval of the Conception of Development of Criminal-Executive System of the Russian Federation until 2020" (henceforth, "the Order"), "the process of making the work of the criminal executive inspectorates more social by putting an emphasis on engaging convicted persons in labour as well as giving them the chance to acquire a profession or training for a new profession; the activation of collaboration with the structures of civil society which can have a positive influence on convicted persons; the optimization of social, psychological and educational activity with convicted persons; the involvement of local self-government bodies, job centres, education and healthcare, the public, residential treatment centres and other institutions in the process of social adaptation and reformation of convicted persons" are important elements for improving the activities of the criminal-executive system as regards the execution of punishments and other penal measures not implying a convict's isolation from society. It seems clear that the Order sets the criminal executive inspectorates the task of optimizing both the social work done with convicted persons as well as the execution of punishments and other penal measures not implying isolation from society. In the opinion of some scholars, "at present the criminal executive inspectorates directly or indirectly carry out different directions of social work".[7]

Despite accepting that those who work in criminal executive inspectorates often play a role in the social assistance, support and defence of persons who have been sentenced to punishments without isolation from society, it is quite contradictory to place on criminal executive inspectorates the task of resocializing convicts for a number of reasons.

Firstly, if a task of resocialization is stipulated by the Criminal-Executive Code of the Russian Federation, this will define the relationship which determines the order of social assistance provided to convicts by criminal-executive legislation. However, the Criminal-Executive Code of the Russian Federation "does not relate the relationship in the sphere of social assistance to discharged persons to the relationship which is regulated by the criminal-executive legislation"[8] and, in our opinion, it is also true of the relationship in the sphere of social assistance with those persons who have been sentenced to punishments without isolation from society. These relationships, as Utkin V.A. reasonably believes, "should be related to the relationships which are governed by the legislation on social security and in a wider sense to the relationships which are governed by the legislation on social protection…"[9]

Secondly, the resocialization of people who have been sentenced to punishments without isolation from society is a task which requires the involvement of a wide range of people and organizations. This statement is not denied even by the supporters of the opposing point of view.

Criminal executive inspectorates can only favour such assistance through carrying out the tasks they have been assigned: the execution of

---

[7] See: Luzgin, S. A., M. I. Kuznetsov, and V. N. Kazancev, et al. 2006. "Social'naya rabota v ugolovno-ispolnitel'noy sisteme [Social Work in the Criminal-Executive System]," ed. Kalinin Yu. I., (Ryazan': Akademiya prava i upravleniya Federal'noy sluzhby ispolneniya nakazaniy), 266.

[8] See: Utkin, V. A. 2005. Pravovye osnovy resocializacii osvobozhdennykh iz mest lisheniya svbody (k koncepcii zakonoproekta) [Legal Framework of Resocialization of Persons Released from Custody]," Aktual'nye problemy ispolneniya ugolovnyh nakazaniy: materials of the international seminar, Ryazan': Akademiya prava i upravleniya FSIN Rossii, 45.

[9] *Ibid*, 46.

certain kinds of punishments without isolation from society, the control over the behaviour of those given suspended sentences, pregnant women who have been convicted and women who have children under 14 years; the prevention of the commitment of crimes by those persons who are registered with criminal executive inspectorates.

Thirdly, the provisions of criminal-executive legislation setting out the duties of criminal executive inspectorates regulate the execution of punishments without isolation from society and the activity of the criminal executive inspectorates as an organ executing these punishments and exercising activities regarding the prevention of the commitment of crimes and other offences by those persons who are registered with criminal executive inspectorates.

Fourthly, the rights and duties of criminal executive inspectorates which are listed by those of the opposing opinion are of a different nature.

Thus, for example, “explanation of the order and the conditions of execution of punishment to convicted persons” and “coming to an agreement with local self-government bodies about places where prison labour is to be served by convicts”, concern organizational measures ensuring the execution of punishments. “Organization and implementation of educational work with those convicted persons who have been sentenced to deprivation of the right to hold specific offices or to engage in specific activities and corrective works”, “exercising of control over convicts’ behaviour at the place of work, study and the place of residence, as well as over their executing of duties and bans imposed by the court and the inspectorate”, “granting of permission to convicted persons who have been sentenced to corrective works on voluntary termination of his/her employment contract during the period of the execution of the punishment and concordance an issue of their leave entitlement with the administration of an organization where they work” as well as rights of the criminal executive inspectorates previously mentioned by the authors, are nothing other than means of ensuring the established order of the execution of punishments and the order of probation where there is a conditional conviction or the deferral of serving a punishment.

Therefore, in our opinion, criminal executive inspectorates should participate in rendering social assistance, support and protection of convicted persons who have been sentenced to punishments without isolation from society only by:

- promptly informing other subjects of the necessity to provide targeted help in obtaining identification documents, finding a job placement, resolving housing problems, etc.;

- explaining to convicted people which rights they have, the implementation of which may affect the execution of punishments and other penal measures.

The basic solutions of how to provide general social assistance to convicted persons who have been sentenced to punishments without isolation from society, and how to provide them with a job placement in particular, should be ensured by the relevant social-economic resources and the legal framework, as well as by the purposeful coordination of the activities carried out by the various social institutions, including criminal executive inspectorates. Indeed, the European standards regarding the execution of punishments and other penal measures without isolation from society emphasise this point. The Europe Probation Rules note that the variety of functions of this institution includes the principle of coordination with other state organs and institutions in order to support offenders (p. 12). The European Rules for Juvenile Offenders contain the same provision (p. 15).[10] Moreover, the results of comparative legal research into the functions of probation services conducted by Van Kalmhout convincingly proves that European probation services perform these functions in coordination with other subjects.[11]

In Russian legislation there is a gap in the legal framework regarding the coordination of criminal executive inspectorates with certain state organs and structures of civil society which could have a positive and humanitarian influence on convicted persons through local self-government bodies, job centres, education and health care, residential treatment centres and other institutions. An indication of some areas of coordination can be found only in the Regulations on Criminal Executive Inspectorates and the Norms Regarding their Staff Number: “in their work the inspectorates cooperate with subdivisions of a body of international affairs, the administration of institutions, and organizations where convicted persons work, local self-government bodies, prosecutors’ offices, courts and public associations” (p. 5).

However, this indication does not guarantee the effective coordination of the aforementioned subjects. First of all, it is necessary to resolve the existing problems of how to coordinate the activities of criminal executive inspectorates with the Federal Migration Service, job placement services

---

[10] See: Korovin, A. A., and N. B. Khutorskaya. 2011. “*Pravovoe regulirovanie i organizaciya deyatel’nosti ugolovno-ispolnitel’nykh inspekciy na osnove realizacii evropeiskikh standartov i zarubezhnogo opyta [Legal Regulation and Organization of Activity of Criminal Executive Inspectorates on the Basis of Implementation of European Standards and Foreign Experience]*. Moscow: PRI, 56.

[11] Van Kalmhout A. *Report for the PC-CP meeting*, 11 December 2007, 14-15.

and the public. The absence of joint acts adopted with the Federal Migration Service in some cases does not allow officers of criminal executive inspectorates to execute a court's sentence on people who have been convicted and who do not have any ID, especially if the matter is linked to his/her job placement. In practice, in many cases where a convicted person applies to the territorial bodies of the Federal Migration Service for a passport as a citizen of the Russian Federation or for an interim ID card, the application leads to no positive results.[12] As a general rule, the issuing of these documents is prohibited for convicted persons due to the absence of the registration in the place of the permanent or temporary residence, or the payment document confirming payment of the state fee. It should be pointed out that the term for the issue of a passport of a citizen of the Russian Federation or an interim ID card stipulated in the order of the Ministry of Internal Affairs of the Russian Federation[13] considerably exceeds the term established for executing a convicted person's sentence. The process of issuing ID cards takes longer if the applicant is a convicted person who has not been living in the area of the relevant region of the Russian Federation, and can take even longer if the applicant is a convicted person who is not a citizen of the Commonwealth of Independent States (CIS). The process of the reciprocal informing of

---

[12] Par. 22 of the Instruction "On organization of implementation of punishments and other penal measures without isolation from society" approved by the Order of the Ministry of Justice of the Russian Federation from 20 May 2009 No. 142 does not resolve the problem, although it is necessary. It establishes that during primary conversation with a convict during his/her registration a criminal executive inspectorate shall explain to "a citizen of the Russian Federation who does not have any ID that he/she shall apply to a territorial body of the Federal Migration Service where he/she has a permanent or a temporary place of residence to obtain of a temporary certificate of identity or a passport, as well as the possibility of implementing administrative responsibility for the necessity of the aforementioned documents". The point is that normative acts which are obligatory for bodies of the Federal Migration Service do not establish the order of execution for issuing identification documents to Russian citizens.

[13] See: *"Ob utverzhdenii administrativnogo reglamenta Federal'noy migracionnoy sluzhby po predostavleniyu gosudarstvennoy uslugi po vydache, zamene i po ispolneniyu gosudarstvennoy funkcii po uchetu pasportov grazhdanina Rossiyskoy Federacii, udostoveryayuschih lichnost' grazhdanina Rossiyskoy Federacii na territorii Rossiyskoy FederaciiOrder of the Ministry of Internal Affairs"* [On approval of administrative regalement of the Federal Migration Service concerning the state service on issue and substitution of passports of a citizen of the Russian Federation, as well as on implementation of the state function concerning the registration process of passports of a citizen of the Russian Federation in the Russian area] from 25 December 2006 No. 1105.

two ministries of breaches of the rules for staying in the territory of the Russian Federation which are committed by persons sentenced to punishments without isolation from society cannot be considered proper.

At present, the process of collaboration between criminal executive inspectorates and the federal state job-placement services (henceforth, "job-placement services") is almost non-existent. This can firstly be explained by changes in the law which now provides other mechanisms for the organization of the execution of compulsory and corrective works which do not presuppose the participation of job-placement services.

However, many functions previously performed by officers of the job-placement services are currently undertaken by officers of the criminal executive inspectorates who are more interested (compared to local self-government bodies) in the "working" range of organizations for the execution of these punishments and in various ways of employing convicted persons. Therefore, the exclusion of the job-placement services from the organization of the execution of compulsory and corrective works entails an increase in the amount of work for officers of the criminal executive inspectorates and consequently their "distraction" from exercising their inherent functions regarding the execution of punishments and other penal measures not implying isolation from society.

The issue of involving additional human resources—the public—in the activity of criminal executive inspectorates is no less topical. The Recommendation No. R (92) 16 of the Committee of Ministers to Member States "On the European Rules On Community Sanctions and Measures",[14] namely rules 46-48, recommends involving the community in assisting offenders, with the agreement of the responsible implementing authority, and permits organizations and individuals drawn from the community to undertake supervision only in a capacity laid down in law or defined by the authorities responsible for the imposition or implementation of community sanctions or measures. It should be noted that current legislation (Art. 23 of the CC RF), through admissible representatives of the public, stipulates only public associations and strictly outlines the directions of their activity, namely assistance in the work of institutions and bodies executing punishments, participation in the reformation of convicted persons as well as exercising public control over these institutions in the order established by Russian legislation. If one takes into account that it is not, at present, possible to exercise public control over the activity of criminal executive inspectorates so long as Russian

[14] Adopted by the Committee of Ministers on 19 October, 1992 at the 482nd meeting of the Ministers' Deputies.

legislation does not provide the grounds and the order of its implementation,[15] it becomes obvious that the opinion of V. A. Utkin, according to which current Russian legislation stipulates far fewer opportunities for public participation in criminal executive activity than the Executive Labour Code of the Russian Soviet Federative Socialist Republic of 1970 and the previous acts is sound.[16]

The institution of public assistants which existed in the Soviet period ceased to continue. Only a few regions of the Russian Federation were exceptions to the general rule. The Exemplary Rules "On Public Inspectors of Criminal Executive Inspectorates of the Regional Bodies of the Criminal Executive System of the Ministry of Justice of the Russian Federation", established by the Order of the Public Administration of the Execution of Punishments No. 212 was passed on 22 November, 2010.[17]

However, in less than two years the order was revoked because it was not registered by the Ministry of Justice. Therefore, at present there are no legal acts providing for the organizational and legal mechanism of involving public associations in the activity of criminal executive inspectorates. It should be noted that there is a controversial trend concerning this matter in some European countries. As R. Canton has pointed out, in the near future all the probation activities in England will be 'privatized'. In other words, they will be handed out on a competitive basis to non-profit organizations.[18]

---

[15] In accordance with the Federal law of 10 June, 2008 No. 76-FZ *"Ob obschestvennom kontrole za obespecheniem prav cheloveka v mestakh prinuditel'nogo soderzhaniya i o sodeistvii litsam, nakhodyaschimsya v mestakh prinuditel'nogo soderzhaniya"* [On public control for implementation of human rights in places of compulsion and on assistance to persons who are in places of compulsion], *Sobranie zakonodatel'stva Rossiyskoy Federacii, 2008, No. 24, st. 2789)* public control does not extend to criminal executive inspectorates.

[16] Utkin, V.A. 1997. *"Pravovye osnovy neuchastiya obschestvennosti v realizacii ugolovno-ispolnitel'noy politiki"* [The legal framework of non-participation of the public in the implementation of the criminal-executive policy], *Problemy teorii nakazaniya i ego ispolnenie v novom Ugolovnom i Ugolovno-ispolnitel'nom kodeksah Rossii*: collected articles of an international conference, Moscow, 146.

[17] 2002. "*Organizacionno-pravovye osnovy deyatel'nosti ugolovno-ispolnitel'nykh inspekciy. Sbornik normativno-pravovykh aktov" [Organizational and legal framework of criminal executive inspectorates' activity]*, Moscow, 218-223.

[18] Canton, R. 2007. *Probation in England and Wales: Report at the PC-CP meeting*, 1–8; "Materialy zasedaniya Soveta po penologicheskomu sotrudnichestvu Soveta Evropy" [The report of the Council for Penological Co-operation], Strasburg, 11 November, 2007, 2.

There is no doubt that the aforementioned situation has an effect on the activity of the criminal executive inspectorates and requires not only the adoption of interdepartmental orders, but also the creation of a system of social assistance (social support) for different kinds of convicted persons, including their employment. In our opinion, the social support of a convicted person should be individual. It should be accepted that such issues are resolved in the most effective way in those regions where local self-government bodies cooperate with public institutions. It is necessary to establish a public-state system of social aid for convicted persons which includes not only bodies and institutions executing penal punishments to prepare convicted persons during the period of the execution of the punishment for outside life, but also regional services of social support for the aforementioned persons which can assist convicts when released from the place of confinement and help those who were sentenced to punishments without isolation from society in the solution of such issues as accommodation, job placement, establishing and restoring social useful relations and accessing free psychological and legal aid. These services should be subordinated to the social protection services and be based on a partnership between the public and the state.

References

Canton, R. 2007. *Probation in England and Wales: Report at the PC-CP meeting.*

Chubrakov, S. V. 2006. *Ugolovnoe nakazanie v vide obyazatel'nykh rabot [Compulsory Works as a Penal Punishment].* Tomsk, 181–182, 185.

Decision of the Government of the Russian Federation of 25 February 2000 No. 163 "On approval of the range of jobs with harmful and/or dangerous work conditions where the employment of persons under the age of eighteen is prohibited".

Federal law from 10 June 2008 No. 76-FZ *"Ob obschestvennom kontrole za obespecheniem prav cheloveka v mestakh prinuditel'nogo soderzhaniya i o sodeistvii litsam, nakhodyaschimsya v mestakh prinuditel'nogo soderzhaniya"* [On Public Control for Implementation of Human Rights in Places of Compulsion and on Assistance to Persons who are in Places of Compulsion], *Sobranie zakonodatel'stva Rossiyskoy Federacii, 2008,* No. 24, st. 2789.

Instruction "On Organization of Implementation of Punishments and other Penal Measures without Isolation from Society" approved by the Order of the Ministry of Justice of the Russian Federation from 20 May 2009 No. 142.

Korovin, A. A., and N. B. Hutorskaya. 2011. "*Pravovoe regulirovanie i organizaciya deyatel'nosti ugolovno-ispolnitel'nykh inspekciy na osnove realizacii evropeiskikh standartov i zarubezhnogo opyta"* [Legal regulation and organization of activity of criminal executive inspectorates on the basis of implementation of European standards and foreign experience]. Moscow: PRI, 56.

Lisauskaite, V. V., and M. V. Sadovnikov. 2008. *Ohrana prav nesovershennoletnikh i razvitie al'ternativnogo nakazaniya: sravnitel'no-pravovye aspekty* [Protection of Minors' Rights and Development of an Altermative Punishment: Comparative Legal Aspects], Utkin, V. A, and F. Dunkel, (Tomsk: Izdatel'stvo "Pechatnaya manufaktura").

Luzgin, S. A., Kuznetsov, M.I., Kazancev, V.N., et al. 2006. *Social'naya rabota v ugolovno-ispolnitel'noy sisteme* [Social work in the criminal-executive system], Yu.I. Kalinin (ed.), 2nd ed., Ryazan': Akademiya prava i upravleniya Federal'noy sluzhby ispolneniya nakazaniy.

Utkin, V. A. 1997. "Pravovye osnovy neuchastiya obschestvennosti v realizacii ugolovno-ispolnitel'noy politiki [The Legal Framework of Non-participation of the Public in the Implementation of the Criminal-executive Policy]," *Problemy teorii nakazaniya i ego ispolnenie v novom Ugolovnom i Ugolovno-ispolnitel'nom kodeksakh Rossii*: collected articles of an international conference, Moscow.

—. 2002. "*Razvitie al'ternativ lisheniyu svobody v ramkakh eksperimenta"* [Development of Alternatives of Imprisonment within an Experiment], *Sodeistvie stanovleniyu mekhanizma realizacii al'ternativnykh mer nakazaniya v Rossiyskoy Federacii*: materials of the international seminar, Samara, 24-27 March, 2002.

—. 2005. "Pravovye osnovy resocializacii osvobozhdennykh iz mest lisheniya svbody (k koncepcii zakonoproekta) [Legal Framework of Resocialization of Persons Released from Custody]," Aktual'nye problemy ispolneniya ugolovnykh nakazaniy: materials of the international seminar, Ryazan': Akademiya prava i upravleniya FSIN Rossii.

Van Kalmhout, A. 2007. *Report for the PC-CP Meeting.*

REGULATING CONVICTS' LABOUR IN CONTEMPORARY RUSSIA

VLADIMIR UTKIN

Over the 20th century, prison labour has been extensively applied to convicts either in the former USSR or in Russia. This aspect also emerges from the contemporary history of the Russian criminal and executive system. In the Soviet period, prison labour and the declared objectives of "correcting and re-educating" referred to a specific branch of law ("corrective labour"), to the Codes on the Execution of Punishments (the 1924, 1933, 1970 "corrective labour" Codes), to some institutions executing such punishments ("correctional facilities"), as well as to a set of social and educational measures applying to convicted persons ("initiatives concerning corrective measures and labour"). The need on the part of the State to attract convicts to reach economic development and increase the power of defence eventually resulted in the establishment of labour camps which are different from prisons in Western Europe.

In the centralized Soviet economy, almost all the convicts who were fit for work were assigned to these tasks, and the fulfilment of the economic objectives on the part of correctional facilities was regarded as the most important criterion to assess their efficiency and that of the prison system, more generally. Significantly, in the 1970s, the Ministry of Internal Affairs of the USSR—which had control over such correctional facilities—was ranked fifth among the other ministries involved in industry-related activities because of its contribution to total production.

The transition to a market economy, political changes and Russia's integration in the international community fundamentally altered the social and economic components of the national criminal and executive system.

A thorough review was then necessary to meet the standards of a democratic society, which also affected prison labour and its legal regulation, being that imprisonment is still one of the most widespread punishments in modern Russia.[1]

In the Criminal-Executive Code of the Russian Federation which came into effect on 1 July 1997 (hereafter CEC RF) labour is considered as one of the main corrective measures for convicted persons (Art. 9). Art. 103 of the CEC RF establishes that "the productive activity of convicted persons shall not prevent the fulfilment of the basic objective of correctional facilities, namely the rehabilitation of convicted persons". Such provisions are mostly in line with international standards regarding the treatment of prisoners. The Standard Minimum Rules for the Treatment of Prisoners, adopted on 30 August 1955[2] sets out that "sufficient work of a useful nature shall be provided to keep prisoners actively employed for a normal working day" (Par. 71.3). In the same spirit, the Recommendation Rec(2006)2 of the Committee of Ministers to Member States on the European Prison Rules of 11 January 2006,[3] provides that "work in prison shall be approached as a positive element of the prison regime […]" (Par. 26.1).

In Russia—and in the former USSR—the labour of convicts in the institutions of confinement is traditionally regulated by two branches of law—employment law and criminal-executive law (previously referred to as "correctional labour law"). The latter regulates the employment of convicts only where its legal objectives and conditions differ from the employment of those without criminal records. Since these objectives and conditions are closely connected with serving a sentence, the special norms are not integrated into specific chapters of Part IV of the Labour Code of the Russian Federation ("Special features regulating the labour of specific categories of workers"), but in chapter 14 of the CEC RF concerning the Labour, Vocational Education and Training of Convicted

---

[1] In 2012, 28.5 percent of convicts were sentenced to imprisonment. Moreover, Russia ranks first in Europe in the number of inmates (560) per 100,000 people. However, the prison population is gradually decreasing. In 2010 the number of convicts serving jail terms was 838,000, decreasing to 693,000 in 2013. The 2013 figure includes: 574,000 inmates in 736 correctional facilities, 39,000 convicts in 128 open prisons, 1,800 convicts in 5 facilities for those serving life sentences, 2,200 convicts in 46 education facilities for young people, and 1,000 convicts in 7 prisons.

[2] Adopted by the First United Nations Congress on the Prevention of Crime and the Treatment of Offenders, U.N. Doc. A/CONF/611, annex I, E.S.C. res. 663C, 24 U.N. ESCOR Supp. (No. 1) at 11, U.N. Doc. E/3048 (1957), amended E.S.C. res. 2076, 62 U.N. ESCOR Supp. (No. 1) at 35, U.N. Doc. E/5988 (1977).

[3] Adopted by the Committee of Ministers on 11 January 2006 at the 952nd meeting of the Ministers' Deputies.

Persons". Yet only a few articles in the CEC RF (Art. 103-107) deal with this issue, with some of them directly referring to employment law. For instance, Par. 2, Art. 103 CEC RF states that "convicted persons under 18 must engage in labour activities in accordance with Russian employment legislation". Par. 1, Art. 104 of the CEC RF establishes that the working time, job safety and occupational hygiene of convicted persons should be dealt with by Russian employment legislation. Art. 105 of the CEC RF also determines that "persons sentenced to deprivation of liberty have the right to remuneration pursuant to Russian employment legislation". In this and other cases, it is employment law which regulates convict's labour in the absence of special norms of the CEC RF, even without expressly referring to it.

In addition to the Criminal-Executive Code of the Russian Federation, specific aspects concerning the employment of convicts in institutions of confinement are regulated by Law of 21 July 1993 of the Russian Federation "*Ob uchrezhdeniyah i organah, ispolnyayuschih ugolovnye nakazaniya v vide lisheniya svobody*" [institutions and bodies inflicting punishments in the form of deprivation of liberty] and other secondary provisions. The most relevant are "*Pravila vnutrennego rasporyadka ispravitel'nyh uchrezhdeniy*" [the internal regulations of correctional facilities] adopted by the order of the Ministry of Justice on 3 November 2005 No. 205 and "*Pravila vnutrennego rasporyadka vospitatel'nyh koloniy ugolovno–ispolnitel'noy sistemy"* [Internal regulations of educational facilities of the criminal and executive system] adopted by the order of the Ministry of Justice on 6 October 2006 No. 311. These provisions determine the positions for which the employment of convicts is prohibited, among others: the upkeep and repair of security equipment and the storage and distribution of medicines, explosives, and poisonous substances. Evidently, such bans should be considered as preventive measures.

The CEC RF and Law of 21 July 1993 also provides a list of production facilities where the employment of convicts is allowed, among others:

1) So called "centres of labour adaptation (labour workshops)". Being that these centres are part of the correctional facilities, they are not independent in legal, organizational and financial terms. In the past, they were known as "domestic manufacturing units of the correctional facilities". In 2012, there were 587 "centres of labour adaptation", 41 workshops for production and training and 52 workshops for production and treatment.

2) Federal state unitary enterprises, which are legal entities and independent in financial and manufacturing terms. At present, the total number of these enterprises is 53.
3) Enterprises having different organizational and legal forms (state-owned, private, and so on) which employ convicts in and outside correctional facilities provided that their proper isolation and surveillance is ensured.
4) Correctional facilities where convicted persons are involved in their maintenance.

The annual output of the institutions making up the Russian criminal and executive system exceeds 25 billion roubles (more than €600 million).

With regard to production activities, wood harvesting and processing are historically relevant for the Russian criminal and executive system. The system accounts for 103 institutions located in nine regions of the Russian Federation where large amounts of wood raw material are available, particularly in the northern area (Ural and Siberia).

Agriculture is also important in the criminal and executive system. Currently, there are 17 federal state unitary enterprises and more than 800 production enterprises which produce, process and supply agricultural products to criminal and executive institutions.

Like the previous provisions in force in the Soviet era, the CEC RF establishes a general duty to work for convicted persons. Art. 103 of the CEC RF states that "every person who has been imposed measures involving deprivation of liberty shall operate at the places and jobs determined by the administration of the correctional facility". The administration shall employ convicts considering "their sex, age, ability to work, health status, specialisation (if possible), and job openings".

However, male and female prisoners respectively aged 60 and 55 or over, as well as persons classified as group I or II disabled are allowed to choose whether or not to be employed.

According to the law (Par. 6, Art. 103, Par. 1 Art. 116 of the CEC RF), the refusal on the part of convicts or any work interruption without valid reasons is considered as a gross violation of the imposed punishment. Further, convicted persons in institutions of confinement do not have the right to strike.

The foregoing provisions of the CEC RF pursuant to which convicts serving their sentence in institutions of confinement have a general duty to work, comply with Par. 71.3 of the Standard Minimum Rules for the Treatment of Prisoners, with Par. 8 of the International Covenant on Civil and Political Rights,[4] and with Art. 4 of the Convention for the Protection of Human Rights and Fundamental Freedoms. The latter establishes that the term “forced or compulsory labour” shall not include “any work required to be done in the ordinary course of detention, [...] imposed according to the provisions of Art. 5 of the Convention or during conditional release from such detention”.

The ILO Forced Labour Convention, 1930 (No. 29) which was ratified by the USSR in 1956 establishes that the term “forced or compulsory labour” does not include, in particular, “any work or service exacted from any person as a consequence of a conviction in a court of law, provided that the said work or service is carried out under the supervision and control of a public authority and that the said person is not hired to or placed at the disposal of private individuals, companies or associations”.[5]

The Labour Code of the Russian Federation includes a similar statement in Par. 3, Art. 4 prohibiting forced or compulsory labour, and specifying that the notion of forced or compulsory labour does not include “work performed as a result of a court ruling that has become final under the supervision of those governmental bodies ensuring compliance with legislation enforcing the ruling”.

Taking into account what has been discussed earlier, the arguments of some employment law experts and criminal-executive law experts about the inadmissibility of prison labour for convicted persons in correctional facilities violating Par. 2, Art. 37 of the Constitution of the Russian Federation—which prohibits forced or compulsory labour—appear to be ill-founded.[6] In addition, two provisions of the Constitution of the Russian Federation which run counter to these assumptions should be mentioned.

In accordance with Par. 3, Art. 55 of the Constitution of the Russian Federation “the rights and freedoms of men and citizens may be limited by federal law only when it is necessary for the safeguard of the fundamental

---

[4] Adopted and opened for signature, ratification and accession by the General Assembly resolution 2200A (XXI) of 16 December 1966. Entry into force: 23 March 1976, in accordance with Art. 4.

[5] 1930. *Mezhdunarodnaya zaschita prav i svobod cheloveka [International Protection of Human Rights and Freedoms]*. Moscow: Yuridicheskaya literatura, 202.

[6] See, for example: Gubenko, A. V. 2005. *“Osobennosti pravovogo regulirovaniya truda osuzhdennykh k lisheniyu svobody [The Specific Features of the Legal Regulation of Labour of Persons Sentenced to Deprivation of Freedom]*. Chelyabinsk: Thesis, 10; Deruga, N. N. 2003. *“Organizacionno-pravovye problemy zanyatosti osuzhdennykh, soderzhaschikhsya v mestakh lisheniya svobody* [The Organizational and Legal Issues of Employment of Convicted Persons who are Kept in Institutions of Confinement]: Vladivostok: Thesis. 6-7.

principles of the constitutional system, morality, health, the rights and lawful interests of other people, in order to ensure that the country and its security are guaranteed". The CEC RF establishes a general duty to work in institutions of confinement for convicted persons, and so does the LC RF, which does not include it under the rubric of "forced or compulsory labour". Being that these are federal laws, they do not contravene the Constitution of the Russian Federation.

The other relevant provision is laid down in Par. 4, Art. 15: "the universally-recognized norms of international law and international treaties and agreements of the Russian Federation shall be integral to its legal system. If an international treaty or an agreement of the Russian Federation establishes rules other than those envisaged by the law, the rules of the international agreement shall apply". The Covenant on Civil and Political Rights of 1966, the Convention for the Protection of Human Rights and Fundamental Freedoms of 1955, and the ILO Forced Labour Convention of 1930 are international agreements ratified by the Russian Federation (and previously by the USSR). None of these agreements treats the employment of convicts in institutions of confinement as forced or compulsory labour.

Yet the legal grounds for employing convicts under 18 are somewhat ambiguous. In accordance with Par. 2, Art. 103 of the CEC RF "convicted persons who have not reached the age of 18 shall be given employment pursuant to Russian employment legislation". The same paragraph further provides some exceptions to the general duty to work for disabled and elderly convicts.

As is generally known, employment legislation is based on the principle according to which labour should be provided on a voluntary basis. Therefore, it can be assumed that convicted persons under 18 shall engage in labour only upon their consent. This is also confirmed by the United Nations Rules for the Protection of Juveniles Deprived of their Liberty of 1990[7] and the Standard Minimum Rules for the Treatment of Prisoners of 1955 which do not provide a duty to work for convicted persons under the age of eighteen. The UN document only states that: "With due regard to proper vocational selection and to the requirements of institutional administration, juveniles should be able to choose the type of work they wish to perform" (Par. 43). However, things are different in reality. This is because as opposed to other categories of workers, there is no obvious exception to the general duty to work for young people.

---

[7] Adopted by General Assembly resolution 45/113 of 14 December 1990.

However, if the legislator makes labour mandatory for young people, in order to clear the ambiguity of the relevant provision, young people's labour should be excluded from Par. 2, Art. 103 and included in Art. 104 ("Working conditions of persons sentenced to deprivation of freedom").

At the same time, the issue on whether convicts' labour should be treated as compulsory or voluntary is not the most important one in practice.

The majority of convicts wish to work, and prison wardens at correctional facilities do not usually impose disciplinary penalties if a convict refuses to perform paid work. However, fewer jobs are available for convicts in the Russian developing economy as compared to the Soviet period. As a result, the scope for employing convicted persons has considerably reduced. In 2012, only 215,000 convicts were given paid employment, 160,000 of whom were recruited in the production sector and 55,000 in service work in institutions. Only 35% of convicts in institutions of confinement in 2012 were engaged in paid work.

Compounding the picture is the fact that while the number of persons who are given a custodial sentence is reducing, an increase has been reported in the share of convicts with low levels of education or literacy, those without a family or a permanent place of residence, those with a disability or those suffering from chronic diseases. Every year, over 150,000 convicts enter correctional facilities. Over a period of six years (from 2005 to 2012) a downward trend was reported in the number of convicts who are fit for work (from 618,000 to 575,000 persons), and in those recruited in the production sector (from 183,000 to 160,000 persons).

Over 30% of convicts under the age of 25 did not work or study before being detained. Further, they are not used to performing work which is planned and organized.

Art. 108 of the CEC RF specifies that convicts should receive training in line with their main occupation which helps them to perform their work and to adopt a more positive attitude towards their activities.

The fulfillment of these goals requires time and financial resources. Drawing on the official data of the Federal Penal Service, the average cost to convert a workplace into a correctional facility which meets today's standards is 1.1 million roubles (about €27,000), without including the investments to be made in technical equipment of production facilities (4.2 billion roubles). The institutions of the criminal and executive system are unable to bear these costs. In considering the dramatic drop in orders, the 2005 to 2008 assignments given to the criminal and executive system were not sufficient to ensure convicts' full and efficient employment. If we consider that most convicts in Russia serve their sentence in labour camps, the reduction in the job openings made available to convicts leads to a deterioration of law and order in such institutions. This explains the objective set by the Federal Penal Service to substitute correctional labour camps with prisons by 2020. Yet this goal is unrealistic, being that this reorganization will cost up to 1.8 billion roubles.

In accordance with the CEC RF, the working conditions of those serving a prison sentence are similar to those established by employment legislation concerning working time (including days off and holidays), job safety, occupational hygiene and other employment-related issues. The CEC RF establishes that paid work performed by a convict while serving a sentence in a correctional facility shall be counted in the calculation of one's length of service. It is up to the facility administration to calculate the number of hours worked by convicts. If convicts systematically refuse to perform their work, the administration can decide that the hours which have not been worked will not be considered to calculate their seniority. This decision can be legally challenged by a convict.

Convicts are entitled to paid leave after working in a correctional facility for six months. However, for the purpose of calculating their length of service and ensuring their right to annual paid leave, the time that the convict has spent as a disciplinary penalty in a cell (up to six months), in a common cell (up to one year), or in a one man-cell special regime colonies (up to six months) is not taken into account, irrespective of whether or not a convict has performed work. Annual paid leave is equal to 18 working days for persons who serve their sentence in educational facilities and 12 working days for those who are confined in correctional ones.

Annual paid leave can be increased up to 18 working days, and up to 24 working days for young convicts who exceed their production quotas or properly perform their tasks, and for those operating in dangerous working conditions. This extension also involves those operating in the Far North and nearby regions, and male workers over 60, female workers over 55, and people with a certified disability (group I and II) operating on a voluntary basis.

In some cases established by the law (Art. 97 of the CEC RF) convicts are allowed to spend their holidays outside the correctional facilities. This right can be granted by the facility administration upon the assessment of such aspects as the crime committed, the term served, and convicts' personality and behaviour.

At present, the remuneration of convicts is almost entirely regulated by employment legislation. Those sentenced to deprivation of liberty who performed and completed their monthly amount of work are entitled to monthly remuneration above the minimum wage. If hired on a part-time basis, remuneration is paid in proportion to their working time or the amount of work performed. On average, in 2012 convicts performed 60% of the work assigned in a correctional facility, receiving a daily wage of 170 roubles (a little more of €4). Of course the gap between the gross and the net wage needs to be taken into account, as a significant difference emerges due to deductions, the modes of which are laid down in Art. 107 of the CEC RF and the Civil Procedural Code of the Russian Federation.

Yet a "guaranteed minimum" wage is always ensured which is calculated pursuant to Par. 3 Art. 107 of the CEC RF and amounts to 25% or 50% of the gross wage.

Referring to international legislation, some scholars and practitioners argued that convicts' labour in institutions of confinement should not necessarily generate profits.[8] In accordance with Par. 72.2 of the Standard Minimum Rules for the Treatment of Prisoners of 1955 "The interests of the prisoners and their vocational training, however, must not be subordinated to the purpose of making a financial profit from an industry in the institution". Clearly, this statement does not imply that the objective of making a profit should not be considered in prison labour, but it stresses that this should not necessarily be the only goal.

This assumption is confirmed by Par. 72.1 stating that: "the organization and methods of work in institutions shall resemble as closely as possible those of similar work outside institutions, so as to prepare prisoners for the conditions of normal occupational life".

Nowadays, increasing attention is being placed on efficiency and therefore on profit, which is becoming an indispensable economic condition. Therefore, taking into account the foregoing provisions, profit cannot be entirely excluded from the objectives of convicts' labour.

However, this should not result in a throwback to the Soviet era, when the criminal and executive system and the production activities were considered as a source of income and an important resource in terms of budget accumulation.

---

[8] For example, Smirnov, A. M. believes that "in accordance with international laws and Russian legislation convicts' labour cannot be used to generate revenue" (see: Smirnov, A. M. 2005. "Ob organizacii trudovoy adaptacii osuzhdennykh v lechebno-proizvodstvennykh (trudovykh) masterskikh [On the organization of convicts' labour adaptation in workshops concerning their treatment and production]," *Ugolovno-ispolnitel'naya sistema: pravo, ekonomika, upravlenie* [The Criminal-executive System: Law, Economics, Administration], No. 3:10.

It seems that the terminology adopted in legislation and occasionally used by scholars and practitioners at the time of investigating convicts' labour in some cases is also somewhat anachronistic and contrary to a humanistic approach. For example, it concerns the use of the term "use of convicts for work" (*trudoispol'zovanie osuzhdennyh*). Thus, the appendix to the internal regulations of correctional facilities earlier discussed is titled "List of occupations where it is prohibited to employ convicts.

Another example deals with an article where an authoritative author has pointed out that "the employment of disabled persons and those with reduced work ability is exercised in compliance with employment legislation".[9]

Obviously, Russian employment legislation does not provide for any "use for work" of disabled persons and those with a limited capacity for work. In accordance with civil law (Art. 209 of the Civil Code of the Russian Federation) the term "use" is an indispensable component to determine the right of ownership. In addition, international law, and the international treaties and agreements of the Russian Federation (pacts, conventions) clarify that: "slavery is the status or condition of a person over whom any or all of the powers attaching to the right of ownership are exercised" (Art. 1 of the ILO Slavery Convention of 1926).[10]

It is clear that the foregoing statements should not be considered as an attempt to restore or preserve convicts' slavery by the criminal and executive system. However, the functional approach adopted since the establishment of the Gulag system—where convicts were employed to cope with large-scale production—is still in place.

Further, this perspective affects the awareness of those within the criminal and executive system, undermining such aspects as the reformation, social rehabilitation and "labour adaptation" of convicts.

---

[9] See: Kononets, A. 2005. "Trudovaya adaptaciya osuzhdennykh v lechebno-proizvodstvennykh (trudovykh) masterskikh [Convicts' Labour Adaptation in Treatment-and-production Workshops]," *Prestuplenie i nakazanie* [Crime and Punishment] No. 9:16. See also Shamsunov, S.H. 2005. "*Organizaciya i pravovoe regulirovanie truda osuzhdennykh k lisheniyu svobody v celyakh ikh social'noy reabilitacii'* [Organization and Legal Regulation of Convicts Sentenced to Deprivation of Freedom for the Purpose of their Social Rehabilitation]. Ryazan': Thesis, 15, 17, 47.

[10] Signed in Geneva on 25 September 1926; entry into force: 9 March 1927. See also Art. 7 of the Supplementary Convention on the Abolition of Slavery, the Slave Trade, and Institutions and Practices Similar to Slavery, 226 U.N.T.S. 3, entered into force on 30 April 1957.

Those aspects can be found in some official statements and are viewed as the underlying objectives to reform the productive sector in the criminal and executive system.

Yet in the author's opinion the terminology itself does not adequately reflects the nature of these processes. For instance, the term "labour adaptation" (*trudovaya adaptaciya*) is a translation from Latin where the term "adaptation" means "adjustment" (*prisposoblenie*). This term is widely and aptly used in legislation and in the scientific analysis of issues related to the labour and living arrangements of persons released from the place of confinement.

The term "adaptation" implies the individual adjustment to conditions encountered by people today and not in the future. In other words, adaptation to freedom can only be at large. In other cases, it is appropriate to only discuss the prerequisites for future successful adaptation. The expression used to denote the productive units of the criminal and executive system as "centers of labour adaptation" cannot be considered appropriate either. Without some existing stereotypes, which to some extent are ideological, such productive units can be appropriately named "correctional labour centres" of correctional colonies and "educational labour centers", as educating (pursuant to Art. 9 of the CEC RF) is still one of main aims of the punishment, with labour being one of the means to meet this objective.

The recent and widespread use of the term "social rehabilitation" in relation to convicts in institutions of confinement also seems ill-founded.

As is widely understood in the medical, legal and social sciences, the term "rehabilitation" refers to the rehabilitation or compensation for the worsening of one's medical, legal or social conditions, either unfairly, undeservedly or due to some objective circumstances (e.g. a disease). This meaning is employed by medical practitioners to refer to the recovery of the disabled and the mentally ill and by lawyers when they consider the rehabilitation of victims of political repression or convicts. In accordance with Art. 133 of the Criminal-Procedural Code of the Russian Federation (hereafter CPC RF) "the right to rehabilitation shall incorporate the right to compensation for property damage, the right to the elimination of consequences from the moral harm suffered, the right to reinstatement and many others, including employment, pension, housing, and others". A convict can be rehabilitated only in the event of the full or partial cancellation of a verdict already enforced or in the event of the termination of a criminal case on the grounds envisaged in items 1 and 2 of the first part of Article 27 of the CPC RF (the lack of involvement in the execution of a crime and other grounds laid down by Art. 24 of the CPC RF).

In the author's view, such "terminology revolution" may be justified only when the existing one cannot adequately reflect a new state of affairs.

However, nobody has argued that "reformation" (in its realistic interpretation fixed by authoritative international legislation), and "re-socialization" (not rehabilitation) are now void of their informative and constructive sense.

Recent experience shows that the legislator swiftly excluded from the CEC RF such disciplinary measures as an additional duty to clean the premises and the institutions of confinement (Art. 53 of the Corrective-Labour Code of the Russian Soviet Federative Socialist Republic of 1970).

This move was formally explained by Art. 28.1 of the Standard Minimum Rules for the Treatment of Prisoners of 1955 according to which "no prisoner shall be employed, in the service of the institution, in any disciplinary capacity". Concurrently, on the one hand, Art. 28.2 provides that "this rule shall not, however, impede the proper functioning of systems based on self-government, under which specified social, educational or sports activities or responsibilities are entrusted, under supervision, to prisoners who are formed into groups for the purposes of treatment". On the other hand, the Standard Minimum Rules for the Treatment of Prisoners establishes that "in view of the great variety of legal, social, economic and geographical conditions of the world, it is evident that not all of the rules can be applied in all places and at all times".

In the author's opinion, since labour camps are the most widespread correctional facilities in Russia (as opposed to Western prisons), a more reasonable approach for the implementation of Art. 28.1 of the Standard Minimum Rules for the Treatment of Prisoners is required. Further, another important legal gap exists in the system of disciplinary penalties established by Art. 115 of the CEC RF in the event of an indigent convict who is unable to pay the fine of up to 200 roubles (Par. "b" Art. 115) with the alternative being either a reprimand or imprisonment (in Russia they are called "disciplinary cells"). This contradicts the principles of differentiation and individualisation of punishment, the principle of rationality in imposing sanctions established by Art. 8 of the CEC RF, and may give rise to the unlawful compulsion or violence.

Another interesting aspect is that pursuant to Art. 28.2 of the Standard Minimum Rules for the Treatment of Prisoners, convicts can be tasked with carrying out some activities. Does this provision also include the unpaid work of convicts operating in a given institution? This question arises as the foregoing clause only states that "no prisoner shall be employed, in the service of the institution, in any capacity". Accordingly, unpaid employment seems to fall under the scope of this provision. The legal framework for engaging convicts in unpaid work is laid down in Art. 106 of the CEC RF. It states that unpaid work is allowed only in relation to tasks aimed at the improvement "of correctional facilities and their contiguous areas". Convicts who have the right instead of a duty to work as well as pregnant women can also be engaged in unpaid work only upon their consent.

Convicts are assigned to works in their free time in order of precedence. The duration of the tasks to be performed can be extended in two cases: upon a convict's written application or following the decision of the facility administration when urgent works are needed (Par. 3, Art. 106 of the CEC RF).

However, the formulation of this provision leaves some unsolved issues. The first relates to the wording "urgent works"; it is unlikely that the legislator refers to activities aimed at the "improvement of the correctional facilities and their contiguous areas" as laid down in Par. 1, Art. 106 of the CEC RF. However, this norm clearly has a restrictive character, with Par. 1 which seemingly contradicts Par. 2. Accordingly, it would be necessary to reformulate Par. 1 as follows: "persons sentenced to deprivation of freedom can engage in unpaid work if work is aimed at the improvement of the corrective facilities and their contiguous areas, and in the exceptional cases following the decision of the head of a corrective institution where it is necessary to carry out rescue works, emergency and reconstruction works, as well as urgent works to ensure the essential functioning of the institution".

It is rather unclear why the legislator excluded certain categories of convicts from unpaid work considering the simplicity and the ease of works concerning improvements and self-service. Drawing on that, it would be necessary to formulate Par. 2 Art. 106 as follows: "convicts with a certified disability falling in group I or II, convicted men who have attained the age of 60, convicted women who have attained the age of 55, and pregnant prisoners can only be engaged in unpaid work aimed at the improvement of correctional facilities and their contiguous areas with due regard for their ability to work, job safety, and occupational hygiene which are established for these categories of workers by employment legislation of the Russian Federation".

Finally, it seems also unfair that the legislator has established a limit of two hours per week for all convicts. Convicted persons who are provided employment and those who do not engage in working activities should be treated differently, the latter having more free time. It would be reasonable therefore to increase to a minimum of twelve hours per week the duration of unpaid work for them. The same time limit must be established for urgent works in accordance with the decision of the administration of correctional facilities (for which provisions have not been laid down yet).

Moreover, the order of precedence at the time of giving such assignments—established by Par. 3, Art. 106 of the CEC RF—should not be considered in absolute terms.

Therefore, Par. 3, Art. 106 of the CEC RF may be reformulated as follows: "Convicted persons engage in work during the time they do not work or study. The duration of the working activities for convicts already carrying out paid work should not exceed two hours a week. The duration of work shall not exceed twelve hours in the case of a written consent on the part of convicts already performing paid work, convicts who do not perform any work at all, or those who are engaged in rescue activities, emergency and reconstruction works, and urgent works related to correctional facilities".

References

Deruga, N. N. 2003. *Organizacionno-pravovye problemy zanyatosti osuzhdennykh, soderzhaschikhsya v mestakh lisheniya svobody [The Organizational and Legal Issues of Employment of Convicted Persons Who are Kept in Institutions of Confinement]* Vladivostok: Thesis, 6-7.

Gubenko, A. V. 2005. *"Osobennosti pravovogo regulirovaniya truda osuzhdennykh k lisheniyu svobody" [The Specific Features of the Legal Regulation of Labour of Persons Sentenced to Deprivation of Freedom],* Chelyabinsk: thesis, 10.

ILO. 1926. *ILO Slavery Convention* Geneva: ILO.

United Nations. 1966. *International Covenant on Civil and Political Rights* adopted and opened for signature, ratification and accession by General Assembly resolution 2200A (XXI) of 16 December 1966 entry into force 23 March 1976, in accordance with Article 4.

Kononets, A. 2005. "Trudovaya adaptaciya osuzhdennykh v lechebno-proizvodstvennykh (trudovykh) masterskikh [Convicts' Labour Adaptation in Treatment-and-production Workshops]," *Prestuplenie i nakazanie [Crime and Punishment]*, No 9: 16.

Council of Europe. 2006. *Recommendation Rec(2006)2 of the Committee of Ministers to member states on the European Prison Rules* adopted by the Committee of Ministers on 11 January 2006 at the 952nd meeting of the Ministers' Deputies. Strasbourg: Council of Europe.

Shamsunov, S. H. 2005. "*Organizaciya i pravovoe regulirovanie truda osuzhdennykh k lisheniyu svobody v celyakh ikh social'noy reabilitacii'*

[Organization and Legal Regulation of Convicts Sentenced to Deprivation of Freedom for the Purpose of their Social Rehabilitation]. Ryazan: thesis, 15, 17, 47.

Smirnov, A. M. 2005. "Ob organizacii trudovoy adaptacii osuzhdennykh v lechebno-proizvodstvennykh (trudovykh) masterskikh [On Organization of Convicts' Labour Adaptation in Treatment-and-Production Workshops]," *Ugolovno-ispolnitel'naya sistema: pravo, ekonomika, upravlenie* [The Criminal-executive System: Law, Economics, Administration], No 3:10.

United Nations. 1955. *Standard Minimum Rules for the Treatment of Prisoners* adopted 30 August, 1955 by the First United Nations Congress on the Prevention of Crime and the Treatment of Offenders.

United Nations. 1957. *Supplementary Convention on the Abolition of Slavery, the Slave Trade, and Institutions and Practices Similar to Slavery*, 226 U.N.T.S. 3, entered into force April 30, 1957.

United Nations. 1990. *United Nations Rules for the Protection of Juveniles Deprived of their Liberty* adopted by General Assembly resolution 45/113of 14 December 1990.

THE RESOLUTION OF COLLECTIVE LABOUR DISPUTES AND THE REALIZATION OF THE RIGHT TO STRIKE IN RUSSIA

ELENA GERASIMOVA

1. Introduction

Russia is party to a number of international agreements recognizing the right to strike. Russia is also a member of the International Covenant on Economic, Social and Cultural Rights[1] which recognizes the right to strike provided that it is exercised in conformity with the laws of the country in question (p.(d) part 1 art. 8) and the ILO fundamental conventions on freedom of association No.87.[2] In addition, Russia is party to certain regional treaties which refer to the freedom of association in a general sense, notably the European Social Charter (amended in 1996), the European Convention on Human Rights and certain human rights acts defined within the Commonwealth of Independent States and other regional organizations. In accordance with part 4 Art. 6 of the European Social Charter, and with a view to ensuring that the right to bargain collectively can be exercised effectively, the parties undertake to promote the right of workers and employers to collective action in cases of conflicts of interest, including the right to strike, subject to obligations that might

[1] International Covenant on Economic, Social and Cultural Rights, 16 December 1966. Ratified by the USSR 18 September 1973. http://www.ohchr.org/EN/ProfessionalInterest/Pages/CESCR.aspx (accessed 08 January 2014).

[2] Freedom of Association and Protection of the Right to Organize Convention of 1948 (No.87), Right to Organize and Collective Bargaining Convention of 1949 (No. 98). ILO Database of international labour standards Normlex: http://www.ilo.org/dyn/normlex/en/f?p=1000:1:0::NO:::. (accessed 08 January 2014). All ILO Conventions and Recommendations henceforth are taken from this database.

arise out of collective agreements previously entered into.[3]

Collective labour disputes and strikes became a legal instrument for the protection of rights and interests in Russia in 1989, when the law of the USSR "On the procedure of collective labour disputes (conflicts) resolution" was adopted.[4] This law imposed rules governing the long and complicated mediation, conciliation and arbitration procedures, as well as prohibiting the right to strike for a large number of employees, thus effectively making it an anti-strike law.

The Constitution of the Russian Federation of 1993 declared that recognition shall be given to the right to individual and collective labour disputes with the use of methods fixed by federal law, including the right to strike (part 4 art. 37).[5]

In 1995 the Federal Law of the Russian Federation "On the procedure of collective labour disputes resolution" was adopted, on the whole continuing the concept of Soviet law.

The detailed regulation of the right to collective labour disputes and the right to strike is now contained in the Labour Code of the Russian Federation (chapter 61), adopted in 2001[6] (henceforth "the Labour Code"), which codifies norms concerning social partnerships, including collective labour disputes and strikes, collective bargaining, collective agreements, and workers' representation. The provisions concerning collective labour disputes and strikes have been amended a number of times, but the most important changes were made in 2006[7] and then in 2011,[8] both times

---

[3] European Social Charter (revised). Strasbourg, 3.V. 1996. http://conventions.coe.int/Treaty/en/Treaties/Html/163.htm (accessed 08 January 2014).

[4] Zakon SSSR. "O poryadke razresheniya collectivnich trudovich sporov" [Law of the USSR "On the Procedure of Collective Labour Disputes (Conflicts) Resolution"] 9 October 1989. No. 580-1. Vedomosti SND SSSR I VS SSSR, 1989, No. 18, Art. 342).

[5] Konstituziya Rossiyskoy Federatsii [Constitution of the Russian Federation]. Rossiyskaya Gazeta, No. 237, 25 December 1993. The English text of the Russian Constitution is available on the internet: http://www.constitution.ru/en/10003000-01.htm.

[6] Trudovoy Kodeks Rossiyskoy Federatsii [Labour Code of the Russian Federation], 2001. Sobranie Zakonodatelstva RF, 7 January 2002, No.1, Art. 3.

[7] Federalniy Zakon "O vnesenii izmeneniy v Trudovoy Kodeks Rossiyskoy Federazii, priznanii ne deiystvuyuschimi na territory Rossiyskoy Federacii nekotorich normativnich pravovih aktov SSSR I atrativshimi silu nekotorih zakonodatelnih aktov Rossiaskoy Federacii", [Federal Law "On Changes to the Labour Code of Russian Federation, Recognition of Invalid Provisions of Normative Acts of the USSR on the Territory of Russian Federation and Finding

acting on recommendations made by the Committee on Freedom of Association of the International Labour Organization (ILO), which revised the Russian Labour Code following complaints made by Russian trade unions (Cases No. 2216 and 2251), and approved a number of recommendations submitted to the Russian government.

The 1996 Law on Trade Unions, their Rights and the Guarantees of their Activities (henceforth "the Trade Unions Act")[9] declares that trade unions have the right to participate in the resolution of collective labour disputes, the right to organize and conduct strikes, meetings, demonstrations, pickets and other collective actions in accordance with the federal law, and to use these actions as a means to protect social-labour rights and the interests of workers.[10] As we shall see, however, after the adoption of the Labour Code, trade unions lost the independent right to start collective labour disputes and organize strikes and must now depend upon the voting of employees.

Since the adoption of legislation regarding collective labour disputes and strikes, and above all since the adoption of the Russian Labour Code, the need to improve the legislation on this topic has been much debated.

Indeed, trade unions and researchers have been questioning the effectiveness of the established norms and procedures for many years.

In spite of their broad social influence, collective labour disputes and strikes have not been widely discussed in Russia over the last decade, either by the media or by experts in the field of labour relations and conflicts.

This is mainly the result of the fact that the number of strikes in Russia has been comparatively low for a number of years. Official statistics have recorded very few since 2008; in 2013 Rosstat registered only 3 strikes, with a total of 196 participants.[11]

---

not Applied of Some Normative Legislative acts of Russian Federation"], June 30, 2006 No. 90-FZ. Sobraniye Zakonodatelstva Rossiyskoy Federazii, 3 July 2006, No. 27, Art. 2878.

[8] Federalniy Zakon "O vnesenii izmeneniy v Trudovoy Kodeks Rossiyskoy Federazii", [Federal Law "On Changes to the Labour Code of RF], 11 November 2011 No. 334-FZ. Sobraniye Zakonodatelstva Rossiyskoy Federazii, 28 November 2011, No. 48, Art. 6735.

[9] Federalniy Zakon o professionalnih Soyuzah, ih pravah i garantiyah deyatelnosti [Federal Act on Trade Unions, their Rights and the Guarantees of their Activity], 12 January 1996. Sobraniye Zakonodatelstva Rossiyskoy Federazii, 15 January 1996, No. 3, Art. 148.

[10] Art. 14 of the Trade Union Act.

[11] Federal State Statistics Service:
http://www.gks.ru/bgd/regl/b13_01/IssWWW.exe/Stg/d12/3-2.htm (accessed: 17 February 2014).

Table 11-1. Number of Strikes Registered by Rosstat.

	1991	1992	1993	1994	1995	1996	1997	1998	1999	2000	2001
No. of organizations where strikes took place	1,755	6,273	264	514	8,856	8,278	17,007	11,162	7,285	817	291

	2002	2003	2004	2005	2006	2007	2008	2009	2010	2011	2012
No. of organizations where strikes took place	80	67	5,933	2,575	8	7	4	1	0	2	6

Federal State Statistics Service:
http://www.gks.ru/bgd/regl/b11_36/IssWWW.exe/Stg/d1/05-12.htm;
http://www.gks.ru/bgd/regl/b12_13/IssWWW.exe/Stg/d1/05-29.htm;
http://www.gks.ru/bgd/regl/b12_01/IssWWW.exe/Stg/d12/3-2.htm (accessed 01 July 2013).

However, Rosstat's statistics do not represent the situation realistically, because, due to the methodology used, Rosstat does not register all strikes but only those which were reported as a strike by the employer. If the employer considers that the employees' refusal to work was not a strike, but, for example, an "illegal stoppage of work", he or she simply does not report it. The Centre for Social and Labour Rights (CSLR) has been monitoring labour protests, including strikes,[12] since 2008. This monitoring uses information gathered about collective labour disputes and strikes from Internet sources (information agencies, trade-union and employer websites, independent information projects and so on). It considers not only legal collective actions, but all labour conflicts and cases of stoppages of work.

According to CSLR's findings, there were at least 60 cases where employees stopped work in 2008, 106 in 2009, 88 in 2010, 91 in 2011, 95 in 2012 and 102 in 2013.[13]

Fig. 11-1. Number of "Cases of Stop-actions" and Strikes According to CSLR and Rosstat data.

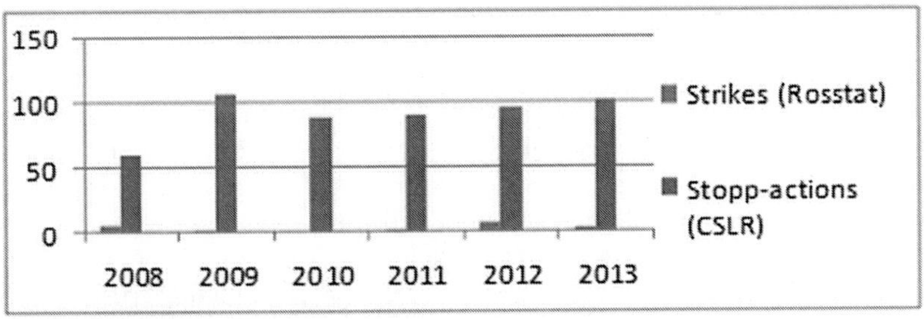

Source: Federal State Statistics Service: http://www.gks.ru/bgd/regl/b11_36/IssWWW.exe/Stg/d1/05-12.htm; http://www.gks.ru/bgd/regl/b12_13/IssWWW.exe/Stg/d1/05-29.htm; http://www.gks.ru/bgd/regl/b12_01/IssWWW.exe/Stg/d12/3-2.htm (accessed 1 July 2013).

[12] For more about monitoring see: Bizyukov, P. 2011. "Labor Protests in Russia, 2008–2011," *Russian Analytical Digest*, No. 104, 27 October 2011. http://www.css.ethz.ch/publications/pdfs/RAD-104.pdf.

[13] Analytical Report "Labour Protests in Russia in 2008-2012," on the basis of CSLR (Centre for Social and Labour Rights) monitoring. http://www.trudprava.ru/index.php?id=2228 (accessed 01 July 2013).

CSLR's research shows that a variety of forms of protest are used by employees. The most popular forms of protest include applying to the court, rallies outside companies and applications to governmental bodies of varying levels. A stoppage of work (full or partial)—the classic strike—was only fourth in the list of the most common forms of protest in 2012.

This indicates an attempt to demonstrate the stability of the socio-economic sphere by misrepresenting the real number of strikes. However, employees themselves do not always consider a strike as the most effective way to settle collective labour disputes. The reasons for this are complex, though restrictive legislative norms and procedures concerning the resolution of collective labour disputes and strikes, as well as lengthy law enforcement procedures, may be contributing factors. Further on we shall examine the legislative norms on collective labour dispute resolution in greater detail.

2. Collective Labour Disputes

In Russia the two main types of labour dispute, individual and collective, are regulated by law. Individual labour disputes can be resolved by commissions for labour disputes created at a local level, in court, and through the process of mediation. In collective labour disputes, workers participate collectively. To settle a collective labour dispute, mediation, conciliation and arbitration procedures can be used. Collective labour disputes can also be settled using the right to strike, which is recognized in Russia as a means for the resolution of collective labour disputes only.

Individual labour disputes are usually *legal* disputes, concerning the implementation of norms; collective disputes are mainly (though not solely) *economic* disputes and *disputes of interest*, concerning the creation of norms.

According to the law, collective labour disputes are unregulated disagreements between employees (their representatives) and employers (their representatives) concerning the establishment and/or changes of working conditions (including salary). These are effectively changes in the implementation of collective agreements, often as a result of the employer's refusal to consider the views of the representative body during the adoption of local normative acts.[14] Collective labour disputes may exist at different levels of social partnership, including local and all higher levels.

---

[14] Art. 398 of the Labour Code.

There are three important factors in collective labour disputes: the parties of the dispute, the reason for the dispute (the topic) and the procedure of the dispute.

Employers (their representatives) and employees are the *parties* of the collective labour dispute. At a local level collective labour disputes may be initiated by the employees of an organization, its representation or branch office, and a separate structural division of the company. The trade union or trade union federation (confederation) may represent employees if they wish to start a collective labour dispute at a higher level.

Employees who may have a conflict of interests in the dispute because they belong to a particular group, for example members of the trade union to which members of a particular profession are affiliated, cannot initiate a collective labour dispute.[15]

The law provides no definition of what may be considered a separate structural division, though this has effectively been defined by the practice of the courts.

The *reason* for the collective labour dispute is defined by law[16] and may fall into one of three categories:

1. working conditions (including salary): if employees wish to create new working conditions or change those previously established;
2. collective agreements negotiated at any level of social partnership,[17] including disagreements concerning the procedure of negotiations, conditions of the draft of the collective agreement, changes or the implementation of the signed agreement;
3. the refusal of employers to consider the opinions of the employees' representative body during the adoption of local normative acts.[18]

Should a disagreement concern other matters, the dispute will not be considered a collective labour dispute and the procedure is not applied. No other procedures are applied either.

---

[15] See: Lyutov, N., and E. Gerasimova. 2014. "Non-trade Union Employees' Representation in Russia," in *Bulletin of Comparative Labour Relations 85, Workers' Representation in Central and Eastern Europe Challenges and Opportunities for the Works Councils' System,* eds. Blanpain, R., and N. Lyutov, (Aspen: Wolters Kluwer), 183-201.

[16] Art. 398 of the Labour Code.

[17] In Russia two different terms are used to define collective agreements according to the different levels of social partnership: "*collectivniy dogovor*" for the local level and "*collectivnoye soglasheniye*" for higher levels (Art. 45, 45 of the Labour Code).

[18] Art. 398 of the Labour Code.

As mentioned earlier, strikes in Russia are considered a means of resolution for *collective* labour disputes only, and they cannot, by law, be used to achieve any other goals. As a result Russian employees are not entitled to use their right to strike in a number of situations when the right to strike is recognized by ILO soft-law.[19] This problem was raised in a complaint made to the Committee on Freedom of Association by the Confederation of Russia (case #2251). The following recommendations of the CFA were approved by the Governing Body: "... (g) The Committee recalls that workers and their organizations should be able to call for a strike aimed at recognizing a trade union, as well as in order to criticize a government's economic and social policies and should be able to take a sympathy strike, provided the initial strike they are supporting is itself lawful".[20]

Though almost ten years have passed since these recommendations were introduced, no changes have been made to legislation. As a result, in a number of cases where employees in other countries might choose to strike in order to defend their interests, it is unlawful for Russian employees to do so.

Another problem concerning the subject of collective labour disputes is how to interpret the legislative provision "implementation of the collective agreement", which, in accordance with Art. 398 of the Labour Code, can legitimately be the subject of a collective labour dispute.

According to Art. 381 of the Labour Code, unregulated disagreements concerning the implementation of collective agreements can be the subject of an individual labour dispute.

Over the last few years there has been a growing tendency in court practice to consider a dispute as collective if its demands regard the implementation of collective agreements. One of the more recent decisions of the Supreme Court of the Russian Federation on this topic is dated 25 January 2013 No. 44-КГ12-5.[21] In this case, the primary trade union organization of a company, "Permskiy svinocomplex", applied to the court

---

[19] ILO. 2006. *Freedom of Association. Digest of Decisions and Principles of the Freedom of Association Committee of the Governing Body of the ILO*. Fifth (revised) edition. Geneva: ILO, par. 526, 527, 529, 531, 534-544.

[20] ILO. 2004. *ILO Committee on Freedom of Association Report No. 333*, March 2004, case 2251, par. 1001 (g). Normlex Database: file:///G:/%D0%BB%D0%B5%D0%BD%D0%B0_%D0%BC%D0%B4/%D0%9C%D0%9E%D0%A2/%D0%A2%D0%B5%D0%BA%D1%81%D1%82%D1%8B/Report%20333%20case%202251.htm.

[21] The website of the Supreme Court of the Russian Federation: http://www.supcourt.ru.

with a complaint concerning the indexation of employees' wages on the basis of the collective agreement. The trade union based their demand on the provision of the collective agreement and the employer's order, issued on the basis of this collective agreement, which required the indexation of wages. The Supreme Court of Russia ruled that there was an unregulated disagreement between the employer and employees concerning a change of working conditions, specifically the indexation of wages on the basis of a collective agreement; this is therefore a collective labour dispute between employer and employees which should be settled through the use of mediation and arbitration procedures. The court did not therefore have the competences to analyse the case. There are a number of other examples where courts demonstrate the same understanding of the issue.

Employees' cases are rejected by the court when their demands are based on collective agreements.

This position can be considered dangerous for the stability of labour relations as it decreases the importance and obligatory mandate of collective agreements. *De facto* courts require employees to start a collective labour dispute on a topic which has been previously discussed by both parties and on which an agreement had already been reached. The Committee on Freedom of Association has commented that the solution to a legal conflict as a result of a difference in the interpretation of a legal text should be left to the competent courts.[22] Besides, in Russia, as we will show, the initiation of collective labour disputes, their resolution and the use of the right to strike, are overly complicated procedures which cannot easily be utilized by employees to protect their interests.

If there is a problem that can be the subject of a collective dispute according to the law and employees are ready to start one, they should *initiate* a collective labour dispute. This procedure is very formal and rather complicated.

Employees and their representatives (including trade unions) are granted the right to make demands to the employer. On a local level the employees' demands must be approved by all employees in one of the following three ways:[23]

- employees can formulate demands themselves during a conference or general meeting of all employees;

[22] ILO. 2006. *Freedom of Association. Digest of decisions and principles of the Freedom of Association Committee of the Governing Body of the ILO*. Fifth (revised) edition. Geneva: ILO, 532.
[23] Art. 399 of the Labour Code.

- employees' representatives formulate demands, and employees then approve them during a conference or general meeting of all employees;
- if it is impossible to organize a conference or general meeting of all employees, the employees' representative body can approve the demands by collecting the signatures of more than 50% of employees.

A conference is valid if over 2/3 of the delegates participate; the general meeting is valid if over 50% of all employees participate; demands must be voted by over 50% of participants present in order to be approved.[24]

If the collective labour dispute is organized at a higher level, demands should be formulated by trade unions, their federation and confederations in accordance with their charters, and do not have to be approved by employees.

The regulations described are complicated to follow in practice; the violation of this procedure is considered a reason to declare a strike called during the collective labour dispute resolution illegal. The CFA has criticized this procedure because of its restrictive nature,[25] and it was partially improved in 2006 and 2011.

We mentioned above that collective labour disputes at a local level may be initiated by an organization's employees, their representatives or by a branch office as a separate structural division. The law provides no definition of the *separate structural division* as applied to labour relations, and this creates numerous problems for employees and trade unions.

Employees never know for sure whether or not the court will consider the structural division where they work as being "separate", and whether the strike they organize will consequently be declared illegal.

Since the adoption of the Labour Code, the definition of a "separate structural division" has been formulated in court practice during the analysis of the legality of strikes. The Supreme Court of Russia ruled that a structural division can be considered "separate" if it works independently (in autonomy) from the main organization and if, should a strike be called, the stoppage of work in this division would not influence the work of the rest of the organization.[26] For example, a coal mine can be considered a

---

[24] Part 3 Art. 399 of the Labour Code.

[25] ILO. 2004. *ILO Committee on Freedom of Association Report No. 333*, case 2251, par.1001.

[26] *Ruling of the Supreme Court of the Russian Federation* from 18 July 2008 No. 45-Г08-12; *Ruling of the Supreme Court of the Russian Federation* from 10 February 2006 No. 74-Г06-4.

separate structural division according to the courts.[27] On the other hand, the technical base of an airline company,[28] a theatre orchestra[29] or the transportation division of a coal mine,[30] cannot be recognized as separate structural divisions.

However, the implementation of this rule in practice still leaves a number of unanswered questions. In many cases this definition does not help groups of employees to fully understand whether or not they can legitimately start a collective labour dispute.

3. Beginning a Collective Labour Dispute

By law, employees' demands should be sent in writing to the employer (or the employer's association). At a local level the employer should answer employees within two working days of receiving their demands; the employers' association should answer their demands within three weeks of receiving the demands—in both cases in writing.[31] The employer may agree to all the demands and if so there is no collective labour dispute. Should the employer (or employers' association) reject the employees' demands in full, in part, or should no answer be given by the end of the term established, the collective labour dispute is considered begun.

A serious problem concerning the initiation of a collective labour dispute is the absence of special rules applicable to disputes arising from collective bargaining. During collective bargaining parties can sign a protocol of disagreements if they do not agree on all issues under negotiation, and here they must include all positions concerning the topics discussed. Due to the current regulations in the Labour Code, even in cases where the protocol has been signed, employees still have to formulate their demands and have them approved at a conference or general meeting, send them to the employer and wait for a reply. Before

[27] *Ruling of the Supreme Court of the Russian Federation from* 18 July 2008 No. 45-Г08-12.

[28] *Ruling of the Supreme Court of the Russian Federation* from 10 February 2006 No. 74-Г06-4.

[29] *Ruling of the Supreme Court of the Russian Federation* from 1 December 2006 No. 48-Г06-20.

[30] *Ruling of the Supreme Court of the Russian Federation* from 26 August 2005 No. 93-Г05-14.

[31] Art. 400 of the Labour Code.

the Labour Code was amended in 2006,[32] the date of signing of the protocol of disagreements during collective bargaining was considered to be the date on which the collective labour dispute began; employees did not need to conduct the procedure of initiating the dispute because the lack of agreement was obvious to both parties.

The existing regulations constitute a serious complication for employees trying to settle disagreements rising from collective agreements with their employers, and do not favour the development of the social partnership system.

Unfortunately, due to the large number of such regulations, employees often feel that the aim of the legal regulations governing the resolution of collective labour disputes is much more about complicating the procedure in order to drain the employees' strength and energy, rather than finding a genuine solution to the dispute.

4. Procedures of Collective Labour Dispute Resolution

Conciliation procedures in Russia are mainly based on the ILO Recommendation No. 92 concerning Voluntary Conciliation and Arbitration, 1951.[33] The procedure for the resolution of collective labour disputes (conciliation procedures) in Russia comprises three procedures: conciliation commission, mediation and labour arbitration.

The only compulsory phase is that of the conciliation commission. The parties involved in the dispute can use the mediation procedure if they both agree that it is appropriate. Labour arbitration is used if both parties agree on it and if they both accept that the arbitrator's decision is binding and obligatory, or if the parties are obliged to use the arbitration process because the group of employees in question are prohibited from going on strike.

---

[32] Federalniy Zakon "O vnesenii izmeneniy v Trudovoy Kodeks Rossiyskoy Federazii, priznanii ne deiystvuyuschimi na territory Rossiyskoy Federacii nekotorich normativnich pravovih aktov SSSR I atrativshimi silu nekotorih zakonodatelnih aktov Rossiaskoy Federacii", [Federal Law "On Changes to the Labour Code of Russian Federation, Recognition of Invalid of Provisions of Normative Acts of the USSR on the Territory of the Russian Federation and Finding not Applied some of the Normative Legislative Acts of the Russian Federation"], 30 June 2006 No. 90-FZ. Sobraniye Zakonodatelstva Rossiyskoy Federazii, 3 July 2006, No. 27, Art. 2878.

[33] Voluntary Conciliation and Arbitration Recommendation, 1951 (No. 92). http://www.ilo.org/dyn/normlex/en/f?p=NORMLEXPUB:12100:0::NO::P12100_I LO_CODE:R092 (accessed 06 January 2014).

The resolution of a collective labour dispute may therefore comprise between one and three steps:

1. conciliation commission;
2. conciliation commission—mediation;
3. conciliation commission—labour arbitration;
4. conciliation commission—mediation—labour arbitration.

The law obliges the parties involved in the dispute to participate in its resolution, and states that penalties of administrative responsibility may be applied should one refuse to participate; the amount of the fine is defined by law as between one and three thousand roubles (around 20 to 60 euros),[34] though this penalty is not effectively applied in practice. If one party refuses to resolve the dispute through the use of one of these channels, the other party can initiate negotiations using the next procedure.[35] If an employer refuses to participate in the resolution of the collective labour dispute by labour arbitration, the employees can begin to organize a strike.[36]

As mentioned previously, a debate has been going for many years concerning the ineffectiveness of the procedures for the resolution of collective labour disputes in Russia. One argument is that the procedures are too lengthy, and the period from the beginning of the dispute until the possible moment of a strike is unreasonably protracted. In response to this argument, changes were made to Chapter 61 of the Labour Code in 2011.[37]

The time frames of all procedures were shortened, and different time frames were established for the resolution of collective labour disputes at different levels (for example disputes at a local level have shorter time frames than those at a higher level).

[34] Art. 5.32 Kodeks Rossiyskoy Federatsii ob administrativnih pravonarusheniyah [Russian Federation Administrative Offences Code]. Sobraniye Zakonodatelstva Rossiyskoy Federazii, 7 January 2002, No. 1, Art. 1.

[35] Articles 402-404 of the Labour Code.

[36] Art. 409 of the Labour Code.

[37] Federalniy Zakon "O vnesenii izmeneniy v Trudovoy Kodeks Rossiyskoy Federazii", [Federal Law "On changes to the Labour Code of RF], 11 November 2011 No. 334-FZ. Sobraniye Zakonodatelstva Rossiyskoy Federazii, 28 November 2011, No. 48, Art. 6735.

Table 11-2. Time Frames for the Resolution of Collective Labour Disputes as Given in the Labour Code before and after the Law of 2011 (in working days).[38]

Actions during the Resolution of Collective Labour Dispute	**Local level since 2011**	**Other levels since 2011**	**Terms before 2011**
Creation of the conciliation commission	*2*	*3*	*3*
Dispute resolution in conciliation commission	*3*	*3*	*5*
Taking decision on invitation of the mediator	*1*	*1*	3
Taking decision on person of the mediator	2	2	
Dispute resolution with the mediator	3	5	7
Taking decision on resolution of the dispute in labour arbitration	*1*	*1*	7
Taking decision on person of labour arbitration	2	4	
Dispute resolution in labour arbitration	3	5	5

During the resolution of a collective labour dispute, the parties can organize mass actions in accordance with the law.[39]

We shall briefly describe the procedures used for the resolution of collective labour disputes in Russia.

1. Conciliation commission. Creating a conciliation commission is the only obligatory procedure. Each party independently chooses its representatives for the commission, the number of which normally varies from two to five.[40] The commission develops its own working regulations. The employer is responsible for creating appropriate conditions in which the commission can work, including providing space and technical supplies. A decision is made if both parties agree on it. The conciliation commission's decision is binding for both parties and should be implemented as defined by the commission.

---

[38] Terms of obligatory procedures are marked in italics.

[39] Federalniy Zakon "O sobraniyah, mititngah, demonstrciyah, shestviyah I piketirovaniyah", [Federal Law "On Meetings, Rallies, Demonstrations, Processions and Picketing"], 19 June 2004 No. 54-FZ. Sobraniye Zakonodatelstva Rossiyskoy Federazii, 21 June 2004, No. 25, Art. 2485.

[40] Regulation of the Ministry of Labour "Ob utvergdenii Recomendaciy ob organizacii raboty po rassmotreniyu kollektivnogo trudovogo spora primiritel'noy komissiey" [Recommendations on the resolution of collective labour disputes by conciliation commissions"] 8 August 2002, No. 57. Bulletin of the Ministry of Labor of Russia, 2004, No. 8.

Should the parties be unable to reach a decision they must sign a protocol on their disagreements. They must then negotiate on whether they will use the mediation or labour arbitration procedure.

2. *Mediation* is a voluntary procedure, but parties should discuss whether they wish to invite a mediator for the resolution of the dispute if it is not possible to reach a settlement in the conciliation commission or if the employer avoids resolving the dispute in the conciliation commission. If both parties agree to use mediation, they have up to two days to decide who to choose as mediator. There are no obligatory requirements for the candidature; anyone can be invited to be a mediator. The State Body responsible for the resolution of collective labour disputes may suggest a candidate, but its recommendation is not binding.

The procedure of dispute resolution by mediation also depends on the parties' agreement. They can use the recommendations[41] approved by the Russian Ministry of Labour to develop the procedure. During mediation a decision is taken if both parties agree on it; the decision is binding for both parties. If an agreement cannot be reached, the parties must sign a protocol on their disagreements and start discussing the initiation of the labour arbitration process. In practice parties do not often use mediation for the resolution of disputes.

If parties are not able to reach an agreement through the process of mediation, they start discussing the initiation of the labour arbitration process.

3. Labour arbitration. Prior to 2011, labour arbitration in Russia could only be initiated as an *ad-hoc* body. Following changes to the Labour Code in 2011, tripartite commissions were granted the right to create permanent labour arbitrations at various levels of social partnership.

As mentioned above, parties are free to decide whether they wish to use the arbitration procedure. Arbitration is used if parties agree on the binding nature of the arbitrator's decision; this agreement must be signed by both parties. The procedure for the creation of *ad-hoc* arbitration is similar to that for the conciliation commission and mediation: members of the arbitration board are chosen by the parties with the participation of the

---

41 Regulation of the Ministry of Labour "Ob utvergdenii Recomendaciy ob organizacii raboty po rassmotreniyu kollektivnogo trudovogo spora s uchastiem posrednika" [Recommendations on the Resolution of Collective Labour Disputes by Mediator"] 8 August 2002, No. 58. Bulletin of Ministry of Labour of Russia, 2004, No. 8.

state body responsible for the resolution of collective labour disputes (State Body);[42] arbitration usually involves between three and five people.

Parties are also free to pass the dispute to the permanent labour arbitration board if there is one in the region. The procedure of dispute resolution by *ad-hoc* labour arbitration is to be developed by the parties and the State Body together on the basis of recommendations[43] approved by the Russian Ministry of Labour. Permanent labour arbitration works by basing itself on the regulations developed by the social partners. Members of the labour arbitration board cannot represent parties involved in the dispute.

Arbitration is compulsory if employees do not have the legal right to go on strike.[44] If parties cannot agree on the members of the arbitration commission, its procedures or whether to give the case over to permanent arbitration, decisions regarding these matters will be made by the State Body.

Decisions made during the process of labour arbitration are binding for all parties. If these decisions are not adhered to, an administrative fine can be imposed on either or both parties. This fine, however, is not particularly high—between two and four thousand roubles[45] (around 40-80 euros) and is not effectively imposed in practice. A more serious consequence is that

---

[42] Federal'naya slugba po trudu i zanyatosti (Rostrud) [Federal Service on Labour and Employment] is appointed to represent the state body, exercising state services for the settlement and resolution of collective labour disputes. It works under the Jurisdiction of the Ministry of Labour and has a number of regional divisions. See President's Decree of 9 March 2004 No. 314 "O systeme I struktute federal'nich organov ispolnitel'noy vlasti" [On the System and Structure of Federal Bodies of Executive Power]. Sobraniye Zakonodatelstva Rossiyskoy Federazii, 15 March 2004, No. 11, Art. 945; Ruling of the Russian government of 30 June 30, 2004 No. 234 "Ob utvergdenii pologeniya o Federal'noi slugbe o po trudu I zanyatosti" [On Federal Service on Labour and Employment (Rostrud)]. Rossiyskaya gazea, 8 July 2004, No. 144.

[43] Regulation of the Ministry of Labour "Ob utvergdenii Recomendaciy ob organizacii raboty po rassmotreniyu kollektivnogo trudovogo spora v trudovom arbitrag" [Recommendations on the Collective Labour Dispute Resolution by Labour Arbitration"] 8 August 2002, No. 59. Bulletin of Ministry of Labour of Russia, 2004, No. 8.

[44] Parts 1, 2 Art. 421 of the Labour Code.

[45] Art. 5.33 Kodeks Rossiyskoy Federatsii ob administrativnih pravonarusheniyah [Russian Federation Administrative Offences Code]. Sobraniye Zakonodatelstva Rossiyskoy Federazii, 7 January 2002, No. 1, Art. 1.

employees are given the right to organize a strike if their employer ignores the arbitrator's decision.[46]

All employee representatives participating in the resolution of collective labour disputes are protected by a set of guarantees: disciplinary action cannot be taken against them, they cannot be moved to a different job or dismissed by the employer without the prior agreement of the workers' representative body.

5. The Right to Strike

As in many other countries the right to strike was only recognized in Russia after many years of finding strikes illegal, imposing fines on strike participants and arresting them. In 1905 strikes on economic grounds were legalized,[47] but striking was prohibited at all state companies. Strikes were actively used during the revolutionary events in 1917 and continued to take place until 1921, though at that time they were used less and less frequently. During the Soviet period strikes were not mentioned in legislation and were not recognized *de-facto*. Formally there were no strikes in the Soviet Union; there was considered to be no reason for them.

Some strikes, however, did take place (17 strikes in the 1960s, 25 strikes in the 1970s, 31 strikes in the early 1980s),[48] but participants were seriously punished. After the increase in spontaneous labour protests at the end of the 1980s the new period of strike regulation began.[49]

---

[46] Article 408 of the Labour Code.

[47] "Vremenniye pravila o nakazuemosti naibolee opasnich proyavleniy v zabastovkah" [Temporary Rules for the Punishment of the most Dangerous Exercising of Strikes], 2 December 1905. See about this period: Shelymagin, I. I. 1947. *Fabrichno-zavodskoye zakonodatel'stvo v Rossii (vtoraya polovina XIX veka), [Industrial Law in Russia (Second Half of XIX Century)]*. M.: Lagal edition of the Ministry of Justice, 36, 173; Shelymagin, I. I. 1952. *Zakonodatel'stvo o fabrichno-zavodskom trude v Rossii [Legislation on Industrial Work in Russia]*, M.: Gosyurizdat, 171.

[48] Milovodov, Y. N., and A. N. Krestyaninova. 1995. "Social'no-trudovieye issledovaniya. Rabochee dvigeniye v segodnyashey Rossii: stanovleniye, sovremennniye problem, perspektivy, [Social-labour Research. Labour Movement in Today's Russia: Development, Contemporary Problems, Perspectives]," in *Zabastovki. Zarubegniy I otechestvenniy opyt" [Strikes. Foreign and Russian experience],* (Institute of world economy and international relations), Edition 1:13.

[49] See Ashwin, S., and S. Clarke. 2002. *Russian Trade Unions and Industiral Relations in Transition.* Basingstoke and New York: Palgrave.

As we discussed earlier, strikes are only recognized as a means of resolving collective labour disputes in Russia, a fact which has been criticized by ILO bodies.

According to the Labour Code,[50] employees are granted the right to organize a strike if:

- conciliation procedures have not succeeded in settling a collective labour dispute;[51]
- the employer refused to participate in the resolution of the collective labour dispute;
- the employer is not adhering to the decisions made during the collective labour dispute resolution.[52]

Organizing a strike is a complicated procedure in Russia; it requires the fulfilment of a number of formal obligations, the violation of any of which may result in the strike being declared illegal by the court.

At a local level the decision to strike should be taken by employees themselves taking into account advice from the employee's representative body.[53] Therefore, two decisions (that of the representatives' body and that of the employees') need to be made before going on strike.

If the collective labour dispute is held at a higher level, the decision on whether to strike should first be taken by the trade union (or trade union federations) and then the employees of each employer should vote on the strike.

In both cases the employees' decision should be made in a general meeting or conference of employees; the requirements are the same as for a general meeting (conference) aimed at starting a collective labour dispute. An employees' general meeting is valid if over 50% of employees participate; a conference is valid if over 2/3 of delegates participate. The decision to go on strike is made if over 50% of participants vote for a strike.[54] If it is impossible to organize a general meeting or conference, the employees' representative body can organize a vote by collecting the signatures of over 50% of all employees.[55] The employer is obliged to provide a location and the necessary conditions for the meeting (conference).

---

[50] Art. 409 of the Labour Code.
[51] Art. 406 of the Labour Code.
[52] Art. 408 of the Labour Code.
[53] Part 5 Art. 409 of the Labour Code.
[54] Art. 410 of the Labour Code.
[55] Part 5 Art. 410 of the Labour Code.

The requirement of obtaining an absolute majority of workers before being able to call a strike was criticized by the CFA[56] in connection with the complaints of Russian trade unions (cases No. 2216 and 2251) and by the CEACR. The first edition of the Labour Code required the presence of 2/3 of participants both for the general meeting and conference for calling a strike. The CFA requested that the government amend section 410 of the Labour Code in order to lower the quorum required for a strike ballot.[57] In 2006 the Labour Code was amended, but as pointed out above, only the amount of participants required for the general meeting was decreased.

In 2006 new terms limiting the duration of strikes were added to the Labour Code: a strike can be started no later than two months after the decision to strike is taken.[58] If the strike is not started within this period employees lose the right to strike, and must restart conciliation procedures from the beginning.[59]

The Labour Code also determines certain obligatory requirements regarding the content of the decision to strike; the following issues must be indicated in the content of the decision to strike:[60]

- a list of disagreements between the parties;
- the date and time when the strike should start and the estimated number of participants;
- the employees' body leading the strike, the list of workers; the representatives appointed to conduct further negotiations about the collective labour dispute with the employer;
- recommendations concerning minimum safety requirements during the strike.

Any violations of the content of the written decision to strike may be considered reason to find the strike illegal in court, and these rules are indeed widely applied by courts in order to declare strikes illegal.

Employees are required to give written notice to the employer before going on strike. This notice should be of at least five working days at a local level, and no less than seven working days at other levels. The

---

[56] ILO. 2006. *Freedom of Association. Digest of Decisions and Principles of the Freedom of Association Committee of the Governing Body of the ILO.* Fifth (revised) edition. Geneva: ILO, par. 556. 557.

[57] ILO. 2004. *ILO Committee on Freedom of Association Report No. 333*, March 2004, case 2251, par. 1001 (i). Normlex Database: http://www.ilo.org/dyn/normlex/en/f?p=1000:50002:0::NO:50002:P50002_COMPLAINT_TEXT_ID:2907631 (accessed 06 January 2014)

[58] Part 9 Art. 410 of the Labour Code.

[59] Part 11 Art. 410 of the Labour Code.

[60] Part 9 Art. 410 of the Labour Code.

employer is responsible for informing the State Body responsible for the resolution of collective labour disputes of the strike.

5.1. Minimum Safety Services

The law does not specify the type of organizations where a list of minimum safety requirements should be provided. However, under the Labour Code, the inclusion of a particular type of industry in the minimum safety service list should be based upon whether there is a danger to the health or life of the population;[61] the list of minimum safety services cannot include industries not listed in sectoral minimum safety services lists. Thus, we can conclude that minimum safety services can only be requested in certain sectors where sectoral minimum safety service lists have already been developed.

Particular levels (lists) of minimum safety services should be established on the basis of the sectoral lists of minimum safety services developed by federal state bodies and agreed upon by an all-Russia trade union (trade unions) acting in the relevant sectors of the economy.[62] The Labour Code requires that such lists be drawn up for sectors which operate in areas connected with people's safety, their health or essentially important interests of society.[63] In some sectors where the CFA finds that minimum services are in place, the law still prohibits strikes (e.g. railroads).[64]

The procedure for the development of sectoral minimum safety services lists is established by the Russian government.[65] Eighteen lists have so far been developed for various sectors of the economy, including the shipbuilding industry; the industry regular arms industry; the ammunitions and special chemicals industries; the light industry; medical and biotechnical industries; chemical and oil industries; state enterprises under the jurisdiction of the Russian Ministry of Culture; rocket and space industry; agricultural and fishing companies; education organizations; the peat industry; the power industry; gas-distributing companies; health organizations; coal and metallurgical industries.

---

[61] Part 5 Art. 412 of the Labour Code.

[62] Art. 412 of the Labour Code.

[63] Part 3 Art. 412 of the Labour Code.

[64] ILO. 2004. *ILO Committee on Freedom of Association Report No. 333*. Geneva: ILO, case 2251, par.1001 (n).

[65] Ruling of the Russian Government of 17 December 2002 No. 901. Rossiyskaya gazeta, 24 December 2002.

On the basis of sectoral lists of minimum safety services, regional lists of minimum safety services should be developed and approved by regional governmental bodies with the consent of regional trade unions. Together they should aim to concretize the content and define how the lists should be applied. In practice, however, few regional lists are ever developed.

For any given strike minimum safety services should be established on the agreement of both employers and employees, and with the participation of a municipal body on the basis of employees' suggestions, within three days of the decision to strike being made (after the call for a strike). If no agreement on the list is reached within three days, the regional governmental body must make a decision on the content of the list. The list of minimum safety services can be revised by the court following a complaint from one of the parties,[66] although in practice this never occurs due to time constraints in the preparation of a strike.

Non-compliance with minimum safety services is a reason for the court to issue an order suspending the strike until such a list is provided.[67]

Before Federal Law No. 334-FZ of 2011 entered into force, non-compliance with minimum safety services was considered just cause for the court to find the strike illegal,[68] and this reason was widely used by courts in their decisions on the illegality of strikes.

5.2. Prohibited Strikes

Under the Labour Code[69] and in accordance with article 55 of the Russian Constitution, strikes are prohibited and therefore illegal in a wide range of cases:

a) during periods of military state, during a state of emergency or other exceptional cases when special measures are in place in accordance with the legislation governing states of emergency; in organizations of military services and other military organizations responsible for the defence of the country and security of the state; for employees in the professional emergency and rescue services, in fire-prevention services or services operating for the prevention or in the aftermath of natural disasters or states of emergency; in law-enforcement bodies; in organizations (branch offices, outlets, other separate structural divisions) directly supplying

[66] Part 7 Art. 412 of the Labour Code.

[67] Part 8 Art. 412 of the Labour Code.

[68] Part 8 Art. 412 of the Labour Code before the changes introduced by Federal Law No. 334-FZ of 2011, para 59 of Ruling of the Plenum of the Supreme Court of Russia from 17 March 2004 No. 2.

[69] Part 1 Art. 413 of the Labour Code.

particularly dangerous products or equipment; at ambulance or first aid stations;

b) in organizations (their outlets, branch offices, other separate structural divisions) directly working to maintain the well-being of the population (energy supply, heating and heat supply, water supply, gas supply, air and railroad transportation, communication) if the strike endangers the defence of the country and security of the state, or the life and health of the population.

Though paragraph (b) of art. 413 part 1 specifies the conditions which would render a strike illegal: "if the strike endangers the defence of the country and security of the state, or the life and health of the population", in practice, courts consider strikes in these sectors to be dangerous *per se*, and do not seriously analyse the extent to which they may or may not actually be dangerous.

Furthermore, the federal law defines other cases where strikes are prohibited. For example, strikes are prohibited by federal law for air traffic controllers;[70] railroad employees;[71] military forces;[72] employees of the Federal State Communication Services;[73] heads of state and municipal unitary organizations;[74] state employees[75] and civil municipal servants.[76]

---

[70] "Vozdushniy kodeks Rossiyskoy Federacii" [Air Code of Russian Federation] of 19 March 1997 No. 60-FZ, Art. 52. Sobraniye Zakonodatelstva Rossiyskoy Federazii, 24 March 1997, No. 12, Art. 1383.

[71] Part 2 Art. 26 of Federalniy Zakon "O geleznodorognom transporte" [Federal Law "On Railroad Transportation"] from 10 January 2003 No. 17-FZ. Sobraniye Zakonodatelstva Rossiyskoy Federazii, 13 January 2003, No. 2, Art.169.

[72] Art. 7 of Federalniy Zakon "O statuse voennoslugascih" [Federal Law "On Military Servants Status"] from 27 May 1998 No. 76-FZ. Sobraniye Zakonodatelstva Rossiyskoy Federazii, 1 June 1998, No. 22, Art. 2331.

[73] Art. 9 of Federalniy Zakon "O feldegerskoy svyazi" [Federal Law "On Federal State Communication Services"] from 17 December 1994 No. 67-FZ. Sobraniye Zakonodatelstva Rossiyskoy Federazii, 19 December 1994, No. 34, Art. 3547.

[74] Part 2 Art. 21 of Federalniy Zakon "O gosudarstvennih I municipalnich unitarnih predpriyatiyah" [Federal Law "On State and Municipal Unitary Organizations"] from 14 November 2002 No. 161-FZ. Sobraniye Zakonodatelstva Rossiyskoy Federazii, 02 December 2002, No. 48, Art. 4746.

[75] Part 15 Art. 17 of Federalniy Zakon "O gosudarstvennoy gragzhdanskoy slugzhbe" [Federal Law "On State Service"] from 27 July 2004 No. 79-FZ. Sobraniye Zakonodatelstva Rossiyskoy Federazii, 2 August 2004, No. 31, Art. 3215.

[76] Art. 11 of Federalniy Zakon "Ob osnovah municipal'noy slugzhby v Rossiyskoy Federacii" [Federal Law "On Basics of Municipal Service in the Russian Federation"] from 8 August 1998 No. 8-FZ. Sobraniye Zakonodatelstva Rossiyskoy Federazii, 12 January 1998, No. 2, art. 224.

Strikes outside nuclear facilities and storage areas are also restricted if they could infringe upon the working conditions of those facilities and storage area personnel, or if they entail any other danger to the safety of others, the environment or the health, rights and lawful interests of others.[77]

This list is broader than the list of essential services recognized by the CFA,[78] and includes some sectors where, according to the CFA, the right to strike should be guaranteed.[79] This particularly concerns civil servants, municipal employees and railroad workers;[80] the CFA has requested that the Russian government "amend its legislation so as to ensure that railroad employees, as well as those engaged in the public services but not exercising authority in the name of the state, enjoy the right to strike", but no changes regarding these points have as yet been made.

5.3. Illegal Strikes

The Russian Labour Code considers strikes illegal if they are prohibited,[81] or if they are organized without due consideration of the terms, procedures and requirements listed in the Labour Code.[82] The latter is, in practice, interpreted widely, and even an unintentional break of the Labour Code's provisions can be seen as a reason for declaring a strike illegal.

The decision to find a strike illegal may be taken by a court subject to the Russian Federation (a second level court of general jurisdiction). The case may be initiated either by an employer or a prosecutor.

---

[77] Art. 39 of Federalniy Zakon "Ob ispol'zovanii atomnoy energii" [Federal Law "On the Use of Nuclear Energy"] from 21 November 1995 No. 170-FZ. Sobraniye Zakonodatelstva Rossiyskoy Federazii, 27 December 1995, No. 48, Art. 4552.

[78] ILO. 2006. *Freedom of Association. Digest of Decisions and Principles of the Freedom of Association Committee of the Governing Body of the ILO.* Fifth (revised) edition. Geneva: ILO, par. 585.

[79] *Ibidem*, par. 587.

[80] ILO. 2004. *ILO Committee on Freedom of Association Report No. 332*, November 2003, case 2199, par. 992. Normlex Database: http://www.ilo.org/dyn/normlex/en/f?p=1000:20030:0:FIND:NO:::. Geneva: ILO. ILO. 2004. *Committee on Freedom of Association Report No. 333*. Geneva: ILO. case 2251, par.1001. Normlex Database: file:///G:/%D0%BB%D0%B5%D0%BD%D0%B0_%D0%BC%D0%B4/%D0%9C%D0%9E%D0%A2/%D0%A2%D0%B5%D0%BA%D1%81%D1%82%D1%8B/Report%20333%20case%202251.htm (accessed 03 January 2014).

[81] Part 1 Art. 413 of the Labour Code.

[82] Part 3 Art.413 of the Labour Code.

Having observed a lawyer who has represented employees in this type of court case for many years, I have noted that almost all strikes connected with the resolution of collective labour disputes, the legality of which is analysed in court, are found to be illegal.

According to statistics of the Judicial Department of the Supreme Court, the number of court cases finding strikes illegal is notably high, and greatly exceeds the number of officially registered collective labour disputes and strikes.

Table 11-3. Court Cases Disputing the Legality of Strikes: Information on Case History.[83]

			No. of cases on which court decisions were taken					
	No. of cases issued	No. of cases from previous year	Total No. of cases	No. of claims satisfied / % of cases considered	No. of claims rejected	No. of cases terminated	No. of cases left without consideration	No of cases concluded
2009	79	20	64	40 / 62.5%	24	18	4	90
2010	38	9	34	24 / 70%	10	8	3	45
2011	39	2	31	21 / 67%	10	7	3	41
2012	100	0	27	19 / 70%	8	65	4	97

As we can see, about 2/3 (62-70%) of strikes are found to be illegal in court, and the reasons for this are very often based on formalities connected with various violations of the procedures and terms required by the Labour Code. It is clear from the analyses of particular court decisions that, judges, on the whole, have anti-strike views and make use of insignificant violations of procedure in order to find strikes illegal.

Court cases may be initiated by employers or prosecutors when the decision to strike has already been taken but the strike itself has not yet taken place. In practice, applications to the court are used to receive a decision from the court on the illegality of a strike which effectively tells the employees that a strike will not be allowed to take place.

Such a situation is a vivid illustration of anti-strike trends in social-labour relations in Russia. We can say that not in all cases of collective labour disputes and strikes do employers or prosecutors apply to the court in order to have the strike declared illegal, but when they do this is usually what happens.

---

[83] The data provided by the Judicial Department of the Supreme Court of the Russian Federation, published on its website www.cdep.ru, has been used in this table. http://www.cdep.ru/index.php?id=79&item=1775 (accessed 01 July 2013).

The main legal consequence of courts' decisions on the illegality of strikes is that employees are obliged to interrupt the strike and return to work. The employees' body leading the strike must inform workers of the court's decision immediately. Employees must go back to work the day after the leading body is informed of the court's decision. If this rule is violated employees can legally be dismissed.

Participation in an illegal strike deprives employees of their guarantees. Employees participating in a strike which has been declared illegal by the court can have disciplinary action taken against them for participating in the strike after they have received official notice of the court's decision.[84] Furthermore, the representative body heading the strike may be responsible for damages incurred from the illegal strike.[85]

5.4. Guarantees for Employees Participating in Strikes

Lockouts are prohibited in Russia, although a lockout is defined simply as the dismissal of employees because of their participation in legal strike action[86]. Other actions which an employer may take against workers are not prohibited. In practice, cases of direct violations of this legislative provision or of discriminatory measures being taken against participants in strikes are not rare. Courts also tend to show little regard for the law prohibiting lockouts.

There are illustrative examples of the lack of protection provided for participants in strikes. Participants in a strike are not protected against discrimination as we can see in the decision of the European Court of Human Rights (ECtHR) in the case of *Danilenkov and Others v. Russia.* In this case the applicants were members of a local branch of the Dockers' Union of Russia and worked in a private company called Kaliningrad Commercial Seaport. In 1997 their trade union began a two-week strike over pay, better working conditions and life insurance. Subsequently, trade union members were moved to special work teams, transferred to part-time positions, and, finally, dismissed by the employer as a result of a structural reorganization of the company.[87] In this case ECtHR ruled that the negative action taken against those belonging to the trade union

---

[84] Part 1 Art. 417 of the Labour Code.

[85] Part 2 Art. 417 of the Labour Code.

[86] Art. 415 of the Labour Code.

[87] *Danilenkov and Others v. Russia*, 2008, ECHR. ECHR, section five. http://hudoc.echr.coe.int/sites/eng/Pages/search.aspx#{"fulltext":["Danilenkov and Others v. Russia"], "documentcollectionid2": ["GRANDCHAMBER", "CHAMBER"], "itemid": ["001-93854"]} (accessed 18 February 2014).

constituted discrimination against the employees in the enjoyment of their rights guaranteed by Article 11 of the Convention. ECtHR ruled that the State should provide effective and clear judicial protection against discrimination on the grounds of trade-union membership, which can, if necessary, be deliberated in a civil proceeding. The same problem was raised in complaints made by the Russian Confederation of Labour to the CFA in 2002 (Case No. 2199)[88] and in 2011 (Case No. 2758)[89].

Unfortunately, the legislation has not been changed to provide better protection against discrimination on the basis of trade-union membership and activity. Employees are still put under serious pressure if they decide to participate in a strike.

Conclusion

We can see that existing procedures for the resolution of collective labour disputes do not, in practice, satisfy the needs and constraints of the social partners and of employees above all.

According to CSLR research, strikes are usually spontaneous or illegal. Moreover, when analysing the forms of protest used by employees, we can see that legitimate forms of protests (the stoppage of work because of the non-payment of wages; collective labour disputes, followed [or not] by a strike) constituted just 11% of all protests in 2008 and 2009; 9% in 2010; 8% in 2011; 6% in 2012. As we can see, the number of legitimate forms of protest is decreasing from year to year.

Another finding of the CSLR research was that the number of strict forms of protests, such as hunger-strikes, plant take-over, road blockages) is particularly high. 17%, 18% and 17% of all protest actions in 2008, 2009, and 2010 respectively, were organized under these forms. In 2011, the number of such actions decreased to 4.5%, but in 2012 it rose again to 9%. 7% of all protests in 2012 were organized as hunger-strikes.

These figures show that though legislation governing the resolution of collective labour disputes and strikes exists in Russia, but it is not used effectively. The reasons for this are manifold.

---

[88] *Committee on Freedom of Association Report No. 331*, June 2003, case 2199. http://www.ilo.org/dyn/normlex/en/f?p=1000:50002:0::NO:50002:P50002_COMPLAINT_TEXT_ID:2907091 (accessed 18 February 2014).

[89] *Committee on Freedom of Association Report No. 365*, November 2012, case 2758.
http://www.ilo.org/dyn/normlex/en/f?p=1000:50002:0::NO:50002:P50002_COMPLAINT_TEXT_ID:3087064 (accessed 18 February 2014).

Social partners in Russia do not genuinely believe in social dialogue; employers rarely comply with their employee's demands, even when the validity of the demands is evident.[90]

Legislation on the resolution of collective labour disputes and strikes is complicated for employees, and leaves considerable room for the employer to exploit bureaucracy in order to avoid serious negotiations aimed at genuinely resolving the labour conflict. Employers can fall back on a number of formalities in order to avoid negotiations and apply for a court ruling to find the strike illegal, and so on. The result of all this is that employees and their representatives go to great lengths to follow the legislative procedures prescribed by the law, but these efforts do not help them to resolve the dispute. Employees who initiate collective labour disputes and participate in their resolution often face pressure from law-enforcement bodies which consider labour protests to be virtually extremist activity.[91] The law limits the right to strike for a broad number of categories of workers and its provisions are not always clear and logical.[92] The majority of strikes are found to be illegal by courts.

These questions have been raised by trade union leaders, researchers and a part of the academic community for years, but serious changes have not followed. As a result, year after year we come to the same conclusion: protest movements in Russia mainly develop spontaneously. The law does not accomplish its task of creating an effective mechanism for the resolution of collective disputes in social and labour relations.

---

[90] A clear illustration of this can be found in the case of Pikalevo, a little town in Leningradskaya oblast. A documentary film, *Three Sides,* by N. Veligzhanin presents examples and reasons of the conflict: http://www.youtube.com/watch?v=l8suJhG2hcE&feature=youtu.be (accessed 01 February 2014).

[91] The Confederation of Labour of Russia made a complaint to the ILO Committee on the Freedom of Association, describing numerous instances of such violations. Case #2758. Report #365, November 2012. Normlex. Informational system on International Labour Standards: http://www.ilo.org/dyn/normlex/en/f?p=1000:50002:0::NO:50002:P50002_COMPLAINT_TEXT_ID:3087064 (accessed 01 February 2014).

[92] Gerasimova E. S. 2012. "Zakonodatel'stvo Rossii o kollectivnih trudovih sporah I zabastovkah: problem I napravleniya sovershenstvovaniya [Legislation of Russia on the Resolution of Collective Labour Disputes and Strikes: Problems and Directions for Improvement]" *//Trudovoye pravo v Rossii I za rubegom [Labour Law in Russia and abroad]* No. 1:29-35.

References

Analytical report "Labour protests in Russia in 2008-2012" on the basis of the CSLR (Centre for Social and Labour Rights) monitoring. http://www.trudprava.ru/index.php?id=2228 (accessed: 01 July 2013).

Ashwin, S., and S. Clarke. 2002. *Russian Trade Unions and Industiral Relations in Transition.* Basingstoke and New York: Palgrave.

Bizyukov P. 2014. *Labour Protests in Russia, 2008–2011.* Russian Analytical Digest, No. 104, 27 October 2011. http://www.css.ethz.ch/publications/pdfs/RAD-104.pdf (accessed 15 January 2014).

Bizyukov, P. V. 2011. *Kak zashishayut trudoviye prava v Rossii: kollektivniye trudovie protest i ih rol' v regulirovanii trudovyh otnosheniy [How Labour Rights are Defended in Russia: Collective Labour Protests and their Role in the Regulation of Industrial Relations]*, Moscow: Tsentr sotsial'no-trudovyh prav [Centre for Social-Labour Rights], 30-33. Available at: http://trudprava.ru/download/bizukov_kak_zaschitit_1pdf (accessed 08 January 2014).

Federal Service on Labor and Employment. 2013. *Number of Collective Labor Disputes Registered during 2006-2012.* http://rostrud.ru/activities/34/22831/22835.shtml (accessed 27 November 2013).

Gerasimova E. S. 2012. "Zakonodatel'stvo Rossii o kollectivnih trudovih sporah I zabastovkah: problem I napravleniya sovershenstvovaniya [Legislation of Russia on the Resolution of Collective Labour Disputes and Strikes: Problems and Directions for Improvement]," *//Trudovoye pravo v Rossii I za rubegom [Labour law in Russia and abroad]*, No. 1:29-35.

—. 2012. "Poryadok razresheniya kollektivnyh trudovyh sporov i organizatsii zabastovok izmenen. Dostignuta li tsel'? [The Procedure for the Resolution of Collective Labour Disputes and Use of Strikes has been Changed. Has the Goal been Achieved?]," *Trudovoe pravo* [*Labour Law*] 1, 51-59.

Lyutov, N. 2012. *Rossiyskoye trudovoe zakonodatelstvo i mejdunarodniye trudoviye standarty: sootvetstvie i perspectivy sovershenstovaniya [Russian Labour Legislation and International Labour Standards: The Issues of Compliance and Perspectives for Modification].* Moscow: Tsentr sotsial'no-trudovyh prav [Centre for Social-Labour Rights]. Available at "Centre for social and labour rights" website: http://trudprava.ru/files/pub/rostrudzak.pdf (accessed 15 February 2014).

Lyutov, N., Gerasimova, E. 2014. Non Trade Union Employees' Representation in Russia in *Bulletin of comparative Labour Relations 85, Workers' Representation in Central and Eastern Europe: Challenges and Opportunities for the Works Council System*, eds. Blanpain, R., and N. Lyutov, (Aspen: Wolters Kluwer), 183-201.

Milovodov, Y. N., and A. N. Krestyaninova. 1995. "Social'no-trudovieye issledovaniya. Rabochee dvigeniye v segodnyashey Rossii: stanovleniye, sovremennniye problem, perspektivy, [Social-labour Research. Labour Movement in Today's Russia: Development, Contemporary Problems, Perspectives]," in *Zabastovki. Zarubegniy I otechestvenniy opyt" [Strikes. Foreign and Russian experience],* (Institute of world economy and international relations), Edition 1:13.

CONTRADICTIONS IN THE ANTI-DISCRIMINATION PROTECTION OF EMPLOYEES IN RUSSIA AND THE INFLUENCE OF THE EUROPEAN COURT OF HUMAN RIGHTS

ELENA SYCHENKO

The prohibition of discrimination was one of the main innovations of post-Soviet labour laws. The Labour Code of the RSFSR[1] was amended in 1992 to incorporate rules prohibiting discrimination in employment and wages (Art. 2, p. 16). The new Labour Code of the Russian Federation,[2] adopted in 2002, prohibits discrimination in employment (although the list of discriminatory grounds remains open). It also allows for the possibility to claim for moral damages (*moralny vred*) in case of discrimination.

Russian anti-discrimination laws therefore comply—at least superficially—with the international standards adopted by the UN and ILO Conventions.[3]

More in-depth research, however, immediately highlights two main contradictions in the system of anti-discrimination protection of employees. The first contradiction is that anti-discrimination rules are laid down only in fundamental principles, thus on the "surface" of the legal system. The adoption of a common principle did not lead to the review of present legislation and modification of the numerous discriminatory provisions.

---

[1] The Code of Labour Laws of the RSFSR adopted by the RSFSR Supreme Soviet 09.12.1971. Available at: http://www.consultant.ru/document/cons_doc_LAW_32447/ (accessed 04 November 2013).

[2] The Labour Code of the Russian Federation N. 197-FZ adopted 30 December 2001. Available at: http://www.consultant.ru/popular/tkrf/#info (accessed 04 November 2013).

[3] The Convention on the Elimination of All Forms of Discrimination against Women (CEDAW), ILO Convention C111—Discrimination (Employment and Occupation) Convention, 1958 (No. 111) and C156—Workers with Family Responsibilities Convention, 1981 (No. 156).

The first contradiction lies therefore in the existence of discriminatory provisions in contemporary Russian labour laws.

The second contradiction relates to the absence of clear and effective mechanisms of anti-discrimination protection granted by the common principles. Further on we will examine both issues presenting cases brought to court vs Russia at the European Court of Human Rights (ECtHR). In conclusion, we will analyse ECtHR's approach to the problem of discrimination and discuss whether its practices might be applicable in Russia.

1. Discriminatory Labour Laws

The discriminatory provisions of labour law are a very complicated issue, because of the constant need to find a balance between discrimination (which is officially prohibited) and differentiation (which is officially permitted). According to Art. 3 of the Russian Labour Code, discrimination can be defined as the restriction of employment rights and freedoms or the receiving of any advantage on the grounds of sex, race, colour, nationality, language, origin, property, family, social or professional status, age, place of residence, attitude to religion, convictions, membership or non-membership of public associations or any social groups, as well as other circumstances not related to the professional qualities of an employee. According to Art. 2 and Art. 242 of the Russian Labour Code, differentiation can be understood as special employment regulations required by the nature and conditions of the work, psycho-physiological characteristics of the organism, climatic conditions and the presence of family responsibilities, as well as other grounds established by law for the special care of people who need enhanced social and legal protection. These definitions show that the notions of discrimination and differentiation are closely related.

The Constitutional Court of Russia has interpreted the difference between these concepts in a wide range of cases,[4] emphasizing that differentiation can be justified by the "traditional role of women in the

---

[4] See for example: Ruling of the Constitutional Court of the Russian Federation No. 378-OP 15.05.2007 on the refusal to consider the non-constitutionality of the provision of the Labour Code on the possibility of concluding fixed-term employment contracts with persons who reached retirement age, or the Judgment of the Constitutional Court 6 December 2012 that established the non-constitutionality of the provision admitting dismissal of pregnant civil servants in case of disciplinary offence. The rule was considered discriminatory, being dismissals of pregnant women never allowed, except in this case for civil servants.

society", social justice and the "public support of family", thus not constituting discrimination.

In many cases, the Constitutional Court found that differentiation was unjustified and the corresponding provisions were held to be discriminatory and invalid. A case in point is the abolition of the norms on maximum employment age for the post of faculty deans, or heads of department in higher education institutions,[5] or the extension of dismissal protection for fathers who have children under 3 years old (in cases where the mother is absent or is unemployed).[6]

There are also cases where the position of the Constitutional Court might be viewed as questionable because of a poor justification of special provisions. As an example we can consider the case of Anna Klevetz heard by the Constitutional Court in 2012.[7] The applicant was refused entry to study courses to become an assistant train driver as this profession was in the list of jobs prohibited to women. Anna Klevetz claimed that the relevant provisions of the Labour Code were unconstitutional and the list of works discriminatory. The Constitutional Court rejected the claim stating that such a restriction was based on the necessity to protect women's "reproductive health". Since the Court's decision does not mention the age of the applicant, the reference to the concept of "reproductive health" is without sufficient grounds. Russian legislation places a general prohibition on the employment of women in harmful or dangerous conditions and in "difficult" or physically demanding jobs, regardless of age. In this decision, the Court avoided the issue of the legality of such a prohibition for women of non-childbearing age and confirmed the constitutionality of an evident case of discrimination against a middle-aged woman.

An analysis of Constitutional Court case law leads us to the conclusion that the main task of the Court with respect to discriminatory provisions of labour laws is that of finding a balance between the competing interests of, on the one hand, the social protection of a "weaker" party (often women) and the economic freedom of the employer. Although the Court emphasizes that ensuring this balance is particularly important for the

---

[5] Ruling of the Constitutional Court of the Russian Federation N 213-O, 11.07.2006, see also Decision of the Constitutional Court of the Russian Federation N 19-P, 27.12.1999. Available at: http://www.ksrf.ru/ru/Decision/Pages/default.aspx.

[6] Decision of the Constitutional Court of the Russian Federation of 15.12.2011 N 28-P, "Collection of Laws of the Russian Federation", 26.12.2011, N 52, art. 7639.

[7] Ruling of the Constitutional Court of the Russian Federation No. 617-O-O issued 22.03.2012.

Russian welfare state, it is not always able to strike a balance in its judgments. In some cases, the Court leans more towards protecting the State's interests rather than the interests and rights of individuals. This is particularly dangerous in the field of anti-discrimination protection, because of the risk of trampling on the right for equality and not respecting the dignity of those concerned.

The best illustration of this argument can be found in the case of Konstantin Markin,[8] who, on 11 August 2008, resorted to the Constitutional Court claiming that the provisions of the Military Service Act entitling only women to take three-year parental leave were incompatible with the equality principle laid down in the Constitution.[9]

The Constitutional Court rejected his application concluding that servicemen under contract are prohibited from combining their military duties with parental leave. The ruling of the Court is of particular interest: "non-performance of military duties by military personnel *en masse* must be excluded as it might be a detriment to the public interests". The Court found the vague "public interest" to be more important than the individual right not to be discriminated against, and concluded that the non-granting of the right to parental leave cannot be regarded as a breach of constitutional rights or freedoms, including a person's right to take care of children. Furthermore, the Court underlined that this limitation is justified by the voluntary nature of the military service contract.

Contradictions of this approach seem evident when taking into account provisions of the Russian Constitution regarding the welfare state, the right to dignity, special support for families and so on. The infringement of important rights such as childcare, the respect for one's private life and non-discrimination may be considered a rather high price to pay for an abstract concept such as "public interest". Ronald Dvorkin wrote, "if the Government does not take these rights seriously, then it does not take the law seriously either".[10] This citation, together with the Konstantin Markin

---

[8] The applicant got divorced after the birth of his third child who was born on 30 September 2005. On 6 October 2005 the applicant and his ex-wife entered into an agreement under which their three children would live with the applicant and their mother would pay maintenance. After this decision the mother of the children left the town. On 11 October 2005 the applicant asked the head of his military unit for three years' parental leave. On 12 October 2005 the head of the military unit rejected his request because three years' parental leave could only be granted to female military personnel.

[9] Ruling of the Constitutional Court N 187-O-O, 25.01.2009.

[10] Dworkin, R. 1978. *Taking Rights Seriously*. Harvard University Press: 205.

case, helps us understand the real situation of anti-discrimination protection in Russia.

The judgment of the European Court of Human Rights in the case of Konstantin Markin is encouraging as the approach of the Russian Constitutional Court was strongly criticised. Konstantin Markin brought the case to court against the Russian Federation on 21 May 2006. In the Chamber Judgment issued on 7 October 2010 the ECtHR declared that the position of the Constitutional Court showed "gender prejudice" which "cannot, by itself, be considered by the Court a sufficient justification for a difference in treatment, any more than similar prejudice based on race, origin, colour or sexual orientation".[11] The ECtHR stated that the exclusion of servicemen from the entitlement to parental leave, while servicewomen are entitled to it, is discriminatory on the grounds of gender and therefore violates Art. 14 of the European Convention when taken in conjunction with Art. 8.

The ECtHR shifted the focus from social rights—such as the right to parental leave—to a broader question of civil rights and equal treatment in Russia.[12] The ECtHR extended the anti-discrimination protection granted by Art. 14 to employment and social security, though Russia has not yet ratified Protocol 12 of the European Convention, which provides a common framework for the prohibition of discrimination.

The Chamber judgment stated that the Russian government did not offer convincing and substantial reasons to justify the difference in treatment between male and female military personnel and found this to be a widespread problem in Russian legislation, affecting a considerable number of people.

Russia took the judgment very hard and appealed the original decision to the Grand Chamber, which upheld the original decision on 22 March 2012.

Valerii Zorkin, Russian Chairman of the Russian Constitutional Court published an article, "The Limit of Pliability", where he called into question the legitimacy of ECtHR's conclusions on the incompatibility of Russian legislation with the Convention.[13] Mr Zorkin said that the position of the European Court might well be seen as a challenge to Russia's national sovereignty and warned that Russia might elaborate a "defence

---

[11] Par. 58 of the Chamber Judgment Markin v. Russia, App. No. 30078/06, 48, ECtHR 2010

[12] Pomeranz, W. E. 2012. "*Uneasy Partners: Russia and the European Court of Human Rights,*" *Human Rights Brief* 19, No. 3:18.

[13] Zorkin, V. 2010. "Predel ustupchivosti," *Rossiyskaya Gazeta*, 29 October 2010. Available at: http://www.rg.ru/2010/10/29/zorkin.html, accessed 07 October 2013.

mechanism" against such decisions of ECtHR should they be "questionable from the point of view of the essence of the European Convention on Human Rights, directly affect national sovereignty, and Russian fundamental constitutional principles".[14]

We are of the view that the official Russian reaction to the ECtHR's judgment reveals the systematic error in Russian law in general and anti-discrimination laws in particular. Personal rights are still made to give way to abstract public interest.

Discriminatory provisions still existing in Russian Labour Laws discredit the system of anti-discrimination protection of employees and call into question the significance of the common principle of non-discrimination defined in the Constitution of the Russian Federation and in the Labour Code.

2. The Inefficiency of Anti-Discrimination Protection

The adoption of common principles prohibiting discrimination in employment relations in Russia has not been accompanied by systematic changes in the corresponding civil procedure legislation resulting in a very limited number of special provisions aimed at combatting direct and indirect discrimination. For instance, the publication of job advertisements containing discriminatory requirements was prohibited after more than 20 years of discussions, at a time when about 50% of all advertisements contained some discriminatory requirements.[15]

The academic debate on the need to introduce the notion of "victimisation", "protection from harassment", as well as proposals to impose the burden of proof on the employer did not reach the Russian legislator.[16]

---

[14] Zorkin, V., see supra note 13.

[15] Russian Federal Law of 02.07.2013 No. 162 "On Amendments to the Law of the Russian Federation on Employment in the Russian Federation" Official site of legal information http://www.pravo.gov.ru accessed 03 July 2013.

[16] See for example: Isaeva, E. A. 2008. "Predotvrashcheniye diskriminatsii v trudovykh otnosheniyakh: teoreticheskiye aspekty i yuridicheskaya praktika :po opytu USA [Prevention of Discrimination in the Employment Relationship: Theoretical Aspects and Legal Practice: The Experience of the United States]," summary of PhD Thesis. Yaroslavl or Mironova, A.V. 2008. "*Mezhdunarodno-pravovoye regulirovaniye truda zhenshchin*" [International legal regulation of women's work] Moscow; Kaurov, V. G. 2001. "Zashchishchennost' rabotnikov po mezhdunarodnomu trudovomu pravu, trudovomu pravu SSHA i Rossii: Sravnitel'noye issledovaniye [Protection of Workers in International Labor Law,

The non-availability of official court statistics makes it difficult to demonstrate the need for change. The reports of the domestic courts in Russia do not include information on cases of discrimination, whereas in the United States 99,412 applications for discrimination protection were registered in 2012[17] and in the UK employment tribunals considered 28,550 claims of discrimination between April 2011 and March 2012.[18]

This lack of judicial practice can be seen as evidence of the ineffectiveness of anti-discrimination protection and of the absence of real remedies in Russia where the problem of discrimination against women (according to official statistics the salary of women is, on average, only 64.1% of the male wage)[19] and migrant workers is evident.

Confirmation of this argument can be found in various research papers on employment discrimination published during the last 20 years,[20] as well as in the reports made by a number of public organizations.[21]

Employment Law of the United States and Russia: A Comparative Study]," Summary of PhD Thesis. Vladivostok; Comandirov, A. A. 2011. "Konstitutsionnyy printsip zapreta diskriminatsii v sfere truda v Rossiyskoy Federatsii [Constitutional Principle of Non-discrimination in Employment in the Russian Federation]," Summary of PhD Thesis. Saratov.

17 Data of private sector workplace discrimination during fiscal year 2012: U.S. Equal Employment Opportunity Commission Press release PRESS RELEASE 1-28-13 . Available at: http://www.eeoc.gov/eeoc/newsroom/release/1-28-13.cfm.

18 Employment Tribunals and EAT Statistics, data from April 2011 until March 2012, available at:
https://www.gov.uk/government/uploads/system/uploads/attachment_data/file/218497/employment-trib-stats-april-march-2011-12.pdf

19 Russian Federal Sate Statistics service report. Available at:
http://www.gks.ru/bgd/regl/B12_04/IssWWW.exe/Stg/d06/3-plat.htm (accessed 24 August 2013).

20 See for example: Lyghin, R. N. 2003. "Voprosy obespecheniya prav i svobod cheloveka i grazhdanina pri zaklyuchenii trudovogo dogovora [The Issues of Human Rights and Freedoms at the Conclusion of the Employment Contract]," PhD Thesis, Moscow; Mitina, N. M. 2006. "Zapreshcheniye diskriminatsii v sfere truda kak odin iz osnovnykh printsipov trudovogo prava [Prohibition of Discrimination in Employment as one of the Basic Principles of Labour Law]," PhD Thesis, Moskva, 2006; Kozlova, M. S. 2006. Diskriminatsiya zhenshchin na rossiyskom rynke truda :regional'nyy aspekt [Discrimination against Women in the Russian Labour Market: Regional Aspect]," PhD Thesis, Saratov.

21 See for example Public hearings organised by the Civic Chamber of the Russian Federation on the topic *State Policy of Equal Rights, Freedom and Equal Opportunities for Women and Men in the Russian Federation: Legislation and Practice*". Available at: http://women.trudprava.ru/50-gosudarstvennaya-politika-

The most vivid illustration of the inefficiency of anti-discrimination protection in Russia is provided by the case of Danilenkov and Others vs Russia[22] heard by the European Court of Human Rights on 30 July 2009.

The applicants were employees of the Kaliningrad Commercial Seaport Co. Ltd. and members of the Kaliningrad branch of the Dockers' Union of Russia (DUR). On 14 October 1997, the DUR began a two-week strike for an increase in wages, better working conditions, and health and life insurance. The strike failed to achieve its goals and was discontinued on 28 October 1997. Since then the management of Kaliningrad seaport had been harassing DUR members attempting to penalise them for the strike and to get them to renounce their union membership.

DUR members subsequently found themselves reassigned to special work teams, transferred to part-time positions, and ultimately made redundant and dismissed, apparently because of a structural reorganisation of the seaport company.

The applicants responded to these and other actions by bringing a number of cases to local courts where they complained of being the object of unlawful and discriminatory treatment because of their union membership. Discrimination charges were repeatedly dismissed on the grounds that applicants could not prove discriminatory intent on the part of the port administration. A number of civil courts stated that discrimination could only be established in the framework of criminal proceedings.

In addition to going to court, the DUR complained to the International Transport Workers' Federation (ITF) and the Kaliningrad Regional Duma (the regional assembly). Both the ITF and the Duma recognized the existence of discrimination based on trade union membership and called for the DUR members' rights to be respected. Despite these measures DUR membership decreased from 290 in 1999 to only 24 in 2001.

The European Court's judgment emphasized the importance of the possibility to challenge discriminatory treatment and exercise the right to take legal action in order to claim damages and other forms of compensation. Under articles 11 and 14 of the European Convention of Human Rights, states are required to set up a judicial system, which ensures real and effective protection against anti-trade union discrimination.

The Court considered that the Russian Federation had failed to fulfil its positive obligations to adopt effective and clear judicial protection against discrimination on the grounds of trade union membership. We

---

ravnih-prav-svobod-i-ravnih-vozmozhnostey-dlya-zhenshin-i-muzhchin-v-rf-zakonodatelystvo-i-realii.html (accessed 20 September 2013)

[22] ECtHR, Danilenkov and others v. Russia (*no. 67336/01)* 30 July 09.

believe that effective protection against other types of discrimination does not exist either.

The aforementioned case demonstrates all the difficulties related to anti-discrimination protection in Russia even in cases, such as the one described above, where discriminatory actions were evident. The reported events took place before the adoption of the new Labour Code by the Russian Federation, but we can presume that the situation has not changed significantly since then. The Russian Labour Code includes provisions concerning the possibility to apply to a civil court to claim for compensation for material damages and/or moral damages in cases of discrimination. Accordingly, civil courts can no longer insist upon resorting to criminal proceedings for discrimination cases, as occurred in the case of Danilenkov, whose case is nevertheless significant as it shows that no effective and clear judicial protection against discrimination as required by the European Court has, as yet, actually been put in place.

Russian scholars note that "research using open-access data revealed that only 19 cases of discrimination were brought before Russian courts in the period between 2008 and 2012".[23] Only in one case did the court acknowledge discrimination and award compensation to the employee. In most cases, the courts used a standard phrase: "The court considers that the arguments of the plaintiff are unreasonable and do not prove discrimination".[24]

In this context, mention should be made of a particularly significant case. On 20 June 2013, the Tverskoy District Court in Moscow found employment discrimination in the case of Yury Idigeshev vs. "Di Alkor" Ltd.[25]

Yury Idigheshev was registered as unemployed with the public employment services. In January 2013, the plaintiff was referred for employment to "Di Alcor" Ltd for the position of barman in their café.

[23] Mikhaylichenko, N. A. 2013. "Voprosy kvalifikatsii ponyatiya «diskriminatsiya v sfere truda» v sudebnoy praktike [Questions of qualification of the concept of "discrimination in employment" in judicial practice]," Paper presented at the Lomonosov conference, Moscow State University, 2013. Available at: http://lomonosov-msu.ru/archive/Lomonosov_2013/2391/57654_5573.pdf (accessed 20 Sempteber 2013).

[24] *Ibid*

[25] Information on the case No. 2-2633/2013 was found in the article "The person who does not look Slavic" of the Center of Social-labour rights, available at: http://cstp.trudprava.ru/novosti/175-litso-neslavyanskoy-vneshnosti.html (accessed 20 October 2013).

However, the café manager refused to hire him after the interview. In the document that the plaintiff delivered back to the public employment services, the reason for refusal was the following: "Yury Idigheshev has Russian citizenship, but is not Slavic by appearance". The Court found proof of discrimination and awarded the applicant 30,000 roubles (about 750 euros) compensation for moral damage.

This case indicates the kind of evidence that is needed to prove discrimination in Russia. This was also a very special case, as written proof is not generally available in the majority of discrimination claims.

Compensation in this case was awarded to the victim of discrimination only because of the employer's ignorance. We can only imagine how many potential discrimination claims are hushed up because of the lack of "evident" proof of discrimination.

The limited number of discrimination cases reflect the shortcomings of Russian Civil Procedure Law. According to the Code of Civil Procedure, plaintiffs in civil cases (including discrimination cases) must provide evidence justifying their claim (Art. 56). Some exceptions to the standard rules on the burden of proof have been made by the Supreme Court of the Russian Federation. In Art. 23 of Resolution no. 2 of 17 March 2004, "On the Application of the Labour Code of the Russian Federation", the Supreme Court states that the burden of proof must shift to the employer in the case of unfair dismissals. In such cases, the employer has to prove the existence of a legitimate reason for dismissal and compliance with the established procedure of dismissal. The plaintiff claiming unlawful dismissal on discriminatory grounds can therefore reasonably expect the employer to provide evidence of the non-discriminatory reasons that led to the dismissal.

In other cases of discrimination (concerning the employment contract, equal pay, working hours, promotions, and so on) the Russian approach to the distribution of the burden of proof follows the standard. We maintain that it complicates anti-discrimination protection and obstructs its efficiency.

A comparative analysis of European anti-discrimination laws[26] shows that it would possible to create more efficient mechanisms of anti-discrimination protection in Russia.

---

[26] Council Directive 76/207/EEC on the implementation of the principle of equal treatment for men and women as regards access to employment, vocational training and promotion, and working conditions (09/02/1976), Council Directive 79/7/EEC on the progressive implementation of the principle of equal treatment for men and women in matters of social security (19/12/1978), Council declaration on the implementation of the Commission Recommendation on the protection of the

We suppose that, in the short-term, the Russian system of anti-discrimination protection must be improved by shifting the burden of proof to the employer (modern European law[27] has similar provisions that could be partly adopted), through the creation of a special body providing conciliation and information services to employees, allowing statistics to be used as proof in cases of discrimination.[28] In the long-term, significant progress could be made by ratifying the 12th Protocol of the European Convention of Human Rights (stating the general prohibition of discrimination) and by creating special labour courts.

3. The European Court of Human Rights: Cases of Discrimination and their Applicability in Russia

We have so far illustrated contradictions regarding anti-discrimination protection in Russia looking at cases brought to the European Court of Human Rights. In these cases, the ECtHR granted effective protection to the applicants who had suffered discrimination. We consider the issue of the applicability of ECtHR decisions in Russian judicial practice and the legal knowledge of the European Court's position on discrimination particularly important both for scholars and practitioners.

According to the Russian Federal Law "On the Ratification of the Convention for the Protection of Human Rights and Fundamental Freedoms and its Protocols",[29] the decisions of the ECtHR are binding for Russia in cases of alleged violation on the part of the Russian Federation.

---

dignity of women and men at work, including the code of practice to combat sexual harassment (19/12/1991), Council Directive 2000/78/EC establishing a general framework for equal treatment in employment and occupation (27.11.2000), Council Directive 2000/43/EC implementing the principle of equal treatment between persons irrespective of racial or ethnic origin (29/06/2000), Directive 2006/54/EC of the European parliament and of the Council on the implementation of the principle of equal opportunities and equal treatment of men and women in matters of employment and occupation (recast) (05/07/2006).

[27] See Council Directive 2000/78/EC, 27/11/2000.

[28] Russian courts have never relied on statistical data when considering discrimination cases though the use of statistics can be deemed acceptable according to a broad interpretation of norms of Civil Procedure Code (Art. 55). We are of the view that the problem can be resolved by issuing a corresponding Resolution of the Supreme Court of the Russian Federation.

[29] The Federal Law 30.03.1998 N 54-FZ// Collection of Legislation of the Russian Federation 06.04.98 N 14, art. 1514

Other decisions made by the ECtHR and its relevant legal positions are acknowledged to be a very important part of the Russian system by the Constitutional Court of the Russian Federation and the Russian Supreme Court.[30] The recent Resolution of the Plenum of the Supreme Court of the Russian Federation[31] was issued specifically to interpret the applicability of the European Convention and of the decisions of the ECtHR in Russia.

The Plenum specifies that binding legal positions of the European Court of Human Rights, which are expressed in the final judgment of the Court in cases vs. Russia, and legal positions expressed in decisions vs. other countries must be taken into account by Russian courts in similar cases. It is recommended that domestic courts take into account the interpretation of the European Convention by the ECtHR.

The Russian Constitutional Court is almost the only one to refer to ECtHR case law in its practice. According to the Constitutional Court's report, Russia referred to ECtHR case-law in 80 Decisions (*Postanovlenya*) and 91 Rulings (*Opredelenia*) of the Constitutional Court. The Constitutional Court always emphasised the importance of ECtHR's views for the development of the Russian legal system.

The aforementioned case of K. Markin v. Russia has changed the absolute willingness of the Constitutional Court to implement legal positions of ECtHR. Since the Chamber decision in the Markin case, the Constitutional Court has become more accurate in its estimation of the role of ECtHR for the Russian legal system, and the emphasis of its importance is now accompanied by the words "if not in contradiction with the Constitution of the Russian Federation". This approach is also applied in the report prepared by the Constitutional Court for the European Congress of Constitutional Courts.[32]

---

[30] Resolution of the Plenum of the Supreme Court of the Russian Federation N. 5, 10.10.03 "On the application of the universally recognized principles and norms of international law and the international treaties of the Russian Federation by the courts of general jurisdiction," Decision of the Constitutional Court of the Russian Federation 05.02.2007 N 2-P or Decision of the Constitutional Court on 25.01.2001 N 1-P.

[31] Resolution of the Plenum of the Supreme Court of the Russian Federation dated 27.06. 13 N 21 "On the application by the courts of general jurisdiction of the European Convention for the Protection of Human Rights and its Protocols," in Rossiyskaya gazeta 05.07.2013 г., No. 6121.

[32] Report of the Constitutional Court of the Russian Federation for the XVIth Congress of the Conference of European Constitutional Courts. Available at: http://www.vfgh.gv.at/cms/vfgh-kongress/downloads/landesberichte/LB-Russie-EN.pdf (accessed 24 October 2013)

Generally, however, the European Convention and the cases brought before the ECtHR are only seldom referred to in other Russian courts. Studies on the impact of the ECtHR's practice in Russian courts reveal the very low level of awareness of ECtHR's legal positions.[33] Russian courts are generally not willing to use the Court's practice in decision-making processes, though it does provide elaborate "ready-to-use" patterns for the consideration of many cases. The Constitutional Court noted that the low level of application of ECtHR practice in Russian courts might be due to the rejection of the precedential nature of judicial acts rooted in the national legal tradition and is also complicated by the absence of any official translation of ECtHR decisions in the Russian language.[34]

Research carried out by Russian human rights organisations identified possible ways of increasing Russian courts' awareness of the European Court's practice. Lawyers of the NGO Sutyajnik steadily and continuously referred to decisions of the European Court in applications to domestic courts and throughout proceedings. Although domestic courts often ignored these references, further decisions on similar matters contained information on ECtHR case law which was taken into account by the Courts.[35]

The experience of the NGO Sutyajnik shows that the lawyer's role is very important in contributing to introducing ECtHR values into the Russian legal system. In situations where there is the need for judicial consideration of ECtHR decisions, Russian lawyers, as well as judges and prosecutors, must be aware of the Court's approach towards discrimination. Although the binding nature of ECtHR case law in the Russian Federation has only been established unofficially,[36] we believe it can be successfully applied, especially in discrimination cases. We have to bear in mind that the application of the ECtHR approach in domestic courts might help reduce the number of cases brought to the European Court.

Turning to ECtHR practice on discrimination, it should be noted that employment discrimination cases are rare, as the European Convention of Human Rights does not specifically cover employment relations. This is

---

[33] See for example Burkov, Anton 2007 "*The Impact of the European Convention on Human Rights on Russian Law: Legislation and Application in 1996-2006*" Stuttgart.

[34] Report of the Constitutional Court, see supra note 26:15, 16.

[35] *Ibid*: 56-58.

[36] It was said by V. Zorkin, Chairman of the Russian Constitutional court, in internet interview, available at: http://www.consultant.ru/law/interview/zorkin/ (accessed 10.10.13)

why, in these few cases, the Court often refers to other rights, such as the right to respect individuals' private life pursuant to Art. 8 (see also the aforementioned case of K. Markin v. Russia), or individuals' right to manifest a religion pursuant to Art. 9 (see Eweida and Others v. the United Kingdom).[37]

In most of the cases where applicants claim they are victims of discrimination, the Court affirms that Art. 14 only complements the other provisions of the Convention and its Protocols which contain the substantive rules.[38]

The Court's approach to discrimination can be analysed by looking at a number of employment and social security discrimination claims.

According to the Court, **discrimination** takes place when individuals are treated differently, without an objective and reasonable justification, as compared to persons in similar situations. "No objective and reasonable justification" means that the difference in treatment does not have a "legitimate aim" and there is no "reasonable relationship of proportionality between the aim and the measures applied".

States, however, enjoy a certain margin of discretion in assessing whether and to what extent situations that appear to be similar might justify a different treatment.

There are three main criteria which can be used to determine discrimination, following the ECtHR:

1. a difference in treatment (also including the absence of a difference in treatment where, in fact, there should have been);
2. special cases where difference in treatment is required to protect specific characteristics;
3. the absence of an "objective and reasonable justification" for discriminatory provisions or acts.

A difference in treatment can be identified through a comparison with someone in a similar situation. In the case D. H. and Others vs. The Czech Republic,[39] for example, the Court investigated whether the education of Roma children assigned to special schools was different from the education given to other children in the city of Ostrava. It was found that the applicants had received a substantially inferior education compared to non-Roma children and had therefore been victims of discrimination on the grounds of ethnic origin.

---

[37] ECtHR, Eweida and Others v. the United Kingdom (No. 48420/10), 15.01.2013

[38] See for example: ECtHR, Bigaeva v. Greece (No. 26713/05), 28/05/2009

[39] ECtHR, D. H. and Others v. the Czech Republic [GC] (No. 57325/00), 13 November 2007.

There have been some cases where Courts have rejected discrimination claims as applicants were not in a situation akin to that of another group treated more favourably. In Carson and Others v. the UK,[40] the applicants (immigrants to South Africa, Australia, Canada) argued that they had been treated differently with regard to pension increases for pensioners living in the UK, as compared to those who had emigrated. The Court did not consider that an act of discrimination had taken place, stating that the conditions of pensioners in the UK and those abroad were incomparable in view of the rise of the standard cost of living in the UK.

We emphasise the importance of following the ECHR approach at the time of dealing with cases of discrimination in Russia. The three aforementioned criteria should be adopted and used as a basis for discrimination claims.

Indirect discrimination in the cases deliberated on by the ECtHR must taken into account by Russian lawyers as these cases are generally not considered in Russian jurisprudence. Indirect discrimination, according to the information available open-access, is never mentioned in judicial practice.[41] This is due to the shortcomings of the Russian Labour Code, which does not mention indirect discrimination (only in Art. 64, on access to employment, are indirect "disadvantages" prohibited on various grounds). The ILO interprets the Discrimination (Employment and Occupation) Convention N. 111, ratified by Russia, as covering both direct and indirect discrimination and recommends that States address both types of discrimination in the preparation of legal texts at the national level.[42]

One might, in theory, claim protection against indirect discrimination before a Russian court by referring directly to the Convention and the practice of ECtHR.

Indirect discrimination is understood by the Court as a "difference in treatment that takes the form of disproportionately prejudicial effects of a general policy or measure which, though couched in neutral terms, discriminates against a group".[43]

[40] ECtHR, Carson and Others v. UK [GC] (No. 42184/05), 16 March 2010.

[41] Text search for "indirect discrimination" was carried out on the sites of the Constitutional court and the Supreme Court of the Russian Federation. See http://www.vsrf.ru/, www.ksrf.ru (accessed 23 October 2013).

[42] ILO. *Guidelines for Labour Law Development.* Geneva: ILO. Available in Russian at: http://www.ilo.org/legacy/russian/dialogue/ifpdial/llg/ (accessed 28 October 2013).

[43] ECtHR, Opuz v. Turkey (No. 33401/02), 9 June 2009, par. 183; ECtHR, Zarb Adami v. Malta (No. 17209/02), 20 June 2006, para. 80.

An analysis of ECtHR's case law[44] reveals a pattern of judicial work in such cases: the main focus is on the effects of a neutral treatment, which have to be much more negative for a protected group. The Court uses statistical data when considering the significance of negative effects on the protected group and compares it with the effects on other groups.

In Thlimmenos vs. Greece[45] the ECtHR found indirect discrimination on religious grounds and stated that "discrimination can be found when States [...] fail to treat differently persons whose situations are significantly different".

The circumstances of the case and the way in which the Court made its decisions are very interesting. The applicant was convicted for insubordination—he had refused to wear a military uniform during a general mobilization because of his religious beliefs as a Jehovah's Witness, manifesting his pacifism. He was later turned down for the post of chartered accountant because of his previous conviction.

The Court took into account the sentence served by the applicant for his refusal to wear the military uniform and considered the applicant's exclusion from the profession of chartered accountants as an additional sanction, therefore disproportionate and discriminative. The ECtHR found that relevant Greek legislation violated the applicant's right not to be discriminated against under Art. 9 of the European Convention as it did not treat the applicant differently than others convicted for more serious crimes.

In this context, mention should be made of a similar case heard by the Russian Constitutional Court where applicants claimed that the provisions of the Russian Labour Code prohibiting the appointment of people with past convictions to posts related to teaching activities were unconstitutional.[46] The Constitutional Court examined the case in the light of the infringement of the right to work and stated that not every crime listed in articles 331 and 351.1 of the Labour Code can lead to the unconditional and permanent prohibition of employment in teaching activities. The Court affirmed the need to consider different factors such as the severity of the crime or personal characteristics with regard to the employment of people who have been convicted for crimes other than

---

44 See European Court of Human Rights. 2011. *Handbook on European Non-discrimination Law* 2011. European Union Agency for Fundamental Rights, European Court of Human Rights, Council of Europe: 29-31.

45 ECtHR, Thlimmenos v. Greece [GC] (No. 34369/97), 6 April 2000, para. 44. Similarly, ECtHR, Pretty v. UK (No. 2346/02), 29 April 2002, par. 88.

46 Decision of the Constitutional Court of the Russian Federation N 19-P issued 18.07.2013.

those considered serious and very serious, or crimes against sexual inviolability and sexual freedom. The unconditional and permanent prohibition of working as teacher for those who have committed serious and very serious crimes, crimes against sexual inviolability and sexual freedom was held to be constitutional and must be enforced without any exception.

We suppose that if the applicants had related their claim to the anti-discriminatory provisions of the Constitution and to ECtHR's decision in Thlimmenos v. Greece, the decision of the Constitutional Court of Russia might have been different. The Court, on the basis of the ECtHR's decision, may have been able to give a broader interpretation of Constitutional norms, including the necessity "to treat differently" even the people who have been convicted of serious crimes.[47]

Drawing on the above the importance of taking into account ECtHR practice in Russian courts clearly emerges. The binding character of decisions issued by ECtHR is acknowledged in Russia, although all the other decisions might be considered as mere legal "positions" of the Court, and despite not being binding, they should be taken into account anyway.

The Russian legal system itself should be interested in learning from the approaches and conclusions of the ECtHR to avoid resorting to the European Court but also with a view to developing anti-discrimination protection in the field of employment, making it more efficient and compliant with European standards.

3. Conclusions

In concluding this paper on the contradictions of anti-discrimination protection in Russia, it should be noted, with optimism, that the above-mentioned problems can be resolved. Orienting anti-discrimination protection towards European standards and taking into account the positions of the European Court of Human Rights would be very helpful for Russian labour law.

The revision of discriminatory provisions of Russian Labour law by the legislator and the Constitutional Court would be more successful if it were based on the priority of individual human rights over public ones.

---

[47] In the present decision the Constitutional Court found fair and legal the prohibition of employment connected with teaching activities for persons convicted, for example, for refusal to provide information to the Federal Assembly of the Russian Federation (art. 287 of the Criminal Code of Russia) or for violation of the rules of safety in the operation of military aircraft, resulting in serious consequences (art. 351 of the Criminal Code of Russia).

References to the decisions of ECtHR in everyday legal practice and the implementation of the Court's understanding of discrimination are particularly important for the development of anti-discrimination protection of employees. However, an assessment of Russian anti-discrimination law by the ECtHR would be extremely useful.

Effective judicial anti-discrimination protection can be achieved by amending Russian Civil Procedural Law. EU legislation and the ECtHR practice might again serve as a pattern of efficiency, and as an opportunity to shift the burden of proof and to legitimize the use of statistical data as evidence in discrimination claims.

References

Legislation

European Union. 1976. *Council Directive 76/207/EEC on the Implementation of the Principle of Equal Treatment for Men and Women as regards Access to Employment, Vocational Training and Promotion, and Working Conditions.* Brussels: European Union.

—. 1978. *Council Directive 79/7/EEC on the Progressive Implementation of the Principle of Equal Treatment for Men and Women in Matters of Social Security.* Brussels: European Union.

—. 1991. *Council Declaration on the Implementation of the Commission Recommendation on the Protection of the Dignity of Women and Men at Work, Including the Code of Practice to Combat Sexual Harassment.* Brussels: European Union.

—. 2000. *Council Directive 2000/78/EC Establishing a General Framework for Equal Treatment in Employment and Occupation.* Brussels: European Union.

—. 2006. *Directive 2006/54/EC of the European Parliament and of the Council on the Implementation of the Principle of Equal Opportunities and Equal Treatment of Men and Women in Matters of Employment and Occupation (recast).* Brussels: European Union.

—. *Council Directive 2000/43/EC Implementing the Principle of Equal Treatment between Persons Irrespective of Racial or Ethnic Origin (29 June 2000).* Brussels: European Union.

ILO. 1958. *ILO Convention C111—Discrimination (Employment and Occupation) Convention (No. 111).* Geneva: ILO.

—. 1981. *ILO Convention C156—Workers with Family Responsibilities Convention (No. 156).* Geneva: ILO.

Russian Federal Law N 54-FZ, 30.03.1998.

Russian Federal Law No. 162, 02.07.2013 "On Amendments to the Law of the Russian Federation", "On Employment in the Russian Federation".

The Code of Labour Laws of the RSFSR adopted by the RSFSR Supreme Soviet 09.12.1971.

The Labour Code of the Russian Federation N 197-FZ adopted on 30.12.2001.

United Nations. 1979. *Convention on the Elimination of All Forms of Discrimination against Women (CEDAW).*

Russian Jurisprudence

Resolution of the Plenum of the Supreme Court of the Russian Federation N 5, 10.10.2003 "On application of the universally recognized principles and norms of international law and the international treaties of the Russian Federation by the courts of general jurisdiction".

Resolution of the Plenum of the Supreme Court of the Russian Federation dated 27 June 2013 N 21 "On application by the courts of general jurisdiction of the European Convention for the Protection of Human Rights and its Protocols".

Decision of the Constitutional Court of the Russian Federation N 19-P, 27.12.1999.

Decision of the Constitutional Court on 25 January 2001 N 1-P.

Ruling of the Constitutional Court of the Russian Federation N 213-O, 11.07.2006.

Decision of the Constitutional Court of the Russian Federation on 5 February 2007 N 2-P.

Ruling of the Constitutional Court of the Russian Federation No. 378-OP 15.05.2007.

Ruling of the Constitutional Court No. 187-O-O, 15.01.2009.

Decision of the Constitutional Court of the Russian Federation No. 28-P, 15.12.2011.

Ruling of the Constitutional Court of the Russian Federation No. 617-O-O issued on 22.03.2012.

Decision of the Constitutional Court of the Russian Federation No. 31-P, 06.12.2012.

Decision of the Constitutional Court of the Russian Federation No. 19-P issued on 18.07.2013.

Practice of the European Court of Human Rights

ECtHR, Chamber Judgment Markin v. Russia, App. No. 30078/06, 2010.

ECtHR, Danilenkov and others v. Russia (*no. 67336/01)* 30 July 2009.

ECtHR, Eweida and Others v. the United Kingdom (No. 48420/10), 15 January 2013.

ECtHR, Bigaeva v. Greece (No. 26713/05), 28 May 2009.

ECtHR, Andrejeva v. Latvia [GC] (No. 55707/00), 18 February 2009.

ECtHR, D.H. and Others v. the Czech Republic [GC] (No. 57325/00), 13 November 2007.

ECtHR, D.H. and Others v. the Czech Republic [GC] (No. 57325/00), 13 November 2007.

ECtHR, Carson and Others v. UK [GC] (No. 42184/05), 16 March 2010.

ECtHR, Opuz v. Turkey (No. 33401/02), 9 June 2009.

ECtHR, Zarb Adami v. Malta (No. 17209/02), 20 June 2006.

ECtHR, Thlimmenos v. Greece [GC] (No. 34369/97), 6 April 2000.

ECtHR, Pretty v. UK (No. 2346/02), 29 April 2002.

Books

Burkov, A. 2006. *The Impact of the European Convention on Human Rights on Russian Law: Legislation and Application in in 1996-2000.* Stuttgart.

Dworkin, R. 1978. *Taking Rights Seriously*. Harvard University Press.

European Court of Human Rights. 2011. *Handbook on European Non-discrimination Law* 2011, European Union Agency for Fundamental Rights, European Court of Human Rights—Council of Europe.

Isaeva, E. A. 2008 "Predotvrashcheniye diskriminatsii v trudovykh otnosheniyakh: teoreticheskiye aspekty i yuridicheskaya praktika :po opytu USA [Prevention of Discrimination in the Employment Relationship: Theoretical Aspects and Legal Practice: The Experience of the United States]," summary of PhD Thesis, Yaroslavl.

Kaurov, V. G. 2001. "Zashchishchennost' rabotnikov po mezhdunarodnomu trudovomu pravu, trudovomu pravu SSHA i Rossii: Sravnitel'noye issledovaniye [Protection of Workers in International Labor Law, Employment Law of the United States and Russia: A Comparative Study]," Summary of PhD Thesis. Vladivostok

Komandirov, A. A. 2011 "Konstitutsionnyy printsip zapreta diskriminatsii v sfere truda v Rossiyskoy Federatsii [Constitutional Principle of Non-discrimination in Employment in the Russian Federation]," Summary of PhD Thesis. Saratov.

Mironova, A. V. 2008 "Mezhdunarodno-pravovoye regulirovaniye truda zhenshchin [International Legal Regulation of Women's Work]," Moscow.

Lyghin, R. N. 2003 "Voprosy obespecheniya prav i svobod cheloveka i grazhdanina pri zaklyuchenii trudovogo dogovora [The Issues of Human Rights and Freedoms at the Conclusion of the Employment Contract]," PhD Thesis, Moscow

Mitina, N. M. 2006. "Zapreshcheniye diskriminatsii v sfere truda kak odin iz osnovnykh printsipov trudovogo prava [Prohibition of Discrimination in Employment as One of the Basic Principles of Labor Law]," PhD Thesis, Moskva, 2006;

Kozlova, M. S. 2006 "Diskriminatsiya zhenshchin na rossiyskom rynke truda :regional'nyy aspekt [Discrimination against Women in the Russian Labor Market: Regional Aspect]," PhD Thesis, Saratov.

Articles and Papers

Mikhaylichenko, N. A. 2013. "Voprosy kvalifikatsii ponyatiya 'diskriminatsiya v sfere truda' v sudebnoy praktike, [Questions of qualification concept of 'discrimination in employment' in the judicial practice]," Paper presented at the the Lomonosov conference, Moscow State University. Available at: http://lomonosov-msu.ru/archive/Lomonosov_2013/2391/57654_5573.pdf (accessed on 20 September 2013).

Pomeranz, William E. 2012 "Uneasy Partners: Russia and the European Court of Human Rights," *Human Rights Brief* 19, No. 3:18.

Zorkin, V. 2010 "Predel ustupchivosti," *Rossiyskaya Gazeta*, 29.10.2010. Available at: http://www.rg.ru/2010/10/29/zorkin.html, accessed on 07.10.2013.

Online Resources

Center of Social-labour Rights. *The Person Who does not Look Slavic*, available at: http://cstp.trudprava.ru/novosti/175-litso-neslavyanskoy-vneshnosti.html (accessed 20 October 2013).

Data of private sector workplace discrimination during fiscal year 2012: U.S. Equal Employment Opportunity Commission, P*ress release 1-28-13*. Available at: http://www.eeoc.gov/eeoc/newsroom/release/1-28-13.cfm (accessed on 23 September 2013).

Employment Tribunals and EAT Statistics, data from April 2011 until March 2012, available at https://www.gov.uk/government/uploads/system/uploads/attachment_data/file/218497/employment-trib-stats-april-march-2011-12.pdf (accessed 23 September 2013)

ILO. *Guidelines for Labor Law Development*. Available in Russian at: http://www.ilo.org/legacy/russian/dialogue/ifpdial/llg/ (accessed 28 October 2013)

Internet interview with V. Zorkin, Chairman of the Russian Constitutional court, available at: http://www.consultant.ru/law/interview/zorkin/ (accessed 10 October 2013).

Public hearings organised by Civic Chamber of the Russian Federation on the topic: "State Policy of Equal Rights, Freedom and Equal Opportunities for Women and Men in the Russian Federation: Legislation and Practice". Available at: http://women.trudprava.ru/50-gosudarstvennaya-politika-ravnih-prav-svobod-i-ravnih-vozmozhnostey-dlya-zhenshin-i-muzhchin-v-rf-zakonodatelystvo-i-realii.html (accessed 20 Sempteber 2013).

Russian Federal Sate Statistics service report. Available at: http://www.gks.ru/bgd/regl/B12_04/IssWWW.exe/Stg/d06/3-plat.htm (accessed 24 August 2013).

Report of the Constitutional Court of the Russian Federation for the XVIth Congress of the Conference of European Constitutional Courts. Available at: http://www.vfgh.gv.at/cms/vfgh-kongress/downloads/landesberichte/LB-Russie-EN.pdf (accessed 24 October 2013).

CONTRIBUTORS

Elena Boltanova, Associate Professor at the National Research Tomsk State University (Russia).

Daria Chernyaeva, Associate Professor at the National Research University Higher School of Economics.

Olga Chesalina, Researcher at the Max-Planck Institute for Social Law and Social Policy (Germany).

Elena Gerasimova, Associate Professor at the National Research University Higher School of Economics, Director of the Center for Social and Labor Rights (Russia).

Svetlana Golovina, Professor at the Urals State Law University (Russia).

Anastasiya Kashlakova, Associate Professor at the Altai State University (Russia).

Vladimir Lebedev, Professor at the National Research Tomsk State University (Russia).

Andrey Lushnikov, Professor at the Yaroslavl State University (Russia).

Marina Lushnikova, Professor at of at the Law faculty of the Yaroslavl State University (Russia)

Nikita Lyutov, Associate Professor at the Kutafin Moscow State Law University, Associate Professor at the National Research University Higher School of Economics (Russia).

Nikolay Olkhovik, Associate Professor at the National Research Tomsk State University (Russia).

Elena Radevich, Associate Professor at the National Research Tomsk State University (Russia).

André Scharrer, Judge at the Labour Court of Munich (Germany).

Elena Sychenko, PhD student at the University of Catania (Italy).

Vladimir Utkin, Professor at the National Research Tomsk State University (Russia).

INDEX